The Changing World
of the American Military

Also in This Series

Blue-Collar Soldiers: Unionization of the U.S. Military, edited by Alan N. Sabrosky

Westview Special Studies in Military Affairs

The Changing World of the American Military
edited by Franklin D. Margiotta

As the U.S. military moves into an uncertain future dominated by rapid change, traditional modes of thought will no longer suffice. Contributors to this volume focus on some of the major factors that will shape the American military in the 1980s: a complex, interdependent international arena, a changing domestic political context, broad societal forces and trends, the imperatives of advanced technology, conflicting bureaucratic and management orientations, and the emergence of new elites.

The articles collected here present the diverse views of civilian scholars, of all services and ranks of the military, and of Department of Defense and congressional civilians; they feature the results of surveys conducted at the three service academies and among other civilian and military populations that number in the tens of thousands. The focus moves from a historical and current assessment of military professionalism to potential influences in the changing international and domestic environments. A major section is devoted to important military manpower issues. Analyses of organizational dynamics and change address the implications of advanced technology, bureaucratization, and centralization of control. The book concludes with contrasting views of the future demands on military professionalism and with a final summary that suggests future research avenues.

Colonel Franklin D. Margiotta is a career air force pilot with an extensive B-52 operational background. Educated in political science at Georgetown University and Massachusetts Institute of Technology, he is research professor of political science at Air University and is director (dean) of curriculum, Air Command and Staff College. His publications include chapters in *Civilian Control of the Military*, *American Defense Policy* (4th ed.), and several journal articles.

The Changing World
of the American Military
edited by Franklin D. Margiotta
Foreword by Morris Janowitz

Westview Press / Boulder, Colorado

Westview Special Studies in Military Affairs

This volume was made possible by the cooperation of the Inter-University Seminar on Armed Forces and Society and the United States Air Force's Air University (Air Training Command).

The views and conclusions expressed by government and military personnel in chapters contained in this volume are those of the authors and are not the policy or position of the Air Command and Staff College, the Air Force, the Department of Defense, or any other governmental agency.

Published in 1978 in the United States of America by
   Westview Press, Inc.
   5500 Central Avenue
   Boulder, Colorado 80301
   Frederick A. Praeger, Publisher

Library of Congress Cataloging in Publication Data
Main entry under title:
The Changing world of the American military.
   (Westview special studies in military affairs)
   Bibliography: p.
   Includes index.
   1. United States—Armed Forces. 2. Soldiers—United States. 3. Military education—United States. I. Margiotta, Franklin D. II. Series.
UA23.C513   355'.00973   78-6765
ISBN 0-89158-331-9
ISBN 0-89158-309-2 pbk.

Printed and bound in the United States of America

This volume is dedicated to all the families who waited patiently while the authors developed their research, but especially to my wife Goldsby. Throughout the planning of the conference and the editing and publication of this book, she has been a source of ideas, a helpmate, and patient beyond all reasonable expectations.

—F.D.M.

Contents

Part 6.   Prescriptions for the Future

Part 7.   A Summary Perspective

Figures

Chapter 17

Chapter 18

Chapter 19

Tables

Chapter 8

Chapter 9

Chapter 10

Chapter 21

Foreword

Scholarship on military institutions and civil-military relations in the United States has passed through the normal "natural history" of any field in the social sciences. In the first phase, initial interest and efforts produced a series of comprehensive formulations and theories supported by limited data and prepared essentially by civilian scholars. For the study of the military profession, this was the case in the decade following World War II, when a number of pioneer monographs appeared. The second phase saw an increased, but still circumscribed, development of empirical studies testing and elaborating the pioneer formulations. In this phase, government and military-based researchers began to participate. Almost two decades later, the emergence of a third stage has brought determined efforts to chart basic changes through time and to reconceptualize earlier formulations about the American military.

The symposium organized by Franklin Margiotta and this resulting volume on the *Changing World of the American Military* represent the arrival of this new phase. The accumulation of basic and trend data by both civilian and government specialists is indeed impressive. I am pleased that the Inter-University Seminar on Armed Forces and Society is a cosponsor of this research enterprise. Each contribution represents the work of individuals rather than of particular universities, research groups, or agencies. Franklin Margiotta has performed the role of conference chairman and editor with commendable skill and persistent concern for objectivity in the responsible and meaningful sense of the term.

The materials presented in this volume provide the bases for the emerging phase—namely, the new efforts at synthesis and reformulation, including partial recasting or reaffirmation of earlier concepts and theories. There is a natural tendency for the original writers to hold to their first ideas. Of course, conceptual continuity is necessary for comparing changes over time. But I have no doubt that the period of conceptual reassessment has begun and will be pressed vigorously by the new generation of Fellows in the Inter-University Seminar on Armed Forces and Society.

Morris Janowitz
Chicago, Illinois

Acknowledgments

This book represents more than the excellent efforts of the many authors who contributed the results of their research and experience. Professor Morris Janowitz, University of Chicago, must be given unique credit, since this volume is the result of a meeting of the Inter-University Seminar on Armed Forces and Society (IUS). As chairman, Professor Janowitz had the foresight to obtain the support of the IUS Executive Committee for the first IUS meeting ever held on a military installation. I also thank Morris Janowitz for becoming a friend and a mentor; for the past four years, he has inspired me to explore many dimensions of my changing military profession.

Of equal importance were the commanders of Air University: General F. M. Rogers, USAF, and Lieutenant General Raymond B. Furlong, USAF. Their vision and support were crucial to the success of the conference. Generals Rogers and Furlong created the climate of open academic inquiry that brought the diverse views contained in this book to the Air Command and Staff College. A debt of gratitude is due my immediate commanders who insured the efficient conduct of the conference: Brigadier General Robert F. C. Winger and Major General William L. Nicholson, III. The conference would not have been possible without the organizing skills and devoted efforts of Lieutenant Colonel Charles Thomas, ably assisted by Lieutenant Colonel Ed White and Major Frank Tantillo. Their attention to details made the conference a pleasant experience for each of our guests.

We are grateful to the several publishers and journal editors who have published versions of these revised conference papers. Two chapters in this volume were already scheduled for publication elsewhere when they were presented: Professor Huntington's in *Civil-Military Relations*, published by the American Enterprise Institute; Professors Russett and Nincic's in *Public Opinion Quarterly*. The following chapters have been published since the conference: Professor Pfaltzgraff's in *Air University Review*; Professor Sarkesian's in *Military Review*; Dean Odiorne's in *Southern Review of Public Administration*; Colonel Taylor's in *American Defense Policy* (4th ed.), published by Johns Hopkins University Press; and Professor Moskos's in *Armed Forces and Society*.

A special note of thanks is due the staff of the Air Command and Staff College who made this final volume possible. Mrs. Jana Carter gave invaluable assistance in administering the conference and in later efforts to revise and publish this book. Captain Mike Duffee helped with the numerous details of a project of this sort. Others who assisted include Major Wayne Anders, Ms. Jean Blackmon, Vi Pitts, Barbara Smilie, Carrie Smith, Dot Stubbs, Marion Gorrie, and Mildred Suydam. Mr. J. C. Smith was our patient, effective, and diligent editor. Finally, we must salute Mr. Frederick Praeger, who challenged, encouraged, and sought quality throughout the production of this book. In a very special way, this volume represents more than a conference and bits of research: it represents the efforts of many strangers who joined together in helping us to understand a complex future. In our joint efforts, we have grown to know one another; for this, I am truly grateful.

Franklin D. Margiotta
Maxwell AFB, Alabama

Introduction

The future will make unique demands on the American military and its leaders. To respond rationally to these demands, both the military and the nation must understand the dimensions of recent changes and their potential for shaping the future. An important purpose of this volume is to aid understanding and focus research on some of the major factors that will affect the American military in the 1980s.

In October 1976, the Inter-University Seminar on Armed Forces and Society (IUS) held a two-day research conference cosponsored by Air University and hosted by the Air Command and Staff College as an integral part of its curriculum. A major feature of the conference was the recognition that wisdom and knowledge reside in no one particular group or discipline. The conference thus served as a forum for mixing the diverse views and disciplines of IUS and non-IUS civilian scholars, all military services and ranks, and civilians from the Department of Defense and Congress. This volume is a collection of selected conference papers that have been revised and edited for publication.

The conference stimulated primary research in previously unexplored subject areas. Featured in this collection are analyses of surveys conducted at the three service academies and polls of other military and civilian populations numbering in the tens of thousands. Certain chapters are introductory and overarching for each major part of the book and are given further development in subsequent chapters.

One purpose of the conference was to create and disseminate new information, insights, and understanding and to foster original research on the military profession. The papers avoided duplication of research areas that have adequately described a number of specific issues facing the military. Consequently, this volume does not contain in-depth coverage of international political trends; arms control; the effects of technology on military hardware; warfare concepts and doctrine; debates concerning particular weapon systems, roles, or missions; or the changing roles of minorities and women. In each of these subject areas, either a rich body of literature is already available, or a substantial number of scholars and staff literature is already available, or a substantial number of scholars and staff agencies is currently examining the issues.

The volume focuses, instead, on other major factors and trends that might shape the future of the American military. The contributors to this book implicitly suggest new directions for future research and offer some answers to several specific questions. What important international and domestic trends will influence the American military in the late twentieth century? How will public attitudes, youth attitudes, and attitudes on college campuses affect the recruitment of enlisted and officer personnel? What new social factors might require the attention of the military profession in the future? What are the implications of advanced technology, organizational dynamics, and bureaucratization? Who are the cadets at the service academies, and how well prepared are they to deal with the uncertain future described in this book? Based upon the analyses and forecasts in this volume, what are the future demands of military professionalism? What, in fact, is the current state of military professionalism?

A Current Assessment of Military Professionalism

Part 1 provides a three-part analysis of current military professionalism by exploring fundamental tensions between American norms and traditional military values. Despite differences in the methods and levels used by the authors, their conclusions are relatively congruent.

In the first chapter, Samuel P. Huntington reviews his earlier findings in his classic *The Soldier and the State* and updates his conclusions with a discussion of the Vietnam war and its aftermath. He states that American society moved away from a traditional mistrust of the military during the cold war period, when society accommodated to many of the pragmatic and conservative military attitudes. He suggests that the hostile antimilitary attitudes among many segments of the population during and immediately after the Vietnam war have recently changed to indifference. In his opinion, the United States will be much less likely to engage in future intervention, and he predicts a strategy that will limit U.S. participation in conflicts by time rather than by levels of force. The importance of military readiness logically follows from this argument.

Sam C. Sarkesian uses empirical survey data from five recent studies to view the issue of civil-military relations from the perspective of the professional officer. He sees the military professional as dissatisfied with military status and influence, and he speculates that Vietnam may be at the root of this dissatisfaction. Although the military professional rejects the convergence of military and civilian society and yearns to retain a unique military life-style, Sarkesian cannot find much evidence of a "military mind."

He also finds the professional officer deeply concerned with ethics, institutional demands, and individual values because individual norms often conflict with a military system that presses for conformity and institutional values. Sarkesian concludes that the U.S. military is recovering from the trauma of the Vietnam war and its impact on professional value systems. He agrees with Huntington on the divergence between military values and American societal values and finds the military more conservative on the issues of military autonomy and security.

James Clotfelter and Guy Peters report on panel interviews with the same group of U.S. Army officers in 1971 and 1975; their interviews and surveys reinforce the conclusions of Huntington and Sarkesian. Clotfelter and Peters find that military officers see major changes in their environment and in the tasks that they may be asked to perform. Over a period of four years, the officers felt a growing separation from civilian society. There was some consensus that the military was adapting to the changing environment and that the army was applying some modern management practices. Although the Vietnam war was a factor in these officers' views, it did not seem to split the officer corps from the broader society. General value differences and a more liberal American society, rather than the effects of war, seem to be the features that create distinctiveness.

International and Domestic Influences

Part 2 focuses on major features of the international and domestic environments in which the military will operate during the 1980s. Robert L. Pfaltzgraff, Jr., analyzes emerging major power relationships of the late twentieth century and suggests possible military implications. He notes that the diffusion of power will continue because of demands for resources found in the Southern Hemisphere and because of the spread of sophisticated weapons technology.

Pfaltzgraff describes a world incredibly more complex than the world of the recent past. Relations between the United States and the Soviet Union will still be the most important, but growing centers of power will emerge on other continents. Smaller states will challenge for supremacy in their regions and, in the process, may generate conflicts with their neighbors. Localized and internal conflicts appear as future norms and may focus on territorial boundaries, food, and resources. Such conflicts will be exacerbated by nongovernment actors such as terrorists, ethnic minorities, and international corporations.

Pfaltzgraff suggests that bipolar strategic deterrent concepts must be adjusted and that lethal nonnuclear weapons will make stability operations much more difficult. The Soviet Union's emergence as a global power capable of projecting its forces overseas and the growth of important regional powers threaten U.S. security with unique circumstances. Within this context, Pfaltzgraff questions traditional U.S. military notions about the efficacy of naval forces and tactical air power.

The complexities of the future international scene will be duplicated in the domestic political environment. Robert Trice's chapter surveys the impact of domestic politics on U.S. national security policy. Trice presents a working definition of national security policy and a description of the numerous domestic actors who shape the directions of that policy. He traces the recent growth in the power of Congress, the news media, the public, and special interest groups. He predicts that professional policy-makers will have weakened roles in the national security arena and that nonexecutive control over national security matters will increase.

James Hogan supports Trice's analysis with the suggestion that congressional staffs will have an increased role in shaping future U.S. national security policy and military programs. He supports his argument by tracing significant improvements in staff capabilities since 1965. The Department of Defense (DOD) will no longer be able to "outstaff and outinformation" congressional committees on Capitol Hill. Improved executive capabilities in the Department of State and the Office of Management and Budget will also be factors in DOD's future.

Chapter 7 continues the analysis of congressional-executive relations with Russell Hale and Leland Jordan's discussion of codified congressional power in the 1974 Congressional Budget and Impoundment Control Act. This act created new organizations and funding techniques that permit Congress to view the whole federal budget and to consider trade-offs between domestic social programs and military hardware. Traditional committee allies of the DOD now must contend with an active budget committee that allocates the total budget and gauges its impact on U.S. economic events. It is still too early to determine the ultimate effects of these developments. However, our congressional and DOD budget analysts conclude that Congress will exert more influence over DOD and other executive budget matters.

Surveys of the American public also suggest a changing role for the executive and a diminished relevance for traditional military power. Through an analysis of polls, Bruce Russett and Miroslav Nincic show that the willingness of the American public to use American troops to defend other countries has declined to its lowest point since 1940. The public approves of defense against external attack to a much higher degree than it approves combating internal insurgencies; this supports Huntington's view that the U.S. military will probably not be used to intervene. Willingness for the United States to provide military defense for other countries is highly selective, and public approval of the use of nuclear weapons is also very low. In an all-volunteer environment, the ability of the military to recruit depends upon these attitudes toward defense in general and toward the military institution in particular.

Military Manpower Issues in a Changing Social Institution

The U.S. military faces a very difficult future in meeting its manpower needs and in satisfying its recruits after they enlist. The survey data in Part 3 signal that it may be impossible to maintain an active force of more than two million men plus a large Reserve and National Guard. Several authors also believe that the U.S. military must adjust to fundamental social changes.

John Blair identifies emerging youth attitudes toward the military in a report based on a continuing survey of more than 17,000 high school seniors. Blair finds a high regard for the military as a social institution, but he also finds the same cautious approach reported by Russett and Nincic on the use of military force. Indeed, there is an increased reluctance to serve, even in a necessary war. Young people perceive that the military provides considerable job opportunities but that it deals with people in an arbitrary, unjust manner. Thus, paradoxically, they consider the military environment as a place where they may get ahead, but they also view it as the least desirable or acceptable work setting. Future recruiting efforts will probably be more successful among blacks, who indicate greater willingness to serve than whites. Although the military may be forced to recruit more women, most young women do not view the military as an acceptable job place. Educational incentives can expand the recruiting market and help continue a broad-based social representativeness in the all-volunteer force.

The recruiting picture for officers may be brighter. Conventional opinion holds that the Reserve Officer Training Corps (ROTC) is relatively unwanted on most college campuses. Two sociologists, Larry W. Reed and L. Anthony Loman, polled almost 1,000 faculty members about ROTC. As expected, faculties in small state colleges in rural southern areas were the strongest supporters of ROTC. Even in the more liberal schools of the Northeast, there was a surprisingly positive attitude toward the military and a rather high acceptance of the need for ROTC on college campuses. This support is generated by one faculty group that views national defense and the military as legitimate and necessary and by a second group that perceives ROTC as a democratic, leavening influence within the military.

Attitudes among youth will affect recruitment potential, but attitudes within the military will affect retention and the capacity to fight. In Chapter 11, Charles Moskos provides a challenging model of changes stemming from the adoption of an all-volunteer force in 1973. He suggests that marketplace recruitment strategies have shifted the military toward an "occupational" outlook, and away from traditional views of the military as a "calling" or a profession. These traditional outlooks tend to set the military apart from civilian society and encourage a relatively all-encompassing life-style. High reliance on monetary rewards to attract enlistees suggests to many military members that their service is only another job. Higher remuneration has permitted more individual freedom of choice and less reliance upon the institution. Moskos views these as threatening trends, speculates on the efficiency of the military to fight, and concludes that unionization could be a logical product of a military occupational model.

The authors of the next three chapters of the book assume the validity of the Moskos analysis as they consider the impact on the future military of changing family structures, job attitudes, and concepts of unionism. In many respects, the military has become a family institution, with growth in the numbers of married personnel from 20 percent of the force in the 1950s to more than 85 percent in some officer categories. The occupational model helps to explain, and is reinforced by, higher interest among many military members in family matters and less interest in institutional matters. Feminist and other movements have created more educated and independent spouses who are less likely to appreciate a total institutional life-style. Hamilton McCubbin and Martha Marsden critique current assumptions that underlie DOD policies, or lack of them, toward the military family. Their research suggests that families will be less likely to tolerate frequent moves, separations, and other traditional demands of military service. Their chapter proposes methods for expressing more concern for the family in military policymaking.

The occupational trend is influencing the military in several other areas. Fundamental assumptions underlying the all-volunteer concept treat the military as a competitor in the workplace. In Chapter 13, David Segal reports that surveys of thousands of military and civilian employees demonstrate that military personnel desire the same characteristics from their jobs as civilians. However, civilian employees perceive that their jobs provide these characteristics to a higher degree. The organizational climate in the military is less favorable than the work climate in industry. Segal suggests that modern management practices may resolve this civilian-military organizational differential but that they will never be completely successful nor address major potential sources of dissatisfaction: pay, fringe benefits, bureaucratization, and unresponsiveness to individual needs. Segal forecasts increasing demands for "worker representation" manifested in efforts to unionize the military, as has been the case in several Western European countries.

William J. Taylor, Jr., reviews recent trends in unionizing public employees and suggests that these trends may have important implications for the future military. Almost every public employee sector has resorted to formal organization, work stoppages, and even strikes. Taylor describes the claims of union advocates and those of opponents who point to the inevitable clash between national security and a unionized military. In reviewing court cases, Taylor suggests that the courts would probably uphold statutes prohibiting unionization in the military as overriding the rights of individuals under the First Amendment. He assumes that unionization must and will become more publicly discussed and that one alternative is a better, more sensitive military leadership.

Organizational Dynamics and Change

In Part 4, other authors permit speculation that growing technology and modernity may be just as important as the underlying dynamics of the phenomena discussed in Part 3. John C. Toomay, Richard H. Hartke, and Howard L. Elman suggest that the fundamentals of military leadership have not changed but that technology has dramatically altered the environment of weapons, people, the military system, and interactions with other organizations. The modern military leader requires more educated people who desire to know organizational goals and methods. Technology has forced the military organization itself to accept the idea of longer-range planning. The need for narrowly specialized individuals and functions has brought larger staffs and increased bureaucratization. Furthermore, growth in the size and complexity of military resources increases the required interactions among numerous organizations. The amount of information that now affects any military choice has expanded exponentially.

Toomay, Hartke, and Elman conclude that modern military leaders must modify traditional leadership methods and adopt styles somewhere on a continuum from authoritarian to permissive, depending upon the circumstances, goals, and nature of their tasks. At times, subordinates must respond instantly, and at other times, they must participate in or actually make the decisions. The fostering of innovation becomes more important in a high-technology environment. This environment will create problems for higher-level commanders who cannot acquire experience in the varied disciplines that they must coordinate.

In the next chapter, Frank R. Hunsicker narrows the focus from military technology to the military organizational challenges and responses that will develop through 1985. He elaborates on the earlier chapter and suggests that the bureaucratic model of military leadership will persist but that it must be adapted to changing circumstances. The conflict between centralization of control and division of labor will continue as a fundamental tension. Commanders will face more complex tasks, more available information, and better educated personnel, but centralization will narrow their control and choice of resources. Commanders will confront situations with personnel whom they have not chosen and with budgets that they cannot control. Hunsicker agrees that the military will respond with a systemic approach to bureaucracy and a behaviorally oriented treatment of people. He also suggests that situational management will become increasingly important.

The final chapter in Part 4 does not assume that these trends are benign; instead, it criticizes the growth of military bureaucratization as counterproductive. George S. Odiorne, a noted author on industrial management, decries military bureaucratization as a super activity trap. He points out that in large organizations, members often forget goals and objectives and focus instead on methods in a continuing and increasingly frenzied manner. Odiorne cautions that the trends described in Chapters 15 and 16 may be inevitable but not desirable. The natural effects of bureaucracy may be angry clients, apathy, alienation from organizational goals, and absurd activities. The bureaucracy consumes inputs but gives few outputs; the activity trap devastates human beings; costs rise because simple operations are complicated; and lower-ranking, smart bureaucrats are able to resist command and authority. Odiorne warns that either the military must reform or others will seek to diminish bureaucratization.

Developments at the Academies

In his chapter, John Lovell describes the practical effects of recent bureaucratization on the service academies and thus bears out Odiorne's theoretical arguments. The academies will have important roles because they provide the leadership cadres to deal with the uncertainties described in this book. Lovell finds that the academies have moved cyclically from a Spartan mode to an Athenian mode. When war threatens, the academies emphasize military skills. When the international scene is relatively quiet and when top leadership remains in place for longer periods, the academies permit academic innovation and less rigid disciplinary and behavioral standards.

Lovell hints strongly that attrition has increased with the growth in the number of academy staff and students. Institutional malaise developed when bureaucratic, impersonal regimentation replaced the earlier intimate seminary existence. Alienation resulting from bureaucratic regulations and procedures seems to be a major cause of cadet resignations. In addition, cadets are subjected to a high level of stress as Athenian academic demands compete with Spartan military demands. A cadet must be intellectually open-minded but must still pass tests on how well he shines his shoes as late as his senior year. These conflicting demands will keep the academies in a difficult position.

Despite these tensions, these future officers are relatively high-quality young Americans. Surveys at the three academies document this conclusion and represent a first attempt to describe the cadres that will provide military leaders into the twenty-first century. This research also describes the types of students who remain at the military academies and defines attributes or values that might explain success in the academy environment.

Ronald Schloemer and Gus E. Myers's analysis of data on the Air Force Academy classes of 1976 and 1977 permits refinement of earlier conclusions about academy students. They found that future military elites will come overwhelmingly from urban and nonsouthern areas and will have family backgrounds found in other careers and professions. Chapter 19 describes these family backgrounds, socioeconomic origins, religious and political identification, and future career aspirations. Several correlations suggest variables that help to explain cadet attrition or success.

The study at the U.S. Naval Academy used the same questionnaire with somewhat different results. John A. Fitzgerald and Charles L. Cochran also suggest the need to modify earlier views about the populations attending the academies. Midshipmen at the Naval Academy differ slightly from Air Force Academy cadets in career perspectives and in predictable indicators of success. Fitzgerald and Cochran make some useful suggestions about further improvements in these research methods.

Robert F. Priest takes a different view in reporting on cadet characteristics at the U.S. Military Academy. Using ten-year survey data, Priest describes evolutionary changes among entering cadets and then predicts that the admission of women to West Point will reinforce these trends. He finds significant and complementary differences between *all* West Point cadets and four-year college students. A sex difference occurs on some dimensions, but in certain other traits, West Point women reverse the typical male/female pattern of sex differences found on college campuses. Priest concludes that because of the unique vocational mission at West Point, some remaining attitudinal and academic differences between the sexes must be further reduced by future training or selection.

Prescriptions for the Future

Part 6 provides three diverse views of the appropriate professional response to the future: Chapters 22 and 23, written by military officers, personalize the frustrations and tensions described in Part 1, and Chapter 24 presents a controversial view of education as an important feature for the future military. G. E. Miller, a retired admiral, focuses on the corporate body. In his view, the most important future demand upon military professionalism will be the challenge to regain lost authority. Military foundations are rooted in the Constitution and the statutes that determine military service. Admiral Miller agrees that technological, social, and international developments will change the military, but he resists the centralization and diminution of military authority of the past two decades. Diminished authority reduces the attractiveness of the military profession for high-quality individuals. Admiral Miller concludes that the military profession can regain its authority by taking concerted action on key issues and by joining associations aimed at gaining particular benefits and advantages. Unionization may come, not because of "occupation," but as a means to redress the decline in authority.

Major James R. Golden provides a different generation's view from his faculty position at West Point. He concludes that the demands of military professionalism will be addressed by the individual's ability to make personal choices. One boundary is the Huntington view that professionalism requires the development of narrowly focused military skills and the provision of politically neutral military advice. The other boundary is the Janowitz view that a military professional should be broadly recruited and should cultivate a broad perspective on civilian, military, domestic, and international affairs while maintaining "the warrior spirit."

In Golden's prescription, the individual professional must seek the essential core values for retention, but he must still adapt to the continuing divergence of military career patterns caused by functional specialization. Golden argues for a renewed commitment to the principles of duty, honor, and country. To the extent that professional officers view military service as merely an outlet for ambition, the future of the profession will be doubtful. Each professional must interpret duty as a broad commitment to contribute to the limits of his own potential. He must create an atmosphere of mutual trust through commitment to personal honor. The country must be served not by a blind commitment to its leaders but by a dedication to its constitutional process.

Thomas W. Carr, former director of defense education, suggests that education will play a more important role in the future military. His analysis reinforces John Blair's findings that youth populations will be smaller, not interested in joining the military, and open to educational incentives as a method of recruitment. By 1985, the military must recruit one of every two male eighteen-year-olds who will not pursue a college education. Carr suggests that the only possible hope is to focus more closely on educational opportunities and predicts a series of innovative cooperative ventures between the military and higher education. The military may become a major instrument of youth socialization, and education will provide a primary focus of new programs to recruit specially qualified personnel. If these predictions come true, a relatively authoritarian military system that stresses established procedures and hierarchy must adjust even further to a broader education that implies the goals of creativity and improvement of the human condition.

A Summary Perspective

The final chapter weaves together the themes and conclusions of this volume. We examine major features of the international and domestic scene, manpower issues and changing military society, organizational dynamics and change, developments at the academies, and the future dimensions of military professionalism. Morris Janowitz's challenge, contained in his Foreword, is accepted, and research implications are proposed for the future study of the military institution and civil-military relations. Several broad research hypotheses are developed, and many earlier assumptions about the U.S. military are questioned.

This synthesis of the research implications of the first twenty-four chapters permits us to identify several central trends that will affect the U.S. military in the 1980s. One draws the conclusion that this may be a truly unique period in U.S. military history; the outlook is hardly optimistic. This summary perspective portrays a future that seems troubled and dominated by uncertainty and rapid change. Few readers will accept these conclusions in their entirety; the analyses will be questioned, debated, and reinterpreted. This volume does not solve these anticipated problems of the future but is intended to help focus and begin to clarify the many dimensions of the changing world of the U.S. military.

A Current Assessment
of Military Professionalism

The Soldier and the State in the 1970s

Samuel P. Huntington

The Problem of the Soldier and the State

"The military institutions of any society," in the opening words of *The Soldier and the State,*

> are shaped by two forces: a functional imperative stemming from the threats to the society's security and a societal imperative arising from the social forces, ideologies, and institutions dominant within the society. Military institutions which reflect only social values may be incapable of performing effectively their military function. On the other hand, it may be impossible to contain within society military institutions shaped purely by functional imperatives. The interaction of these two forces is the nub of the problem of civil-military relations.[1]

The military institutions of most societies embody a changing pattern of balance and accommodation between the societal imperatives and the functional ones. There is, however, no guarantee that the societal and functional imperatives will be reconcilable. Indeed, they sometimes clash head-on in such a way that one or the other has to give. Why should the patterns of political and technological development happily spare any particular society this unhappy choice? Why should other states frame their challenges to a particular society so that the society can meet those challenges in ways that are compatible with its basic political values and not discomforting to its ruling classes? Faced with certain threats, some societies may be incapable of providing for their own security except at the price of becoming something different from what they are.

Editor's note: This chapter was delivered in abbreviated form as the opening plenary address at the October 1976 IUS Conference. It had already been committed for publication and is reprinted with permission from *Civil-Military Relations*, the American Enterprise Institute for Public Policy Research, © 1977.

The interaction between societal and functional imperatives manifests itself in a variety of ways. Of central importance, however, is the relationship between the military officer corps and the political institutions and leadership. The emergence of modern, developed societies has transformed the historical problem of civil-military relations. In less highly institutionalized and differentiated societies, the problem of civil-military relations centers on the twin issues of *military intervention* in politics through coups d'etat and insurrections and of *military rule* of the polity, once the military have seized power and decide to keep it. In modern, developed societies, these are seldom the major problems. Such societies are characterized by relatively highly institutionalized political structures and patterns of rule (of which the communist variant and the liberal democratic variant are the principal examples in today's world) and by relatively highly institutionalized and professionalized officer corps. The central problem of civil-military relations thus becomes the relationship between the military professionals and the political leadership.

In theory, this problem is not dissimilar from the broader issue of the relations between the generalist and the specialist, the politician and the expert. In the case of the military, however, it is often particularly intense and of central political importance to the society because of the nature of the functional imperatives that the military professional represents and because a highly professionalized and bureaucratized military establishment is, by its very nature, a potential source of political power and influence.

The modern officer corps is a highly professional body. It has its own expertise, corporateness, and responsibility. The existence of this profession tends to imply, and the practice of the profession tends to engender among its members, a distinctive outlook on international politics, the role of the state, the place of force and violence in human affairs, the nature of man and society, and the relationship of the military profession to the state. This professional military ethic tends to be one of conservative realism. Clearly, not all military officers adhere uniformly to it; indeed, in any military establishment very few officers possess the professional "military mind" in toto. It is instead an ideal type in the Weberian sense, and the interesting questions concern precisely why, how, and to what extent officers in different societies at different times deviate from this ideal type.

The ability of the officer corps to develop and maintain high standards of military professionalism and to adhere to the conservative realism of the military ethic depends upon the nature of the society it serves. If the values and ideology predominant in the society differ sharply from the conservative realism of the military ethic, the officer corps can acquire power in the society only by altering its attitudes and outlook to correspond more closely with those of the society. A totalitarian system cannot tolerate a military institution that controls substantial power but does not adhere to the political ideology of the regime. Civil-military relations in such regimes are almost always in a state of latent or actual crisis, as the all-encompassing demands of the state interact with the professional imperatives of the officer corps for autonomy. Political commissars, secret police, periodic purges, ideological indoctrination are the result: political control of the military, like political control of every-thing else, tends to be exerted in its most extreme form in the totalitarian state, whether Fascist or Communist.

The conservative realism of the professional military ethic also contrasts dramatically with the Lockean liberalism that has predominated in American society. In large degree, there has been an American consensus, and it has been a liberal, antimilitary consensus. Military forces, particularly professional military forces, and military institutions have been viewed with suspicion and hostility. The ideals of liberty, democracy, equality, and peace have contrasted with the military's concern with authority, hierarchy, obedience, force, and war. In theory and in practice, this fundamental ideological conflict can be resolved in one or more of three ways:

1. The political power and functional importance of the military can be reduced so that the military exists as a conservative institution on the periphery of a liberal society, a policy of *extirpation*;

2. The values and outlook of the military can change from conservative to liberal, thereby bringing the military into congruence with the society, and military functions can be broadened to include normally civilian ones, a policy of *transmutation*;

3. The prevailing societal values can shift away from traditional liberalism in the direction of conservatism, society thereby adopting a policy of *toleration* with respect to the military.

These are the three theoretical options for accommodation between military institutions and a liberal society. At one time or another each has played a role in the American experience.

Military Institutions and Liberal Society: The Historical Patterns

Phase I: The Traditional Pattern

For the bulk of our history between 1815 and 1940 major threats to American security were few and remote. National security was a product of geographical location and of European politics, over neither of which the United States could exercise much control. National security was, in a sense, the starting point of policy, the assumption upon which policy was based rather than its product. Unconsciously and without concern, a liberal society could pursue a policy that was predominantly one of extirpation but partly too one of transmutation. Each successive group that rose to a preeminent role in American society had its own reasons for being suspicious of the military: to the eighteenth-century Whigs and Jeffersonians large military forces were a threat to liberty; the Jacksonians saw them as a threat to democracy; the dominant industrial and business groups after the Civil War saw them as a threat to economic productivity and prosperity; and the progressives and liberals saw them as a threat to reform. Almost everyone thought large standing military forces were a threat to peace.

The instrumental roles of the military forces were limited and relatively unimportant. In peacetime, these were, in the nineteenth century, largely confined to the pacification of the Indians and the protection of commerce from exotic pirates. In the twentieth century, the navy and Marine Corps were also used for various small-scale interventions in the Caribbean and Central America. The military forces maintained in peacetime were, in wartime, supplemented and largely overwhelmed and supplanted by militia units, reserve organizations, and other nonprofessional forces. Until World War I, even the major commands in wartime were in large part occupied by citizen-soldiers. The irrelevance of the standing forces in peacetime embodied the policy of extirpation; in wartime, their subordinate role reflected the ideals of transmutation: wars were too important to be fought by professional soldiers rather than by citizen soldiers. A sharp distinction was thought to exist between war and peace, and the role of regular military forces in either was limited.

As a result, the resources devoted to military purposes in peacetime were minimal throughout the nineteenth century and remained, by present-day standards, extraordinarily modest even after the beginning of the buildup of the navy early in the twentieth. An autonomous professional military officer corps did not emerge until the latter part of the nineteenth century, considerably later than in most major European countries. Before that time nonprofessional officers, of whom Jackson was the exemplar, often played leading political roles: this reflected the extent to which military functions were diffused through society. After the development of an autonomous profession, military officers faded from political roles outside the military establishment, which was itself too small to be a significant power base.

By and large, then, during Phase I the potential tensions between military institutions and liberal society remained latent because the lack of significant security threats made it possible to maintain, outside the mainstream of society, small military forces with little political influence, few economic resources, and marginal instrumental roles.

Phase II: The Cold War Pattern

After World War II, all of this, of course, changed drastically. National security suddenly became the overriding goal of policy rather than its starting point. Political elites and opinion makers saw the Soviet Union and the Communist bloc as posing major threats to that security, and the United States, they thought, must make substantial efforts to counter them. This produced five major changes in the traditional pattern of civil-military relations.

First, there was a tremendous qualitative and quantitative change in the instrumental roles of the armed forces. Military forces were necessary for nuclear deterrence, for deployment overseas in support of our allies in Western Europe and East Asia, and for rapid response to aggression and conflict in other parts of the world. Theories and policies were developed for deterrence, alliance management, and flexible response. Military force came to be viewed as a prime instrument of policy to prevent large-scale war and to deal with small-scale conflicts. Probably nothing is more striking in the contrast between the pre-World War II and post-World War II attitudes concerning civil-military relations than this change in attitude toward military force as an instrument of policy.

Second, the economic role of the military expanded tremendously. For twenty years beginning with the rearmament effort of the early 1950s—which brought into existence the military forces designed for the cold war—the military establishment commanded approximately 10 percent of the gross national product. A substantial armaments industry concentrated largely in aircraft, missiles, electronics, and shipbuilding came into existence to support the needs of that establishment.

Third, new governmental institutions were developed to organize and to control the military establishment, and significant changes took place in the roles of existing political institutions with respect to the military establishment. The National Security Acts of 1947 and 1949 legitimated the Joint Chiefs of Staff and created the Department of Defense, but they still left that department with one major deficiency, which was pointed out in *The Soldier and the State*. This was the relative weakness of the Office of the Secretary of Defense. The 1958 Defense Reorganization Act went a long way toward correcting this deficiency, and Secretary McNamara completed the task in the early 1960s with his vigorous administration of the office and his strengthening of its staff. With this, the organization of the department as a whole came close to achieving the "balanced" pattern that is most desirable for maximizing both civilian control and military effectiveness.

Coincidentally, significant changes took place in the roles of the

President and Congress with respect to military policy. Prior to 1940, Congress did not hesitate to make strategic decisions on the weapons, force levels, and base systems of the armed forces. During the cold war, however, the primary locus of strategic "legislation" moved to the executive branch, with congressional groups at times playing significant roles as lobbyists and pleaders on behalf of one program or another, but not, by and large, exercising decision-making authority over such programs. Instead, the executive branch exercised that authority on force levels, weapons, deployments, and the use of force. Congress, however, continued to play its traditional role with respect to the "structural" side of the military establishment, that is, to such issues as recruitment, pay, and other aspects of personnel policy, organization and administration, procurement policies and procedures, and issues connected with the reserve forces.

Fourth, the cold war period saw an end to the earlier isolation of the military establishment from other important segments of American society. In the immediate post-World War II years, large numbers of career officers moved into civilian roles in government and business. Subsequently, close relations developed between the military services and the business component of what was generally referred to as the military-industrial complex. Reliance on selective service for the procurement of enlisted men and the major role of the ROTC in officer procurement circulated through the armed forces more or less representative samples of noncollege and college youth. The horizons of military education broadened, with the liberal arts and sciences playing a greater role in the curricula of the military academies and civilian lecturers and experts participating in greater numbers in the work of war colleges, staff colleges, and other military educational institutions. Even more important, large numbers of military officers were sent to civilian universities for advanced study in a variety of fields. Through Operation Bootstrap, more than 11,000 service personnel earned the bachelor of general studies degree in the twenty-five years after the program's inception in 1950-1951. The military services, which had previously been isolated from American society, were now interacting vigorously with it.

Fifth, and perhaps most important because it was in a sense a precondition for these other changes, major shifts took place in the attitudes of the American public and elites toward the military services and military force. In effect, liberal antimilitary presuppositions and attitudes were at least temporarily weakened or suppressed, thus resolving in some measure the tension between military security and the liberal society. Some indications of this trend in the direction of a more conservative realism compatible with the professional military outlook were briefly sketched in the final chapter of *The Soldier and the State*. Indeed, the publication of

The Soldier and the State, with its unabashed defense of the professional military ethic and rejection of traditional liberalism, was itself evidence of this changing intellectual climate. At the same time a large number of other books by scholars and journalists appeared that treated the military with a respect, and military needs with a consideration, most unusual in American history. The political and governmental elites of this period shared, by and large, an understanding and appreciation of the role of military force with respect to foreign policy matched only by that of the Federalists in the 1790s and the "Neo-Hamiltonians" in the 1890s.

These attitudes held by the intellectual and policy elites paralleled those that prevailed among the public. From the late 1940s until the mid-1960s, opinion surveys showed the mass public overwhelmingly opposed to reductions in U.S. military forces and budgets and a significant portion of the public in favor of increases in military strength. The Democratic majorities that dominated Congress through almost all of this period more often tried to increase spending for military programs than to reduce it significantly. On the use of force abroad, both the public and Congress generally deferred to the President.

The Disruption of the Cold War Pattern

In the early 1970s, the cold war pattern of civil-military relations—a variant of the toleration option—clearly began to disintegrate as a result of the changes in the external and domestic environments that had made it possible in the first place. These changes may have been part of a broader antimilitary trend throughout the industrialized democracies as a result of higher levels of affluence and education, the decline of traditional authority, and changes in basic values. In addition, however, these changes had three distinct sources in the American experience.

First, the 1960s witnessed a momentous and dramatic change in the temper, scale, direction, intensity, and activity of American public life. This "democratic surge" involved the expansion of political participation, the introduction of new forms of participation, a significant polarization of opinion over social and foreign policy issues, the increased relevance of ideology to political behavior, and, most significant, a renewed commitment by various groups in American society to traditional American ideals of equality, liberty, democracy, and openness in government and a concomitant challenging of the authority of established political, economic, and social institutions. One key aspect of this surge was the redirection of public attention away from foreign affairs and concerns to the "neglected" priorities of domestic affairs: welfare, health, education, the environment, the cities. In somewhat paradoxical fashion, the surge thus produced both a major expansion of governmental activity (in domestic programs) and a major decrease in governmental authority.[2]

This mobilization of opinion on behalf of reform had many similarities to the democratic surges that occurred in the Jacksonian and Progressive eras. The patterns of thought and behavior, the values that were articulated and the priorities that were set forth, had their precedents in these earlier periods. In the context of this reaffirmation of democratic and liberal values, continued adherence to the toleration option of the 1950s (which had involved the neglect or suppression of precisely those values) was no longer feasible.

A second major factor disrupting the cold war pattern of civil-military relations was, of course, the Vietnam War. Not only did this serve to galvanize and crystallize antimilitary sentiments latent beneath the surface of public opinion, but also it directly challenged the military's own perception of the proper balance in civil-military relations. It raised again in more acute and agonizing fashion the whole question of the limited use of military force for political purposes. This issue had, of course, come to the fore during the Korean War, but in that case had simply involved the imposition by political leadership of the government of restraints on how the military could fight a familiar type of war between sovereign states. In Vietnam, by contrast, the problems of guerrilla warfare, counter-insurgency, nation building, and political development were central to the conflict, at least in its early phases. And these problems raised critical issues as to the role of military force in a civil war. In addition, the operation of the draft during the conflict brought into the military the "democratic surge" with its challenge to established authority, the counterculture, and the racial tensions then characteristic of American society. Instead of being tolerated by liberal society, the military establishment was now being invaded by it.

Third, changes in the international environment in the middle and late 1960s appeared to reduce the actual and potential external challenges to national security. On the one hand, there was the improvement in relations with both the Soviet Union and China, which seemed to decrease the probability of military conflict with either. On the other hand, there was a redefinition of American security interests; developments that had previously been conceived to be major threats were downgraded in terms of their implications for American security. Hence the impetus to maintain large, diverse, and extensively deployed military forces in the post-Vietnam era was considerably less than it had been previously. In the post-Vietnam, postcontainment, post-cold war era of détente, what were large-scale military forces needed for? The Vietnam War became the only war in American history immediately after which military manpower levels and budget levels (in constant dollars) were significantly lower than they had been at the war's outset.

As a result of these three developments, civil-military relations in the 1970s entered a phase of confusion and flux. The brief cold war reign of the toleration option clearly is ending or being substantially modified. But what will take its place? A return to the traditional pattern? Some compromise between the traditional and cold war patterns? Some new arrangement differing from either of these historical models? In terms of maximizing military security at the least sacrifice of other social values, what pattern of civil-military relations should be developed?

Constraints on the Level of Military Force

"Previously the primary question was: what pattern of civil-military relations is most compatible with American liberal-democratic values? Now this has been supplanted by the more important issue: what pattern of civil-military relations will best maintain the security of the American nation?" This proposition in *The Soldier and the State* accurately reflected the prevailing attitudes and concerns of the 1950s. In the 1970s, however, as Douglas Rosenberg and Raoul Alcala accurately observe, "Huntington's statement appears curiously inverted today. Critics, scholars and policy-makers have all begun to lose their preoccupation with external threats and to shift their attention to the effects of U.S. defense policy."[3] The 1970s, in short, witnessed a reversal of the reversal of the traditional liberal priorities that occurred in the 1950s.

This change in attitude was broadly visible across the board among elites, the attentive public, and the mass public. At the level of the mass public, opinion surveys showed a dramatic shift away from the permissive attitude toward military forces that characterized the 1950s and early 1960s to widespread opposition. In the 1950s about 15 percent of the public wanted smaller military forces; in the early 1970s about 50 percent did. A Gallup poll for February 1957, typical of the era, revealed, for instance, that only 9 percent of the public favored a decrease in military spending, while 60 percent favored the existing level, and 22 percent favored an increase. In contrast, a poll taken in March 1971 showed that 50 percent of the public favored a decrease in military spending, 31 percent endorsed the existing level, and only 11 percent were in favor of an increase. "Recent antimilitary feeling," Bruce Russett wrote in 1974 in his summary of the poll data, "is absolutely unprecedented from the beginning of scientific opinion-sampling."[4] Opinion in Congress toward defense spending underwent comparable changes; in particular, the Democratic majorities of the 1950s, which had consistently attempted to increase military spending, were replaced in the 1970s by Democratic majorities that regularly attempted to reduce defense spending.

Widespread as it was, this change in attitude was, nonetheless, more marked among the elites and the attentive public than among the mass public. In the 1950s the "defense intellectuals" dominated the public debate of military matters. By the end of the 1960s, they had been superseded by a new corps of antidefense intellectuals, whose warnings of the dangers of militarism gave a very different tone to public discussion. "Anti-militarism," as Charles Moskos observed, "has become the anti-Semitism of the intellectual community."[5] The outpouring of antimilitary literature between 1968 and 1972 was, indeed, overwhelming. The old ideas of American liberalism in connection with military affairs came again to the surface. An overweening military establishment was a threat to peace, justice, liberty, the revisionists said. The attack on the military-industrial complex, on military institutions (such as the military academies), on military heirarchy and discipline—all sounded familiar themes that had been articulated many times before in American history.

Here we see another manifestation of the paradox of power in America. Ten years earlier, in 1961, President Eisenhower had spoken of some of the dangers inherent in the emergence of the military-industrial complex—whereupon the Kennedy administration had swept into power, dramatically increasing U.S. nuclear and conventional military strength. The power of the complex was, in a sense, reflected in the extent to which Eisenhower's warning was ignored. Ten years later, with military force-levels and budgets declining rather than rising, the intellectual elite became obsessed with the dangers of militarism. Their cries of warning about the power of the military, however, were testimony not to the extent of that power but rather to its waning. In American society, whenever the power of an organization or groups is being exposed, it is also in the process of being reduced.

In the 1950s, the attitudes of the college-educated tended to be some-what more promilitary than those of people with only a grade-school education. In the 1970s, however, the roles were reversed: both groups were more antimilitary than they had been before, but the survey data show the college-educated group to be more antimilitary than those with grade-school education by about 15 percentage points. As Russett comments: *"Antimilitarism is now strongest in the attentive public.* In other words, it is concentrated precisely in that part of the population most likely to vote, to express its opinions, to make campaign contributions and to participate in some form of organized political activity."[6] The anti-militarism of the late 1960s and early 1970s reached an intensity unequaled since the 1920s and 1930s.

In 1975, however, the new wave of antimilitarism showed some signs of abating. The October 1973 Middle East War, the difficulties in negotiating SALT II, the collapse of South Vietnam, and the Soviet-Cuban intervention in Angola all modified somewhat the perceptions of the international environment that had prevailed five years earlier. In addition, the decline in democratic regimes in the less developed countries and the confrontations between developed and less developed countries over raw materials, trade, and the appropriate arrangements for the new international economic order all conjured up the image of a United States at odds with a hostile world. These factors, particularly when combined with a severe economic downturn, at least temporarily stilled the voices of antimilitarism, suspended congressional efforts to cut the military budget, and instead produced a general sympathy in Congress and the executive branch, among Democrats as well as Republicans, for modest increases in military spending. The idea that the military budget would increase gradually in real terms for the next several years became widely accepted.

Whether this recent turnabout in opinion is anything more than a temporary deviation from a more general trend remains uncertain at the present time. Antimilitary attitudes are particularly prevalent not only among the educated but also among the young. Consequently, it seems likely that they will have an influence on public policy for some while to come. On the other hand, the passion that characterized these attitudes during the Vietnam War has clearly abated. It thus seems possible that antimilitarism will become less fervent and more conventional, more like our traditional wisdom with respect to military matters, in which case a fair amount of discretion to determine the size and composition of the military forces will rest with political leaders. Just as antimilitarism is subsiding into indifference, so indifference may make way for a new toleration. But in the absence of a major international crisis, a return to anything resembling the cold war pattern of civil-military relations seems very unlikely.

Nevertheless, as long as antimilitarism is with us, particularly among the educated and the young, it will have two implications for the level of U.S. military forces. First, in the absence of a major international crisis, it will impose a real and important constraint on the level of those forces. Given the decline in the intensity, if not the scope, of antimilitary feeling, however, it seems likely that executive and congressional leaders will retain some freedom of action. Second, any significant reduction of this constraint will occur as the result either of a major international crisis or of actions taken by administration leaders to make it appear that a major international crisis exists. The latter course might well be adopted by an administration eager to reverse what it considered a long-term decline in relative U.S. military strength. The two major U.S. military buildups of the cold war years, indeed, were made politically possible by the accidental crisis of the Korean War and the largely manufactured crisis of the "missile gap." In the future, if administration leaders believe a military buildup is necessary to avert a crisis, they may have even greater incentives than did the leaders of the 1950s to create the appearance of a crisis in order to make that buildup acceptable to Congress and the public.

Constraints on the Use of Military Force

Until the 1950s the prevailing American view on the use of military force emphasized the distinction between war and peace. During peacetime, military force had little role to play except to furnish the base and the cadre for the mobilization of the forces that would be used in wartime. During war, on the other hand, military needs took precedence over all else; the policy was, in Woodrow Wilson's phrase, "force, force to the utmost," and the goal was total victory. The sharp distinction between diplomacy and war was appropriately symbolized by Secretary of State Hull's remark to Secretary of War Stimson, a few days before Pearl Harbor, concerning our deteriorating relations with Japan: "I have washed my hands of it, and it is now in the hands of you and Knox—the Army and the Navy."[7] During World War II, this view was, of course, reflected in the emphasis on unconditional surrender and the general unwillingness to consider the implications of the military conduct of the war for postwar politics and diplomacy. Diplomacy had no role in war, military force little or no role in peace.

During the 1950s, the Korean War, the conflict between General MacArthur and the government in Washington over the conduct of that war, and then Secretary of State Dulles's pronouncements on massive retaliation produced a remarkable change in the prevailing American attitudes on the use of force. The traditional dichotomy between war and peace, force and diplomacy, was replaced by a new stress on a continuum of conflict from war to peace and on the role of force as an instrument of policy and diplomacy. In effect, American strategists and policymakers came to think of military force in Clausewitzian terms: war is the instrument of politics, the continuation of politics by other means, and hence the use of force should not necessarily be "total" but instead limited to that necessary to achieve the political goals of the government. "The subordination of the military point of view to the political," is, therefore, as Clausewitz expressed it, "the only thing which is possible." The recognition by the defense intellectuals—of whom Bernard Brodie, William Kaufmann, Robert Osgood, and Henry Kissinger were most notable—and by others of the intimate relation between force and policy naturally led to the development of theories of limited war and graduated response. Since the government had to be prepared to exercise various military options across the spectrum of conflict, this also meant, of course, that the government had to maintain diverse and hence substantial military capabilities. The military buildup of the Kennedy years reflected, in large part, the impact of this doctrine.

The idea that force could be used for a variety of more or less important political purposes had implications for the constitutional and political processes by which the decisions of the use of force were made. Implicitly, the congressional power to declare war became equated with the power to declare total war. The commitment of forces to something less than total war was, in practice, done under the authority of the President, who acted with such consultation with Congress as he deemed appropriate.

The early 1970s saw a major reaction against this view of the relation of force to policy and against the related ideas of limited war, flexible response, and compellence as guides to the use of force. This reaction stemmed from many sources and manifested itself in many forms. It may well be the most portentous aspect of the disintegration of the cold war pattern of civil-military relations. It was expressed not so much in any decline in our military capabilities to engage in limited war but rather in political, legal, doctrinal, and psychological constraints upon our willingness to use those capabilities. Three of these constraints deserve particular attention.

First, there were some significant shifts in the willingness of mass public opinion to contemplate the use of force overseas. One 1974 poll, for instance, found that a majority of the American public with an opinion on the issue were opposed to the use of U.S. troops to defend Western Europe, West Berlin, or Yugoslavia against attack by the Soviet Union, Taiwan against attack by Communist China, South Korea against attack by North Korea, the Dominican Republic against attack by Cuba, or Israel against defeat by the Arabs. Interestingly, the relationship between elite and mass attitudes on the use of force tended to be the reverse of what it was on the level of force. Foreign policy elites were substantially in favor of the use of U.S. troops to defend Western Europe and West Berlin and were ambivalent about their use to protect the Dominican Republic and Israel. They were about as overwhelmingly opposed as the mass public to the use of U.S. forces to defend Taiwan, South Korea, or Yugoslavia. This hesitancy among both opinion leaders and the mass public concerning the use of U.S. forces overseas was, of course, one aspect of a much broader swing toward isolationism. In 1964, for instance, 8 percent of the American public could be classified as "total isolationists," while 65 percent were identified as "total internationalists." In 1974, the total isolationists had risen to 21 percent of the public, while the total internationalists had shrunk to 41 percent of the public.[8]

Public opinion surveys posing hypothetical questions and general questions are not necessarily a reliable guide as to what public opinion will be in the crunch or how it will respond to vigorous executive leadership. But public opinion does now constitute a potential constraint on the decision to use force that must be taken into account by policy makers. Beyond the question of the *initial* use of force by the government in response to conflict or aggression abroad, the Vietnam experience, when added to that of Korea, underlines the fact that public opinion clearly will not support the *sustained* use of force abroad. It is conceivable that if such sustained use were possible without recourse to conscription, it might be tolerated for a short while. There are, however, few contingencies that could involve the United States in combat for a sustained period of time without the government's resorting either to the draft or to a call-up of reserves, and even in contingencies where such measures were not necessary, public opinion would undoubtedly impose serious temporal limits on the use of U.S. forces.

Second, some indication of the nature of those temporal constraints is furnished by the legal limitations on the executive use of force contained in the War Powers Resolution of 1973. Under the act, the President must report promptly to Congress any introduction of U.S. forces into combat or any major new deployment of U.S. forces abroad. Such use of forces must then be terminated within sixty days unless Congress either declares war or specifically authorizes such use. When coupled with other legislation prohibiting the use of U.S. forces in Indochina (1973) and in Angola (1975), the likelihood seems small that Congress would authorize the sustained use of force under the War Powers Resolution for anything other than response to a major and direct challenge to vital U.S. security interests. Limited war on the model of the 1950s and 1960s has become a legal impossibility for the United States.

Third, the ideas of limited war and graduated response are being rejected on theoretical grounds. The Korean War inspired the doctrine of limited war; the Vietnam War did just the opposite. Vietnam is now being interpreted as a case in which the limited war theories of the 1950s were applied and found wanting. Flexible response and the gradual escalation of U.S. force did not produce the desired results. Instead, the prevailing argument now—advanced by both ex-hawks and ex-doves— is that a massive application of American power to North Vietnam in the early phases of the conflict might well have produced a relatively quick and satisfactory resolution of the conflict. Graduated response was, in General Westmoreland's words, "ill-considered," a "lamentable mistake," the product of "nebulous nonmilitary" considerations. The military judgment of the effects of the policy was well summed up by one air force officer: "We taught the bastards to cope."[9] And while the lessons drawn from Korea did not seem to work in Vietnam, the lessons drawn from Vietnam have been reapplied to Korea: "One of the lessons of the Vietnamese conflict," Secretary of Defense Schlesinger observed with Korea in mind, "is that rather than simply counter your opponent's thrusts, it is necessary to go to the heart of the opponent's power: destroy his military forces rather than simply being involved endlessly in ancillary military operations."[10]

Thus, prevailing American opinion on the use of force appears to have reverted to the pre-World War II assumption of a sharp dichotomoy between war and peace. In fact, there has been a marked decline in the past eight years in the peaceful use of force by the United States to support its diplomacy.[11] But is the separation of force and diplomacy a realistic and constructive assumption with which to confront the 1970s and the 1980s? At the end of the Korean War, the then secretary of defense, Charles E. Wilson, remarked, "I do not think we could fight another Korea and not use all the resources necessary to win the war. . . . I do not think the American people would be in favor of another one like that." Vietnam proved Wilson a good political prophet. On the other hand, Wilson's successor during the Vietnam War, Robert McNamara, had, at least for a while, a somewhat different view:

> The greatest contribution Vietnam is making—right or wrong is beside the point—is that it is developing an ability in the United States to fight a limited war, to go to war without the necessity of arousing the public ire. In that sense, Vietnam is almost a necessity in our history, because this is the kind of war we'll likely be facing for the next fifty years.[12]

McNamara could be right in his judgment about future military contingencies; Wilson could be right in his judgment about the constraints on how we can deal with these contingencies.

Political, legal, and military factors thus all lead to a rejection of what seemed to be the sophisticated doctrines of the 1950s on limited war and graduated response. The reaction of the doves against the way we got into the Vietnam War reinforces the reaction of the hawks against the way we fought it. A future Vietnam is more likely to last seven weeks than seven years. The United States will probably be slower to resort to force in the future than it has been in the past, but when it does, it will apply overwhelming force in order to achieve its objectives quickly and decisively. The emphasis will be on limiting the duration of the conflict, not on limiting the means. In this sense, future aggressors may well end up paying part of the cost of the failure of the U.S. military strategy in Vietnam.

The Military and Society: Congruence and Interaction

The changes in the environment of the military have also had an impact on the military establishment itself. They have raised the question whether the military establishment will continue to tend toward "civilianization" and convergence with social institutions or whether this trend has been reversed in the direction of remilitarization and a renewed stress on traditional military values and behavior. And beyond this, which tendency ought to be encouraged? Is convergence or insulation the more desirable course for the military establishment in the post-Vietnam world? Military officers, principally field-grade officers, have engaged in a wide-ranging and most impressive discussion of these questions.

A useful analysis of these issues requires that a sharp distinction be made between two dimensions of the convergence-isolation dichotomy. On the one hand, there is the issue of the *congruence* between the military establishment and society or other social institutions, that is, the extent of their similarity or difference in terms of personnel, functions, structure, and other salient characteristics. Second, there is the issue of *interaction* between the military establishment and society or other social institutions, that is, the extent to which military institutions and individuals have a multiplicity of contacts with nonmilitary institutions and individuals.

The distinction between congruence and interaction is important because, as David Segal and his associates have usefully reminded us, there is quite possibly a tendency for levels of congruence to vary inversely with levels of interactions. A military establishment, they argue, that encompasses many nonmilitary functions and that operates in a civilianized manner is likely to be more autonomous—freer from civilian contacts and, potentially, civilian control—than a military establishment that is purely military and that, precisely because of its specialization, is dependent upon civilian society for support.[13] Clearly, there is a certain logic to this argument. On the other hand, it is perhaps more useful to envision congruence and interaction as two separate dimensions of civil-military relations susceptible to a variety of possible combinations in both theory and practice (see Table 1). A self-sufficient military establishment would indeed be characterized by a high level of congruence and a low level of interaction. As Segal and his associates suggest, such a situation has been approximated by U.S. forces stationed abroad in their relations with the surrounding societies. On the other hand, a high level of congruence could also exist in a military establishment with a very high level of interaction, and even identification, with society; this is the pattern implied by the nation-in-arms concept and embodied in some measure in the practice of countries like Israel and Switzerland. Third, a military establishment with a low level of congruence with civilian society—that is, one highly specialized in its military functions—might also have a low level of interaction, as tended to be the case with the U.S. military establishment in the late nineteenth century. Finally, a professional relationship might be said to exist when there is a relatively low level of congruence,

TABLE 1

ALTERNATIVE RELATIONS BETWEEN THE MILITARY AND SOCIETY

Level of Interaction	Level of Congruence	
	Low	High
Low	Insulation	Self-sufficiency
High	Professionalism	Identification

reflecting specialization, but a relatively high level of interaction, reflecting responsiveness to civilian society.

Recent trends in the U.S. military establishment have been in the direction of lower levels of congruence and, to a lesser degree, lower levels of interaction in relation to civilian society. During the cold war period, for instance, both the officers and the enlisted personnel of the armed forces were recruited from fairly diverse sources in civilian society. The shift to purely volunteer recruitment of enlisted personnel undoubtedly will make the enlisted personnel of the armed services less representative of the civilian population as a whole. How drastically the social composition of the military will be altered, however, at the moment remains unclear and is, indeed, a matter of considerable dispute. The expanded role of the military academies in providing officers is likely to raise the proportion of officers whose values and attitudes, if not necessarily their social origins, differ from those of civilian leadership groups. In addition, the increasing predominance among ROTC programs of those operated by smaller colleges and universities, particularly in the South and West, may reinforce a growing gap between military leaders and economic and political elites. As we have noted above, the latter tend to have fairly strong latent if not active antimilitary attitudes. Thus, in terms of personnel, the level of congruence between the military and other social institutions appears to be declining.

With respect to functions, recent analyses have stressed the extent to which the trend toward convergence between the military occupational structure and the civilian occupational structures has ceased and perhaps even been reversed. In addition, as between military and civilian institutions, there seems to be "a reaffirmation, in the current decade, of a traditional division of labor that perhaps did get blurred in the early 1960s."[14] Or, as another observer put it, with the decline of the mass army, there is a tendency toward "remilitarization" and an abandonment

of the "school of the nation" functions that modern armies have sometimes assumed."[15] In military educational institutions, broad courses on
international affairs have yielded to a stress on more "purely military"
topics. At the same time, however, sharply differing views are held by
analysts, both civilian and military, as to whether this or the reverse
course is the more desirable. Some have argued for a wider concept of
military professionalism, challenging the argument of *The Soldier and the
State* that the essential task of the military is "the management of violence"
and positing a much broader administrative and managerial role for
professional military officers. Other officers have urged a reaffirmation
of the traditional concept. Similar debates have gone on over the desirability
of the armed forces' assuming responsibility for "domestic action" or
"civic action" programs unrelated to their national security functions.[16] But
while these debates have been raging, the trends toward military role
expansion and functional congruence between the military establishment
and civilian institutions have shown signs of coming to a halt.

Finally, with respect to the structure of the military, strong tendencies
existed in the late 1960s and early 1970s toward convergence with
civilian patterns. Much of the civil turmoil, many of the changes in
life-style of those years, manifested themselves in the armed services as
well as in civilian society. Traditional concepts of rank, discipline, and
social relations were reexamined, and efforts were made—in the navy
under Zumwalt, for example—to stress the similarities between life-styles
and human relations within the military establishment and those outside.
One recruitment slogan read, "The Army wants to join you!" Some
officers suggested even further alterations in the traditional military
structure, such as abolition of the "two-caste" division between officers
and enlisted men in favor of a single nondiscontinuous heirarchy.[17] At
present, however, the trend toward structural congruence between military
and civilian institutions, like the trend toward functional congruence,
seems to have leveled off.

In general, then, the level of congruence in terms of personnel, function,
and structure between the military establishment and civilian institutions
seems to be declining. The evidence concerning patterns of interaction
is more mixed, but here again the dominant trends appear to be downward.
In the long run, voluntary recruitment will reduce the interaction between
the military and society as well as having its impact on the level of congruence. Congressional efforts to reduce the numbers of military officers
attending civilian institutions of higher education are further evidence
of the decline of both interaction and congruence between military and
civilian institutions. One proposal espoused by many army officers in the
early 1970s was that the military itself be sharply divided into "combat
forces" and "support forces."[18] The former would, in most respects,

be very noncongruent with civilian institutions and would have little interaction with the civilian sector. The various components of the support forces, on the other hand, would be very similar in operation and function to parallel civilian groups and would have significant interaction, including personnel interchanges, with those groups. The prospects for such a neat sorting out of these relationships seem remote. Indeed, if this proposal were implemented, the problems of congruence and interaction between the military and society that now exist would merely be duplicated within the military in the relations between the combat forces and the support forces.

Conclusion: The Dilemma Revisited

The argument advanced in *The Soldier and the State* in 1957 was that, given the existing international situation, "the requisite for military security" was a shift from liberalism to a "sympathetically conservative" attitude toward the needs of military professionalism. To a surprising extent, that shift occurred. In some measure, also, it has now been reversed. The immediate future would thus appear to involve a combination of the liberal attitudes dominant before World War II (Phase I) but repressed during the cold war (Phase II), with the security threats nonexistent in Phase I but predominant in Phase II. The dilemma that was partially resolved in the 1950s has returned.

For the immediate future, civil-military relations in the United States will be characterized by loosely constraining public attitudes and more tightly constraining elite attitudes on military force-levels. More important, both public and elite opinion will impose severe constraints on the future uses of our military forces. At the same time, although a variety of conflicting pressures will be at work, the prevailing trend will be toward less congruence and possibly less interaction between the military establishment and other social institutions. The toleration that characterized the cold war period of civil-military relations is not likely to be superseded by traditional extremes of either extirpation or transmutation. As the effects of the democratic surge, the Vietnam War and the enthusiasm for détente fade into the past, the prevailing attitude of American society toward its military forces is likely to be one of modified or contingent toleration. This attitude will be reinforced if the military limit the extent to which they turn inward and instead emphasize their professional military functions and characteristics without self-consciously breaking their ties with civilian society. In the end, the dilemma of military institutions in a liberal society can only be resolved satisfactorily by a military establishment that is *different from but not distant from* the society it serves.

Notes

1. Samuel P. Huntington, *The Soldier and the State: The Theory and Politics of Civil-Military Relations* (Cambridge, Mass.: Harvard University Press, 1957), p. 2.

2. See the argument in my chapter on the United States in Michael Crozier, Samuel P. Huntington, Joji Watanuki, *The Crisis of Democracy* (New York: New York University Press, 1975), pp. 59 ff.

3. Douglas H. Rosenberg and Raoul H. Alcala, "The New Politics of National Security: A Selected and Annotated Research Bibliography," in Bruce M. Russett and Alfred Stepan, eds., *Military Force and American Society* (New York: Harper and Row, 1973), p. 197.

4. Bruce M. Russett, "The Revolt of the Masses: Public Opinion on Military Expenditures," in John P. Lovell and Philip S. Kronenberg, eds., *New Civil-Military Relations: The Agonies of Adjustment to Post-Vietnam Realities* (New Brunswick, N.J.: Transaction Books, 1974), p. 76.

5. Charles C. Moskos, Jr., "Foreword," in Lovell and Kronenberg, *New Civil-Military Relations*, p. xi.

6. Russett in Lovell and Kronenberg, *New Civil-Military Relations*, p. 77. See also William Schneider, "Public Opinion: The Beginning of Ideology?" *Foreign Policy*, no. 17 (Winter 1974-1975), p. 117: "The persistence of antimilitarism as an attitude associated with education represents a basic change in the traditional structure of foreign policy opinion."

7. Quoted in Huntington, *Soldier and State*, p. 317.

8. John E. Reilly, ed., *American Public Opinion and U.S. Foreign Policy 1975* (Chicago: Chicago Council on Foreign Relations, 1975), p. 18; *New York Times*, June 16, 1974, p. 3. For evidence of some shift in mass opinion in 1976 toward a greater willingness to aid in the defense of Western Europe and Japan, see William Watts and Lloyd A. Free, "Nationalism, Not Isolationism," *Foreign Policy*, no. 24 (Fall 1976), pp. 16-19.

9. General William C. Westmoreland, *A Soldier Reports* (Garden City, N.Y.: Doubleday and Co., 1976), pp. 112, 119, 195-96, 410; Franklin D. Margiotta, "A Military Elite in Transition: Air Force Leaders in the 1980s," *Armed Forces and Society*, vol. 2 (Winter 1976), p. 162. For a definitive analysis of the views of the top military commanders and civilian advisers on the use of force during the cold war years, see Richard K. Betts, "Soldiers, Statesmen, and Resort to Force: American Military Influence in Crisis Decisions, 1945-1975" (Ph.D. thesis, Harvard University, 1975).

10. *U.S. News & World Report*, May 26, 1975, p. 25.

11. Barry Blechman of the Brookings Institution has developed quantitative data demonstrating this decline.

12. Quoted in Samuel P. Huntington, "Democracy Fights a Limited War: Korea, 1950-1953," in Merrill F. Peterson and Leonard W. Levy, eds., *Major Crises in American History: Documentary Problems* (New York: Harcourt, Brace and World, 1962), vol. 2, p. 481; and Douglas H. Rosenberg, "Arms and the American Way: The Ideological Dimension of Military Growth," in Russett and Stepan, *Military Force*, p. 170.

13. David R. Segal et al., "Convergence, Isomorphism, and Interdependence at the Civil-Military Interface," *Journal of Political and Military Sociology*, vol. 2 (Fall 1974), pp. 157 ff.

14. Ibid., p. 169.

15. Jacques van Doorn, "The Decline of the Mass Army in the West: General Reflections," *Armed Forces and Soviet*, vol. 1 (Winter 1975), p. 155.

16. For some of the views held by military officers on these issues, see Richard F. Rosser, "A Twentieth Century Military Force," *Foreign Policy*, no. 12 (Fall 1973), pp. 156ff.; Edwin A. Deagle, Jr., "Contemporary Professionalism and Future Military Leadership," *The Annals of the American Academy of Political and Social Science*, vol. 406 (March 1973), pp. 162ff.; Robert G. Gard, Jr., "The Future of the Military Profession," in *Force in Modern Societies: The Military Profession*, Adelphi Paper No. 103 (London: International Institute of Strategic Studies, 1973), pp. 1-8; Zeb B. Bradford, Jr., and Frederic J. Brown, *The United States Army in Transition* (Beverly Hills: Sage Publications, 1974), Chapters 13, 14; William L. Hauser, *America's Army in Crisis: A Study in Civil-Military Relations* (Baltimore: Johns Hopkins University Press, 1973), Chapter 12; William R. Corson, "Towards a Concept of Military Domestic Action" (Unpublished paper, Inter-University Seminar on Armed Forcs and Society, September 1971).

17. See, for example, Rosser, "Twentieth Century Military Force," and the ideas canvassed in *Rapporteur's Report: First Inter-Service Defense Policy Conference, 10-12 May 1972* (Department of Political Science, United States Air Force Academy and the National Security Program, Graduate School of Public Administration, New York University).

18. This was proposed by Charles C. Moskos, Jr., "The Emergent Military: Civil, Traditional or Plural," *Pacific Sociological Review*, vol. 16 (April 1973), pp. 255ff. Similar arguments are advanced in Rosser, "Twentieth Century Military Force"; Hauser, *America's Army*; and Bradford and Brown, *Army in Transition*.

2
An Empirical Reassessment of Military Professionalism

Sam C. Sarkesian

In retrospect, the issues for the U.S. military in Vietnam were not whether the war was just or unjust or whether the military should serve in that area. The issues were the effectiveness of the military in defeating the enemy and the impact of the total experience on the military institution and the profession.[1] This latter concern has caused much debate and discussion in the aftermath of Vietnam. Obviously, the Vietnam war can be blamed neither for all the ills of the military establishment nor for all of the professional issues that subsequently surfaced.[2] Nevertheless, insurgency required the U.S. military to engage in operations characterized by a broad political-psychological dimension and by the ambiguity of a traditional Asian culture. The result of the Vietnam war was a highly critical environment fostering self-analysis and a major reassessment of military professionalism.[3]

This chapter reexamines military professionalism with reference to the major themes developed in recent empirical studies; it also analyzes the relationship of these themes to general propositions regarding the military profession in the post-Vietnam era. We focus, in particular, on value convergence and empathy between the military and society and on officer perceptions of the military institution and profession.

Five studies are particularly relevant to these purposes: The Army War College's *Study on Military Professionalism* (1970); Moellering's "Future Civil-Military Relations" (1973); Russett's "Political Perspectives of U.S. Military and Business Elite" and (with Hanson) *Interest and Ideology* (1974 and 1975); Bachman and Blair's *Soldiers, Sailors and Civilians* (1975); and Margiotta's "A Military Elite in Transition" (1976).[4] Although there are other useful empirical studies, the works noted here are especially significant to the study of professionalism.

The *Study on Professionalism* by the Army War College (hereafter called the Army War College Study) in 1970 was designed to "assess the professional climate of the Army, to identify any problem areas, and to formulate corrective actions." It involved approximately 250 officers from six army schools and 165 members of the Army War College Class of 1970 and army members of the faculty. Data were gathered in questionnaires supplemented by interviews (at schools outside the Army War College) and in seminars. The officers involved in the sample ranged in grade from second lieutenant to general, with most of the respondents in the grades of captain to colonel.

Moellering conducted his study in February 1972. He used questionnaires to survey 970 Army Command and General Staff College students and faculty regarding their perceptions of the profession and civil-military relations. His purpose was to assess the presumption that the army had turned inward as a result of the Vietnam experience.

Russett examined the perspectives of U.S. military and business elites in 1973 by assessing survey data from 567 vice-presidents and senior vice-presidents from "Fortune 500" industrial corporations and leading financial institutions. He also used questionnaires to survey 619 U.S. military officers enrolled in the five U.S. war colleges (Air, Army, Navy, National, and Industrial College of the Armed Forces). The survey dealt with various U.S. foreign and domestic policy matters, international relations, and issues of peace and war.

Bachman and Blair examined samples from the army, navy, and the civilian population regarding value preferences and perceptions about the military. The data sampling years were 1972 to early 1975. They collected data from thirty-eight different navy sites and included 2,522 officers and enlisted personnel. Civilian data were collected in February and March 1973 as part of a larger interview study conducted by the Survey Research Center. This study included 1,327 dwelling units in which a trained interviewer conducted an interview with a designated respondent, male or female, aged eighteen or older. This approach resulted in a 75 percent rate of response from interviews and approximately 90 percent from questionnaires. The army sample was collected from November 1974 to April 1975; it included a population of 2,286 army officers and enlisted personnel from a cross section of units.

Margiotta based his study on biographical, demographic, and career information on 351 line air force general officers in active-duty status on January 1, 1974. He also collected twenty-three items of biographical, demographic, and career data in a computer search of personnel files of early promotees. The major part of the study was based on responses by 680 students who were enrolled at the Air War College and the Air Command and Staff College in 1974. Their responses included answers to a series of questions supplemented by interviews concerning air force careers, perceived social status, and civil-military relations.

Although these studies cover a variety of matters, several significant issue areas emerge: professional ethics and behavior, military and civilian value systems, and the nature of professional perceptions regarding society, the military institution, and the profession. One should understand at the outset, however, that any examination of professionalism, its boundaries and substantive elements, lacks a generally accepted and coherent perspective. The elusiveness of professional boundaries and the imprecise definitions and measures of substantive professional matters—such as honor, ethics, and morals—invite an intuitiveness and subjectivity. Nevertheless, the significance of these studies is the amazing consensus that appears on substantive issues among different populations and services at different times.

Identifying ethical criteria and their underlying moral content is difficult enough for most scholars, but for the professional officer, it is a dilemma resolved primarily by reference to organizational behavior and institutional loyalty. Equally important, behavior and professed ethical standards do not necessarily coincide. Indeed, as many people argue, even the best military professionals are rationalizing individuals. The impact of socialization and institutional behavior on professionalism is likewise not clear. These matters are difficult analytical concepts in themselves, but the difficulty in assessing cause-and-effect relationships compounds the problem. Finally, there is a wide gap between macroanalytical and microanalytical perspectives on professionalism. That is, the translation of concepts of "duty, honor, country" to day-to-day behavior is at best an ambiguous undertaking filled with ethical pitfalls and analytical roadblocks. Yet the issue persists—is there a new professionalism in the post-Vietnam era? What impact will a changing professionalism have on the military system?

The Vietnam Heritage

As noted earlier, Vietnam cannot be blamed for all of the problems and dilemmas facing the military profession in the late 1970s, but most people agree that the war catalyzed a number of substantive professional issues. Nowhere is this more evident than in the matters of professional integrity and institutional demands. One of the consistent themes evolving from the Vietnam war is the visible gap between the ideals of the profession and the actual behavior of "professionals." Another major concern attributed to the Vietnam war is the all-volunteer military—a result, according to many sources, of public resistance to the selective service system. Many scholars and military men also view the antimilitary sentiments and antiwar attitudes of important segments of the population as crucial elements in the depreciation of the military's status and prestige. Thus, as a result of a major conflict that involved virtually the entire officer corps, there is sufficient persuasion to conclude that the U.S.

military has been affected institutionally, professionally, and socially.

My Lai, as perhaps no other incident, illustrates these matters. Lt. William Calley and other members of Charlie Company, Task Force Baker of the Americal Division, were accused of murdering Vietnamese citizens— old men, women, and children—in March 1968. The behavior of a number of officers compounded the issue. Yet instead of aggressive investigations and positive procedures to preclude future incidents, evidence suggests that procrastination, delay, self-protection, institutional loyalty, and career concerns characterized the reactions of those who should have been investigating.[5] As one scholar summarized these phenomena: "All the bureaucratic tendencies visible in the Army are characteristic of all organized power in America. But the Army accentuates and exaggerates bureaucracy because it is a bureaucracy without competitors; conformity, careerism, cultivation of the right attitudes and the safe style become almost necessary obsessions, difficult for any but a very few to resist."[6]

Other incidents associated with Vietnam have given rise to professional self-examination and criticism—the actions of the "Khaki" Mafia, the unauthorized bombing raids over North Vietnam and the subsequent falsification of reports, the refusal of officers to engage in bombing missions, riots on navy ships, and "fragging" in army units. The issues raised by such incidents are not limited to the military profession; all professions face ethical problems. Nevertheless, the importance of this matter to the military is clear: because of its uniqueness, its purpose, and its relationship to society, the military profession faces a problem regarding its ethical behavior, professional ideals, and civil-military linkages.

Military Values and Societal Norms

In their concern that military and civilian systems should be closely linked, some scholars and military men argue that the community bestows legitimacy on the military. Thus, to reinforce and maintain this legitimacy, the two systems must have congruent values. The community's perceptions of professional ethics and norms are essential in developing esteem, prestige, and credibility. The central argument is that the military profession is relevant only in terms of the community. The community is the sole client.

However, the profession's authority and identity, although sanctioned by the community, must be continually nurtured and reinforced by military-civilian linkages. The profession must demonstrate not only its expertise at war but also its acceptance of the community's value system and "rules of the game." As Barnes has written:

How, then, are we to assess the vast powers that the military has come to hold over millions of American citizens? Simply, the military's powers are legitimate to the extent—and *only* to the extent—that they are in the first instance, consonant with contemporary standards of justice and humanity, and then only when the foreign policy which the military carries out is both (1) directly related to the defense of the nation or its closest democratic allies, and (2) by elected officials whose decisions are guided by the will of the people as expressed through the political process.[7]

A soldier-scholar differs with this view: "One would be hard pressed to find a mature professional soldier who would accept Barnes' premise."[8]

The distinctions between these views of the civilian and the professional stem from different perspectives: one focuses on political and the other on operational considerations. This difference in perspective lies at the root of the distinctions between societal and military views of ethical behavior; indeed, this is one of the important distinguishing factors between the military and society.

Scholars are prone to state that the military must have links with society and provide an institution that transmits and incorporates the core values of society into the professional system. Therefore, American society considers the profession as supportive of democratic values, even though professional values are more authoritarian and bureaucratic in nature. More important, society expects military men to commit themselves to the basic precepts of the political system. For example, civilian control of the military, individual dignity and worth, and justice before the law must be ingrained in the military professional.

Professional perspectives and dimensions cannot be developed in a vacuum. Presumably, military systems reflect societal norms; thus, professional ethics, attitudes, and beliefs develop a close identification with those of society. Moreover, the socialization of the military professional is not completely divorced from society. This does not suggest that professionalism cannot develop its own dimensions. For example, society temporarily rejects further Vietnams, but the professional should not necessarily reject further study of counterinsurgency. But it does require a shift in professional emphasis to dimensions that are compatible with society.

Therefore, we suggest that a fundamental concern in the study of professionalism should be societal values and the extent to which these values influence the military value system. This naturally leads to a second focus on the degree of congruence between the two systems. A military system in a democratic society cannot long exist without some reference to civilian values. Equally important, the values of society—technical skills, professional ethics, or "proper" political perspectives—must have some visible and meaningful connection with the same values in the military.

There is much disagreement regarding the proper relationships between the military profession and society. Some sources argue for a distinct separation, but others press for a civil-military fusion. For example, Hauser writes: "It seems almost simplistic to conclude that a disjuncture between the Army and society has brought about this long litany of troubles, but that is what the evidence suggests. The Army has been unable to isolate itself from society sufficiently to maintain its authoritarian discipline or to prevent the intrusion of such social ills as racial discord and drug abuse."[9] Thayer, on the other hand, notes: "The concept of professionalism seems to demand that professionals themselves be constantly aware of the delicate balance they must maintain in their own behavior between autonomy and fusion. They cannot be so totally separated as to become the proverbial 'society within a society,' but neither can they afford total integration within the civilian overhead."[10]

Thus, the debate focuses on theories of convergence, divergence, or cautious, limited linkages. The convergence theory presumes that domestic pressures and institutional requirements cause a convergence of military and civilian value systems. The divergence theory presumes a return to a professional isolation of pre-Vietnam years, encouraged by the volunteer system. A middle perspective presumes that the profession recognizes the need for closer association with society and a commitment to societal values but that the military must maintain its separateness and uniqueness.

Separateness and Alienation

The evidence suggests that military men are ambiguous about the proper relationships between the military and society although they are clear about such relationships in certain specific areas. On the one hand, military men accept control by society as legitimate, and they desire a close linkage between democratic values and the military. On the other hand, most military men feel that military influence vis-à-vis civilians should increase in specific areas concerning military matters. Moreover, the evidence shows an underlying dissatisfaction with civilian perceptions of the military and the lack of civilian appreciation for the demands of the military profession.

With respect to military-civilian convergence, Moellering, for example, found that 74 percent of the army officers surveyed believed that the army should "take more cognizance of American civilian society, its values, and its criticism."[11] Both Margiotta and Moellering also found that officers were concerned about the representativeness of the volunteer military. This concern reflected a feeling that the volunteer military should be representative of society to avoid isolation from society.

Interestingly, Margiotta found that two-thirds of his air force sample opposed secondary roles for the military: e.g., remedial education, engineering projects, ecological reclamation, and highway rescue. He states that "younger, lower-ranking ACSC officers expressed less resistance to change in traditional air force roles. Although most officers opposed the suggestion of an expanded role, 40 percent of the ACSC officers expressed at least a qualified agreement."[12] Russett's data also show that most officers prefer a focus on social problems within the military before focusing on problems outside the military[13] and that most military men prefer not to become involved in the broader range of social issues.

Professional attitudes appeared most clearly, however, in views about the uniqueness of the profession. These views show an underlying desire for separation from society and for recognition that the profession is unique.

In the Army War College Study, officers felt that the military should "accept the fact in the Army that the rights, privileges and responsibilities of the military are not and cannot be the same as the rights, privileges, and responsibilities in civilian life. . . . We have democracy in this country but we have an autocracy in the military. And the public ought to be educated along these lines and the military ought to stand up for what it has to have—and that is a disciplined force of people."[14] Of the officers surveyed at the Army Command and General Staff College, 69 percent felt that discipline, sacrifice, and patriotism are found "to a greater or much greater extent in the U.S. Army" than in American society. Ninety percent of the air force officers surveyed by Margiotta responded in the same way.[15]

The gap that professionals perceive between the military and society and the attitude that the military is distinct are also reflected in the military's views regarding society's perception of the profession. Margiotta states that "at least three-fourths of our interviewees cited specific instances in which their friends and families either misunderstood their careers or undervalued the highly competitive criteria for advancement in the Air Force."[16] In other words, immediate friends and relatives outside the military have little understanding of the military profession and, in turn, place little value on it. He concluded:

> Officers believe that the public neither knows nor understands their educational achievements, their lifestyle based on upper-middle-class pay and allowances, the competitive promotion system in the Air Force, and the variety and complexity of jobs that may be required of them. When we added officer experiences in Southeast Asia, their dissatisfaction with media coverage of the military and their feeling that they safeguard important national values, then perceived patterns of status and alienation are more understandable, if not completely realistic.[17]

As is consistent with their perceptions of the Vietnam experience, professionals are apparently concerned about society's views of the military role in the war and are very suspicious of the press. These attitudes seem to reinforce the feeling of separateness from society, and they may also indicate a latent, but deeply felt, resentment of society's treatment of the military.

For example, Moellering found that 67 percent of the officers surveyed felt that "the American public's view of U.S. Army involvement in Vietnam was negative."[18] Similarly, 40 percent of the officers felt that antiwar and antimilitary attitudes had evolved within American society because "politicians got the Army into a war it didn't want to fight and placed undue restrictions on it which precluded its proper mission accomplishment." Another 20 percent felt that antiwar and antimilitary sentiments stem from "the general lack of commitment to traditional values by the youth of our country." Less than 5 percent thought that the army was at fault.

Russett found that more than 52 percent of the business elite surveyed answered "no" to the question, "Do you personally think it was correct for the U.S. to send ground troops to Vietnam?" On the other hand, more than 70 percent of the military officers said "yes." Slightly more than 38 percent of the business elite said "yes" to the question, and approximately 27 percent of the military officers responded "no."[19]

Equally instructive is the fact that 95 percent of the air force officers in Margiotta's study concluded that the "recent media coverage of the military was biased against the military, and fully 48 percent selected the extreme response 'strongly biased against the military.'"[20] In reference to the attitudes about the media, Margiotta noted that "officers comprising the future military elite have, at this moment, a basic distrust of a major and influential national institution." Moellering's study reinforced this perspective with the finding that more than 19 percent of the army officers surveyed "considered the press highly biased and antagonistic." More than 67 percent considered the news media "usually biased against the Army."[21] The Army War College Study reported a series of interviews as follows: "A frustration—a real feeling of frustration—and this is expressed all the way up to the most senior officers we talked to—the senior officers expressing a strong frustration—just as strong as the young captains, that the media is biased."[22]

Although "alienation from society" is a strong term to use in describing the military and society in the 1970s, the evidence suggests that it has some relevance. Focusing specifically on this issue, Bachman and Blair noted that career military men have a "profound sense of dissatisfaction."[23] They have a "feeling that their own kind, the top military leaders, should have a good deal more power over most national military policy than civilian leaders do."

Margiotta observed that "our officers, however, did not feel valued by society. . . . Fully 80 percent of our potential future elite view their status as low or declining."[24] Moreover, according to Margiotta, "we found that two-thirds of our respondents felt that 'alienation' is the best way to characterize present civil-military relations.''[25]

The evidence shows a high degree of professional ambiguity about the relationship between the military and society. There is a recognition that some degree of congruence between military and civilian systems is needed, but recognition stops far short of accepting any linkage that would dilute the uniqueness of the profession and its military focus. An underlying suspicion of society's intentions and attitudes, stemming partly from the Vietnam war, has apparently become ingrained in the profession—a factor that may have serious civil-military repercussions in future crises. However, the fact remains that the profession is not sure how to reconcile its desires for congruence with society with its desires for professional distinction.

The Military Mind

The distinctions between society and the military help to explain a similar phenomenon regarding the concept of the "military mind." There is, of course, considerable doubt regarding the existence of a "military mind" and the notion of a monolithic professional perspective. Indeed, several scholars argue that there is no great divergence between the attitudes of military men and other elites within society.[26] Nevertheless, there is evidence of commonly held professional attitudes regarding the nature of professionalism and military purpose.[27] Moreover, when they are viewed within the context of professional life-styles and professional purpose, these distinctions provide a persuasive argument that the professional perception of the environment and society contrasts with that of other elites in society.

The evidence presented in Moellering and in Bachman and Blair apparently supports this view. Moellering found that more than 82 percent of the respondents felt that the American public perceived a "military mind."[28] On the other hand, in response to a question about professional self-perceptions, only 15 percent felt that the officer corps possessed a military mind. Bachman and Blair reached similar conclusions:

> there is considerable evidence that the belief system of career military men— officers and enlisted—is distinctive from that found among comparable civilian groups. Career men were considerably more pro-military substantively and showed greater homogeneity or consensus in these beliefs. . . .
>
> One of the arguments raised in the debate about the all-volunteer force was the danger of a "separate military ethos" or distinctive "military mind" brought about by a military force made up largely of career men. The findings presented above suggest some basis for concern in this area.[29]

Bachman and Blair also found a distinction between career officers and college graduates: "Career officers are a great deal more favorable toward the military organization, more eager for U.S. military supremacy [rather than parity with the Soviet Union], more willing to make use of military power, and much more in favor of enlarged military [vs. civilian] influence over U.S. policy affecting the military."[30]

Although attempts at categorizing political ideologies can easily distort conclusions about attitudes, a significant point is the general dominance of conservative or "hawkish" attitudes among military officers. Although these attitudes are not surprising, they lend weight to the argument concerning a distinctly military view of the world.

Margiotta found what he calls a "pluralist conservatism," in which 64 percent of the respondents identified themselves as conservative or somewhat conservative.[31] He also concluded that "conservative ideology in the military increased with rank and age" and noted that, although no clearly definable political ideology differentiated military from civilian elites, "issues related to national defense produced the most 'hawkish' or 'conservative' discussion."[32]

In Moellering's survey of officers' self-characterization of their political ideology, he found that more than 48 percent identified themselves as "conservatives," 2 percent as "right," 34 percent as "middle-of-the road," and only 15 percent "liberal" and 3 percent "left." He likewise concluded that this gives some credence to the view that the conservatism of the officer corps is a potential basis for alienation from a more "dynamic" society.[33]

Although Russett eschewed the concept of a military mind, he found an ideological distinction between military men and business elites. He concluded that "On many matters that might be construed as in the sphere of professional military expertise, but where constitutional authority is vested in civilians, the civilian-military differences in policy preferences are great. Especially on matters of weapons acquisition and defense spending levels, conflicts would be further compounded by any military effort to protect bureaucratic interests of their organization."[34] Furthermore, Russett found that slightly more than 33 percent of the business elite said "yes" and more than 59 percent said "no" in response to the question, "Do you think a 25 percent reduction in defense spending would have an adverse effect on the American economy?" More than 61 percent of the military said "yes" and slightly more than 31 percent said "no" in response to the same question.[35]

Although conservative versus liberal distinctions may not in themselves indicate a military mind, a distinct military perspective is clear, particularly when it is combined with separateness, alienation, and general views regarding the values of society. Moreover, if one presumes that socialization does reinforce the military perspective and that there is a self-selection process, as Bachman and Blair conclude, then a distinct conservative or highly promilitary perspective is ingrained in the institution.[36] Although every institution and profession can be expected to develop its own perspective, this is manifested in the military profession in dissatisfaction with the perceived lack of military influence; it encourages a "we-they" syndrome and perpetuates a separateness from society that can easily lead to alienation and a motivation to protect military interests under all circumstances.

The Institutional and Professional Context

The Volunteer System

The question of the volunteer military has evoked wide-ranging debate since the publication of the Gates Commission Report.[37] The first debates focused on the availability of proper levels of manpower for a volunteer system. A new vocabulary developed with such terms as *shortfall, first term accessions,* and *true volunteers.* Later, the debate focused on the black-white ratio; some sources argued that a high percentage of blacks in the volunteer system would tend to make the military less attractive for whites. Moreover, there was concern regarding the representativeness of the force.[38] In addition, there is currently an increasing concern with the total force concept (active military, National Guard, and Reserves), of which the combat readiness and combat capability of the volunteer force are components. Generally, the issues of manpower quantity and quality, racial and sex percentages, combat readiness, and military posture have negatively affected professional perspectives on military capability. Undoubtedly, this is partly attributable to the relative lack of experience with a volunteer system and to the fact that the system has not yet been tested fully.

An observer and participant in the Gates Commission made this astute comment in 1971:

> Although the broader issues have received extensive airing in the media, it is not clear, because of the highly charged rhetoric frequently involved, that all of the probable long-range implications of moving toward an all-volunteer force have been clearly and forcefully set before the American public. Most of the detailed discussions and analyses have dealt with the draft and its individual virtues and shortcomings. While a good case can probably be made, costs aside, for preferring the all-volunteer concept over the draft, it would be imprudent at best to adopt the all-volunteer force without full consideration of the relevant costs and their possible long-term implications for national security policy.[39]

The evidence seems to suggest that professional officers still grope for clear-cut assessments of the impact of the volunteer force on the profession and on the ability of the military to carry out its combat mission.

Army officers appear the most ambiguous and skeptical about the volunteer system. Almost 40 percent of the officers surveyed by Moellering felt that the volunteer army "will be worse than today's Army because it will have been cut off from American society."[40] Five percent of this group felt that the army would be worse because it would be less efficient. More than 27 percent felt that the volunteer army would not be much different from today's army. Interestingly, only 1.8 percent felt that the volunteer army would be an improvement because it could be cut off from American society and thus be more professional. (These observations are also relevant to the examination of military-civilian value convergence.)

According to Margiotta's study, "Only a limited number of officers accept the all-volunteer concept, even though the Air Force should be influenced least by this new manpower policy. Two-thirds of the respondents felt that the all-volunteer force would be worse than 'today's military.'" Almost one-half were concerned that the volunteer system would create a military that did not represent a cross section of American society.[41]

Individual Ethics and Professional Norms

Military men are prone to view the dilemma between individual conscience and institutional demands as unique to their profession. But as the study of history and political philosophy shows, men in various walks of life have faced this dilemma throughout the course of Western civilization.

No one argues that institutional demands and societal order are not crucial considerations. On the other hand, what weight should be given to individual values and conscience? As individuals, we are responsible for our own actions and decisions. If a conflict develops between the institution and the individual, what can be done? In an institution such as the military, this becomes particularly troublesome.

Professional stress on the requirements for integrity and on institutional goals has normally shaped individual behavior to the point that it subordinates dissent or resistance. In other words, integrity and instant obedience are the sine qua non of the military institution. However, the question of conscience in conflict with institutional demands has become a crucial issue of professional legitimacy.

Although these issues have always been a part of the professional dimension, the Vietnam experience not only exacerbated civil-military tensions but also fostered alienation between professionals and the political system and developed some professional antipathy toward professional behavior. This is primarily a perceived professional issue rather than an issue in society at large.

Military professionals' views of the military are linked to the perceptions of the general society. The most articulate groups in society come from the more educated elements, some sectors of the liberal intelligentsia, and many important representatives of the mass media. The antimilitary attitudes of these groups lead military professionals to equate this small articulate sector with the whole of society. The ultimate result is a negative view on the part of military professionals, a view that deprecates the esteem, prestige, and professional legitimacy of the military.

With respect to the dilemma between the individual officer and the profession, the Army War College Study concluded that "officers of all grades perceive a significant difference between the ideal values and the actual or operative values of the officer corps. This perception is strong, clear, persuasive, and statistically and qualitatively independent of grade, branch, educational level, or source of commission."[42]

The same study examined an in-house report by the U.S. Military Academy (USMA) Office of Research on the reasons for the resignations of several officers from the USMA Class of 1966. According to these officers, many senior officers, particularly colonels and lieutenant colonels in command positions, "were forced to abandon their scruples and ignore the precepts of duty and honor; and if necessary to lie and cheat in order to remain successful and competitive."[43] This was primarily attributable to the demands of the "system."

To underscore the point on professional integrity, the study noted the results from four teams who had interviewed officers of all grades at different army posts. One team reported that "dishonesty is across-the-board."[44] Another team noted that "this was a general opinion of all these groups. . . . They brought out the fact that in their judgment, integrity was a luxury that a junior officer could not afford in today's army and survive."[45] The report from a third team concluded that "the word that was used by every one of our four seminar groups, I think it's the key word here, survivability. Unless you are willing to compromise your standards, even ever so slightly, you will not survive in the Army system."[46] The fourth team observed that "junior officers felt that the barrier to their integrity was the senior officers' lack of integrity."[47]

The recent "West Point scandal," as one national magazine labeled it, is another reflection of the issues of honor—professional ideals and actual behavior.[48] Despite the merits or demerits of the honor system at West Point, one should note that the "operationalizing" of the ideals of the profession remains an elusive matter, whether at the service academies or in the profession. An officer is not supposed to lie, cheat, or steal. This has been a fundamental element of professional behavior, but a gap, perhaps an unbridgeable gap, still exists between ideals and reality.

An important insight about professional views on professional integrity and on the gap between ideals and behavior comes from the Army War College Study. In reporting the comments of one interview team, the study noted that "every group pinpointed the fact that the Army would not tolerate a wave-maker or a boat-rocker regardless of how high the officers' personal standards were."[49] It also observed that "pressures to achieve unrealistic goals, whether imposed by design or generated through incompetence, soon strain the ethical fiber of the organization."[50] The study concluded in part:

> It is impossible to forecast future institutional climates with any degree of reliability. Nevertheless, it is not unreasonable to state as consequences of the present climate: it is conducive to self-deception because it fosters the production of inaccurate information; it impacts on the long-term ability of the Army to fight and win because it frustrates young, idealistic, energetic officers who leave the service and are replaced by those who will tolerate if not condone ethical imperfection; it is corrosive of the Army's image because it falls short of the traditional idealistic code of the soldier—a code which is the key to the soldier's acceptance by a modern free society; it lowers the credibility of our top military leaders because it often shields them from essential bad news; it stifles initiative, innovation, and humility because it demands perfection or the pose of perfection at every turn; it downgrades technical competence by rewarding instead trivial, measurable, quota-filling accomplishments; and it eventually squeezes much of the inner satisfaction and personal enjoyment out of being an officer.[51]

As indicated in this conclusion, there is a close relationship between professional integrity and the institutional environment. In the current environment, many professionals obviously decry the pressure to conform, but more importantly, they decry the pressure to conform to what they believe are misplaced values.

In addressing this issue, the study noted:

> The climate . . . is one in which there is disharmony between traditional, accepted ideals and the prevailing institutional pressures. These pressures seem to stem from a combination of self-oriented, success-motivated actions, and a lack of professional skills on the part of middle and senior grade officers. A scenario that was repeatedly described in seminar sessions and narrative responses includes an ambitious, transitory commander—marginally skilled in the complexities of his duties—engulfed in producing statistical results, fearful of personal failure, too busy to talk with or listen to his subordinates, and determined to submit acceptably optimistic reports which reflect faultless completion of a variety of tasks at the expense of the sweat and frustration of his subordinates.[52]

These observations have deep ramifications regarding the professional perspectives of the military institution. They suggest an institutional orientation that places high value on institutional loyalty and doctrinal orthodoxy. Moreover, they suggest that the institution rewards officers who accept existing institutional norms and frustrates those who tend to be more liberal and flexible. Furthermore, this conclusion is supported, to a degree, by the professionals' perception of their own ideology—a basically conservative orientation that inherently supports the status quo and a "don't rock the boat" attitude. As the Army War College Study noted, "The layers of bureaucracy stifle innovative ideas and intuitive thinking. Senior officers shy away from new ideas, fear mistakes. The supervisory mode of the 'squad leaders in the sky' is prevalent."[53]

Moreover, the evidence seems to indicate an acceptance of situational ethics in which individual ethics are subordinated to the requirements of the institution, the demands of the mission, and career demands. In such circumstances, many professionals feel that the profession is forced to accept standards of behavior and ethical norms far removed from the idealistic notions of "duty, honor, country."

Conclusion

The military profession is clearly engaged in serious soul-searching, although the process does not appear to have a coherent focus. The ramifications of this soul-searching, however, are not clear. Nevertheless, two themes emerge from this examination. The first theme is an underlying professional dissatisfaction with the military's status and influence in society. The Vietnam experience may well be the root of current professional dissatisfaction. Not only do professionals blame society for the Vietnam involvement; they also feel that the military has been made the scapegoat for society's mistakes. This feeling is also reflected in the low marks given to the mass media by a great majority of professionals as well as in the cautious and quite limited acceptance of the convergence of military-civilian value systems, an attitude that probably indicates the professionals' desire to remain separate from society. This attitude does not necessarily imply complete isolation but rather a desire to retain a professional life-style unique to the military and to strengthen the autonomy of the profession in its own sphere.

If the term "military mind" means a rigid, uncompromising perspective that focuses on problems through a military intellectual or semi-intellectual view of the world and seeks essentially military solutions, then there is some doubt as to its existence in the U.S. military. This does not deny that the system may include such "minds," but they are probably a distinct minority. If "military mind" means that the profession seeks to insure its autonomy over a unique way of life, then there is a military mind, at least according to the evidence presented here. The desire for this autonomy further motivates professionals to seek an effective voice in policies that affect the military system and reflects a homogeneity of views on military matters. Finally, the military perspective reinforces and perpetuates those values that are distinct from civilian life.

The second major theme is the professionals' concern with ethics, institutional demands, and individual values. This concern is reflected in the perceived gap between professional ideals and professional behavior. Indeed, one can reasonably conclude that professional ethics, in the broadest terms, is the basis of professional restiveness concerning the relationship of the professional to society, the capability of the military institution, and the general character of the military profession. Many professionals feel that institutional demands and organizational behavior encourage "careerism," subordinate individual ethics, erode professional ideals, and develop a career orientation based on unquestioned acceptance of institutional requirements, regardless of the ramifications to the profession and to the individual.

In the profile that emerges from these studies, the military profession is generally conservative. More specifically, there is a commitment to existing institutions, a distinct promilitary philosophy, and "hard-line" views in military matters; and the conservatism becomes more intense as one moves up the rank pyramid. Although a visible divergence between military and civilian values is not apparent in the abstract (i.e., in the broader sense of democracy and domestic policies), there is a distinctly different perspective on matters of war, military policy, and the influence of military leaders. This difference is exacerbated by the professional perception of society's negative and disparaging attitudes regarding the military and military life-styles. This separateness between society and the military is crystallized into a more perceptible form by the homogeneity of professional views on specific matters dealing with the military.

Although there appears to be no major cause for alarm regarding professional perceptions of their roles and status in society, some attention should be focused on the basic causes of these perceptions, since they may well have a direct link to a deeper professional concern. Perhaps the most relevant explanation lies in the succinct observations of de Tocqueville:

> When a nation loses its military spirit, the career of arms immediately ceases to be respected and military men drop down to the lowest rank among public officials. They are neither greatly esteemed nor greatly understood . . . it is not the leading citizens, but the least important who go into the army. . . . The elite of the nation avoid a military career because it is not held in honor, and it is not held in honor because the elite of the nation do not take it up.

> There is therefore no reason for surprise if democratic armies are found
> to be restless. . . . The soldier feels that he is in a position of inferiority
> and his wounded pride gives him a taste of war which will make him needed,
> or a taste of revolution, in the course of which he hopes to win by force
> of arms, the political influence and personal consideration which have not
> come his way.[54]

One need not unconditionally accept de Tocqueville's observations in
order to recognize their relevance to current professional restiveness.
Although it is unlikely that the profession will deliberately seek combat
to restore its perceived status and influence, evidence of lost honor and
self-depreciation reveals a serious dilemma within the profession. The
dilemma results from a perceived gap between professional ethics and
behavior, a gap manifested not only in critical assessments of military
purpose and civil-military relations but also in continuing professional
self-analysis. Although professional self-analysis may be a healthy condition and a characteristic of a dynamic profession, it may also manifest
a more serious problem within the profession.

Reinforced by institutional demands and professional loyalty, this
condition can easily lead to a profession preoccupied with its status,
jealous of its prerogatives, harsh in its response to divergence, and relentless
in its pursuit of professional purity. Such a "military mind," unresponsive
to society, rationalizing its actions as servants of the state, and cloaked
in the barrier of military expertise would be most dangerous to professional
ideals and compatibility with democratic society.

As it looks to the future, the profession has several choices available
to it.[55] First, it can perpetuate the traditional and narrow perception of
professionalism on the basis of the premise that military men are unconditional servants of the state. This choice suggests not only a robotlike
response to political leadership but also a rationale for uncritical response
with limited intellectual perspectives. Second, the profession can assume
an occupational model based on a civil service role in which civilian
politics, unionization, salary concerns, and fringe benefits become the
underlying professional motivation. This can erode the professional ethos
and expose the profession to political manipulation, posing dangers not
only for the profession but also for the entire political system. Finally, the
profession can strive to develop a new rationale in which the military views
itself as something more than an unconditional servant of the state. In
so doing, the military would need to develop political understanding and
expertise. At the same time, it should develop a sense of realistic and
enlightened self-interest and professional perspectives transcending boundaries traditionally associated with duty, honor, and country.

This third approach would provide the greatest opportunity for the
profession to establish a realistic and effective voice in the political system

within the accepted "rules of the game." Moreover, it would allow some individuality in the search for professional satisfaction and purpose, with a degree of recognition that individual ethics and values are components of professionalism. The institutionalization of healthy skepticism, reasonable inquiry, and legitimate dissent would do much to reinforce the worth of the individual and provide a momentum to innovation, imagination, and self-examination. Finally, this approach would provide the greatest opportunity for the profession to respond to professional restiveness and to establish a civil-military relationship that can maintain value systems mutually enriching and supportive of professional ideals and democratic expectations.

Notes

1. This section is from Sam C. Sarkesian, *The Professional Army Officer in a Changing Society* (Chicago: Nelson-Hall Co., 1975), p. 188.

2. For an excellent overview of the literature, see Charles C. Moskos, Jr., "The Military," *Annual Review of Sociology* 2 (1976). See also John C. Lovell, "No Tunes of Glory: America's Military in the Aftermath of Vietnam," *Indiana Law Journal* 49, no. 4 (Summer 1974).

3. See, for example, Morris Janowitz, *The Professional Soldier* (New York: Free Press, 1971); Samuel P. Huntington, *The Soldier and the State* (Cambridge, Mass.: Harvard University Press, 1957); Stuart Loory, *Defeated* (New York: Random House, 1973); William L. Hauser, *America's Army in Crisis* (Baltimore: Johns Hopkins University Press, 1973); and Zeb B. Bradford and Frederic J. Brown, *The United States Army in Transition* (Beverly Hills, Calif.: Sage, 1973).

4. U.S. Army War College, *Study on Military Professionalism* (Carlisle Barracks, Pa., June 30, 1970); John H. Moellering, "Future Civil-Military Relations: The Army Turns Inward?" *Military Review* 53, no. 7 (July 1973); Bruce M. Russett, "Political Perspectives of U.S. Military and Business Elite," *Armed Forces and Society* 1, no. 1 (Fall 1974); Bruce M. Russett and Elizabeth C. Hanson, *Interest and Ideology: The Foreign Policy Beliefs of American Businessmen* (San Francisco: W. H. Freeman and Co., 1975); Jerald G. Bachman and John D. Blair, *Soldiers, Sailors and Civilians: The "Military Mind" and the All-Volunteer Force* (Ann Arbor, Mich.: Institute for Social Research, The University of Michigan, November 1975); Franklin D. Margiotta, "A Military Elite in Transition: Air Force Leaders in the 1980s," *Armed Forces and Society* 2, no. 2 (Winter 1976).

5. Seymour M. Hersh, *My Lai 4: A Report on the Massacre and Its Aftermath* (New York: Random House, 1970).

6. Wilson Carey McWilliams, *Military Honor after My Lai*, Council on Religion and International Affairs, Special Studies no. 213 (New York, 1972).

7. Peter Barnes, *Pawns: The Plight of the Citizen-Soldier* (New York: Alfred A. Knopf, 1972), p. 8. Emphasis in original.

8. Hauser, *America's Army in Crisis*, p. 88.

9. Ibid., p. 186.

10. Frederick C. Thayer, "Professionalism: The Hard Choice," in *National Security and American Society*, ed. Frank Trager and Philip S. Kronenberg (Lawrence: The University of Kansas Press, 1973), p. 568.

11. Moellering, "Future Civil-Military Relations," p. 81.

12. Margiotta, "A Military Elite in Transition," pp. 177-178.

13. Russett and Hanson, *Interest and Ideology*, p. 281.

14. U.S. Army War College, *Study on Military Professionalism*, p. B-1-16.

15. Moellering, "Future Civil-Military Relations," p. 80; Margiotta, "A Military Elite in Transition," p. 168.

16. Margiotta, "A Military Elite in Transition," p. 168.

17. Ibid., p. 180.

18. Moellering, "Future Civil-Military Relations," p. 79.

19. Russett and Hanson, *Interest and Ideology*, pp. 277-278.

20. Margiotta, "A Military Elite in Transition," p. 168.

21. Moellering, "Future Civil-Military Relations," p. 80.

22. U.S. Army War College, *Study on Military Professionalism*, p. B-1-15.

23. Bachman and Blair, *Soldiers, Sailors and Civilians*, p. 15.

24. Margiotta, "A Military Elite in Transition," p. 165.

25. Ibid.

26. Russett, "Political Perspectives," p. 97.

27. David M. Krieger, "A Developmental Model of the Military Man" in *Soldiers in Politics*, ed. Steffen W. Schmidt and Gerald A. Dorfman (Los Altos, Calif.: Geron-X, 1974); see also Huntington, *The Soldier and the State*.

28. Moellering, "Future Civil-Military Relations," p. 78

29. Bachman and Blair, *Soldiers, Sailors and Civilians*, p. 100.

30. Ibid., pp. 12-13.

31. Margiotta, "A Military Elite in Transition," p. 169.

32. Ibid., p. 172.

33. Moellering, "Future Civil-Military Relations," p. 77.

34. Russett, "Political Perspectives," p. 98.

35. Russett and Hanson, *Interest and Ideology*, p. 277.

36. Bachman and Blair, *Soldiers, Sailors and Civilians*, p. 15.

37. Gates Commission, *The Report of the President's Commission on an All-Volunteer Armed Force* (Washington, D.C.: Government Printing Office, February 1970).

38. See, for example, Morris Janowitz and Charles C. Moskos, Jr., "Racial Composition in the All-Volunteer Force," *Armed Forces and Society* 1, no. 1 (November 1974): 109-123.

39. Ames S. Albro, Jr., "Observations on the Costs of an All-Volunteer Armed Force." Unpublished Manuscript, August 26, 1971.

40. Moellering, "Future Civil-Military Relations," p. 80.

41. Margiotta, "A Military Elite in Transition," p. 175.

42. U.S. Army War College, *Study on Military Professionalism*, pp. iii-iv.

43. Ibid., p. 17.

44. Ibid., p. B-1-10.

45. Ibid., p. B-1-17.

46. Ibid., p. B-1-19.

47. Ibid., p. B-1-23.

48. *Time*, June 7, 1976.

49. U.S. Army War College, *Study on Military Professionalism*, p. B-1-20.

50. Ibid., p. 24.

51. Ibid., pp. 28-29.

52. Ibid., pp. iii-iv.

53. Ibid., p. B-29.

54. J. P. Mayer, *Alexis de Tocqueville: Democracy in America*, trans. George Lawrence (New York: Doubleday and Co., 1969), p. 648.

55. A fuller explanation of these choices can be found in Sam C. Sarkesian and Thomas M. Gannon, eds., "Introduction: Professionalism," *American Behavioral Scientist* 19, no. 5 (May-June 1976).

3

The Military Profession and Its Task Environment: A Panel Study of Attitudes

B. Guy Peters
James Clotfelter

Earlier chapters by Huntington and Sarkesian described changes in the dimensions of military professionalism and in civil-military relations. Their analyses summarize historical forces and a major body of survey literature. They provide a useful backdrop for this more narrowly focused chapter, which examines similar issues by using in-depth interviews and a panel study of selected army officers to test hypotheses suggested by public administration studies. In general, our findings reinforce the conclusions of these earlier chapters.

Important research in the field of public administration states that public bureaucrats confront an increasingly unstable task environment created by rapid social changes. These studies also suggest that this unstable environment has not limited the flexibility of public bureaucrats; it has permitted them increasing autonomy to deal with their organizational tasks.[1]

We are interested here in a different category of public bureaucrat—the professional military officer. In 1971, we personally interviewed a relatively small sample of active-duty U.S. Army officers and reinterviewed them by mail in 1975. These interviews focused on the officers' attitudes toward, and perceptions of, their environment and their tasks. This research design of gathering the same data over time is known as a panel study. It allows us to assess whether officers perceived environmental changes; that is, whether the officers thought that outside groups that deal with the military and provide its resources view the military and its responsibilities in a new light. We also wished to determine whether the officers perceived that their tasks are changing, but the sampling of officers reported few changes in this respect, at least in regard to foreign policy tasks.

Contrary to the findings of some administrative studies in other functional areas, we found that many middle-level officers in the sample perceive that the military has *not* adjusted successfully to the problems produced by its unstable environment and that is has *decreased* autonomy.

To the extent that it does exist and is perceived, this inability to adjust is probably related to perceived hostile attitudes among important components of the civilian population. That is, officers who feel that civilian groups treat the military unfairly also probably feel that this situation restricts professional autonomy. They perceive that instability in the environment restricts autonomy because the instability stems from changes in attitudes toward military bureaucrats and, consequently, lessens the respect and autonomy granted to them. More speculatively, increased negative perceptions of the military by civilians would perhaps erode the professional mystique that sometimes discourages outside efforts to participate in decision making on military issues. Thus, we find that the army professional represents a class of public employee with reactions to a changing environment quite different from the reactions reported for other types of public workers.

Another important trend found in the sample of officers is that perceived managerial styles within the military in 1975 are more similar to styles outside the military than in 1971. The impact of the participative management style, in particular, has increased in the military. This is a long-term trend brought about by the Vietnam war, by the manpower situation under an all-volunteer army, by efforts of professional officers to become less differentiated from civilian society, and by conscious study and adoption of these management methods.[2]

To explore these questions and relationships, albeit incompletely, we used data derived from our panel study of U.S. Army officers. In 1971, we interviewed 153 active-duty officers at the Georgia Institute of Technology in Atlanta, the Army Infantry School at Fort Benning, Georgia, and the Command and General Staff College at Fort Leavenworth, Kansas. At the time of the original interviews, all but three of the officers were majors and captains. We make no claims that this sample is representative either of the officer corps in general or of this particular stratum of officers. However, the sample was quite useful as a quasi-experimental group to examine the effects of certain career and environmental changes on attitudes.[3] Results of the 1971 interviews have been reported in four earlier papers.[4] In the spring of 1975, the current addresses of 131 of the 153 officers were obtained. A questionnaire containing many of the same questions used in 1971 and some different items related to specific changes since that time was mailed to those officers. Of the 131 officers, 76 returned completed questionnaires; these 76 officers constitute the panel on which we report results in this chapter. Analysis indicates that these 76 officers are not significantly different from the total sample of 154 officers in terms of their backgrounds and attitudes in 1971.

In this chapter, we consider three sets of variables. The first set comprises the perceived relationships of the officers to civilian society, to the profession's external task environment, and to the groups that participate in setting the profession's tasks and providing the support necessary to achieve them. Within this set of variables are indicators of respondent perceptions of civilian society. These indicators include measures of a perceived gulf between the military and civilians and the fairness with which the military is treated by various important groups.[5] The second set of indicators deals with the officers' opinions of their profession, including management styles, the perceived openness of the profession, the profession's success in adjusting to problems and pressures, and the extent and causes of officer career motivations. The third set of indicators deals with the foreign policy tasks—specifically, with the officers' perceptions of past foreign policy events and their expectations concerning future foreign policies. The study also includes several variables describing the personal and professional backgrounds of the responding officers.

The Military and Society

As described in earlier papers, the officers questioned in 1971 indicated that they felt separated from the larger civilian society, that the general population had insufficient respect for the army officer's responsibilities, and that selected civilian groups and the mass media treated the military unfairly. This gulf between the military and civilian communities is the principal means used to measure the officers' reactions to their changing environment. Officers with more contacts with civilian society were less likely to perceive a gulf between themselves and civilian society.[6]

In 1975, we found that more officers perceived a gulf between themselves and civilian society. As shown in Table 1, the proportion of officers who

TABLE 1

PERCENT OF OFFICERS WHO BELIEVE
CIVILIANS HAVE SUFFICIENT RESPECT FOR OFFICERS

	Percent 1971	Percent 1975
Yes	34	25
No	60	57
Don't Know	6	18
	N = 76	N = 76

TABLE 2

PERCENT OF OFFICERS WHO BELIEVE THE MILITARY IS TREATED FAIRLY

| | By Civilian Groups | | | | | |
| | Faculty | | Congress | | Civilian Leaders | |
	1971	1975	1971	1975	1971	1975
% fairly or very fairly	24	13	55	25	45	25

| | By Media | | | | | | |
| | TV News | | TV Programs | | Newspapers | | Magazines | |
	1971	1975	1971	1975	1971	1975	1971	1975
% fairly or very fairly	17	20	29	14	34	25	35	29
	N = 76							

felt that civilians had sufficient respect for the professional military officer declined between 1971 and 1975: only 25 percent of the respondents in 1975 reported that civilians had sufficient respect. The proportion of officers who believed that civilian groups treated the military fairly also declined between 1971 and 1975. Table 2 shows the decline of perceived fair treatment, with the decline particularly pronounced for Congress and civilian political leaders. Thus, the officers in the sample *do* perceive significant changes in their task environment. They perceive that civilians whose support is necessary for their profession have become even less supportive than in 1971. This is true despite the end of the Vietnam war and a lessening of obvious civilian reaction to the military establishment.

We were also interested in learning whether the officers felt that the profession had adapted successfully to changes in the environment. Table 3 shows that almost all of the responding officers felt that significant changes had occurred in patterns of military leadership. They divided almost evenly between those who felt that the changes had been adaptive (e.g., greater need to explain orders and persuade men, more responsibility given to junior officers, a more open hierarchy) and those who identified less adaptive changes (e.g., less integrity, less professionalism). Officers who felt that the mass media treated the military unfairly and officers who acknowledged that they felt conspicuous when they wore their

TABLE 3

RELATIONSHIP OF PERCEIVED CONSPICUOUSNESS TO PERCEIVED CHANGES IN
MILITARY LEADERSHIP (1975 INTERVIEWS)

	Feel Conspicuous in Uniform	
Military Leadership has been:	Percentage With High Feeling	Percentage With Low Feeling
Adaptive	38	73
Not Adaptive	62	27
N =	38	34

uniforms off base were much more likely to identify nonadaptive changes within the military profession (see Table 4). Thus, officers who felt apart from civilian society also tended to believe that changes in their profession have been negative and that the profession has not adapted to changes in the environment.[7] This was also true of officers who perceived hostile attitudes within the media.

Another instrument for measuring the successful adjustment of the military to its environment was a set of four items asking whether the officers believed that the army provided sufficient guidelines to deal with problems more likely to occur in the army today than in previous eras: disobedience, racial disturbances, political dissent, and drug abuse.

TABLE 4

RELATIONSHIP OF PERCEIVED MEDIA FAIRNESS TO PERCEIVED CHANGES IN
MILITARY LEADERSHIP

	Believe Media is Fair to Military	
Military Leadership has been:	Percentage With High Belief	Percentage With Low Belief
Adaptive	67	48
Not Adaptive	33	52
N =	44	32

TABLE 5

RELATIONSHIP OF PERCEIVED CONSPICUOUSNESS TO PERCEIVED
SUCCESSFUL ADJUSTMENT OF ARMY TO PROBLEMS

	Feel Conspicuous in Uniform	
In dealing with problems the Army has been:	Percentage With High Feeling	Percentage With Low Feeling
Adaptive	39	68
Not Adaptive	61	32
N =	38	34

As shown in Table 5, the extent to which an officer felt conspicuous in uniform off the base was related to these measures of perceived army successful adjustment. Officer perception of media fairness was also significantly related to this measure of adjustment.

Opinions of the Profession

These findings are consistent with our earlier findings on the perceived distinctiveness of officers and their attitudes toward changes occurring within the military. One of the most interesting findings is that officers who believe that a gulf exists between the military and civilians also tended to espouse more traditional methods of leadership and motivation. Thus, the officers who perceived their jobs as relatively similar to the jobs performed by civilian managers were more likely to adopt the more participative management style practiced in civilian society; i.e., these officers felt that the best method of motivating men to do their jobs was to involve them in decisions, explain orders, and allow for greater initiative and responsibility for the lower echelons of the organization. They were also asked whether this style of leadership was as successful in combat situations as in noncombat situations. We coded as "participative managers" the officers who answered these questions affirmatively.

Between 1971 and 1975, an apparent change occurred in the style of management practiced by these officers. In 1971, we asked what is the "best way to get subordinates to do what you want?" Twenty-three percent of the respondents gave answers that were coded as relatively authoritarian or traditional, e.g., giving orders and treating men firmly. They stated that this style of leadership was most useful in both noncombat and combat situations. In 1975, *none* of the respondents reported such a traditional view of management styles, although some officers stated that more traditional styles of leadership may be more useful in combat situations. Morris Janowitz reported this shift from traditional or authoritarian leadership to modern or participative management in 1960, and insofar as this sample represents a trend within the military, the shift continues.[8]

One may hypothesize that inception of the all-volunteer force led to more participative leadership styles. As more men enter the army voluntarily from civilian society, we might expect that the techniques will become more like civilian techniques. However, all the officers did not agree that the all-volunteer force was a major factor in the shift to participative management. Most of the officers responding in 1975 reported that the all-volunteer force had had no effect on leadership, and 38 percent felt that the all-volunteer force had stimulated more emphasis on participation. Only 5 percent identified a major negative effect on discipline as a result of this shift in recruitment patterns.

One might also expect that participation in the Vietnam war and the types of tasks performed by officers would contribute to the trend toward participative management. Some sources have suggested that the war produced changes in leadership patterns and that officers who perform tasks similar to civilian tasks (e.g., support branches as opposed to combat branches) would more readily accept participative styles. However, neither the number of combat positions held by the officers nor the branch of service had any significant relationship with the acceptance of modern leadership styles. This finding suggests a more general permeation of military leadership styles by the surrounding society. It further suggests that the *perceived* similarity of tasks performed by officers to tasks performed in civilian society may be more important in the adoption of modern leadership styles than the *objective* similarity of the tasks (see Table 6).

TABLE 6

RELATIONSHIP OF PERCEIVED JOB DIFFERENCES TO STYLE OF LEADERSHIP

	Military Jobs are Much Like Civilian Jobs	
Leadership Style Chosen	Percentage Who Think They Are	Percentage Who Think They Are Not
Modern	63	46
Traditional	37	54
N =	43	33

In other words, an officer's belief that his tasks are similar to civilian tasks is more likely to produce "modern" leadership than the actual similarity of the tasks.

A third pattern perceived by the officers was the changing of the military hierarchy or, more specifically, the opening of the hierarchy to more alternative means of promotions and different types of careers. The military has long held that command experience is necessary for promotion or, at least, that long periods in specialist positions damage an officer's career mobility.[9] As the army responds increasingly to the technological environment and its tasks, the hierarchy should become more open to technically specialized careers. Officers obviously perceived changes in the openness of the profession between 1971 and 1975. Many more officers reported that informal contacts were not crucial to promotion and that long periods in specialist careers had relatively little negative impact on their careers. Less clear, however, is the relationship between the perceived distinctiveness of the military career and the perceived openness of the profession. As shown in Table 7, we found a statistically significant relationship in the 1975 responses between the perceived conspicuousness of officers and the perceived effects of time spent in specialist positions. But several other potential relationships were not significant, though they showed tendencies in the predicted direction. Therefore, as officers regard their careers as distinct from other professions, they also stress factors that make them distinctive, such as command positions and combat positions.

Another possible explanation of the officers' perceived openness of

TABLE 7

PERCEIVED CONSPICUOUSNESS COMPARED TO BELIEFS ABOUT EFFECT
OF TIME SPENT IN SPECIALIST POSITIONS ON PROMOTION

Effect of Specialist Time on Promotion	Feel Conspicuous in Uniform	
	Percentage With High Feeling	Percentage With Low Feeling
Helps	9	14
Depends	61	74
Hurts	30	12
N =	38	34

the profession is their success in achieving promotion. We hypothesized that officers who were denied promotion during the period in question would find it easier to rationalize their own relative lack of success by blaming the system. We did find that officers who had not been promoted were significantly more likely to claim that informal contacts were important for promotion than officers who had been promoted. However, there are few significant differences among the officers as to how they perceive the effects of specialist or staff positions on their career prospects. Neither those who have been promoted nor those who have not been promoted tend to fear that these positions will damage their careers, although many noted that this change had been recent.

Foreign Policy Tasks and the Military

The Vietnam war was clearly the most traumatic experience for the U.S. military in recent history. Although it by no means represented all current foreign policy tasks, it structured much contemporary thinking on foreign policy. Among the possible effects, one might expect to find that officers who felt most strongly that the war had been unsuccessful and that the army had been misused would develop the most negative views of civilian society, feel the most remote from civilians, and be the most pessimistic about the ability of the army to adapt to its new task environment. In other words, those officers who felt the most hindered by civilians during their experience in Vietnam might tend to take the most pessimistic views of civilians and of the military's ability to cope with changing civilian society.

Only a few officers regarded the Vietnam war as anything other than an unqualified defeat. Respondents could classify the war as a success, a limited success, a stalemate, a limited defeat, or a defeat. Of the seventy-six respondents in 1975, only one considered the war a U.S. victory; another viewed it as a limited U.S. victory; and two viewed it as a stalemate. The rest, with almost equal frequency, viewed it as either a limited or a total U.S. defeat. Likewise, as Table 8 shows, only three respondents thought that the army was used wisely in the war; another twenty-four thought that it was sometimes used wisely; but most thought that it was generally used unwisely. When asked why the army had been unwisely employed, the most frequent answer, by far, was that civilian leadership had prevented it from fully using its power and its weapons. Thus, in view of a general feeling that civilians were significant factors in the U.S. defeat, we hypothesized that officers who felt the defeat most strongly would also have the most negative attitudes toward civilians. In general, however, there was little evidence to show that the attitudes of officers who classified the Vietnam war as a total U.S. defeat were different from the attitudes of other officers. Although all of the relationships

TABLE 8

WAS THE ARMY USED WISELY IN VIETNAM?

Feel Conspicuous in Uniform	Percentage Answering No	Percentage Answering Yes, or Sometimes
High Feeling	66	48
Low Feeling	34	52
N =	47	27

among the indicators took the direction hypothesized above, only one was significant: the relationship between the officers' perception of the wise or unwise use of the army in Vietnam and their feelings of conspicuousness in uniform off base. Thus, the feeling that civilians had interfered with the conduct of the war perhaps widened the perceived gulf between officers and civilian society, but there is little evidence to suggest a general separation of the officers from civilians on this basis. This may be related in part to general feelings that the war was at least a partial defeat and in part to the survey instrument's inability to distinguish more gradations of feelings regarding the nature of that defeat.

The officers had another opportunity to react to the role of civilians in the U.S. defeat through a number of attitudinal questions expressing sentiments about the relative abilities of civilian and military institutions to make effective decisions and about the role of the military as the personification of traditional American values.[10] In this instance, several significant differences in the officers' attitudes toward civilians were related to their conception of the outcome of the war and the use of the army in the war. Table 9 shows one of these relationships; several other similar relationships are not included. Officers who perceived the war as a total defeat were more likely to regard civilians in a negative light than officers who characterized the outcome of the war more positively. These results show some direct perceptions of a growing gulf between the military and society or some feelings that society and the media treat the military unfairly. Nevertheless, there is some resentment toward society at large, and officers who felt most strongly about the defeat in Vietnam expressed a degree of moral superiority.

Conclusions

Although these results are only preliminary and not so overwhelming as

TABLE 9

RELATIONSHIP OF CHARACTERIZATION OF THE VIETNAM WAR TO
ATTITUDES TOWARD CIVILIAN SOFTNESS

	Characterization of War	
	Percentage Choosing Total Defeat	Percentage Choosing Other Answers
Civilians are "Soft"		
High Belief	64	41
Low Belief	34	59
N =	37	38

one might expect, we have gained some insights into the relationships between changes in the environment of the military organization and its response to those changes. First, we found that respondents to these questionnaires did perceive changes in their task environment. These perceptions are manifested primarily through feelings of the military's increasing separation from civilian society. The officers felt that the profession is treated unfairly by the media and by significant groups within the society, and they perceive that their organizations and their tasks are different from those in the larger society.

The officers' feelings of separation and distinctiveness were related to their feelings that the military was successfully adapting to important changes in its environment. Officers who felt most strongly that the military is separated from civilian society were more likely to take negative views of adaptations occurring within the military; that is, they viewed these adaptations as manifestations of "softness" coming into the army from civilian society.

Finally, there was relatively little relationship between the officers' evaluations of the Vietnam war and their evaluations of the military's adaptation to changes or their evaluations of the task environment. Major hostility toward civilians as a result of the Vietnam war appears in more personalized statements about the softness and indecisiveness of civilian institutions.

Thus, this experiment apparently does not substantiate the basic hypothesis in the literature concerning the relationship of the environment in which an organization functions and the response of the members of the organization. Officers who perceive changes in the task environment are more likely to see the military as engaging in nonadaptive changes. Thus, the reactions of these officers to environmental changes were apparently different from those of many other public employees. The reasons for these differences are as yet unexplained, but they appear worth further study in understanding the changing relationship between the military and society.

Notes

1. See, for example, Charles Perrow, "Hospitals: Technology, Structure, and Goals," in *Handbook of Organizations*, ed. James G. March (Chicago: Rand McNally, 1965); William R. Dill, "Environment as an Influence on Managerial Autonomy," *Administrative Science Quarterly* 2 (March 1958): 409-443; and Nicholas Henry, *Public Administration and Public Affairs* (Englewood Cliffs, N.J.: Prentice-Hall, 1975), Chapter 4.

2. Morris Janowitz, *The Professional Soldier* (New York: Free Press, 1960); also Rensis Likert, *The Human Organization* (Chicago: Rand McNally, 1967).

3. All interviews in 1971 were conducted personally, with a standardized questionnaire containing open-ended and close-ended items. The interviews were conducted by university students at one location and cooperating officers at the others.

4. James Clotfelter and B. Guy Peters, "Profession and Society: Attitudes of Army Captains and Majors" (Paper for the Workshop on Research in Military Manpower—the All Volunteer Military, Chicago, September 1972); idem, "Mass Media and the Military: Selected Ratings of Fairness," *Journalism Quarterly* 51 (Summer 1974): 332-334; idem, "Post-Vietnam Perspectives of Military Officers: The Profession and Its Tasks" (Paper for the Section on Military Studies [ISA], biennial meeting, Carlisle Barracks, Pa., November 1974); and idem, "Profession and Society: Young Military Officers Look Outward," *Journal of Political and Military Sociology* 4 (Spring 1976): 39-51.

5. Clotfelter and Peters, "Profession and Society."

6. Ibid., p. 45.

7. Our earlier studies have shown that the question on how conspicuous officers felt in uniform off the base was a good indication of the feeling of a gulf between the military and the civilian society. It was also useful in predicting a number of other attitudes.

8. Janowitz, *The Professional Soldier*.

9. The evidence on the actual effects of these positions is less clear.

10. The Vietnam war is now past, but the reaction to that conflict still conditions much contemporary thinking about foreign policy.

Part 2

International and Domestic Influences

4
Emerging Major Power Relationships: Implications for the U.S. Military in the Late Twentieth Century

Robert L. Pfaltzgraff, Jr.

We are at the threshold of an era in which military and economic power will be far more diffused than at any time in the twentieth century. In addition to the superpowers and China, the international system of the last quarter of this century will contain a series of regional powers, as well as smaller actors, in possession of destructive capabilities of unprecedented lethality and accuracy—nuclear and nonnuclear. Patterns of interaction among actors—major powers and lesser powers—will be far more variegated and complex than at any time in the twentieth century. Thus, the world of the next generation, the focal point of this analysis of emerging major power relationships, is likely to hold for the United States and its allies even greater danger than in the recent past.

As in the past, relations among major powers will be the product of many factors—foreign policy objectives and capabilities, domestic stability or instability and political will, and levels of economic and technological development. It is possible, of course, to postulate a variety of scenarios in the U.S.-Soviet relationship based on the Soviet Union in an "imperial phase" and the United States in decline, both in relative military power and in political will. The assumption of this analysis, however, is that the defense capabilities of the United States and the Soviet Union will remain in general parity, although the Soviet leadership will continue to strive for overall military superiority and although the United States, in the years just ahead, will face major decisions about both the adequacy of existing levels of defense and the allocation of resources between strategic and general purpose forces. Both superpowers, especially the Soviet Union, will be engaged in large-scale research and development (R&D) efforts designed to achieve breakthroughs that might prove decisive in altering the existing strategic-military relationship. Among the likely

Editor's note: An earlier version of this chapter was delivered at the October 1976 IUS Conference and then published in the *Air University Review* 28, no. 3 (March-April 1977):2-16.

emphases of Soviet R&D will be ballistic missile defense and antisubmarine warfare. The United States and the Soviet Union will remain adversaries, although their relationship will be punctuated by periods of "détente," whether for "tactical" or other reasons. The Soviet Union will be in an "imperial" phase with global interests and a propensity to seek to extract political advantage by virtue of possession of vast military power. Nevertheless, the Soviets will probably face increasing problems internally as a result of the demands of intellectuals, nationalities, and other dissident groups and externally in their relations with emergent regional actors and even with smaller states whose interests diverge from Moscow's interests. Formidable economic problems will continue to beset the Soviet Union as a result of inefficiencies in economic planning, declining per capita productivity, persistent difficulties in agriculture, including climatic variations and changes, and the continued concentration of Soviet technology and other resources in the defense sector.

In the period ahead, the United States, while endeavoring to reconstitute its domestic consensus on foreign policy in support of allies and interests abroad, will make an effort to redress the military imbalance that appeared to be emerging with the Soviet Union in the mid-1970s.[1] Nevertheless, the United States will have lost, perhaps irretrievably, many of the major qualitative advantages in strategic nuclear systems that it enjoyed until the present decade, even though U.S. forces at levels below the strategic will be based on the substitution of quality for quantity and firepower for manpower. In comparison with the rest of the world, the United States and the Soviet Union will still have the most advanced defense technologies, although technologies now available only to the superpowers will be diffused to other states. The technological edge possessed by the United States and the Soviet Union will result from their superior concentration of R&D, especially in defense, relative to other states.

The U.S.-Soviet-Chinese Relationship

Crucially important to the future of the U.S.-Soviet relationship is, of course, the Sino-Soviet conflict. The deepening of tensions between Moscow and Peking in the late 1960s and the interest of the United States in minimizing its potential for conflict with Peking through the reduction of U.S. interests in the Asian-Pacific region provided the crucially important ingredients for the Sino-U.S. rapprochement symbolized by President Nixon's visit to the People's Republic of China (PRC) in February 1972. Although several factors (including the Soviet need for large-scale imports of grain) accounted for the Soviet interest in the "détente" with the United States in 1972, the possibility of improved relations between Peking and Washington, possibly to the detriment of Soviet interests, contributed to Moscow's eagerness to sign agreements with the United States, including SALT I. From the U.S. perspective, the Sino-U.S. relationship became central to U.S. diplomacy with the Soviet Union. The United States sought to evolve a better relationship with both Peking and Moscow than either could maintain with the other. The essence of the "triangular relationship" and major power interaction within it was competition by each of the powers to preclude a major improvement in relations between the other two. From the U.S. perspective, if not necessarily from the perspective of Moscow or Peking, a condition of neither friendship nor war was, and remains, vital to triangular diplomacy. A Sino-Soviet war, resulting in the destruction of either communist power—in all likelihood China—would leave the Soviet Union in a pre-eminent position in Eurasia. Since the early 1970s, the United States has signaled to Moscow its interest in the preservation of China, whose physical integrity is indispensable to the major power balance.

The problem of assessing future relationships among the major powers—the United States, the Soviet Union, China—is complex and difficult. Widely differing domestic structures, potential changes of profound importance in the leadership of at least two of the major powers, and conflicting and, in some instances, parallel foreign policy goals complicate the search for clarity about the future. In this analysis, for example, we assume, as noted above, a continuation of hostility between China and the Soviet Union. Historically, however, nations have undergone trans-formations in their relations, even in short periods of time. The *renversement des alliances* was a feature of past and recent international systems.

For the Soviet Union, the stakes in a Sino-Soviet rapprochement would be enormous, as the Moscow leadership must have realized when it made renewed overtures to Peking just after the death of Chairman Mao. The substitution of collaboration for competition between the two leading communist powers would perhaps impose insurmountable burdens on the United States. Even in a world of power diffusion, a decision by Moscow and Peking to act in concert to achieve their respective goals in regions of interest to the United States would have incalculable consequences for U.S. foreign policy. Conceivably, the transformation of Sino-Soviet relations from essentially a zero-sum to a non-zero-sum game is an unlikely contingency. It deserves mention in an analysis of emerging major power relationships only because of the horrendous consequences that it would have for the United States and its allies, consequences all the more horrendous if such a rapprochement came at a time of strategic-military imbalance starkly in favor of the Soviet Union. In fact, one may hypothesize that a decline in the position of the United States relative to that of the Soviet Union would provide the incentive for China to repair its rift with Moscow if the Chinese leadership concluded that it had more to gain or less to lose by improving its relations with the Soviets. Therefore, this analysis of future major power relationships assumes the preservation of U.S. military, economic, and technological power at a level of "parity" with the Soviet Union and a fundamental commitment to a minimum strategy of "assured survival" rather than "mutual assured destruction."[2] This assumption is made even though Soviet concepts of nuclear strategy call for patently superior forces not only to deter the United States but also to enable the Soviet Union to prevail in a nuclear exchange.

Major Power Interests at a Regional Level

In addition to competition for the development of strategic systems and general purpose forces, the continued superpower adversary relationship will manifest itself at several levels: efforts to increase polycentrism in alliance systems and, in the case of Soviet policy, to promote tendencies toward neutralism in the alliances of the United States; attempts to retard the emergence of new power centers or to gain influence in such states and regions; and a Soviet interest in exploiting the tensions and conflicts that will be endemic in the global system of the next quarter century, especially in the Third World.

In Western Europe and Japan, the United States and the Soviet Union, as in the recent past, will have largely divergent foreign policy goals. Soviet policy has been, and is likely to continue to be, oriented toward efforts to detach the United States from alliance partners and to achieve a form of neutralization or "finlandization," especially in Western Europe. Political patterns within Western Europe are complex and shifting. There are contradictory tendencies within the European Community, with a movement to the left in some countries (especially Italy and, perhaps, France) and, for the present at least, toward greater conservatism in other countries (Federal Republic of Germany, Great Britain, and Sweden). The accession to power of communist parties in Italy and France would accord with the Soviet interest in neutralization and in the weakening of West European links with the United States.[3] The continued growth of Warsaw Pact capabilities will confront NATO with a variety of defense problems: threats to the stability of the military balance on the NATO central front; uncertainties about sea control, especially in the Mediterranean, where surface navies composed of large ships will become increasingly vulnerable to attack by precision-guided weapons launched from land, submarines, or aircraft; greater nuclear threats to Western Europe posed by new-generation Soviet strategic forces, such as the SS-20 and the Backfire bomber; and the potential for a shift in the overall military balance in Europe toward the Soviet Union.[4] In itself, this phenomenon might be sufficient to achieve a form of "finlandization" if Europeans increasingly perceived a political shadow cast by the Soviet *possession*, not necessarily the actual *use*, of military power. In the absence of an alliance relationship that continued to commit U.S. military power to NATO, Western Europe would be hostage to Soviet goodwill in such a changing military balance.

Likewise, Soviet policy in Northeast Asia, especially toward Japan, will diverge from that of the United States. Japan's high vulnerability to disruption in supply of vital raw materials and its heavy dependence on overseas markets will give the Soviet Union potential leverage against Japan and, indeed, against Western Europe and other countries and regions vitally dependent on trade. Major increases in Soviet naval deployments in the seas adjacent to Japan and in the Indian Ocean may pose a threat to Japanese and European commerce. This is not to suggest that the Soviet Union necessarily will take action to interdict shipping. However, the potential Soviet threat to interdict vital shipping from the Persian Gulf to Japan or Western Europe will pose difficult choices for U.S. allies in the event of protracted crises between the United States and the Soviet Union.

Conceivably, the Soviet Union will attempt, as it has attempted in the past, to normalize its relations with Japan. The prospects for success will be severely limited so long as the Soviet Union refuses to return to Japan territory seized at the end of World War II. Moreover, Soviet diplomacy, like that of Japan, will be conditioned by the quadripartite power balance that exists in Northeast Asia. Japan will seek to use the Sino-Soviet conflict to minimize potential threats from either China or the Soviet Union. Conceivably, it will evolve a somewhat closer relationship with Peking than with Moscow. The Japanese government may be drawn increasingly into trade-technology transfer agreements with both China and the Soviet Union, although neither Moscow nor Peking will wish to have the other's industrial capabilities strengthened so long as they remain in confrontation. Thus, the Chinese leadership apparently viewed with apprehension the possibility that Japan, together with the United States, might make substantial investments in the development of Siberian oil and natural gas.

The Emergence of Regional "Superpowers"

The alliance issues confronting the United States in its relationships with the Soviet Union are, in some cases, the legacy of the past generation and, in others, new manifestations of a competitive relationship in which the stakes revolve around the world's greatest industrial-technological-economic power centers outside the United States and the Soviet Union. In this respect, if not in military power, Western Europe and Japan represent economic power centers in the emerging international system, although they are highly vulnerable, as we saw in the immediate aftermath of the October 1973 war, to international political and economic forces over which they have little or no control. But the world of the last quarter of this century is likely to contain other emerging power centers that, if not as vast economically as Japan and Western Europe, will nevertheless have impressive capabilities. Within the next generation, a series of regional "superpowers," such as Brazil and Iran, will probably emerge. The regional "superpowers" will have attained their status in the international system by dint of economic growth based, in some instances, on resources and on major progress toward industrialization, with technology transfer and investment from the industrialized countries of the West and Japan. The problems of international security will have become far more difficult and complex as a result of the power diffusion within each of the world's regions and the presence of numerous conflict-laden issues. The capacity of the United States and the Soviet Union to influence the behavior of regional "superpowers" will have diminished, even though major regional actors will remain dependent on the United States and the Soviet Union for certain of the most advanced military capabilities.

Diffusion of Military Power

Rapid growth in the defense capabilities of major regional actors will provide potential threats to superpower interests and even military forces (for example, naval forces deployed in oceans where regional powers maintain substantial naval power, especially "inshore navies" consisting of small ships equipped with precision-guided weapons and other advanced capabilities that can threaten superpower forces). There will be a growth in R&D capabilities and weapon production facilities among regional "superpowers" as technologies and skills are transferred from the most advanced countries.

The continuation and, in some cases, the growth of adversary relationships within regions will create new opportunities for intervention, directly or indirectly, by one or both superpowers. The continued propensity of the Soviet Union to exploit regional problems for unilateral advantage will provide a destabilizing element in virtually all regions. The potential for conflict among regional powers and for superpower involvement in regional conflict will increase. Major regional powers will possess, or will be capable of acquiring, nuclear capabilities for the deterrence of other powers within their respective regions. In some instances, other regional powers, in addition to Great Britain and France, will have the capability to strike superpowers with nuclear weapons. On balance, the Soviet Union will be more vulnerable than the United States to nuclear attack by smaller nuclear powers, especially in the 1980s, although by the 1990s the United States will also have become more vulnerable than in any earlier period to attack by such powers. The relatively greater vulnerability of the Soviet Union to smaller nuclear forces will result both from the geographic proximity of the Soviet Union to other nuclear powers and from the conflict potential of issues dividing the Soviet Union and nations or groups of nations on the Eurasian land mass and rimlands. The possibility of the emergence of a series of such regional powers in possession of nuclear forces gives added incentive to the Soviet Union to seek both to neutralize and to achieve major influence in potential power centers. Thus, the Soviet Union has sought not only to detach Western Europe and Japan from their respective alliance relationships with the United States but also to prevent the emergence of a unified, militarily strengthened Western Europe.

By the late 1980s, such countries as Great Britain and France are likely to have built new-generation strategic forces based, perhaps, on technologies such as those embodied in the U.S. cruise missile programs, although the ability of other states to incorporate such advanced cruise missiles (nuclear and conventional—long-range and short-range) into their weapons inventories will depend on the acquisition, in some cases, of highly sophisticated guidance systems now available only to the United States.[5] Conceivably, Great Britain and France will have achieved substantial technological collaboration in the development and production of new-generation nuclear weapons and, as part of a broader European-Atlantic framework, in other types of weapons as well. The availability of relatively inexpensive delivery systems, such as the cruise missile, will increase the prospects for the emergence of a multinuclear world.

Proliferation of Nuclear Weapons

Within the next generation, as many analysts have noted, other states will have acquired nuclear weapons. Other nuclear powers in Europe and on the periphery of Europe may come into existence. The list of potential nuclear powers in Europe includes the Federal Republic of Germany, Spain, Italy, Yugoslavia, and, by the 1990s, Greece and Turkey.

Outside of Europe, one can envisage hostile pairs of countries, one or both of which will have acquired an atomic weapons capability or will have substantially augmented existing nuclear forces—in the Middle East, Egypt-Israel, Egypt-Libya, Iran-Saudi Arabia, Israel-Iraq, and Algeria-Libya; in Asia, Taiwan-the People's Republic of China, the Philippines-Indonesia, South Korea-North Korea, and India-Pakistan; in Africa, Nigeria-South Africa and Zaire-South Africa; and in Latin America, Argentina-Brazil.

In Europe, the propensity of states to acquire nuclear weapons will depend on several factors. These include, for example, the perception of continued credibility of the U.S. nuclear guarantee embodied in the

Atlantic Alliance. Outside NATO, Yugoslavia may acquire nuclear weapons. Depending on the course of events in Yugoslavia after the demise of Tito, especially the outcome of whatever succession crisis ensues and the Soviet propensity for intervention, Yugoslavia will have an incentive to develop a nuclear weapons capability, although the Soviet Union can be expected to exert pressure to prevent the development of such a nuclear force. The possession of nuclear weapons by states outside Europe, particularly in North Africa and the Middle East, will lead existing European nuclear powers to retain such capabilities and provide a rationale for the development of a European nuclear force or for the acquisition of atomic capabilities by other European states, especially those states on the northern littoral of the Mediterranean. Several Middle East states—Egypt and Libya, for example—will have the potential for developing or acquiring a nuclear capability, a portion of which could be targeted against Western Europe. Other states in the Middle East-Persian Gulf region are likely to have an atomic force capable of reaching targets in the Soviet Union. These include Israel and Iran.

Whatever the outcome of the racial conflicts erupting in southern Africa, there will probably remain in that region a technological infrastructure capable of developing and manufacturing nuclear weapons. The present South African government, if it survives the formidable challenges that it faces, or as part of its strategy to ensure survival, will have great incentive to acquire a nuclear weapons capability. If a black-dominated successor government were to come to power after a protracted racial conflict, it might have within its grasp the capacity for a nuclear force and, thus, the means to remain, for some time to come, the strongest military power in sub-Saharan Africa, although Nigeria can be expected to register major economic gains by the 1980s. This assumption, in turn, depends on Nigeria's ability to prevent internal fragmentation and to attract needed levels of overseas investment.

In South America, Brazil has embarked on programs to acquire technology for the development of a nuclear weapons capability. The achievement of nuclear status appears to accord with Brazilian aspirations to become the dominant power in Latin America and perhaps, eventually, to assume a major role outside of Latin America. Depending upon its success in resolving formidable domestic political and economic problems, Argentina would possess the technological infrastructure needed for atomic weapons development and production in the next generation.

In Asia, Japan may be deterred from the development of nuclear weapons by the continuation of Sino-Soviet rivalry and by security guarantees extended by the United States. In all likelihood, Japan will have increased, as a percentage of its GNP, its defense spending. Japanese defense interests will encompass the sea-lanes through which Japanese commerce must pass and control of air space over and near Japan. Japan will retain a technological infrastructure that will permit a future Japanese government to decide to "go nuclear." Major changes in Sino-Soviet relations—either the defeat of China by the Soviet Union in a war or a rapprochement between Moscow and Peking—would have unsettling effects on Japanese foreign policy, including the issue of nuclear weapons. Especially if it came at a time of strained U.S.-Japanese relations, war or rapprochement between Moscow and Peking could produce either a marked growth of neutralism in Japan or an impetus toward a major defense buildup. The former is more likely than the latter, only because of the lead times that would be needed to produce a *credible* Japanese nuclear force.

Similarly, a sharp increase in the Japanese perception of isolation from the United States and of growing threats to economic well-being could lead to rapid shifts in Japan's foreign policy. At the very least, Japan, in the next generation, can be expected to evince a greater tendency toward independence from the United States.

Within the next decade, both South Korea and Taiwan will have a greater incentive to develop nuclear weapons and, increasingly, the necessary technological infrastructure to do so. Especially in the case of South Korea, a nuclear capability designed for deterrence against attack by North Korea will become feasible. Whatever other incentives may exist for the acquisition of an atomic capability by Taiwan, they will include a desire to preserve independence at a time when the capacity or willingness of the United States to provide a defense guarantee for Taiwan will have diminished. In Seoul, interest in the acquisition of an atomic capability will stem, in all likelihood, from similar considerations, notably from the withdrawal of U.S. ground forces from the Republic of Korea. Conceivably, a decision by South Korea to develop atomic weapons would give rise to an intensified debate within Japan on the nuclear issue.

The Diffusion of Military Power, Regional Balances, and Conflict Potential

The effects of nuclear capabilities on regional power balances and stability are difficult to predict. Conceivably, hostile pairs of states that may possess nuclear capabilities will be deterred from taking military action against each other. Possibly, as noted earlier, superpowers will face additional constraints in intervening *directly* in regional conflicts if their territory becomes vulnerable to a nuclear attack from a regional atomic power. Although the regional possessors of nuclear weapons may find that the risks of nuclear devastation exceed the potential gains (in accordance with deterrence theory in bipolar nuclear relationships), other factors may increase the prospects for regional instability. These include power imbalances between states that have nuclear weapons and states that do not.

In such a multinuclear world, the United States will confront many difficult security problems. The protection of assets of importance to the United States—the territories of allies, vital sea-lanes, especially from the Persian Gulf to the North Atlantic and East Asia, and onshore and offshore resources—will become more difficult. This will result not only from the proliferation of nuclear weapons but also from the acquisition by regional "superpowers" of a broad range of military capabilities. For this reason, technology transfer and the acquisition of indigenous technological infrastructures and weapon development and production facilities will be salient characteristics of the emerging international system.

The diffusion of military power characteristic of the global system of the last quarter of this century will have potentially important implications for the conduct of warfare. Here, it is possible to suggest, only in broad terms, some of the likely implications. New technologies will blur the distinction between nuclear and conventional conflict. As nonnuclear weapons become more lethal and accurate and as nuclear weapons with extremely low yields, i.e., below 0.1 kt, become available, the threshold between the use of nuclear and nonnuclear weapons will be less distinct.[6] Such weapons for use in each of the military environments—land, sea, and air—will be more readily available to a wide variety of actors. Many of the weapons that will be widely available will be easily operated by relatively unskilled persons. Conflict environments in the air, on the battlefield, and on the oceans will be increasingly inhospitable to manned weapon systems and will, therefore, place a premium on the conduct of warfare by weapons directed at remote range.

In recent years, there has been considerable discussion in the literature of international relations about the growing importance of nonstate actors, of which there are many types—from multinational enterprises spanning national economies to organizations employing terror and blackmail to achieve their objectives. The setting for a wide variety of nonstate actors is provided by increased world trade, the continued growth of the economies of many, if not all, states, the development of a more interdependent global economic system, and the diffusion of power in a world fraught with conflict potential. The extent to which such actors, especially those bent upon the use of violence to effect revolutionary change, will use sophisticated weapons to achieve their goal cannot be determined with great accuracy. The emergence of such actors with greater military capabilities poses potential security problems for all states, especially highly industrialized societies. Traditional defense concepts may be largely inapplicable to the problems posed by such actors. These actors may seek redress for grievances against the Soviet Union or against the United States. The Soviet Union, as well as the United States, may be vulnerable to actors possessing such capabilities. Nonstate actors without fixed assets in the form of internationally recognized frontiers and territory will be less affected by deterrence rationales than has been the case with state actors. If targets of great value to nonstate actors cannot be identified and threatened with unacceptable levels of damage, traditional theories of deterrence cannot be applied. Therefore, the potential exists for conflict and for nuclear blackmail between nonstate actors and regional powers and between nonstate actors and superpowers.

Major Power Relationships and the "Global Issues" of the Future

Much has been written in recent years about the issues that supposedly will dominate the foreign policy agenda of the United States and other countries in the next quarter century. It has been suggested that "North-South" issues will hold greater importance than "East-West" relationships in global context. This is not a recent argument. It has formed a basis for criticism of the alleged shortcomings in U.S. foreign policy for at least a generation. But it has become more salient in recent years as a result of new and old issues that include much of the so-called Third World—resources, population, food, trade, investment, and growing dissatisfaction among "have-nots"—especially in Asia, Africa, and Latin America.

The dangers that will exist in the global system of the next generation result, in large part, from such issues as these. For example, there is great potential for conflict arising from demands for scarce resources. We have already witnessed clashes over fishing rights among NATO members and the difficulty of delineating zones for fishing even among members of the European Community. It is not difficult to foresee the development of technologies that will make more profitable the extraction of a variety of resources in addition to oil from the seabed. Control of the seas will be increasingly important to nations or other groups in search of new resources. At the same time, the exploitation of onshore resources will provide new potential for conflict. Much of the mineral wealth of the world lies within the territory of the major powers. Much, but not all, of the competition for resources *outside* the major powers is likely to focus on the so-called Third World, although there is a potential for conflict involving one or more major powers over oil in the North Sea and the Barents Sea, over oil in the East China Sea and the South China Sea, and over fisheries in several parts of the world, to mention only the most obvious. Since the oil destined for Japan, Western Europe, and the United States must travel several thousand miles over oceans and through narrow choke points, the potential for various forms of disruption is enormous, whether from the Soviet Union, from smaller surrogates with inshore navies, or from other powers not aligned with the Soviet Union and bent on disruptive action either against suppliers or consumers.

Major Power Relationships and Subnational Conflict

Furthermore, one may hypothesize that the international system of the last quarter of this century will contain a large number of states faced with many varieties of revolutionary forces. In some instances, they will be based on new or old ethnic-linguistic nationalisms seeking independence from, or control of, an existing state. They will include groups whose goal is the destruction of other groups within an existing state. The "age of nationalism," far from having run its course, may yet produce new nationalisms that will pose threats to the viability and survival of many states. Although the potential for such movements is greatest in the Third World, perhaps only because of the larger number of states and greater endemic political instability, it also exists in some of the oldest nation-states in the industrialized West.

Such actors will have available to them weapons of unprecedented potential for destruction. One or more contending groups may possess nuclear weapons, either by controlling the apparatus of state authority, by capturing nuclear stockpiles, or even by acquiring nuclear weapons from an outside power (not necessarily the United States or the Soviet Union). With the proliferation of nuclear weapons in a world of growing tendencies toward fragmentation within states, the potential for civil conflict between parties at least one of which has nuclear weapons will increase. In subnational wars of the future, decisive engagements will very likely be fought with weapons of unprecedented lethality. It will be less possible to confine civil conflict within state boundaries. The potential for spillover into neighboring states and to nonadjacent powers may be enhanced by at least two factors: the extent to which outside powers, including superpowers, intervene directly or indirectly and the increased range and lethality of weapons available to protagonists in a civil conflict. Whether these factors will deter or restrain would-be superpower intervention is uncertain. One may hypothesize that the growth in superpower vulnerability to devastation, even on a limited scale, by nuclear or other forces controlled by smaller states will introduce into superpower behavior greater restraint in support for one or another of the contending groups in an internal or a regional conflict. But one may also hypothesize that the superpowers will be pressed toward *indirect* forms of intervention in support of one side or the other, or both, in the regional and subnational conflicts of the next generation. Soviet support for Cuban forces in Angola and elsewhere in southern Africa may be a harbinger of future Soviet strategies and tactics based on "proxies." In return for various forms of Soviet assistance and support, other states, in addition to Castro's Cuba, may seek to play a greater role in fomenting and exploiting the revolutionary forces in the world of the late twentieth century, and some states, at least, may be available for Moscow's use by virtue of parallel interests or as a result of extensive superpower-client state leverage between the Soviet Union and smaller powers.

Even in the generation after World War II, East-West issues could not be viewed in isolation from issues associated with the Third World. Many of the confrontations between the United States and the Soviet Union or between forces backed by one or the other superpower related directly to the Third World—the Korean conflict, the Cuban missile crisis, the successive Middle East wars, the Vietnam war, and the Angolan civil war. The pattern of Soviet behavior has been consistent at least in one respect: the Soviet Union has shown great propensity to exploit, to the disadvantage of the United States and the West, the conflicts that have been endemic to the Third World. This pattern is being repeated today in the Middle East and in southern Africa. Therefore, we may infer that the East-West issues of the future will be, in large part, North-South or Third World in nature.

The emergence of new issues does not necessarily preclude the possibility that issues from an earlier period will remain with us. In fact, the dangers posed in the emerging global system for the United States in its relations with the Soviet Union result in large measure from the need to cope effectively with issues that are the legacy of the past and to respond to a series of new challenges. Because the interests of the Soviet Union still diverge from the interests of the United States on many of the problems of the past generation, U.S.-Soviet relations on old and new issues of the last quarter of this century will very likely be characterized more by competition and conflict than by détente and cooperation. In fact, the potential for discord between the Soviet Union and the West may grow as a result of the increasing salience of so-called global issues. Although U.S.-Soviet collaboration on as many issues as possible is a desirable objective, the pattern of past Soviet behavior does not encourage optimism about the future. If Soviet leadership has always been the "scavenger of revolution," why should it necessarily view its interests in the remaining years of this century as more in harmony than in conflict with the interests of the United States and its principal allies? Far more likely, the Soviet Union, especially in a period when Soviet military power may be at its zenith or at least unprecedented in its relative position to the United States, will seek to benefit from the issues offering potential for conflict at many levels— between intranational and regional groups, rich states and poor states, and producer and consumer states—with possible effects highly adverse to the economic prospects for the industrialized, noncommunist world. This has, in fact, been the pattern of Soviet behavior even when the Soviet Union was far weaker than it is in the 1970s.

Implications for U.S. Security

Several important implications of major power relationships can be adduced from this analysis of the emerging international system of the last quarter of this century. At the abstract level, the deterrence concepts that have been central to U.S. force planning at the strategic level and that have been applied within a bipolar U.S.-Soviet strategic relationship will be inadequate or, at least, will need reexamination in a multinuclear world. The diffusion of weapons to other power centers and the unprecedented lethality of their capabilities will decrease the ability to deter conflict and, at the same time, increase the need for deterrence. However, problems of assuring the adequacy of forces against preemption, of determining suitable levels of forces, and even of identifying sources of an attack or targets of value will be rendered more difficult. Problems of threshold between conventional and nuclear conflict and between intervention by regional actors in regional conflicts and by superpowers in such conflicts will become more complex. In turn, problems of determining the adequacy of strategic forces against more than one or, possibly, many potential threats will increase for the United States and for the Soviet Union. Since nonstate nuclear actors are not accessible as targets for the strategic forces of nuclear states, there will be a greater need for technologies of defense against limited nuclear attack as well as against the accidental launching of nuclear weapons, not only by the Soviet Union but also by smaller nuclear powers with less sophisticated command and control systems.

As noted earlier, the problems of protecting U.S. allies will be heightened, both by the diffusion of military power and by the emergence of the Soviet Union as a global military power. Both trends will diminish but will not necessarily eliminate the efficacy of security guarantees provided by the United States in its alliance systems. The continued presence of U.S. forces in vitally important regions and countries, such as Western Europe and South Korea, will help to retard the diffusion of military power, especially at the nuclear level, and it reduces the prospects for "finlandization," especially of Western Europe, by the Soviet Union.

The diffusion of military power and the increasing availability of highly accurate and lethal weapons will have implications of potentially far-reaching magnitude for superpower-client state defense relationships and the protection of superpower interests in the various regions. The problems likely to confront superpowers in direct intervention in regional conflicts have been noted. They result from the greater indigenous capabilities of regional actors in the world of the future and from the possibility that regional powers may have the capacity to inflict destruction at unacceptable levels on the superpowers themselves. Therefore, a premium may be placed on the capacity of superpowers either to pre-position military matériel on the territory of allies and clients or to resupply such states rapidly in a conflict environment characterized by the use of advanced weapons. Western Europe and the Middle East are examples of such conflict environments.

Elsewhere, especially in a large number of Third World environments, the problems facing superpowers, particularly the United States, in assisting allies and client states will, indeed, be enormous. In light of Vietnam, such problems need not be belabored here. To the extent that the United States will need a capability to assist its allies in such contingencies, including indirect support for one side in a subnational conflict, a premium will be placed not only on a capacity for the rapid movement of large quantities of matériel but also on the availability of highly accurate weapons that were initially deployed in the final stages of U.S. military involvement in Vietnam.

The implications of widely diffused new-generation weapon systems and the emergence of new conflict issues are potentially enormous for the structuring and for the roles and missions of U.S. forces. For example, if regional "superpowers" and global superpowers develop naval forces equipped with highly accurate weapons and if such weapons can be launched against ships from land or the air, large surface navies will be more vulnerable to attack and destruction. Highly accurate antiship cruise missiles with an over-the-horizon attack capability will create problems for surface navies and for the protection of other maritime forces, such as convoys, in wartime. Especially at choke points, navies and merchant vessels will become increasingly vulnerable to attack from land or from the air. In seas, such as the Mediterranean, naval forces will face growing problems from highly accurate weapons launched either from submarines or from the air or land.

The use of tactical air power will face increasing contraints in battle-field environments, especially in Western Europe, and possibly the Middle East, as a result of the technologies inherent in electronic warfare. More extensive use of remotely controlled capabilities and other highly accurate weapons, such as cruise missiles, against fixed targets, such as airfields, supply depots, and other military installations, and against other targets, such as tanks, will be both feasible and desirable at an early stage in a future conflict.

Because of the increasing importance of the oceans, both as sources of energy and vital raw materials and for the transit of rising levels of trade in an interdependent world, the need for capabilities for sea-control missions will increase. To these considerations must be added the rise of Soviet naval capabilities, which will enable the Soviet Union to pose a variety of threats to U.S. interests in the years ahead. The emerging technologies noted above will alter the traditional roles of the military services. For example, long-range aircraft equipped with highly accurate air-to-surface weapons may undertake sea-control and surveillance missions to a greater extent than ever before. Submarines or highly mobile, small surface craft may pose major threats to land-based battlefield targets at ranges of at least several hundred miles by virtue of highly accurate weapons with nuclear or conventional warheads. Targets on the oceans may be struck most effectively, especially in narrow seas, by weapons deployed on land.

In sum, the United States faces, in the emerging international system, a far more complex constellation of forces and actors than in any previous era. One can assume that new actors and older ones, such as the Soviet Union, will seek to maximize the potential inherent in new weapon technologies and conflict issues for political gain, even though a major goal of U.S. diplomacy has been to search for areas of parallel interest between the United States and the Soviet Union in order to minimize conflict and build a more stable and peaceful world.

The paradox of the emerging system is that the need for more effective structures and mechanisms to reduce the likelihood of conflict will be greater than in any previous era. At the same time, the potential for exploiting a variety of conflicts for unilateral advantage will be greater than ever. The broad interest of the United States lies, of course, in helping to shape a global system in which the prospects for conflict will be diminished. For this purpose, U.S. military power will remain an indispensable ingredient. Whether the Soviet propensity to exploit regional and subnational conflicts to achieve unilateral advantages can be diminished, even under the best of circumstances, is uncertain. Whatever the chances for reducing such Soviet proclivities, the prospects will depend on the continued ability of the United States to maintain at least overall military parity with the Soviet Union, together with the political will and the conceptual vision necessary to mold regional power balances and protect vital U.S. interests in a world of greater power diffusion, interdependence, uncertainty, and revolutionary change.

Notes

1. See, for example, John M. Collins and John Steven Chwat, *The United States/ Soviet Military Balance: A Frame of Reference for Congress* (Washington, D.C.: Government Printing Office, for the Congressional Research Service, Library of Congress, January 1976); Paul H. Nitze, "Deterring Our Deterrent," *Foreign Policy*, no. 25 (Winter 1976-1977).

2. John Erickson, *The Soviet Military, Soviet Policy, and Soviet Politics*, USSI report 73-3 (Washington, D.C.: United States Strategic Institute, 1973), p. 5.

3. See, for example, James E. Dougherty and Diane K. Pfaltzgraff, *Eurocom-munism and the Atlantic Alliance*, special report (Cambridge, Mass.: Institute for Foreign Policy Analysis, January 1977).

4. John Erickson, *Soviet-Warsaw Pact Force Levels*, USSI report 76-2 (Washington, D.C.: United States Strategic Institute, 1976).

5. Robert L. Pfaltzgraff, Jr., and Jaquelyn K. Davis, *The Cruise Missile: Bargaining Chip or Defense Bargain?*, special report (Cambridge, Mass.: Institute for Foreign Policy Analysis, January 1977).

6. See, for example, Geoffrey Kemp, Robert L. Pfaltzgraff, Jr., and Uri Ra'anan, eds., *The Other Arms Race: New Technologies and Non-Nuclear Conflict* (Lexington, Mass.: D. C. Heath, 1975).

5

The Impact of Domestic Politics on U.S. National Security Policy

Robert H. Trice

The ability of the executive branch to achieve its national security policy objectives has always been subject to some domestic political constraints. From at least the end of World War II until very recently, however, Congress and other domestic political forces generally did not seek an equal and active role in the making of foreign and military policy. Based more on accepted practice than on law, control of national security policy devolved to the president and career officials in the bureaucracies of the executive branch. Congress and the public came to view executive predominance in foreign affairs as necessary to ensure professionalism and continuity in the pursuit of national objectives.

Recently, however, the thick layer of political insulation that for so long separated professional national security policymakers from the concerns of partisan politics has apparently become much thinner. Beginning with the Vietnam war, more and more foreign and military policy issues have become topics of widespread domestic political debate, and more and more actors outside the executive branch have sought roles in determining policy. Such diverse issues as the Strategic Arms Limitation Talks (SALT), U.S. arms sales policy, the United States' role in the United Nations, the Panama Canal, U.S. intelligence operations, Sino-American relations, and U.S. commitments to the North Atlantic Treaty Organization (NATO) have become the focus of considerable interest and discussion not only among career professionals in the executive branch but also among members of Congress, the media, and interest groups. As the number of domestic actors seeking an active role in the making of foreign and military policy has increased, the flexibility and freedom of action of officials within the executive branch have apparently declined. Moreover, this recent trend toward greater involvement in national security affairs shows no signs of weakening. If anything, the long-term prospects are that nonexecutive actors will probably exercise even greater control over the direction of national security policy.

This discussion explores some of the constraints that domestic political forces are likely to impose on professional policymakers in the future. As defined here, *domestic* actors include noncareer officials inside the executive branch, such as the president and cabinet members; governmental actors outside the executive branch, such as Congress; and nongovernmental groups, such as the mass media. The term *national security policy* describes decisions involving the use of diplomatic, economic, intelligence, or military instruments to defend the territorial integrity and political sovereignty of the United States against perceived threats or to advance national interests abroad. To understand the impact of domestic politics on national security policy, one must consider three related questions. First, *who* are the actors most likely to seek roles in the making of U.S. foreign and military policy? Second, *how* can these individuals or groups affect policy? What kind of power do they have, and how can they apply this power? Third, *when* are noncareer and nonexecutive actors likely to demand a voice in the formulation of national security policy, and under what conditions are they most likely to have a determining effect on policy?

The Policymaking Process: Actors and Their Impact

This section considers the range of actors that may take an interest in national security policy and their relative abilities to see their policy preferences translated into governmental action. At least three different categories of actors are relevant to this discussion: (1) career professionals in the various national security bureaucracies; (2) elected and appointed federal officials; and (3) individuals and groups outside the government. Each category has unique political characteristics, and each is likely to affect national security policy in a unique way. Interaction among these different types of actors is likely to have a significant influence on the alternatives that are finally selected as "official" governmental policy.

The Executive Bureaucracy

Two very different kinds of governmental actors share responsibility for the conduct of national security policy. The first group includes the professionals who make their careers in the national security bureaucracies: the State Department, the Department of Defense, the Joint Chiefs of Staff and the armed forces, and the intelligence community. These people implement national security policy decisions made by elected officials, identify potential external threats to national security and foreign policy objectives, and suggest alternative courses of governmental action to elected officials. They are prohibited from engaging in overt political activities; they are separated from the public by elaborate tenure and internal judiciary systems; and they are socialized and trained to base their policy positions and actions on conceptions of the "national interest" rather than on narrower, more particularistic concerns. To the extent that these ideals are achieved in the real world, actors in the national security bureaucracy are the least likely to introduce partisan politics into policy debates.

The power of the national security bureaucracies resides in their day-to-day control over the foreign operation of the U.S. government. The central thrust of legislation, recruitment, and socialization has been to produce a corps of professionals who can make important decisions unencumbered by the need to satisfy the demands of any constituency in the domestic political environment. The goal has been to ensure that the nation as a whole is the primary focus for the loyalties and obligations of the diplomatic, intelligence, and defense communities.

Differences in the organizational interests and perspectives of various parts of the national security bureaucracy make political competition and conflict an integral part of bureaucratic decision making. Generally, however, a consensus among the participants on basic goals has tended to limit the ferocity of bureaucratic infighting and has created a willingness to accept the outcomes of bureaucratic struggles. When members of the national security bureaucracies fail to reach a consensus on fundamental values or refuse to accept bureaucratic defeats, when they appear overly responsive to the demands of domestic interest groups, or when they appear to violate the expectations of nonpartisanship, they invite the intrusion of a second group of actors and risk the loss of internal control.

Elected and Appointed Government Officials

The second group of relevant governmental actors includes those elected and appointed officials who have one foot in the domestic political arena and another foot in the professionally dominated foreign and military policymaking arena. These individuals and groups share formal power for making national security policy with the professionals in the executive bureaucracy, but they depend on continued domestic popularity for their political livelihoods. These individuals and groups are most likely to introduce partisan political considerations into policy debates. The relevant actors in this category are the president, members of Congress, presidential appointees who serve as ambassadors and cabinet members, and others who serve as under secretaries and assistant secretaries in the bureaucracy. Particularly when the president and members of Congress base their positions on personal or partisan political concerns rather than on the national interest (no matter how vaguely defined), the policy impact of the bureaucracy is likely to decline. When dominance over the formulation of foreign and military policy shifts from bureaucrats to politicians, noticeable and sometimes dramatic changes are likely to occur in national policy.

The president's power resides in his constitutional roles as commander in chief and highest executive officer of the government. However, a person attains these powers only after he has been duly elected by the American people. To stay in office or to maintain the presidency for his party, he generally concentrates his efforts on political decisions likely to increase his popularity with the public and holds to a minimum the decisions that are likely to reduce his base of electoral support. On many issues, the president experiences little conflict between his political ambitions and his perceptions of what is best for the nation. In general, he is likely to be less accountable to the public for his foreign and military policies than for his domestic policies.

Periodically, however, major national security decisions force the president to choose between two distinct roles—the role of politician and head of his political party and the role of guardian of the national interst. Such situations are likely to arise when short-term political goals, such as winning an election, conflict directly with longer-term strategic goals. Subordination of national goals to domestic political considerations is most likely to occur when a president decides for or against a particular policy alternative on the basis of anticipated reactions from other politicians and the public.

It is impossible to uncover the "true" motivations behind any presidential decision. However, many analysts contend that the domestic concerns of presidents can have significant, long-term effects on national security policy. For example, it has been argued that John Kennedy wanted to withdraw U.S. troops from Vietnam in 1963, but that he decided that he would wait until after the 1964 election to avoid Republican charges of being "soft on communism." In the fall of 1968, in a very close presidential race, Lyndon Johnson approved the first sale of Phantom jets to Israel in an attempt to win the Jewish vote for Hubert Humphrey. Richard Nixon reportedly accelerated the withdrawal of U.S. troops from Vietnam in order to defuse George McGovern's single-issue campaign. Gerald Ford could sacrifice Vice-President Rockefeller and thereby woo Republican conservatives only if he also sacrificed Secretary of Defense Schlesinger in an attempt to appease the liberal wing of his party. When such instances occur, they are generally accepted as realistic responses to the hard facts of political life. But there is also at least a twinge of disappointment in the realization that the president is not always "above politics" on matters of national security.

On the other hand, few illusions surround the role of Congress in the making of foreign policy. Although greater consensus can be expected among members of Congress on foreign and military issues than on domestic issues, Congress still provides a direct channel through which partisan and nongovernmental forces can influence national security policy. Senators and congressmen represent the interests of particular state and local constituencies. Consequently, their policy positions on foreign affairs are likely to reflect the diverse interests and involvement of various segments of the population. Congressional consistency on national security issues is difficult to maintain because congressmen have a high rate of turnover and because they tend to respond to the changing demands of their constituents. These particularistic and transitory tendencies introduce a strong element of unpredictability into the policymaking equation when Congress demands a major role.

Congress has always had the potential to exert substantial control over foreign and military policy. It derives its power through control of the nation's purse strings, its legislative capabilities, its authority to declare war and ratify treaties, its capacity to veto presidential appointees, and its responsibility for overseeing the operations of the executive branch. Historically, however, at least three factors have limited the congressional role in national security policymaking. Most members of Congress have traditionally shown much less interest and expertise in foreign affairs than in domestic policy issues. Congressional powers are decentralized among a large number of committees, each of which jealously guards its piece of national security turf. The result has been a lack of intracongressional communication and an inability to reach consensus on the directions that foreign and military policy should take. Inadequate staffs have also hindered congressional capacity to keep close tabs on the activities of the executive bureaucracies. For example, in 1970, total staff support for both the Senate Foreign Relations Committee and the House Foreign Affairs (now International Relations) Committee included fewer than seventy people. Yet these committees and the Armed Services and Government Operations committees were expected to carry the major burden of conducting hearings and writing legislation on foreign policy. Their tasks also included overseeing the relevant actions of the Department of Defense, the National Security Council, the State Department, the Central Intelligence Agency and the rest of the intelligence community, and some elements of the departments of Labor, Commerce, Agriculture, and Treasury. Because of these limitations, Congress traditionally was very selective in challenging the executive branch on national security matters.

However, beginning with the period of the Vietnam war and continuing through the present, Congress has demanded and achieved a major role in the policymaking process, primarily through its singular control over appropriations. For example, such legislation as the Cooper-Church amendment forced an end to U.S. involvement in Indochina; the Jackson amendment threatened to block the administration's trade agreements with the Soviet Union; and Congress unilaterally ended U.S. operations in Angola by denying funds to the administration. The dramatic increase in the scope and depth of congressional oversight activities has also had profound effects on national security policy. The recent investigations by Senator Church's Senate Select Committee on Intelligence, in particular, are likely to produce significant, long-term consequences for the worldwide operations of the U.S. intelligence network. These examples show that despite its limitations as an effective and responsible foreign policy actor, Congress can almost always override the policy preferences of the president and the professional bureaucracy when it is sufficiently aroused. As the record of the last decade has demonstrated, a number of national security matters no longer come under the sole control of the president. Congress has clearly staked out for itself a more direct and active role in the policymaking process.

Nongovernmental Forces

Various actors and elements in the political environment surrounding the government can also affect foreign and military policy. Three domestic nongovernmental forces are particularly relevant: interest groups, the mass media, and public opinion. Although all of these forces can affect policy, they share a common handicap in the sense that they have no formal policymaking authority. Thus, to influence policy, they must work through actors, such as the president and Congress, who are willing and able to translate their policy preferences into governmental action. Nongovernmental sources often stimulate decision makers into action and help to guide their behavior in certain directions, but their impact on policy will almost always be indirect and mediated through governmental actors.

Businesses, religious organizations, ethnic groups, professional societies, and other voluntary membership associations petition the government when their organizational interests are adversely affected by actors beyond their control, such as foreign governments, or when they seek to commit the resources of the government to the advancement of their foreign policy objectives. The primary tools used by interest groups to gain consideration from policymakers are campaign contributions, bloc votes, and, occasionally, a legitimacy of purpose that rallies support from the media and public opinion. Congress is generally the most accessible and responsive governmental target for interest groups; the professional bureaucracies are generally the least responsive. The president's receptivity to interest groups is likely to vary greatly, depending on the issue, the strength of the group, the legitimacy of its cause, and specific short-term political considerations.

When interest groups succeed in mobilizing the interest and support of nonexecutive, governmental allies, they can effectively override professionals in the national security bureaucracies. For example, at least since 1968, the pro-Israel lobby has consistently been able to persuade the president and Congress to provide credits and grants to Israel for weapon systems that, according to many professionals, are needed for U.S. defense and are too sophisticated and numerous for maintaining stability in the Middle East. Also, at times, a coalition of interest groups and Congress can prevail over both the president and the professionals. The Greek lobby, for example, marshaled congressional support for its objections to the U.S.-Turkish aid agreement of 1976. Congress refused to ratify the accord, which was designed to stabilize relations in the wake of an earlier congressional decision to impose an arms embargo on Turkey after the Cyprus war. The agreement would have guaranteed Turkey one billion dollars in grants and loans over the next four years in return for the continued operation of twenty-six U.S. military installations in Turkey. The administration argued, to no avail, that the refusal of Congress to approve the agreement would lead to a worsening in U.S.-Turkish relations, the closing of U.S. bases, and a serious weakening of NATO's eastern flank. These effects of interest group activities on foreign and military policy tend to be sporadic but dramatic. The mass media, on the other hand, represent another group of actors who are likely to have a greater and more consistent impact on policymaking.

The mass media—television, newspapers, and popular journals—play several important roles in the conduct of U.S. foreign affairs. They serve as the primary link between the government and the American people by providing information from government decision makers to the public and feedback from the public to policymakers. They are the primary sources of information for the professionals about world happenings. The media can support governmental actions by providing favorable analyses and explanations of complex situations and decisions. However, they can also play the role of adversary to the government by questioning the wisdom or motivation behind policy decisions. In their adversary role, they are most likely to have an observable effect on national security policy.

The media can exert significant nongovernmental influence because of their ability to conduct and publicize independent investigations that can trigger more powerful actors such as the president or Congress into action. For example, Seymour Hersh's investigation of My Lai, Joseph Treaster's stories on Dr. Frank Olson's fatal overdose of LSD given by the CIA and the subsequent cover-up, and the CBS special on the "Selling of the Pentagon" set in motion processes that brought the behavior of professionals under close public scrutiny. The media can also affect policy by serving as conduits and amplifying devices for sensitive materials "leaked" by people within the government. The *New York Times*'s publication of *The Pentagon Papers*, the publication of Daniel Schorr's "Pike Papers" (the classified report of the House Select Committee on Intelligence) by the *Village Voice*, and the listing of active CIA operatives by the magazine *Counter-Spy* are the most obvious examples of this trend toward more direct media involvement in national security affairs. The publication of secret materials by the mass media can have an impact at the general policymaking level and, in some instances, at the operational level as well. The murder of CIA station chief Richard Welch in Athens in late 1975, for example, followed the disclosure of his role by *The Athens News*, which reportedly obtained its information from *Counter-Spy*.

The impact of public opinion is generally weaker and more diffuse than that of interest groups or the media. By and large, public opinion can affect foreign and military policy only over the long term. It sets broad parameters that define the range of policy choices that are available to government decision makers and "acceptable" to the American people. Only when decision makers step across these vague and constantly shifting lines of tolerability are they likely to feel directly the weight of an aroused public. The attitudes and opinions of most Americans rarely impinge on specific national security decisions because, in general, the public is slow to mobilize on foreign policy issues; it rarely reaches a consensus about what should be done; and it tends to follow, rather than lead, executive decision makers in particular policy directions. However, when the public does mobilize, as it did in the 1950s in support of the administration's hard line on cold war issues and in the late 1960s and early 1970s when a large and articulate minority opposed the politics of the Johnson and Nixon administrations on Indochina, it can exercise very real constraints on government officials.

Up to this point, we can conclude that several nonexecutive and nongovernmental actors and forces can, on occasion, affect national security policy. However, we have yet to discuss the conditions under which partisan, domestic political considerations are likely to enter into the decision-making process. And we have not yet considered how the interests and authority of professionals in the national security bureaucracies are likely to be affected when the policymaking arena is widened to include domestic political actors.

National Security Policymaking: Occasions for Domestic Impact

A number of situations are likely to result in a diminution of professional control over national security policy. This discussion includes some typical occasions that provide opportunities for nonexecutive and nongovernmental actors to have a significant impact on policy. Some of these situations, such as general elections and the annual budget, are recurring events that need little discussion. However, other equally important, but perhaps less obvious, conditions are likely to weaken the traditionally strong roles of professional policymakers in the decision-making process.

Presidential Elections

The year preceding a presidential election is usually characterized by a noticeable decline in substantive foreign policy activity. Incumbents are generally cautious about providing rivals with political ammunition that may be used against them in the course of the campaign. Moreover, foreign governments are usually reluctant to enter into major new agreements with the United States if they feel that a change in administration is probable. As a result, many of the important planning and negotiating activities of professionals in the national security bureaucracies are "frozen" until the election is decided.

If an election produces a change in leadership, another period of in-activity is likely to extend anywhere from three to four months to a year or longer. During this time, the national security bureaucracy waits for new foreign policy directives. A new president can always be expected to reject some of the proposals that have taken professionals years to develop; on others, he may demand further analyses based on premises that differ significantly from the premises of his predecessor. New cabinet officers and other political appointees add to the confusion of the transition period as they simultaneously acquaint themselves with their duties and attempt (generally with little success) to carry out ubiquitous campaign promises to bring the foreign policy bureaucracy under control. In time, relationships between professionals and their political superiors are sorted out; new norms are established; and the active process of national security policy-making resumes.

Defense Budget

Congress and nongovernmental actors affect national security policy routinely through the annual process of determining the size and composi-tion of the defense budget. Congress's control over appropriations permits it to rearrange the defense priorities of the professionals by deleting monies for unacceptable programs and adding funds to projects that it seeks to emphasize. The complexity of the budget, the relatively crude analytical devices used to compare U.S. spending levels with those of major adversaries, the number of congressional committees, and the importance of the outcome make the budgetary process a significant test of executive and congressional strength.

Some members of Congress, such as Senator William Proxmire (D.-Wis.) and Representative Les Aspin (D.-Wis.), have built their political reputations largely on their roles as "watchdogs" for military overspending. In contrast to the recent past, however, most members of Congress seem willing to accept the administration's arguments for an increase in military spending. A majority of Congress has found the president's evidence of a growing "dollar gap" between Soviet and U.S defense budgets persuasive and has overridden the objections of congressional critics. However, as congressional personnel and perceptions of threat change, professionals can periodically expect strong challenges to elements of national security strategy reflected in the budget. Presidential elections and the budgetary process provide regular opportunities for politicians and the American public to make their imprint on foreign and military policy. But a number of more specific occasions—budgetary, bureaucratic, and military—are also likely to signal a shift in policy control from professionals to noncareer and nonexecutive actors.

Strategic Weapon Systems

Domestic political considerations are likely to become important whenever policy decisions involve the extended commitment of funds for expensive strategic weapon systems whose functions or missions are open to debate. Because of the extraordinary cost of these systems, advocates must justify their need in cost-benefit terms. Not only must professionals satisfy the concerns of politicians that the money, once spent, will produce a viable, operational system; they must also be prepared to explain *how much better* a new system will fulfill a given strategic mission than existing systems. If professionals cannot provide convincing responses, they run a high risk of losing the systems. The fate of the ABM system, for example, was determined, in part, when the professionals could not provide conclusive evidence that an expenditure of $50 billion would make the population appreciably safer from a nuclear attack.

Although a consensus is likely on the strategic value of some systems, professionals should expect such agreement to be the exception rather than the rule. All three services currently face strong opposition in their fights for weapon systems that they consider crucial to the fulfillment of their missions: the army's request for 3,300 XM-1 (Abrams) tanks at a cost of $1.3 million per tank, or a total cost of about $4.5 billion; the navy's request for more Nimitz-class "supercarriers" at $2 billion per copy; and the air force's request for billions to develop a mobile missile system for the 1980s. In each case, questions of cost, vulnerability, and existing capabilities will interact with the prevailing mood of elected officials to determine the future of these proposed systems.

Extended Troop Commitments

Elected officials will probably demand a major role in any future policy decision that involves an extended commitment of military forces or that can produce significant U.S. casualties. The Vietnam and Angolan experiences and the 1973 passage of the War Powers Resolution clearly reflect a new willingness on the part of Congress to challenge the unilateral commitment of troops by the president. Any president who attempts to circumvent Congress in matters involving the extended use of troops is likely to fail and pay a heavy price in the domestic political arena. In the absence of overt hostilities, existing troop commitments, such as those to NATO and South Korea, are likely to come under increasing congressional criticism. Professionals should expect especially strong domestic opposition to any action that may be construed as a de facto commitment that could lead to a spiral of military escalation similar to the escalation in Vietnam. In the near term, for example, Congress will probably keep very close tabs on military assistance to Zaire, on the reactions of the administration to any calls for help from South Africa, and on any proposed increases in the U.S. military presence in the Panama Canal Zone.

Military Failure

Professionals should expect a considerable decline in their political power and prestige in the policymaking process when a high-risk, potentially high-gain military or quasi-military operation fails. Nonexecutive actors have virtually no control over tactical military operations, but their reactions to success or failure can produce significant political consequences. When tactical operations are relatively successful, as in the case of the *Mayaguez*, the administration is likely to receive a vote of thanks and support from politicians, the media, and the public. When these operations fail, however, as in the Bay of Pigs, the blame is likely to shift rapidly from the president and the administration to the specific agencies directly responsible. Following such an incident, the policy preferences of those agencies are likely to carry little weight either with the president, who will predictably keep his political distance from the "tainted" professionals, or with Congress, which is likely to initiate a postmortem investigation and call for bureaucratic reorganization.

Bureaucratic Infighting

Professionals invite the participation of noncareer and nonexecutive actors and loss of control over the formulation of policy when infighting leads them to search for political allies outside the national security bureaucracy. Inability to resolve bureaucratic disputes at the interagency level will generally result in "pushing up" the decision to the National Security Council, the cabinet, or the president. However, when a professional feels that an important issue is not handled properly within the executive branch, he may "leak" relevant information to members of Congress or the media. When leaks occur, they tend to broaden the range of domestic actors who participate in the resolution of the problem. As a result, issues are likely to be withdrawn from the policymaking domain of professionals and resolved in more open political forums.

Loss of Popular Control

Finally, the professional national security establishment should expect a diminution in authority when other domestic actors perceive that it has exceeded or violated its mandate to defend national interests. Two different types of actions can lead to the apparent loss of popular control, and in both of these actions, professionals are likely to lose much of their power in the conduct of foreign and military policy. First, professionals face such situations when they appear to act without the approval of higher authority within the government. The Church Committee, for example, uncovered numerous abuses of organizational power within the intelligence committee. One of the more disturbing cases was the admission by the National Security Agency (NSA) that from 1967 to 1973, it monitored the overseas telephone calls and cables of approximately 1,650 Americans and those of some 6,000 foreign nationals and groups without the approval of the president or the attorney general. This NSA program, called Project Minaret, supplemented the CIA's Operation CHAOS, which sought to investigate the links between U.S. antiwar protestors and foreign governments. These violations of the prohibition against internal activities illustrate what can happen when powerful but misguided organizations lose sight of their basic missions.

Other situations likely to bring charges of organizational misconduct occur when professionals become too closely tied and too responsive to the interests of particular groups within the domestic environment. Charges of a "military-industrial complex" have periodically aroused the suspicions of politicians and the public alike concerning the primary loyalties of certain appointed civilian officials in the upper echelons of the national security bureaucracy. The increasing trend toward greater direct involvement of professional military personnel in the sale of U.S. arms abroad is likely to produce significant domestic repercussions in the near future. Suspicions that the organizational interests of government professionals and corporations in the private sector may be becoming too intertwined are fueled by the intercession of the Defense Department on behalf of Lockheed's interests in Japan, the disclosure that Rockwell International entertained military officers (such as the former chairman of the Joint Chiefs of Staff, Admiral Thomas Moorer, and Vice Admiral Vincent de Poix, former director of the Defense Intelligence Agency) at Chesapeake Bay hunting lodges, and the 1976 admonishment of thirty-eight high-ranking DOD officials for accepting entertainment by Northrop. If professionals become identified with the particularistic interests of any sector of society, they jeopardize their role as guardians of the national interest. And if they abandon their role, they are likely to become indiscernible from all the other actors who compete for a piece of the political action. If carried to its logical conclusion, the result would be the loss of a unique and stabilizing force in the making of national security policy.

This discussion has avoided judgement as to whether the shift in power from the professional bureaucracy to noncareer and nonexecutive actors for many foreign and military issues is essentially "good" or "bad." A person's judgment will be determined by this question: good or bad in relation to what set of values? Some people view the introduction of domestic political considerations into national security affairs as frustrating, unnecessary intrusions into decision processes that should be left to professionals, who work "above politics." For others, the move toward greater domestic involvement represents a "democratization" of decision processes that affect the lives of all Americans; therefore, these processes should be open to participation by all people who wish to voice an opinion. Irrespective of one's personal feelings, however, domestic constraints on the activities of professionals in the national security bureaucracies are likely to increase in the future. The manner by which professionals adjust to these changing facts of political life will have significant long-term consequences for the behavior of the United States in the world arena.

6

Increasing Executive and Congressional Staff Capabilities in the National Security Arena

James J. Hogan

For many years, the Department of Defense (DOD) held an advantage in dealing with Congress and various executive offices because it possessed the critical data, the expertise, and the analytical capability to advocate its proposals successfully. Congress and the relevant executive offices, primarily the Office of Management and Budget (OMB), approved or disapproved DOD programs and budget requests more as matters of intuition than as judgment based on factual information and evaluation. Members of Congress did not hesitate to admit their limitations in considering multifaceted problems. They simply stated that the volume of information and the constraints of time reduced their effectiveness in dealing with every aspect of important issues.[1] The executive branch had an advantage over Congress in the sense that it had more direct access to critical information.

Increasing Congressional Power

Government operations, particularly in the executive and legislative branches, have undergone significant changes in recent years. For example, newspapers, political journals, and academic studies cite the diminishing power of the executive branch and the growth of congressional power. Recent congressional concern in the areas of foreign policy, budget actions, and management of the military apparently confirms these assessments. Thus, the generally accepted view is that Congress has taken a revitalized and active interest in determining national security policy. Professor Robert Trice's chapter provides an excellent general description of this development. Our research validates Trice's analysis and describes the growing congressional and executive staff power to question the Department of Defense.

This chapter relies upon Trice's broad working definition of national security. Complex relationships in national security issues and the impact of these issues on domestic programs are the primary motivating forces behind revitalized congressional interest in national security affairs. "Domestic" government activities increasingly face one another in a competitive environment created and drawn together under the aegis of national security. Thus, few issues can be considered as safe or neutral, because any program may be successfully advocated at the expense of another program. The bureaucratic result of this competitive environment is a trend toward increased staff capabilities in both the executive and legislative branches.

Improved congressional staff capabilities are evident in the increasing range of issues before Congress, the depth of research analysis, and Congress's ability to exploit its position. Specialization in such areas as budget accounting, agriculture, or housing and urban affairs has led to cross-referencing of information; thus, hearings conducted by one sub-committee frequently contain relevant points developed in other hearings. Hearings on military weapon systems involve as much discussion on budgetary impacts and domestic programs as discussion on departmental needs and shares of the budget. Congress has increasingly adopted a broader and broader view of national security affairs.

Equally significant is the depth of staff research analysis. Recent congressional staff research demonstrates the advantage of thoroughly exploring conflicting military positions, economic factors and trade-offs, and the case history of each issue. By giving closer attention to various branch positions within DOD and within each service, staff researchers can examine functions and missions for duplication and possible integration. Potential conflicts between plans for personnel cuts and demands for manpower created by new weapon systems are critical points of examination. The congressional staff preparation of research materials is often more than the sum of each individual preparation, because much of the information has multiple applications.

Another important advantage accrues to the staffs through participation in the hearings. The supporting arguments found in air force, navy, or army programs may lead to critical examinations of other programs under study. Thus, in one hearing, a congressional staff member may obtain criteria and evaluation standards that can be used to measure a program in another department. Staff researchers develop a panoramic view because they often occupy an aggregating position regarding national objectives and means.

As Congress exercises and strengthens its ability to operate in the national security arena, it may frequently use a readily available news medium. Members of Congress have free access to television and newspaper coverage on an almost limitless range of subjects. This, and the public's sense that addresses on the Senate and House floors are always significant, can make weak arguments appear strong and valid arguments overwhelming. Equally important in the effort to exploit positions is the employment of the normal political network of influence. This network varies from logrolling to bipartisan cooperation. Congress gains added strength through various forms of reciprocity agreements between individual members.

The more diverse and complex the issues faced by congressional and executive decision makers, the more critical is the staff role. Particularly on issues of national security, these officials depend more and more on their staffs to gather and select data, to examine and develop positions, and to provide feasible courses of action. Thus, staffs exercise considerable power in controlling the decisions of their employers. In some instances, they have so much control that the decision makers are virtually figureheads. Many members of Congress readily acknowledge their problems in attempting to prepare adequately for important issues requiring sound objective judgment.[2]

Factors in Staff Power

Mere possession of a capability does not guarantee effective application of the capability. Any attempt to analyze staff performance rather than capability is not practical for a number of reasons. Staff power may not be consistent from staff to staff or within the same staff across a spectrum of issues. Successful efforts on one issue may produce poor results on another issue. Furthermore, the employer may diminish staff efforts through poor articulation.

The discussion of staff capabilities also presents certain problems in the sense that staff potentials or features are difficult to analyze. However, certain factors in staff operations provide a fairly reliable means of measuring staff capabilities. These factors include staff size, budgets, expertise, continuity, and management procedures. Such factors can be quantified and compared to previous figures to determine changes and improvements during a given period.

Staff Size

The number of people serving on a staff is a crude but useful measurement of staff capability. A large staff can address more issues, develop specialized expertise, tailor ad hoc groups for special projects, develop anticipated programs, and provide an internal evaluation and review system. The list of advantages available to a large staff as opposed to a small staff could be continued ad infinitum. The point is that a large staff can produce more than a small staff. Congressional committee and personal staffs have increased dramatically over the past ten years. Other staffs at the service

TABLE 1

SELECTED SENATE STAFF STATISTICS, 1965–1975

SENATOR	Staff Size 1965	Staff Size 1970	Staff Size 1975	Percentage Increase 1970–1975	Number in Continuous Service 1965–1975
Church	9	12	24	100	3
Jackson	16	14	22	57	5
Javits	30	36	51	42	3
Muskie	17	23	23	0	2
Proxmire	6	10	8	(20)	1
Scott	28	37	45	22	9
Sparkman	17	11	17	55	6

Source: Congressional Staff Directory, 1965, 1970, 1975

TABLE 2

GROWTH IN SENATE COMMITTEE STAFFS

COMMITTEE	Staff Size 1965	1970	1975
Appropriations	35	38	53
Armed Services	18	18	24
Commerce	32	43	40
Foreign Relations	22	25	44

Source: <u>Congressional Staff Directory</u>, 1965, 1970, 1975

of Congress work in the Congressional Research Service (CRS), the General Accounting Office (GAO), and the newly created Office of Technology Assessment (OTA). The personal staffs of members of Congress are not uniform. Some senators and representatives are supported by larger staffs than others, and the geographic or demographic characteristics of their states do not determine the size of their staff. Demographics set an upper limit, but they are not a critical factor in decisions on staff size. A sampling of Republican and Democratic senatorial staffs from large and small states supports this observation. Table 1 indicates an almost continual across-the-board growth in personal staffs. A larger staff is not synonymous with a more favorable worker/work-load ratio. The advantages provided by larger staffs may be offset by increases in functional tasks or in the addition of home state regional offices, which satisfy constituents but are not concentrations of intellectual talent focused on new and substantive issues.

Congressional committees have undergone the same absolute growth in staff membership. Some committees involved in national security have significantly increased their staffs since 1965 (see Table 2).

The number of committees and subcommittees has also increased more than 20 percent during the same period. This double-barreled growth indicates that more staffs and more individuals now support Congress than in the past. According to data provided by the U.S. Civil Service

Commission, employment by agencies of the legislative branch increased by 22 percent from June 1970 to December 1975. Congressional staff increases of more than 5,000 during this period represent a 44 percent increase.[3] One explanation for these increases is that more personnel are necessary for the additional positions created by the proliferation of subcommittees. This is only a partial explanation, since personnel increases have proportionally outpaced the growing number of committees. In addition, staff members serve on several committees and thus derive multiple advantages from their research efforts.

The Congressional Research Service of the Library of Congress has undergone dramatic growth from 286 assigned personnel in 1968 to 714 in 1975. The CRS provides in-depth studies for individual members of Congress and for congressional committees. These studies require the services of senior research staff members and involve approximately two weeks or more in research activity.[4] This service is separate from the standard library functions performed by more than 4,000 other employees of the Library of Congress (up from 3,300 in 1970).

The professional staff and total employment of the General Accounting Office have increased more than 60 percent and 30 percent, respectively, since 1966. The professional staff consists primarily of accountants, auditors, systems analysts, operations researchers, statisticians, and attorneys. The disproportionate increase in professional staff is dramatized by the fact that in 1966, the professional staff represented 54 percent of total GAO personnel, and in 1975, 69 percent. Table 3 illustrates this growing competency. As the congressional overseer of federal spending, the GAO can be intimately involved in all DOD programs and issues, and it is a continuing member of the national security bureaucracy.

The Technology Assessment Act of 1972 created the Office of Technology Assessment to assist Congress in anticipating and planning for the use of new technology. Since it began its operations only in January 1974, it provides little comparative data for accurately tracing its pattern of growth. However, its entire structure and existence constitutes a de facto increase in capabilities, for it provides an entirely new source of staff support to Congress. Several of OTA's 105 study requests have already played a significant role in challenges to DOD proposals. In addition to the twelve-member congressional board comprised of six senators and six representatives, OTA began operations with thirty-six professional staff members and seventeen supporting personnel. The professional staff was increased slightly in FY 1976, which strengthens OTA's research capabilities, staff power, and organizational credibility.

Compared to the overall growth in congressional staff, less growth has taken place in other agencies with purview over DOD programs. Within the executive branch, the bureaucratic structure in the national security arena includes the State Department Policy Planning Staff and the Office

TABLE 3

GENERAL ACCOUNTING OFFICE PERSONNEL STRENGTH

Fiscal Year	Strength	Increase	Profess. Staff	Profess. Increase	Profess. as % of Total
1966	4148	--	2280	--	54.9
1967	4216	68(1.6%)	2326	46(2.0%)	55.2
1969	4544	328(7.8%)	2663	337(14.5%)	58.6
1971	4751	207(4.6%)	2989	326(12.2%)	62.9
1973	4962	211(4.4%)	3358	369(12.3%)	67.7
1975	5490	528(10.6%)	3800	442(13.2%)	69.9

Source: Comptroller General Annual Reports, FY 1966-1975

of Management and Budget. The Department of Defense is obviously a key participant in national security affairs; however, we will not examine the DOD role as initiator and sponsor of proposals, since our focus is upon the changing review and adversary roles held by the other members of the structure.

The Policy Planning Staff has more than thirty professional staff members, which represents a gradual increase since 1970.[5] Its activities have expanded after reorganization in 1971; it now cuts across a wider spectrum of State Department activities. The clerical staff shows no significant increase and is approximately the same size as it was in 1970. Major staff changes focus on tailoring of talent and a reawakened interest in its activities by the secretary of state.

Under Reorganization Plan No. 2 of 1970, the Office of Management and Budget assumed all functions vested by law in the Bureau of the Budget. Between 1970 and 1975, the organizational structure and personnel manning of OMB have varied to meet changes in emphasis in functional areas and increased tasking. Personnel manning experienced a surge of approximately 18 percent in 1971 followed by a period of continuing stability. Present professional and clerical staffs number 661.[6] Since 1973, the office has substantially augmented its work force through the use of part-time consultants and personnel on assignment from other agencies. Some of the consultants are retired OMB executives and, in effect, fill permanent positions. The ratio of professional staff to clerical staff shows a slight decline over the past ten years. In 1965, the Bureau of the Budget had

68 percent in the professional staff category, but in 1975, OMB had 63 percent in this category. This decline may be offset by the part-time consultants and other personnel not included in the calculation.

Budgets

Budgets are another aid in determining changes in staff capabilities. The direct relationship between budgets and staff size is obvious, since an increase in the number of people requires an increase in the budget to meet a larger payroll. Budget increases can also provide for incentive plans designed to motivate increased staff efforts. They provide for upgrading facilities, equipment, training, travel, and recruitment. This list could be extended to continue emphasizing the point—more dollars can purchase more capabilities.

Budget increases for congressional staffs (personal and committee) result from personnel and pay increases. Personal staff budgets of members of Congress have increased from $72 million in 1970 to $141 million in 1976. Committee staff budgets have increased from $10.7 million to $76 million during the same period.[7] The budgets for Senate and House operations provide limited insight as to the potential advantages available to staffs through access to centralized equipment, supplies, and communications. Contingent expenses for the Senate and the House have increased from $13.5 million in 1970 to $36.3 million in 1976.[8] This increase is greater than the amount attributable to inflation; thus, more money is available to support staff activities, directly or indirectly.

The CRS of the Library of Congress experienced a budget increase from $3.6 million in 1968 to $17 million in 1976. The Library of Congress budget increased from $36 million to more than $116 million during the same period. The CRS benefits from this increase because it uses the facilities and equipment supported by funds appropriated for the Library of Congress.

Congress has continued to increase the fiscal resources available to the GAO. In 1966, GAO operating expenses amounted to $47.4 million; this increased by 166 percent to $126.1 million in 1975.[9] Operating expense is usually less than congressional budget appropriations. However, the yearly total application of all funds available to the GAO exceeds operating expenses because the GAO has various receipts available from audit services and funds carried over from prior periods.

The OTA began its operation in 1974 with a $2 million appropriation from Congress. This budget increased to $5 million in 1975 with $0.7 million in unobligated 1974 funds available for use. The 1976 appropriations provide for a continued increase in the OTA budget to a level of $6.5 million.[10]

The State Department Policy Planning Staff presents a difficult problem in any attempt to determine specific budget authorizations and changes during the past few years. Although isolated budget figures for the Policy Planning Staff are not available, the larger State Department Division of Executive Direction and Policy Formulation provides some indication of the direction and magnitude of budgetary changes. Its budget increased from $22.1 million to $32.5 million.[11] This increase is rather modest in comparison with the increases observed in other staffs after the effects of inflation are considered.

From 1970 to 1975, the OMB received increased authorizations that more than covered rising personnel, utility, and other fixed costs. During this period, its total budget increased by 100 percent, coming in at $24.1 million in 1975. Personnel costs increased 65 percent and shifted from 84 percent of the total budget in 1970 to 68 percent in 1975. A larger increase occurred in the areas of rents, communications, printing and reproduction, and other services.[12]

Expertise

Expertise has several impacts on staff capabilities. Experts generally produce better studies, and those who work in close contact with experts generally perform better. Recognized expertise commands a certain authority based upon academic, employment, or achievement credentials. Decision makers can use this authority to supplement the quality of staff work and thereby produce an increased capability.

These three criteria of staff expertise may be used to examine changes over time in staff capabilities. Congressional staffs contain large numbers of well-educated individuals with a wide range of experiences.[13] Competition is very strong, and there is no job tenure. Selection for a staff position often demands impressive credentials. Many long-term staff members are prolific writers in their special fields; others enter the staff community after long service in the armed forces, in industry, or in the academic professions. Many committee staff members bring considerable knowledge with them from their previous positions on the personal staffs of congressmen.

The CRS acquired most of its expertise by directly hiring recognized experts. Recent testimony reveals that it is less difficult to recruit experts in specific technical areas because of current conditions in the labor market. In addition to technical skill, a selection criterion for CRS staff members is their grasp of the legislative process and their understanding of public policy implications in their field of expertise.[14]

A sampling of key, top-level individuals within GAO reveals that highly competent individuals with years of experience in GAO operations direct the activities of the agency. Senior staff members include lawyers, economists, auditors, statisticians, and former assistants to cabinet secretaries. And the GAO training program has been noteworthy for the past ten years. In 1972, the last year in which training data were included in the GAO annual report, 2,735 GAO personnel received training within the organization, and 1,975 personnel received training outside the agency. Training programs ranged from clerical skills to professional and technical education.

Congressional demand for staff expertise in the field of technology was the primary reason for establishing the OTA. The staff personnel on the congressional committees did not have enough technical skills to meet the challenges of advanced science and technology. Thus, from its inception, the OTA was staffed with persons eminent in one or more fields of engineering and the physical, biological, and social sciences. These people are also experienced in the administration of technological activities or qualified on the basis of their contributions to education or other public activities. The initial members have previously held positions in the Defense Department or other executive agencies, such as the President's Scientific Advisory Committee, the Defense Science Board, and the Bureau of the Budget.

Individual and bureaucratic expertise is readily apparent in the executive staff areas of the State Department Policy Planning Staff. Expertise includes knowledge and understanding of bureaucratic procedures, the environment of operations, and informal networks of communications and decision processes associated with the organization. The staff director (1976) previously served in an impressive array of jobs in policy planning in the Defense Department, the National Security Council staff, the Foreign Service, and in the role of senior adviser on China. Other staff members have equally impressive backgrounds. Ranging in age from twenty-eight to fifty-seven, they draw their experiences from the Foreign Service, National Security Council, Defense Department, White House staff, fields of science and technology, and the academic world, where several have served as faculty members.

The backgrounds of staff personnel also provide a means of assessing the level of expertise in the Office of Managment and Budget. During House budget hearings in June 1975, experience summaries of nineteen staff members indicated the level of competence in the OMB. All of the nineteen members had college degrees, and eighteen had more than one degree. Five had Ph.D.s and ten had master's degrees. Two had law degrees in addition to bachelor's degrees. Seven had degrees in economics or finance, and four in government, political science, or public administration. Four other degrees were held in engineering, mathematics, chemistry, and premedicine. Nine of the nineteen members had military experience, and thirteen of the nineteen had worked for one or more federal agencies before joining the OMB.[15]

Continuity

Despite some of the shortcomings cited in management textbooks, continuity provides a number of distinct advantages, such as knowledge of job procedures, techniques, the evolution of present policy, and the weaknesses of abandoned procedures. It represents experience complemented by an expanding network of contacts and callable favors. In government activities where the cycling of proposals is a common phenomenon, a staff member who has experienced previous rounds of proposals and counterproposals is prepared for the next cycle. Continuity is also important within the clerical staff. A bureaucratic structure can impede proposals, programs, and ideas with requirements for detailed coordination and rigid formats. Clerical workers with experience in the same position relieve operating staffs of many time-consuming tasks associated with coordinating and formatting; this may permit operating staffs to devote their energies to more substantive issues.

A review of the *Congressional Staff Directory* over a span of years reveals a consistent roll call. Table 4 indicates that committee staffs have maintained impressive records of continuity during the past ten years. Apparently, long-term working relationships on congressional staffs are intracommittee and intercommittee, since each of the committees interacts in the normal course of events. The continuity of officeholders is also a significant factor, with ten years of service in the same elected office not at all uncommon in either the House or the Senate. Personal staffs often show the same stability as elected officials.

The CRS staff does not display the same stability as congressional staffs. A major reorganization of structures and functions since 1970 may account for part of the personnel turnover, but the changing demand for selective expertise is the major factor in personnel changes.

Although the GAO has also experienced several reorganizations since 1970, they have not produced or eliminated significant blocs of skills and, therefore, have had little disruptive effect on overall continuity. GAO annual reports show that more than 40 percent of the professional staff has served ten or more years with GAO, and this comprises 47 percent of the total GAO force. Internal and external training programs may provide a two-way incentive for stability. The organization invests in the individual, and the individual remains with the organization to obtain entry into a training program. This implied incentive complements the expected stability that results from tailoring expertise through the training programs.

The OTA is such a recent creation that it is rather meaningless to speak of continuity within the staff, but two factors warrant attention. The congressional board included those who maintained professional contacts over an extended period (for example, Congressmen Kennedy, Case, Humphrey, and Udall). The members of the Citizen's Advisory Council have also shared a number of experiences with their fellow members and, therefore, enjoy some of the benefits normally associated with staff stability.

Continuity is less likely within the Policy Planning Staff, a staff closely

TABLE 4

CONTINUITY IN SENATE COMMITTEE STAFFS

COMMITTEE	Staff Size 1965	Staff Size 1970	Continuous Service 1965-1970	Staff Size 1975	Continuous Service 1970-1975	Continuous Service 1965-1975
Appropriations	35	38	29	53	7	7
Armed Services	18	18	11	24	5	3
Commerce	32	43	16	40	11	11
Foreign Relations	22	25	11	44	14	11

Source: Congressional Staff Directory, 1965, 1970, 1975

associated with the Secretary of State. In relation to the congressional staffs, the Policy Planning Staff experiences a more rapid turnover of personnel. However, when one observes the experience backgrounds of the staff members, common membership in the same operating network of the State Department is evident. The advantages of continuity resulting from interdepartmental activities in the State Department are not as numerous or strong as the advantages accruing to intrastaff operation, but they cannot be wholly discounted.

There has been a high turnover rate in the upper personnel structure of the OMB since 1970. Of the thirty-two top positions in 1976, only one-half were manned by personnel with more than three years of experience in the OMB. Four important positions were vacant for extended periods, and the director and two of four associate directors were appointed as recently as 1974. Professional and clerical staffs below the level of associate director have experienced far more stable employment. Almost 40 percent of the professional staff and more than 50 percent of the clerical staff have ten years of experience in their positions.

Management

There have also been improvements in management procedures, such as specialized staffs, the use of private research sources, and technological methods of gathering data. Whether improved procedures are merely the result of factors discussed earlier or of separate factors is immaterial. They warrant separate consideration because they are the means by which other factors improve staff capabilities.

Improved management procedures can be examined in a fashion slightly different from that used for the other factors, because many of the improvements involve interactions among the various staffs. Others appear more exclusive to particular staffs and warrant separate discussion.

Obviously, staff reorganization actions throughout the national security arena have brought increases in staff capabilities. The creation of the OTA provides an entirely new dimension in scientific information for Congress. The congressional budget office is also a new staff entity that has increased overall congressional staff capabilities. Major restructuring of the Library of Congress and the Congressional Research Service, General Accounting Office, and the Office of Management and Budget have been prompted by needs for more responsive and efficient staff resources. And there has been a general increase in the use of computer data. The significance of this change is that the staffs have found ways to extract and retrieve selective data from the wealth of information stored in the computer systems. This procedure is employed most successfully in the CRS and GAO.

The improvements in staff interaction are apparent in the procedures established by the congressional committee staffs. Staff tasks are divided into workable parts and then selectively assigned to various supporting staffs, such as the CRS, CBO, or GAO. The tasking staff then designs an integrated research project specifically tailored to the needs of the originating decision maker. In the past, it was often easy to identify the source of congressional or executive information. Single-source staff work often carried a parochial slant and singular view. The task of allocating information requests and then designing a single staff product is more complicated, but recent congressional actions show considerable improvements in staffing.

Management improvements by individuals have also increased capabilities. The OTA is especially noted for forming ad hoc working groups with resident talent and temporary, direct-line expertise. The tailoring and responsiveness of this method of operation draw strong congressional support for OTA operations. The extensive GAO training programs warrant recognition as a management improvement that produces a continuing flow of individuals with improved skills. The direct hiring of experts by the CRS to meet changing requirements provides immediate improvements in its staff capability. In addition to these specific improvements, the interest and desire of each staff to make improvements indicate a vitality and concern for quality that constitutes a capability improvement in itself.

Implications for the Department of Defense

Congressional staffs and agencies have significantly increased their capabilities in the national security arena. A number of staffs have experienced increases both in personnel and in budget allocations. They have recruited members with impressive credentials, and they have retained substantial numbers of people who provide the priceless advantage of experience. They have instituted management practices to capitalize on individual skills and technological hardware, and they have demonstrated a desire to improve their capabilities. Executive staffs have also increased their capabilities in the national security arena but not to the same extent as the congressional staffs.

These improved capabilities imply expanded staff power, a key factor in national security decision making. As a participant in the national security arena, the military must be keenly aware of these developments. Military programs face stiffer competition because congressional and executive staffs are now able to challenge these programs with their own well-staffed priority listings of national security programs.

When high-ranking Department of Defense officials testify on Capitol Hill, they should not be surprised if they are hit with difficult, well-staffed questions prepared by the professional people who service the congressmen. Since military expertise will be more challenged in the future by others with qualifications, backgrounds, and experience in these "military" areas, ordinary military justifications for major defense programs may not suffice. Military staffs must recognize that the kinds of arguments that persuade military decision makers to choose a particular program may not be as persuasive when that program is described and discussed with decision makers on Capitol Hill or in other executive branch agencies.

This chapter thus documents Robert Trice's analysis that the executive branch is losing its virtually unchallenged control of the conduct of national security affairs. By narrowing our focus to an analysis of growing congressional and executive branch capabilities, we have determined that DOD will be challenged in great detail by credible, competent, and knowledgeable staff experts. In the next chapter, Russell Hale and Leland Jordan carry this research further. They narrow the focus to developments based upon one significant legislative act, the Congressional Budget and Impoundment Control Act of 1974, which is another clear codification of the growing staff capabilities we examined in this chapter. Their conclusions support the central conclusion of this analysis—in the next decade, military and DOD influence on general and specific programs can be expected to diminish.

Notes

1. William C. Olson, "Congressional Competence in Foreign Affairs: The Measure of Information and Analysis," *The Round Table*, no. 250 (April 1973), p. 254.

2. Tax Foundation, Inc., "The Legislative Branch: The Next Billion Dollar Bureaucracy," Government Finance Brief no. 26 (Washington, D.C., May 1976), p. 22.

3. Ibid., p. 9.

4. U.S., Congress, Senate, Committee on Appropriations, *Library of Congress: Hearings before the Committee on Appropriations*, Senate on H.R. 13763, 91st Cong., 1st Sess., 1970, p. 206.

5. John H. Esterline and Robert B. Black, *Inside Foreign Policy* (Palo Alto, Calif.: Mayfield Publishing Co., 1975), p. 218.

6. U.S., Congress, House, Subcommittee on the Committee on Appropriations, *Hearings before the Committee on Appropriations*, 1969-1975.

7. "The Legislative Branch: The Next Billion Dollar Bureaucracy," pp. 24-25.

8. Ibid.

9. Comptroller General Annual Reports, FY 1966-1975.

10. U.S., Office of Technology Assessment, *Annual Report to the Congress* (Washington, D.C.: Government Printing Office, 15 March 1975), p. 5.

11. U.S., Department of Commerce, *Statistical Abstract of the United States (1970-1975)* (Washington, D.C.: Government Printing Office, 1975), p. 376, 389.

12. U.S., Congress, House, Committee on Appropriations, Subcommittee on Treasury, Post Office, and General Appropriations for 1976, *Hearings*, 94th Cong., 1st sess., vol. 3 (Washington, D.C.: Government Printing Office, 1975), p. 285.

13. *Washington Post*, June 2, 1975, p. A3.

14. U.S., Congress, Senate, Committee on Appropriations, Library of Congress, *Hearings*, Senate on H.R. 14012, 93rd Cong., 2d sess., 1975, p. 202.

15. U.S., Office of the Federal Register, National Archives and Records Service, General Services Administration, *United States Government Manual, 1975/76* (Washington, D.C.: Government Printing Office, 1975), p. 579.

7

New Congressional Budgeting Procedures: An Initial Analysis of Effects on the Department of Defense

Russell D. Hale
Leland G. Jordan

The Congressional Budget and Impoundment Control Act of 1974 is historic legislation that created new congressional mechanisms to set fiscal policy and budget priorities. Its stated purpose is to establish (1) a new congressional budget process, (2) a committee on the budget in each house of Congress, (3) a congressional budget office, and (4) a procedure to insure congressional control over the impoundment of funds by the executive branch.

In this act, the Congress also declared that it is essential to: assure effective congressional control over the budgetary process; provide for the congressional determination each year of the appropriate level of federal revenues and expenditures; provide a system of impoundment control; establish national budget priorities; and provide for the furnishing of information by the executive branch in a manner that will assist the Congress in discharging its duties.

In this book, both Huntington and Trice have discussed the War Powers Resolution, adopted by Congress in 1973, as an important political, legal, and symbolic curb on executive power in foreign affairs and national security matters. In its own way, the Budget and Impoundment Act is a similar important signal that Congress is reasserting its constitutional and historic role in fiscal and budget matters as well. After two fiscal years of experience, it is clear that this act has important implications for all agencies of the executive branch; as we shall see, the effects might be viewed as both potentially positive and negative by those who manage the Department of Defense. The one clear effect is that Congress's reform of its budgeting processes will substantially alter traditional relationships and thinking.

Historical Precedents

Budget reform is not new to Congress. In 1909, President Taft requested funds from Congress to "inquire into the methods of transacting the public business." Congress granted the request, and the president appointed the Commission on Economy and Efficiency. The president's message to Congress in January 1912 on *Economy and Efficiency in the Government Service* and the commission's report in June 1912 on *The Need for a National Budget* suggested that the president should assume responsibility for financial planning.[1]

The Budget and Accounting Act of 1921 finally established an executive budget system. It also established the General Accounting Office (GAO) and empowered it to make reports and investigations as directed by Congress; the Legislative Reorganization Act of 1946 increased the GAO's investigatory powers. Congressional concern with the federal budget process and financial planning has continued through the years. But an impetus to new action and reform came in the president's budget message submitted to Congress in January 1973. In that message, President Nixon stated:

> The fragmented nature of Congressional action (on the budget) results in a serious problem. Rarely does the Congress concern itself with budget totals or with the effect of its individual actions on these totals. . . . Backdoor financing . . . provides permanent appropriations authority to contract in advance of appropriations, authority to borrow and spend without an appropriation, and program authorizations that require mandatory spending whether or not it is desirable in the light of current priorities. . . . The Congress must accept responsibility for budget totals and must develop a systematic procedure for maintaining fiscal discipline.

A cursory examination of the fiscal record of Congress over the last twenty years indicates that deficiencies did exist and that budget reform was necessary. Quadrupled federal spending since 1960 emphasized the need for an effective vehicle to control and coordinate budget totals and to determine spending priorities and goals in relation to realistic revenue and debt levels. In the past, Congress reacted to the executive budget piecemeal through individual appropriation, authorization, and revenue measures. Final spending and taxing levels were simply arithmetic totals of collective spending bills passed during a current session and previously enacted spending bills minus the revenues from existing tax legislation. This lack of a procedure for coordinating spending and revenue decisions clearly did not permit Congress to determine the impact of the federal budget on the economy or to make program trade-offs in setting spending priorities.

The Office of Management and Budget, the National Security Council, the Council of Economic Advisors, and similar executive agencies have used the executive budget to formulate, coordinate, and control national policy. As a result, the president and his staff have been considerably more powerful actors than members of Congress in the national policy arena.

Congress has not had sufficient administrative and organizational resources to match or counter executive initiatives in national policy. The Congressional Budget and Impoundment Control Act of 1974 may provide these resources.

The New Budget Act

Despite overwhelming agreement that reform was needed in congressional fiscal decision making, the formulation and enactment of the Budget Act covered a period of more than two years. After legislation was introduced in early 1973, several versions of the act were debated, altered, and finally accepted by both bodies of Congress in June 1974. The fundamental principles that generated this major reform remained valid throughout this legislative process:

1. The separation of spending and taxing decisions did not provide a coordinated basis for determining fiscal policy.
2. Total spending by Congress would not be determined until the appropriations committees completed the piecemeal legislation.
3. Incremental appropriations decisions make the problems of determining national priorities in the aggregate difficult, if not impossible.
4. Backdoor spending that bypassed the annual appropriation process significantly affected total spending without full congressional recognition of its impact on the budget and the economy.
5. Appropriation legislation for the executive was generally not passed by the beginning of the fiscal year (July 1).

A Joint Study Committee was established in October 1972 to recommend legislation for improving congressional control over budgetary outlay and receipt totals. The final report was submitted in April 1973 and referred to the Senate Government Operations Committee and the House Rules Committee for subsequent introduction as legislation. Essentially, the report recommended establishment of a budget committee in each chamber, a legislative budget staff to provide information and analytical expertise, and a congressional timetable based on an early May concurrent resolution to set targets on total new budget authority and outlays. The concurrent resolution would also set the overall level of revenues, debt, budget surplus or deficit, and limitations on guaranteed or insured borrowing for the upcoming fiscal year. The Joint Committee report was introduced in April 1973 as H.R. 7130, a House Rules Committee bill, and as S. 1641, the corresponding Senate Government Operations Committee bill.

Hearings on S. 1641 were held during April and May 1973; the final version was reported from full committee in November and then referred to the Senate Committee on Rules to determine its effect on Senate operations. After hearings and extensive staff work, a consensus bill went to the floor of the Senate in March 1974 and passed, with several amendments, by a vote of 80 to 0. The House Rules Committee held hearings on H.R. 7130 throughout the summer of 1973; after several changes were made, the House passed the final bill by a vote of 286 to 23 in December 1973.

The House and Senate version of the bill were then referred to a Conference Committee, which reported the final bill to the House and Senate in June 1974. Final passage in the House came on June 18 by a vote of 401 to 6 and in the Senate on June 21 by a vote of 75 to 0. The bill was signed on July 12, 1974, as Public Law 93-344.

The act contains the following provisions:

1. a budget committee for each house of Congress
2. a timetable for the congressional budget process
3. a congressional budget office
4. an office of program review and evaluation within the General Accounting Office and a general emphasis on program review and evaluation
5. administrative procedures to coordinate the budget process
6. a four-year projection to be included in the president's budget
7. restriction of presidential authority to impound funds
8. a new fiscal year beginning each October 1

New Procedures

The timetable in Figure 1 shows the key elements of the new budget process. The budget committees receive reports from each standing committee of its house, the Joint Economic Committee, the Joint Committee on Internal Revenue Taxation, and the Congressional Budget Office. After considering each of these reports and the president's budget, the budget committees report the First Concurrent Resolution to their houses. Congress can then review the full federal budget, balance the various functions against one another, and establish national priorities.

Adoption of the First Concurrent Resolution completes the first stage of the new process; that is, information gathering and analysis. This stage culminates with the setting of congressional targets for total budget authority, outlays, revenues, deficit, and public debt. The spending targets are broken down by major function (national defense, etc.) and by budget authority and outlays. May 15 is the deadline for action on the First Concurrent Resolution and also the date by which committees must report legislation authorizing budget authority in the coming fiscal year. Action

Figure 1. New Congressional Budget Timetable

On or Before:	Action to be Completed
November 10	President submits current services budget.
15th day after Congress meets	President submits his budget.
March 15	House and Senate committees submit report to Budget Committee; these contain views and estimates on the upcoming fiscal year's budget.
April 1	Congressional Budget Office submits reports to Budget Committee.
April 15	Budget Committees report First Concurrent Resolution on the budget to their respective Houses.
May 15	Committees report bills authorizing new budget authority.
May 15	Congress adopts First Concurrent Resolution on the budget.
7th day after Labor Day	Congress completes action on bills providing budget authority and spending authority.
September 15	Congress completes actions on Second Concurrent Resolution on budget.
September 25	Congress completes action on reconciliation process implementing Second Concurrent Resolution.
October 1	Fiscal year begins.

on spending and revenue legislation that becomes effective in the coming fiscal year is prohibited before adoption of the First Concurrent Resolution.

The totals agreed to in the first resolution are intended as guides for Congress as it enacts spending and revenue legislation during the summer months. The House and Senate appropriations committees then divide the budget authority provided in the First Concurrent Resolution among their respective spending committees.

Congress must complete action on a Second Concurrent Resolution in September. It can revise the First Resolution totals in the light of current circumstances—the economic situation, the international situation, or other developments. Conversely, Congress can use the Second Concurrent Resolution to direct committees with jurisdiction over spending, revenue, or debt legislation to make adjustments that reconcile budget components with the totals in the First Concurrent Resolution. Changes are reported to Congress in the form of a reconciliation measure.

The Congressional Budget Office

The act established the Congressional Budget Office (CBO) as a separate agency of Congress. The director of the CBO is appointed by the Speaker of the House and the president pro tem of the Senate for a four-year term.

The CBO provides budget information or general staff assistance relating to federal programs to the House and Senate budget committees. It also provides assistance to the appropriations committees, the House Ways and Means Committee, the Senate Finance Committee, and other committees or members of Congress.

By the first of April each year, it prepares a report on alternative budget levels, fiscal policy, tax expenditures, national budget priorities, and alternative functional allocations of outlays and budget authority. This report includes a five-year projection.

The act does not state the purposes of the projection, but the CBO lists its apparent purposes as follows:

1. to provide a baseline for use in measuring budget options
2. to provide members of Congress with an estimate of the expenditures to which they are committed and an estimate of their flexibility in considering future budget options
3. to provide estimates of changes in priorities or relative shares of the budget due primarily to growth in entitlement programs [2]

Program Review and Evaluation

The act addresses program review and evaluation. Committees are authorized to fulfill their oversight responsibilities by contracting for studies or by requiring evaluations by federal agencies. In addition, the GAO has authorized an office of program review and evaluation, and the comptroller general is required to report annually on his evaluation activities. Taken together, these actions substantially increase congressional abilities for review and evaluation of federal activities, both in cooperation with, and independent of, federal agencies.

Initial Experiences: FY 1976 and FY 1977

The Budget and Impoundment Control Act made the new budget process mandatory, beginning in fiscal year 1977, and permitted earlier implementation of the process in conjunction with certain other new budget control procedures. In March 1975, the House and Senate budget committees reported plans to implement major portions of the process for fiscal year 1976. The committees were not prepared to implement the complete process for a variety of reasons. For one thing, committee information systems were still in the developmental stages, and the Congressional Budget Office had just begun to function. Despite these difficulties, the committees desired partial implementation because they believed that the new process would enable Congress to address the nation's mounting economic problems in a comprehensive manner. They also believed that working with the new process would enhance its usefulness in subsequent years.

The committees planned to hold hearings on the budget and economy, receive and consider the views and estimates of other congressional committees, report the First Concurrent Resolution on the budget in April, and report the Second Concurrent Resolution in the late summer or early fall. They contemplated action on the First Concurrent Resolution in May and on the Second Concurrent Resolution in September. They agreed not to break down federal spending by function in the first resolution and to concentrate instead on the macro totals. The prohibition against consideration of spending, revenue, and debt legislation before adoption of the first resolution and the May 15 deadline for reporting legislation were suspended during this initial period.

The budget committees began marking up the First Concurrent Resolution in March. In mid-April they introduced resolutions containing budget aggregates and submitted reports explaining the economic and legislative assumptions. Since the House and Senate resolutions were not identical, a Conference Committee resolved the differences, and a First Concurrent Resolution was achieved.

The floor fight in the Senate over the FY 1976 Authorization Bill for Defense is significant. Senator Edmund Muskie, chairman of the Senate Budget Committee, challenged the Senate Defense Authorization Bill and stated that it exceeded the amount targeted in the First Concurrent Resolution. In a roll-call vote, the Senate (by a vote of forty-eight to forty-two) sent the bill back to the Armed Services Committee for reductions. The Armed Services Committee cut $250 million in new authorization, and the bill then passed the Senate. In early fall, a Second Concurrent Resolution was achieved; Congress had made the new process work, despite what many people had considered great odds.

The act was fully implemented with the submission of the president's budget in January 1976. The president requested $433.4 billion in new budget authority for FY 1977; the allocation requested for national defense was initially $114.9 billion of that amount, but this was later amended to $113 billion.

The budget committees received the views and estimates of the other committees and used the information to prepare a recommended First

Concurrent Resolution. The House Armed Services Committee's recommendation to the House Budget Committee exceeded the president's request for national defense in several accounts with a proposed $114.6 billion for national defense.

The budget committees held extensive hearings on all budget functions, including national defense. Testimony received by the House Task Force on National Security Programs dealt primarily with long-range planning by the Department of Defense and the eventual impacts on outyear budgets. The committees considered such key policy issues as the rate of real growth in equipment modernization.

Although the House and Senate First Concurrent Resolutions were different, they were still slightly less than the president's request of $113.3 billion ($112 billion for the House and $113 billion for the Senate). The conference produced a timely First Concurrent Resolution that included $112.5 billion in budget authority for national defense.

The House and Senate committees adhered closely to the timetable provided by the Budget Act; the Second Concurrent Resolution was passed by the Senate on September 15 and by the House on September 16. The total federal budget was $451.6 billion compared with the president's revised request of $431.4 billion; the national defense budget authority was $112.1 billion compared with the president's request of $113.3 billion.

Significantly, the House Appropriations Committee reported a bill that exceeded the House Budget Committee's allocation to the Defense Subcommittee on Appropriations, and the Appropriations Committee bill was amended on the floor to come within the allocation. It is also significant that the Senate Budget Committee directed the Defense Department to submit a mission-oriented budget with the FY 1978 submission. Most significant, however, is the fact that the Defense Department received its appropriations before the beginning of the fiscal year for the first time in more than twenty years!

Implications

The experiences of fiscal years 1976 and 1977 demonstrate that Congress can meet the new budget timetable, alter spending committee recommendations to conform with a specified *total* federal budget, and propose alternatives to the president's budget. Because of these new budget capabilities, Congress will have an expanded impact on all federal programs and functions. The implications for defense are especially significant.

In many ways, the defense establishment is a large industrial operation. Procurements, maintenance, operations, and modification of bases and equipment have been hampered in the past by consistently late appropriations. Knowledge of funding availability at the beginning of the fiscal year can only enhance the efficiency of defense management.

National defense currently consumes 24 percent of total federal expenditures and more than 50 percent of the expenditures resulting from annual appropriation action by Congress. The defense establishment has received relatively intense budget scrutiny because it has been visible and controllable. In a study prepared for the House Budget Committee, Allen Schick states that defense spending has declined as a portion of the federal budget because other portions have grown at a much faster pace.[3] The steep growth in mandatory entitlements has played a major role in that process. One purpose of the five-year projections is to approximate the change in relative budget shares and priorities caused primarily by growth in entitlement programs. In the future, Congress will explicitly balance defense and domestic priorities on a multiperiod basis. That balancing may favor defense in comparison with previous years, because the high outyear cost of social entitlement programs will be made clearer. A decline in real defense purchasing power similar to the decline in the mid-1970s is less likely in the future. On the other hand, any assumption that there can be real growth in national defense or in any other area of federal spending may no longer be valid. Each year, programs in the aggregate will be balanced against the macro considerations of limited resources and relatively unlimited demands.

The increased program review and evaluation capability of Congress, coupled with specific provisions authorizing committees to require evaluations by federal agencies, will have a significant impact on the Defense Department. Congress will require increasing numbers of more detailed and sophisticated studies by DOD. Such requests may be sufficiently numerous to require a substantial expansion of the analytical staff capabilities within the military departments.

The role of Congress in the development of defense policy and forces will increase. This increase will result from the improved availability of information and from the increasing sophistication and knowledge concerning defense matters. Membership on the budget committees is, by law, rotated among the members of each house. For example, no member of the House Budget Committee can serve more than four of any ten consecutive years. Budget committee members develop expertise in all federal budget matters, but congressmen and senators who might otherwise remain specialists in domestic areas also become knowledgeable in defense matters. As Congress uses the new budget process, it will assume a more direct role in establishing defense policy and force structures. The Defense

Department must prepare itself to interact increasingly with members of Congress and their staffs on matters of military policy and administration.

Notes

1. Jesse Burkhead, *Government Budgeting* (New York: John Wiley and Sons, 1956).

2. U.S., Congressional Budget Office, *Five-Year Budget Projections: Fiscal Years 1978-1982* (Washington, D.C., 1976), p. 1.

3. Allen Schick, *Congressional Control of Expenditures* (Washington, D.C.: Congressional Research Service, December 1976).

8

American Opinion on the Use of Military Force Abroad

Bruce Russett
Miroslav Nincic

Public opinion in the United States is now much less favorably disposed toward the use of American military force abroad than at any time since the beginning of the cold war. In part this indisposition stems from the American failure in Vietnam, but it is also a result of partial East-West détente and other changes in the world at large and in America as well. Nevertheless, the reasons for this change are not well understood, nor are the characteristics of present attitudes well documented. Little systematic comparison has been made with attitudes in earlier periods; there is insufficient appreciation of important differences in the places and circumstances under which the use of force might be approved; and there is insufficient understanding of differences in attitudes among various parts of the population. Here we try to begin to fill these gaps, using systematic public opinion survey data gathered at various points over a period of nearly forty years.

This is not a report on public attitudes toward "involvement" in international affairs generally, or on a variety of important topics such as attitudes toward China and the Soviet Union, detente, arms control, or foreign economic assistance. Material on these questions is available, but the pattern of response is complex and often quite different from that on the use of military force.[1] Rather, this chapter is addressed more narrowly

We are grateful to Yale University for research support and to the Roper Public Opinion Research Center, Williamstown, Massachusetts (both directly and through its monthly publication, *Current Opinion*); Louis Harris and Associates; and Professor Charles Doran of Rice University for making data available to us. Of course, no organization bears any responsibility for the use we have made of the data.

Editor's note: This chapter was presented at the IUS conference and is reprinted with permission from the Academy of Political Science.

to approval of the use of American military forces to defend other nations: as different parts of the American public see it, *who* should be defended, from *what kind* of attack, by *what means*? Three specific aspects will be discussed:

1. A comparison of responses to similar questions at different points in time, especially comparing recent attitudes with those expressed in the 1950s and imediately before World War II
2. Differentiation of attitudes according to (a) the country at issue, (b) the type of attack hypothesized, and (c) different instruments of national security policy that might be employed
3. A discussion of differences of opinion within various segments, elite and mass, of the population

The discussion will concentrate almost exclusively on public opinion itself, rather than on broader questions of the relation of that opinion to actual policy formation and execution in the government. That is, we will *not* assume official American policy will simply reflect the majority opinion of the total populace at any particular time, nor make any simple assumptions about just what the relation between mass opinion and official policy might be. That is a fascinating but very complex matter not easily explored by the standard techniques of empirical social science. Toward the end we shall make a few brief and tentative comments on the matter, but no more. Finally, it should be stated explicitly that this is a report on some available evidence, much of which emerges in a form that is a surprise and occasionally a source of distress to the authors; reporting that *evidence* in no way should be taken as an expression of the authors' *opinion* about what United States foreign policy "ought" to be.

Now and Then

Since so many sweeping comparisons are made about the relation of "isolationism" in contemporary America to the mood prevailing in the years before World War II, it should be useful to make some systematic comparisons. For example, questions about what other countries should be defended from attack have been asked repeatedly of national samples both recently and in the period immediately preceding American entry into World War II. Table 1 presents those cases where the same country is referred to in both periods. Not surprisingly, there are some differences in wording and in labeling the countries in question, but probably not enough to affect the results markedly.[2]

Despite variation in response within each of the two periods (1938-1941; 1969-1975), the greatest difference in results is *between* the two periods. In fact, in a number of instances, the highest percentage of Americans willing

TABLE 1

APPROVAL OF USE OF AMERICAN TROOPS TO DEFEND VARIOUS
COUNTRIES, 1938-1941 AND 1969-1975*

Country Subject to Attack	Pre-World War II				1969-1975		
	Nov 38	Nov 39	Jul 40	Jul 41	Apr 69	Apr 71	Apr 75
Canada	73%	74%	88%	86%	57%	N.A.	57%
Mexico	43	54	76	85	52	45%	42
England[a]	28	N.A.	N.A.	51	N.A.	38	37
Philippines	46	54	65	60	30	N.A.	29
Brazil	27	37	55	N.A.	34	16	15
Indonesia[b]	N.A.	N.A.	17	46	20	N.A.	N.A.
Malaysia[c]	N.A.	N.A.	N.A.	42	20	N.A.	N.A.
Sample size (n)	5,171	5,244	2,590	5,244	1,561	1,518	1,599

Sources: Pre-World War II surveys are Roper surveys for *Fortune* #3, 12, 19,
and 27 courtesy of Roper Public Opinion Research Center. The 1969
survey was by Louis Harris and Associates, partially reported in
Time, May 2, 1969, p. 16; additional data supplied by Louis Harris
and Associates and Professor Charles Doran of Rice University.
The 1971 survey is by American Institute of Public Opinion,
reported in Albert H. Cantril and Charles W. Roll, Jr., *Hopes and
Fears of the American People* (New York, 1971); 1975 survey by
AIPO, reported in *Current Opinion*, June 1975, p. 56.

*Questions in November 1938 to July 1940 were: "If a major foreign power
actually threatened to take over . . . by armed invasion, would you be
willing to see the United States come to its rescue with armed force?"
July 1941 question first employed a map with large areas delineated, asking
"for each area whether you would be willing to defend all of it, part of
it, or none of it with armed forces if Germany or her allies tried to take
it." For those answering "part," they were then asked about specific
countries. Above includes all respondents prepared to defend all of each
area, plus those identifying the relevant country as part they would defend.
April 1969 asked, "If . . . were invaded by outside Communist forces"
whether respondent would favor American action with "U.S. armed forces,"
"military and economic aid," or "stay out." The 1971 and 1975 surveys posed
the event where ". . . is attacked by Communist backed forces" and offered
choices of "send American troops" or "send military supplies but not send
American troops" or "refuse to get involved."

[a]Labeled Great Britain in 1941.
[b]Labeled "Dutch Possessions in the Orient" in July 1940 survey; "Dutch East
Indies" in 1941.
[c]"Singapore" in July 1971.

to use American troops in defense of any of these countries in the recent
period is *lower* than the lowest such percentage in the earlier period.
While the size and consistency of these differences is striking, one
should *resist any temptation to conclude too quickly that Americans necessarily now
are more reluctant* to use military force than before World War II. Most of
the data points here are after the outbreak of the war in Europe, and
after the depths of isolationism had been passed. Unlike the present era,
this was a period of widespread hot war on two continents; invasion of
many of these countries was indeed an immediate threat. As the war

TABLE 2

PERCENTAGE FAVORING MILITARY ACTION IN CASE OF SOVIET ATTACK ON
AMERICAN ALLIES IN EUROPE*

1949–1955					1970–1974		
Oct 49	Jan 50	Apr 54	Jan 55	Nov 55	Sep 70	Jun 72	Dec 74
50	52	51	44	44	51	52	39

Sources: Early surveys are by National Opinion Research Center courtesy
of Roper Public Opinion Research Center; 1970 survey is Louis
Harris and Associates, *The Harris Survey Yearbook of Public
Opinion* (New York, 1971), pp. 86-87; 1972 by AIPO, William
Watts and Lloyd Free, *State of the Nation* (New York, 1973),
p. 281; and 1974 by Louis Harris and Associates, reprinted
in John Reilly (ed.), *American Public Opinion and U.S. Foreign
Policy 1975* (Chicago, 1975), p. 18.

*For question wording 1949-1955 see text. The 1970 question was: "Do
you feel if each of the following happened it would be worth going to war
again or not?" and the item referred to here is "Western Europe were
invaded by communists." The 1972 question asked for agreement or disagreement with the statement, "The United States should come to the defense of
its major European Allies if any of them are attacked by Soviet Russia."
The 1974 question asked whether, "if Western Europe were invaded"
respondents would "favor or oppose U.S. military involvement, including
the use of U.S. troops." "Don't know" responses averaged 10 percent in
the 1970s. Sample size varies from 1,200 to 1,800.

progressed, the percentage of the populace prepared to defend foreign
countries rose pretty consistently. The one prewar poll (November 1938)
shows results somewhat more like those of the 1970s. Also it is important
to be aware that the 1969-1975 surveys offered options of "troops" or
"supplies but not troops," whereas the 1938-1941 surveys asked only for a
yes or no on the use of American "armed force." The latter forced choice
is sure to have inflated the percentage approving the use of force over
what would have emerged from the more nuanced question of the 1969-1975
period.

Nevertheless, the recent results *are* low. This roughly parallels data on
public attitudes toward military expenditures. Surveys since December
1968 have consistently found that 40-50 percent of the populace want to
reduce military spending, as compared with 5-20 percent in 1937-1939.[3]

While not applicable to the pre-World War II period, there is one
other relevant set of trend data. In the early years of the cold war, the
following question was regularly asked: "If one of our allies in Western
Europe were attacked by the Russian army, do you think the United States
would be justified in using atomic bombs against Russia?" (For the 1954
and 1955 surveys discussed below, the question changed to "using hydrogen
bombs against Russian cities.") As will be apparent from Table 2, the
1950s results are not very different from the percentages who would be

prepared to defend Western Europe in the early 1970s, but there was a substantial drop by 1974. Moreover, there is a further difference on closer inspection. The 1970s questions did not specify the use of nuclear weapons, but merely referred to "going to war," unspecified means to "come to the defense" of Europe, or "use of U.S. troops." Asked specifically, "Could you conceive of *any* [italics added] situations in which nuclear war would be necessary, or not?" immediately following the item in the 1970 questionnaire, only 26 percent of the sample could do so. And as we shall see below (Table 3), in a 1969 survey the percentage ready to use *nuclear weapons* for the defense of other countries was very low, varying from 17 percent to 2 percent depending on the country at issue. The rise of the Soviet Union to nuclear parity with the United States has surely made a difference to many Americans' thinking.

Selectivity According to Type and Location of Attack

Warnings against the uncritical reading of percentages from public opinion surveys are very common, and appropriate. Responses are heavily influenced by transitory factors such as question wording, salience of an issue at the moment, the position (or absence of a position) by government and opinion leaders, and respondents' mood. An individual who disapproves of a hypothetical course of action when asked his opinion by a pollster may react very differently if the president of the United States actually initiates or proposes the action. We cannot predict from these figures whether a majority of the American public would, in a crisis situation, approve or disapprove a particular (and probably highly nuanced) American action in support of a country being attacked. Nevertheless, survey data can be useful, if interpreted carefully, for uncovering changes in opinion over time—especially when similar questions are repeatedly employed—and for differentiating the *relative* levels of support for different kinds of responses to different kinds of events. We turn now to a more intensive look at those questions that have on a number of occasions presented respondents with a list of countries which might conceivably be subject to attack. We shall use the answers to suggest what kinds of countries people are most willing to see defended. We shall also see how the answers vary according to the type of threat postulated, and the nature of the American reaction suggested.

We can begin with Table 3. It shows responses to the longest such list of countries—twenty-one—employed in a single survey, and also distinguishes responses according to three different possible American reactions. The question is that referred to in the April 1969 column of Table 1; it becomes important to note here (as it was not in that table) that responses approving use of "U.S. armed forces" were divided according to whether

TABLE 3

PERCENTAGE OF UNITED STATES RESPONDENTS FAVORING VARIOUS KINDS OF MILITARY
ACTIONS IN SUPPORT OF DIFFERENT COUNTRIES IF ATTACKED

Country	U.S. Troops, Nuclear Weapons, or Military and Economic Aid Only	U.S. Troops or Nuclear Weapons	Nuclear Weapons
Canada	74	57	17
Mexico	70	52	15
Bahamas	59	43	7
West Germany	54	38	7
Brazil	47	34	6
South Korea	47	33	5
Philippines	43	30	3
Japan	39	27	5
Italy	38	27	5
Taiwan	38	26	6
Finland	37	25	5
Israel	36	14	4
Thailand	36	25	5
Bolivia	36	25	6
India	33	22	4
Ethiopia	32	22	4
Kenya	30	21	4
Malaysia	29	20	4
Indonesia	29	20	4
Yugoslavia	23	15	3
Romania	20	13	2

Source: April 1969 survey as reported in Table 1

or not the respondent would approve the use of "nuclear weapons." In the third column we have listed the percentage who would approve American use of nuclear weapons, and the second column indicates that number plus the additional number who would approve the use of American troops but without the nuclear option. The first column indicates the number who would employ American troops or at least approve sending military and economic assistance if not troops; that is, the total who would approve some form of American assistance to the country if it were attacked. As should be apparent, the variation is very great, ranging from Canada and Mexico to Yugoslavia and Romania when the differentiation is by country, and sometimes dropping by as much as 30 percent intervals according to the type of action contemplated. And while the rankings of various countries are similar for each of the three instruments, there are some changes worth analyzing.

In an attempt to sort out these differences, we employed a standard statistical method—multiple linear regression—using characteristics of the countries as attempted predictors and approval of the three action categories as responses to be predicted. The following were the predictor characteristics:

1. Distance from the United States, measured by distance from the nation's capital city to Washington, on the hypothesis that people would

be more ready to defend countries closer to the United States (where the threat to America would seem more immediate). We might alternatively have measured border-to-border distances, or from geographical center to center, but given the great distances involved, in most cases such alternatives would not affect the results in any important way.

2. Economic importance to the United States, measured as a country's total trade (exports and imports) with the United States. Hypotheses about the relation of economic interest to foreign policy and military involvement are too common to need argument. An earlier exploratory study[4] did suggest some evidence that both the credibility of a deterrence promise, and a nation's readiness to carry out the promise, were positively related to the strength of economic linkages. Of course economic linkages may be closely associated with other kinds of international bonds of communication and common interest; economic interest alone may not be the operative variable.

3. A measure of sociocultural "distance," on the hypothesis that people will be more willing to fight to defend countries that have a way of life similar to their own. Here we used a composite measure of such "distance" that was devised by the first author in earlier research. It weights equally four different dimensions of society derived by factor analytic techniques: economic development, land-use patterns, a political system dimension, and a religious culture dimension. The measure of sociocultural "distance" between the United States and each of the twenty-one countries comprises the sum of absolute differences between their scores on each factor. While such a measure is unavoidably arbitrary in some degree, this one has been extensively validated and the basic pattern confirmed in studies by a variety of researchers.[5]

4. A measure for type of political system, on the hypothesis that, perhaps especially after past experiences, Americans will be more ready to fight in defense of countries whose governments are perceived as both non-Communist and reasonably representative of the populace. We thus coded all countries in one of these categories, using the results as dummy variables in the regression: Communist countries (Yugoslavia and Romania); parliamentary democracies; and non-Communist but nondemocratic regimes (major electoral system irregularities or major violations of civil liberties). This overlaps in part with the political dimension of number 3, above, but seems important enough to warrant separate examination.

5. Presence or absence of a formal military alliance with the United States coded as a dummy variable.

Table 4 presents the results of the three equations. The first column identifies each of the predictors, the second lists the unstandardized regression coefficient (b) for each predictor, and the third shows the partial correlation coefficient (r) for each predictor when all the others are held constant. The b's indicate the percentage change in each response

TABLE 4

PREDICTORS TO AMERICAN PUBLIC WILLINGNESS TO EXTEND VARIOUS KINDS OF
ASSISTANCE TO ATTACKED NATIONS

	Regression Coefficient(b)	Partial Correlation
Equation 1: *Help of Some Sort (U.S. armed forces and military and economic aid)*		
Trade	0.40	0.25
Geographical distance	-0.28(a)	-0.55
Sociocultural distance	-1.21	-0.16
Democracy	16.70(b)	0.48
Non-Communist, nondemocracy	15.27(b)	0.46
U.S. ally	6.49(c) $R^2=.82$	0.41
Equation 2: *U.S. Armed Forces with or without Nuclear Option*		
Trade	0.40	0.28
Geographical distance	-0.20(b)	-0.49
Sociocultural distance	-1.13	-0.17
Democracy	10.71(c)	0.36
Non-Communist, nondemocracy	10.88(c)	0.38
U.S. ally	5.74(c) $R^2=.78$	0.41
Equation 3: *Troops with Nuclear Option*		
Trade	0.20(c)	0.42
Geographical distance	-0.08(a)	-0.52
Sociocultural distance	-0.31	-0.13
Democracy	2.83	0.29
Non-Communist, nondemocracy	2.96	0.30
U.S. ally	1.10 $R^2=.77$	.24

Note: The parenthetical information in the first column refers to
significance levels: $(a)p < .025$, $(b)p < .05$, (c) $p < .10$.

category associated with a "unit" change in each of the predictors. For
example, as we have measured it, a unit of geographic distance corresponds
to approximately 100 miles; according to the first equation for every
100 miles distant a country is from the United States the percentage of
respondents willing to provide help of some sort decreases by 0.28. The
basic unit of trade is $1 billion. For the political system variables and
alliance the unit is simply presence or absence; e.g., existence of an alliance
with the United States increases by 6.49 the percentage of the population willing to provide help. In the case of sociocultural distance,
an abstract measure, the unit is not easily interpretable.[6] Most readers
will probably find the partial correlations to be the more useful statistic.
In parentheses after the *b*'s we indicate those coefficients that can be

considered statistically significant at various levels of significance. Without taking the notion of statistical significance literally here, the reader may find this useful for identifying influences making a relatively important contribution to "explaining" variation in responses about military support. Beneath each section of the table is given the R^2, or the percentage of the variation in the responses that is accounted for by all the predictors together.

Looking first at the equation for help of some sort, clearly the major contribution is made by *geographical distance* (the closer a country is to the United States, the greater the readiness to assist it), followed by regime type and presence of an alliance with the United States. Both types of *non-Communist regimes* are favored over countries with Communist governments (even relatively independent ones like Yugoslavia and Romania) but *democratic* governments are *not* especially favored. Remember too that 20 percent or more of the population is ready to give assistance to any of the twenty-one countries should they be attacked.

In the second equation, representing readiness to employ American military forces, both geographical distance and regime type recede somewhat (though with alliance they remain important), and trade links with the United States gain slightly in importance. And at the highest level of commitment, a readiness to use nuclear weapons as in the third equation, *trade* volume becomes a substantial predictor, behind geographical distance.

In none of the equations does *sociocultural distance* seem to make anything but the most trivial difference. To check whether our measure of sociocultural distance might be at fault we found an independent measure of a kind of perceptual "distance." In two recent national surveys,[7] respondents were asked to rank various countries "from the highest position of 'plus 5' for a country you like very much, to the lowest position of 'minus 5' for a country you dislike very much." The results for those countries included both in our equations and in the "liking" surveys are reported in Table 5, as for comparative purposes, are the results for China and the Soviet Union (Russia). While no one should take too seriously the rather casual impressions likely to be tapped by such a question, the results agree surprisingly well (inversely, of course) with our measure of sociocultural distance (column 3). More important for our purposes, they confirm that even subjective or perceptual differences in "distances" are not very efficient predictors of readiness to provide help in case of attack. In the Table 3 data for the latter, Brazil consistently ranks above Italy, and Japan ranks about with Italy and Israel (for conventional force much above Israel).

Overall, the results indicate that popular willingness to provide assistance is *highly structured* according to a few, perhaps implicit, criteria. Approximately four-fifths of the variance is accounted for in each of the three equations.[8] Other results may be summarized as follows:

TABLE 5

"LIKING" SCORES FOR VARIOUS COUNTRIES FROM NATIONAL SURVEYS, AND
MEASURE OF SOCIOCULTURAL DISTANCE USED IN EQUATIONS*

| Country | "Liking" Scores | | Sociocultural |
	1973 Survey	1974 Survey	Distance Measure
Canada	332	351	1.60
West Germany	189	N.A.	3.84
Italy	160	N.A.	5.07
Israel	N.A.	142	5.46
Brazil	N.A.	135	4.90
Japan	134	112	6.45
China	−09	−59	9.28
Russia (Soviet Union)	−115	−70	7.10
Sample Size (n)	1,500	1,484	

*"Liking" scores are calculated by multiplying each scale score (from +5
to −5) by the percentage of the population assigning that score; no
opinion and no answer responses are ignored. A number of countries--
largely in the middle range of scores--are omitted because they are not
relevant to this analysis. Sociocultural distance measure is from
Russett, *International Regions.*

Geographical distance is the most powerful predictor at all levels of
commitment.

In these 1969 results, at least, people did *not* systematically prefer
democratic governments as beneficiaries of American military involvement.
This probably dates from the cold war dichotomization of regimes between Communist and non-Communist, disregarding differences within
the latter group.[9]

Trade ties, while unimportant at low levels of commitment, become
increasingly so as the level of commitment *rises* to use of American military forces and ultimately nuclear weapons. Since American direct investment abroad by country is highly correlated ($r = 0.73$) with American trade,
it seems likely that a general dimension of economic linkage is at issue
here—though perhaps compounded with broader links of communication
as suggested above, because the man in the street is unlikely to have
detailed information on trade. But whether or not one believes that economic ties cause such a public willingness to use force, the data indicate
that *if* American elites wished to use force, popular support for the action
would be greater with the degree of American economic involvement
in the country.

Formal *alliance* commitments become quite unimportant at the highest
(nuclear) level of assistance and are superseded by economic linkages.
Interpretation of the last equation, however, should be careful and
tentative. There is relatively little variation in the responses (only from

2 to 17 percent), and the statistical results are heavily influenced by the two exceptional cases (Canada and Mexico with scores of 17 and 15 respectively, with all others at 7 percent or below).

We also have some data on public willingness to use "armed force" to defend various countries in 1940-1941, with the questions as given for Table 1. There are some serious problems with such data, both in comparability between surveys and in measuring the predictors. Nevertheless as an experiment we did run the exercise on a total of eighteen observations from the two surveys combined (four countries were used in both surveys, and thus are double counted in the eighteen). While we are too skeptical about the quality of the results to dignify reporting the equation in a table, it may be worth reporting the very great importance we seemed to find for geographical distance (partial $r = 0.73$)—even more important than in any of the 1969 equations. Perhaps the American public now has a more complex image of other countries and their importance than it did in 1940-1941. Other predictors applicable to that period (sociocultural distance, despite some measurement problems; trade; and a somewhat different regime type variable—independent democracy or not, since many of the observations were colonies as well as nondemocracies) were unimportant except, in a small way, regime (partial $r = 0.55$, with independent democracies favored).

Returning to the 1969 equations, it will be useful to look at the results for specific countries. The regression equation gives us a "predicted" level of support for each country that we can compare with the level observed from the opinion survey. A comparison of observed and predicted levels allowed us to see which countries were "unexpectedly" high in public support and which were low, and to suggest, in a post hoc fashion to be sure, what additional influences may be operating.

Mexico, the Bahamas, and Canada (especially Mexico) were consistently and fairly substantially "underpredicted." Rather obviously, great closeness to the United States exerts an even more important effect than a simple linear measure of miles would suggest. Of the other countries markedly underpredicted by the equations, nearly all—South Korea, Indonesia, Philippines, and, for the first and third equations, Taiwan—had been subjected to some sort of major communist attack, coup attempt, or insurgency before the time of the survey. Where local determination to resist has previously been demonstrated to the American public, and/or where the United States itself has intervened vigorously to support that resistance (e.g., Korea), the American public is especially ready to grant assistance.

One other poorly predicted case is of some interest: Israel, especially in the second equation for military force, where it emerges as a very badly "overpredicted" case. The survey found only 14 percent of the population ready to use American forces in Israel's defense—the second lowest figure of all for American forces—whereas the equation "predicted" 25 percent. Partly this may be due to the phrasing of the question, where for this one instance the standard question wording seems to have been changed to "if it looked as though Israel would be overrun by the Arabs with Russian help," less threatening to Americans, possibly, than "being attacked by Communist-backed forces." Nevertheless, the 1971 and 1975 surveys references in Table 1 also mentioned Israel, and they found the percentages even lower for American troops to Israel (11 and 12 percent respectively). The most important reason for Israel's low rating probably stems from a genuine fear that in this case, particularly, the United States would risk being drawn into a wider war with the Soviet Union if it were to employ its *own* military forces directly in Israel's defense. In the 1969 survey Israel's score for help including military and economic aid was just a little below that for Japan (36 rather than 39 percent) but rose in the 1971 and 1975 surveys (55 and 54 respectively for Israel and 51 percent in both for Japan). Similar questions in several other surveys show roughly half of Americans ready to send military supplies, but not necessarily American troops, for Israel's defense.[10]

Our major regression analysis was based on a 1969 survey, a year which coincided with intense public disillusion with the Vietnam war, and with foreign military commitments in general. An April 1975 survey, however, listed thirteen countries as possible recipients of American assistance. While that is too small a sample of countries to perform a new regression analysis on, we can use the equation derived from the 1969 analysis to

TABLE 6

PREDICTED AND ACTUAL PERCENTAGE OF AMERICANS WILLING TO EXTEND HELP
OF SOME SORT IN RESPONSE TO ATTACK, APRIL 1975

Country	Percentage Predicted from Table 4a Equation	Actual Percentage in Survey	Difference
Canada	80	76	4
Mexico	59	67	-8
England	55	67	-12
West Germany	55	59	-4
Japan	49	51	-2
Brazil	49	48	1
Turkey	46	38	8
Israel	38	54	-16
Taiwan	35	35	0
Philippines	34	63	-29
Thailand	34	42	-8
Saudi Arabia	34	34	0
India	29	41	-12

Note: Sources and question wording given in Table 1. Trade and political
       system data are updated from those used in analysis of Table 4.

TABLE 7

PERCENTAGE OF SENIOR AMERICAN BUSINESS EXECUTIVES AND MILITARY OFFICERS
WHO WOULD APPROVE USE OF AMERICAN TROOPS TO FIGHT EXTERNAL ATTACK
OR INDIGENOUS INSURGENCY, 1973

Country	*Military* Attack	Insurgency	*Business* Attack	Insurgency
Mexico	95	53	78	33
West Germany	92	37	51	15
Brazil	71	17	45	11
Japan	80	21	37	8
Thailand	33	10	7	2
Yugoslavia	8	1	4	1
India	5	1	6	1
Sample Size (n)	621		567	

try to "predict" what the 1975 results would be. That is, using similar measures (distance, trade, etc.) to characterize the countries, and the same coefficients for each measure as given in Table 4, we can "predict" the percentage of the population that would be willing to render assistance. We can then, in Table 6, compare our "prediction" with the results actually observed from the 1975 survey. On the average, we have underpredicted by less than 6 percent. While this indicates a small increase over the 1969-1975 period in public willingness to extend help, the basic stability in this willingness—both in overall level, and in the relative ranking of various countries—is remarkable.

Seeing this stability, we then attempted to predict the percentage of the American public who would have agreed to send help of any sort to Angola—a country which at the time of writing this article was of special importance in international politics. Inserting the appropriate measures for Angola into the equation, we estimated that only 33 percent of Americans would agree to such help, even in response to an "attack" (as contrasted with an "indigenous insurgency"). Awareness of the thinness of this public support might have enabled the American administration to avoid inviting a damaging public defeat in Congress.

Finally, it makes a very great difference whether a country is perceived as "attacked by foreign communist forces" or subject to "a serious insurgency movement led by an indigenous communist movement." This question was asked in April 1973 of a special sample of vice-presidents of the largest industrial and commercial corporations in America, and of a sample of senior military officers enrolled in the five war colleges.[11] Table 7 shows the percentage of each group prepared to use American military forces in either event. While the proportions who would approve the use of troops are not too low (and higher than among the general public, as we shall see below) in the case of an external attack, there is in no case for business executives, and only for Mexico among military officers, a majority ready to use American troops to fight an indigenous insurgency. Depending on the country in question, one-quarter to one-half as many people would use American troops to combat an insurgency as would use them against an attack. Discrimination on this point seems to have sharpened considerably since the Harris survey in 1969, when the figure for insurgency was two-thirds that for attack.

Who Supports Assistance?

Although one man may have one vote in a democracy, in no political system is the influence of each citizen exactly the same. Speaking generally, people of higher income, education, and professional status are more likely to vote, to try to influence others, to be able to make persuasive public statements, to make campaign contributions, and otherwise to be politically

TABLE 8

COMPARISON OF ELITES AND GENERAL PUBLIC READINESS TO SEND
HELP TO COUNTRIES IF ATTACKED

Country Attacked	Elites (1973) Military (1)	Business (2)	Telephone Respondents (1973) (3)	General Public 1969 (4)	1971 (5)	1975 (6)
	Percentage Prepared to Send Troops, or Help but Not Troops					
Mexico	100	96	N.A.	70	71	67
West Germany	100	90	N.A.	54	59	59
Brazil	98	88	N.A.	47	52	48
Japan	99	84	N.A.	38	51	51
Thailand	95	57	N.A.	36	47	42
India	59	46	N.A.	33	47	41
Yugoslavia	63	41	N.A.	23	34	N.A.
	Percentage Prepared to Send Troops					
Mexico	95	78	61	52	55	42
West Germany	92	51	50	38	28	27
Brazil	71	45	N.A.	34	16	15
Japan	80	37	38	27	7	16
Thailand	33	7	34	25	11	10
India	8	6	26	22	7	9
Yugoslavia	5	4	N.A.	15	17	N.A.
Sample Size (n)	621	567	1,014	1,561	1,518	1,599

Sources: For columns 2 and 3, Bruce M. Russett and Elizabeth C. Hanson,
           Interest and Ideology: The Foreign Policy Beliefs of American
           Businessmen (San Francisco, 1975). The telephone survey was
           performed by Daniel Starch & Staff, Inc., January 1973; reported
           in Current Opinion, August 1973, p. 87.
Note: For elite samples, questions are as for Table 7. For telephone survey,
        question was "If . . . is threatened by Communist-supported invasion
        and takeover, should the U.S. send troops?" Questions and sources for
        general public surveys, 1969-1975 are as reported in Table 1.

active. Thus it is essential, in making even the crudest assessment of the impact of public opinion on governmental policy, to have some idea of the distribution of opinions within a population. Table 8 begins the investigation with a comparison of three different kinds of samples and their attitudes on aiding specific countries. The first two columns represent data for the senior military officers and business executives, samples discussed in conjunction with Table 7. While not official policymakers, these certainly represent an "elite" group of special potential influence. (No acceptance of "power elite" theories is required for an attribution of some special influence.) Column 3 represents the responses of people polled in a national survey conducted *by telephone*. While certainly not any kind of "elite" sample, it is well known that telephone survey samples regularly underrepresent low-income, poorly educated people who may not have ready access to a telephone. Thus the sample is inevitably composed of people with a somewhat higher average status than is the case with personal interview surveys conducted on national samples by the large professional survey organizations. Three such surveys are represented in columns 4-6.

Two conclusions emerge. First, higher-status individuals are generally more willing to come to the aid of other countries than are average members of the public. With only a single and trivial exception, this is true for *all* comparisons of elite with mass samples in the upper half of the table, for sending help of some sort. It is also true for all comparisons of telephone respondents with the mass samples in the lower half[12] and for most, but not all, of the comparisons of elites with the general public on this matter. Only in the case of the countries least "popular" for defense—Thailand and India for the businessmen, and Yugoslavia for both elite samples—is this reversed.

Looking at the great spread between most and least favored countries for the elites, however, leads to the second conclusion. A higher-status person has a much more selective, discriminating set of preferences than does the average person. The variation is much wider for the elite samples, with clear majorities ready to defend the top countries and, especially where American troops are at issue, some very low figures for the countries at the lower end of scale.

Similar patterns are clear if we look *within* the general public sample, as in Table 9. Here we have the various answers in each column, controlling first for income and then for education. The basic number in each cell is the *percentage* of respondents in a given income or educational category making a particular response, averaged across their answers for all eleven countries. For the "send troops" and "send supplies" answers, we show, in parentheses beneath, a *selectivity score* (the standard deviation) in the groups' response across the eleven countries. Thus a high number indicates great selectivity, a low number little selectivity. Regularly and sharply,

TABLE 9

AVERAGE LEVELS OF SUPPORT FOR ASSISTANCE, AND SELECTIVITY SCORES,
BY INCOME AND EDUCATION

Income	Send Troops	Only Send Supplies	No Help	Don't Know
Over $15,000	23.0% (17.2)	40.1% (7.7)	28.6%	8.3%
$ 7,000– $14,999	20.6% (15.3)	37.6% (7.1)	30.8%	10.9%
$ 6,999– $ 5,000	17.4% (12.1)	35.1% (6.1)	32.9%	14.6%
Under $ 5,000	11.6% (7.6)	27.8% (5.0)	42.1%	18.6%

Education	Send Troops	Only Send Supplies	No Help	Don't Know
College	21.9% (17.1)	41.0% (8.0)	29.3%	7.8%
High school	19.2% (12.6)	34.3% (5.8)	33.5%	13.1%
Grade school	12.0% (9.1)	30.3% (4.1)	39.6%	18.1%

the *higher* people's social *status* (by income or education), the *more willing* they are, in general, to aid in the defense of other countires, and the *more selective* or discriminating they are according to the country at issue.[13]

A related pattern is apparent in recent American attitudes on Vietnam. In the early stages of that war higher-status Americans were more likely to favor American participation,[14] but as the war dragged on into the 1970s these same individuals were more likely to change their minds, and the association of status with hawkish attitudes on Vietnam became weaker though still discernible. Individuals were more likely to change, the greater their exposure to the mass media of communication.[15] Moreover, whereas in the early cold war years higher-status Americans were most likely to support higher levels of military spending, from 1968 onward they became more ready to cut the military budget than were lower-status people.[16] It is—as one might expect on reflection—higher-status individuals, probably especially those heavily exposed to the media, who are most likely to have a rich, and fluid, set of images and opinions on international affairs. They are both more discriminating at a particular point in time—that is, more responsive to particular pieces of information—and more ready to change their opinions in response to new information or ideas in their social environment. With regard to our concern here, such individuals are likely—and more likely than the average man in the street—to give immediate support to an American government that decided to use force to defend a country from attack if a persuasive case for such action could be made by a reasonably united American government and by major opinion leaders in the media. If, however, the grounds for military action could not so readily be demonstrated, and there were major divisions in the government and/or media or both, then these higher-status people might well become as likely as the average person to oppose the action. Furthermore, these same people—and again, they are the ones more likely to be politically effective—would be more likely to desert the initial commitment if, after a time, major doubts should arise about its purpose or efficacy.

This perspective also helps us to interpret another facet of opinion on Vietnam and to offer some thoughts on the longer-term stability of readiness to help in the defense of other countries in general. Figure 1 shows the percentage of Americans saying "no" to the repeated survey question, "Do you think the U.S. made a mistake sending troops to fight in Vietnam?"[17] The first impression is, of course, an overall decline over time. A second interpretation, necessarily tentative, is that the decline proceeded at varying rates. In the early stages it was quite precipitate, then became much less so after falling below 40 percent at the beginning of 1969. In other words, near the beginning of the war, when its costs were moderate and its difficulty not yet widely understood, most Americans were prepared to support the war effort—but it was not yet very salient to them. As the war and its costs proceeded, however, many of those most attuned to cues and opinions from the media and, one would suppose, from their informal social networks, turned against the war. Toward the later years the minority which supported the war was disproportionately (though surely *not* exclusively) composed of individuals less open to cues from their environment. To use a public health analogy, antiwar attitudes took root in the susceptible parts of the population and spread from individual to individual across a network of social contacts. After most such "susceptible" individuals had been reached, what was left was a core of people who either were less closely linked to that social network or more resistant to change because for reasons of personality or life-experience they were strongly committed to supporting the war.

Or to look from yet a slightly different angle, people may support a policy for three reasons: because doing so satisfies basic personality needs, because on the basis of available information the policy is perceived as consistent with certain interests and beliefs, and because of support for

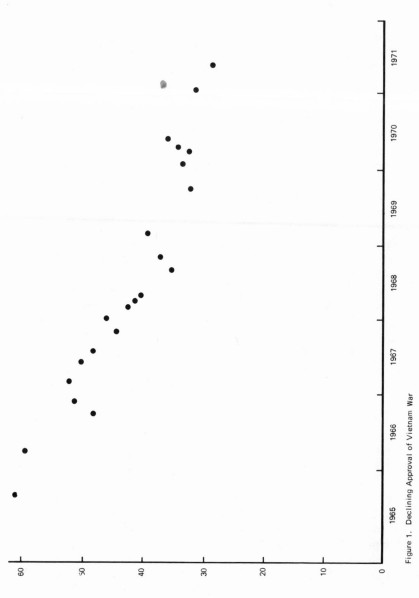

Figure 1. Declining Approval of Vietnam War

PERCENT APPROVING TROOPS IN VIETNAM

their attitudes from that segment of their social environment most meaningful to them. While higher-status people presumably are no more or less likely than others to have certain basic personality needs, they are more likely to be linked with a broad social environment where international affairs are salient and considered important. Thus when cues in that environment change, higher-status people are more likely to change their opinions for two reasons which interact. First, new information that a given foreign policy is inconsistent with his interests and beliefs is especially likely to reach a higher-status person and thus to incite him to reassess his former position. Second, as this likelihood applies to all members of the higher-status group, the general support from his salient social environment can be expected to decrease, providing even less incentive for the particular member to cling to his previous opinion. Such a perspective suggests that the current level of popular support for aid to other countries is not likely to decline much further, at least in the absence of another effort that "goes bad" as the Vietnam one did. The question of military aid to other countries has been very prominent in the media for a number of years now; many people have changed their opinions so as to oppose it, but we would guess that most of the "susceptibles" have now been reached.[18]

Some Conclusions

To summarize the major empirical findings:

1. The willingness of the American public to use United States' armed forces for the defense of other nations is currently *lower* than during the earlier cold war years and is probably at approximately the same level as prevailed in the years immediately preceding American entry into World War II. That level of willingness seems to have held fairly steady during the years 1969-1975, and there is *no reason to expect any continued decline* if our hypothesis concerning trends in such willingness are correct.

2. Public willingness to employ *nuclear* weapons on behalf of allies is extremely *low*, much lower than during the early 1950s.

3. Public willingness to employ American forces, or even to send military supplies for the defense of other countries, is *highly selective*. That willingness tends to be higher for countries the *closer* they are geographically to the United States. *Economic ties* to the United States, existence of a formal military *alliance* with the United States, and rule by a *non-Communist government* (of any variety) also make a positive contribution.

4. Public willingness to employ American forces also depends strongly on the *nature of the threat*. Depending on the country threatened, between two and four times as many people would use American troops to defend against an external attack as against an indigenous insurgency.

5. Public willingness to defend other countries varies markedly among different segments of the public. *Elite* or leadership samples are much more willing than are average members of the general public; among the general public that willingness is greater with higher *income* and *education*. These people are also much more *discriminating* in regard to whom they would assist.

Some further speculations about the political consequences: we have noted the low level of popular support for the commitment of United States' military forces outside the Western Hemisphere. In the elite as well as the mass public, data show few instances where as many as half are ready to approve such action. Presumably, recent official statements, especially by former Defense Secretary Schlesinger, have sought to confront that problem by asserting American readiness to use nuclear weapons in defense of other nations. Nuclear weapons could be used quickly, with existing forces, and—hopefully—produce a rapid outcome that might not directly involve the American homeland. Such action could be taken by a determined American executive even in the absence of any widespread popular support. Yet the irony is that such action would run *directly counter to the wishes of the American public* as expressed in these opinion surveys. The use of nuclear weapons, as indicated earlier in this chapter or in Table 3, would be approved by only a very small portion of the populace. Far more are prepared, at least initially, to support the kind of continuing long-term effort implied by sending military supplies or even conventionally armed American troops into combat.

Until now, we have been discussing only material about public opinion, whether mass or elites, rather than beliefs or attitudes at the very top of the foreign policy decision-making system. More than in domestic policy, foreign policymakers do have some latitude to act independently of public opinion. We *cannot* predict in simpleminded fashion that leaders will follow public opinion on the matters we have addressed. Despite constraints, they may persist in certain policies for a while even if general opinion lags behind, and they may work to influence the public and bring it along to accept the policies that decision makers believe are right. We have good evidence of the decision latitude given for a long time to American presidents on Vietnam, when there was a potential majority available to be mobilized either for moderate escalation or moderate withdrawal, according to the direction in which the president chose to lead. This phenomenon, and that of "rallying 'round the flag" in a crisis, tends most commonly to be found among higher-status people.[19] There is also the risk—or opportunity, depending on one's perspective—that deliberately incurring *some* costs through a rapid military response could be used as a tactic to rally and hold public support even for an initially unpopular purpose. Some American deaths, for instance, could represent a "sunk cost" that had to be "redeemed."[20]

The effects of flag-rallying nonetheless do fade, and the period of its relevance becomes ever shorter the more frequently it is invoked. And many kinds of foreign policy behavior are not suitable for rallying the populace as in a crisis. A quick action can be mounted by the executive with existing military forces and without prior approval; if successful it may be widely applauded. The year-in, year-out maintenance of troop levels and weapons capabilities, however, requires congressional approval under circumstances where the trade-offs in terms of domestic welfare become vividly apparent and politically very salient.

Notes

1. For example, on the question, "Do you think it would be best for the future of this country if we took an active part in world affairs, or if we stayed out of world affairs?," a March 1973 survey found the percentage saying "active part" still a clear majority (65 percent) but at the lowest point since World War II (*Current Opinion*, April 1975, p. 30). However, the percentage favoring foreign economic assistance to less developed countries has risen: 51 percent in 1958, 58 percent in 1966, 68 percent in 1973. See Paul A. Laudicina, *World Poverty and Development: A Survey of American Opinion* (Washington, D.C., 1973), p. 31. For further explication of these complexities, see Bruce M. Russett and Elizabeth C. Hanson, *Interest and Ideology: The Foreign Policy Beliefs of American Businessmen* (San Francisco, 1975), Chapter 3.

2. For samples of this size, due to sampling error differences of less than 5 percent from one survey to another are generally not statistically significant at the 0.01 level; where sampling procedures or question wording differ, the 5 percent spread should be widened.

3. Bruce M. Russett, "The Americans' Retreat from World Power," *Political Science Quarterly* 90, no. 1 (Spring 1975): 1-21; also John Rielly, ed., *American Public Opinion and U.S. Foreign Policy 1975* (Chicago, 1975), p. 16.

4. Bruce M. Russett, "The Calculus of Deterrence," *Journal of Conflict Resolution* 7, no. 2 (June 1963): 97-109; reprinted as Chapter 12 of Bruce M. Russett, *Power and Community in World Politics* (San Francisco, 1974).

5. Bruce M. Russett, *International Regions and the International System* (Chicago, 1967), Chapters 2, 3.

6. In general, data were quite complete, and the need for coding judgments was minimized. Coding of regime types was carried out independently by the two authors, and the only two differences then reconciled on the basis of published analyses of these countries' political systems. Trade data for the Bahamas, and measures of sociocultural distance for the Bahamas, Ethiopia, and Kenya had to be estimated. We have omitted many technical details here. Information on our statistical estimation procedures, and the complete data set, are available from the senior author.

7. American Institute of Public Opinion, April 1973, reported in *Gallup Opinion Index*, June 1973, pp. 14-24; and National Opinion Research Center, March 1974,

reported in *Current Opinion*, September 1974, p. 103.

8. This, incidentally, is nearly 0.10 percent higher than a previous effort that, among other differences, did not include regime type as a predictor. See Charles Doran, "A Theory of Bounded Deterrence," *Journal of Conflict Resolution* 17, no. 2 (June 1973): 243-270.

9. This distinction *may* have become more meaningful by 1975. In his testimony to the Senate Foreign Relations Committee on September 10 (p. 4), Louis Harris reported that by a 67 to 20 percent majority Americans believed "we should not again commit American lives to the defense of corrupt governments abroad." Yet a 51 to 32 percent majority also agreed that "sometimes the U.S. will have to back governments we don't like because a communist takeover would be worse."

10. Louis Harris, "Oil or Israel?" *New York Times Magazine*, April 6, 1975, p. 21ff.; and *Roper Reports*, special report, September 1975, p. 4. Other problems with the 1969 data on Israel compel caution in interpretation.

11. Russett and Hanson, *Interest and Ideology*.

12. This, however, may in part be a result of differences in question wording. As in the 1938-1941 surveys, the option of "help but not troops" was not offered, thus inflating for comparison the percentage approving use of troops.

13. For the data, and this conclusion, see Albert H. Cantril and Charles W. Roll, Jr., *Hopes and Fears of the American People* (New York, 1971), pp. 49, 86-89. Results like this can be observed in other studies: for example, Reilly, *American Public Opinion*, p. 18, who compares a national sample with a special leadership sample on a variety of possible threats to other nations; and *Gallup Opinion Survey*, July 1975.

14. Richard F. Hamilton, "A Research Note on the Mass Support for 'Tough' Military Initiatives," *American Sociological Review* 33, no. 3 (June 1968): 439-445; Andre Modigliani, "Hawks and Doves, Isolationism and Political Distrust: An Analysis of Public Opinion on Military Policy," *American Political Science Review* 66, no. 3 (September 1972): 960-978; John Mueller, *War, Presidents, and Public Opinion* (New York, 1973), Chapter 5.

15. James D. Wright, "Life, Time, and the Fortunes of War," *Transaction* (now *Society*) 9, no. 3 (January 1972): 47-52.

16. Russett, "The Americans' Retreat from World Power."

17. Data are from Mueller, *War, Presidents, and Public Opinion*, pp. 54-55.

18. This inference is supported by the mild reversal that has recently occurred in attitudes toward defense spending. In January 1976 AIPO asked, "Do you think we are spending too much, too little, or about the right amount [for national defense and military purposes]?" Responses were: 36 percent "too much," 22 percent "too little," and 42 percent "about right" and "don't know." Previous AIPO surveys had the percentage saying "too much" in the range 42-46. (Russett, "Americans' Retreat from World Power," p. 3.) Nevertheless note that the advocates of reduced defense spending still outnumber the advocates of increased spending by more than three to two *and* they still outnumber them among south-

erners and among Republicans (by 31 to 28 and 31 to 23 respectively).

19. See Sidney Verba et al., "Public Opinion and the War in Vietnam," *American Political Science Review* 61, no. 2 (June 1967): 317-333; and Mueller, *War, Presidents, and Public Opinion* Chapter 5.

20. See Ralph K. White, *Nobody Wanted War* (Garden City, N.Y., 1970); and Charles Wolfe, "The Present Value of the Past," *Journal of Political Economy* 78, no. 3 (July-August 1970): 783-792. We owe this point to our colleague James Austin.

Part 3

Military Manpower Issues in a Changing Institution

9
Emerging Youth Attitudes and the Military

John D. Blair

The military establishment can no longer depend on direct conscription or on draft-motivated enlistment to assure the accession of sufficient numbers of high-quality recruits. Although the attitudes of American youth toward military service constitute only one component of the accession equation, they are extremely important. Moreover, to assure the cost effectiveness of recruiting efforts, the services need to know not only the aggregate attitudes of youth but also the variations in these attitudes among different "recruiting markets."

In addition, scholars and policymakers concerned with the study of the armed forces and society must attempt not only to delineate the implications of young people's attitudes for recruiting policy. They must also be concerned about broader issues, such as the legitimacy of the military as a social institution and potential problems for civilian control. Indeed, they must examine the recruiting policies themselves—not only in terms of their efficacy but also in terms of their effect on these broader questions of civil-military relations.

Information available through survey research obviously does not translate directly to specific policy decisions. But such information should enhance the planning of recruitment efforts, since it provides insights into the size and nature of available personnel resources, rates of change in the interest and enlistment intentions of young people, and the potential effects of major policy choices, such as changes in GI Bill benefits, affirmative action programs, and new recruiting efforts.

The acquisition of such information, however, requires more than a

The writing of this chapter was supported by a faculty summer grant awarded by the General Research Board of the University of Maryland. Jerald G. Bachman and Lloyd D. Johnston, codirectors of the "Monitoring the Future" study at the Survey Research Center, provided access to their data, and their colleague, Patrick O'Malley, provided valuable assistance in computer operations.

continuation of past research efforts in this field. It requires research on a *large scale* to permit a reliable assessment of levels and rates of change for relatively rare events, for example, the enlistment intentions of young women. It requires *national* research for the findings to be generalizable to the most relevant population. It also requires *longitudinal* research to disentangle developmental changes in the individual from cohort and secular changes in groups and to link these changes to specific individual maturational experiences, such as marriage, employment, or further schooling. Most important, it requires *systematic* and *continuous* research to permit comparisons from one time to another and from one situation to another.

"Monitoring the Future"

A current effort entitled "Monitoring the Future: A Continuing Study of the Life Styles and Values of Youth" is generating data that may provide the necessary information for such analysis. The data are being collected by Lloyd D. Johnston and Jerald G. Bachman at the Survey Research Center of the Institute for Social Research at the University of Michigan. Their annual and longitudinal national surveys of youth include a number of questions dealing with the enlistment intentions of young men and women and their perceptions of the military as a workplace; e.g., job opportunities within the military in comparison to other work settings. Preliminary findings from the first of these surveys are presented below.

Population to Be Studied

The heart of "Monitoring the Future" is a series of annual, national surveys of high school seniors, beginning with the Class of 1975. In addition, annual follow-up surveys track these classes for the first five years following graduation. The samples are large-scale and nationally representative.

The initial survey contact with each cohort occurs in high schools during the senior year. Each year the survey includes approximately 125 to 130 schools to insure a representative sample of high schools throughout the United States. As many as 200 or more seniors are surveyed in each school, yielding a total sample of approximately 16,000 to 17,000. The first data collection for each class (average age eighteen) consists of group-administered questionnaires. Follow-up data collections (average ages nineteen, twenty, twenty-one, twenty-two, and twenty-three) involve mailed questionnaires.

Thus, the population of interest consists of young American men and women, ranging in age from approximately seventeen to twenty-three.

They are monitored through an ongoing series of cohort analyses that permit assessments of, and distinctions among: (1) changes from one high school cohort to another; (2) life cycle or maturational changes that reappear with each new cohort; and (3) period effects reflected across all cohorts without reference to age (secular trends).

Some important practical advantages accrue in building a system of data collection around samples of high school seniors. For example, the last year of high school is the final point at which a reasonably good national sample of an age-specific cohort can be drawn and studied economically. The need for systematically repeated, large-scale samples to insure reliable estimates of changes in attitudes toward military service and enlistment requires considerable emphasis on efficiency and feasibility. The population and methods chosen for "Monitoring the Future" meet these requirements. The author recognizes that this sampling frame under-represents one specific segment of the population—young people who do not graduate from high school. However, defense manpower studies demonstrate that high school graduation is an important indicator of personnel quality.

Data Collection to Date

Samples of high schools were drawn for the first three years of the study. Five separate but interlocking questionnaires were developed for the first study. All forms collected data about enlistment intentions. Data were collected from 16,000 seniors in 128 high schools in the spring of 1975. The findings in this discussion come from these data and usually reflect the responses of slightly more than 3,000 high school seniors who filled out one of five different questionnaires.

A revised sample of schools was selected and contacted for the second cycle of the study. The five base-year questionnaires were shortened by approximately 30 percent after extensive analysis and review, but they continued to collect data on enlistment intentions. Data for the Class of 1976 have been collected from approximately 17,000 seniors in 123 high schools.

Preliminary Findings from 1975 "Monitoring the Future"

Although the findings presented in this discussion shed considerable light on several important issues, they must be considered preliminary for two basic reasons. First, they do not yet reflect the thorough forth-coming analysis, which is based on more powerful statistical techniques. However, they do provide an important description of emerging youth attitudes and the military. Second, as the sample design indicates, "Monitoring the Future" will eventually allow an examination of attitudinal and behavioral changes both in high school seniors as a group and in individual members of each cohort, who will be reexamined at different points after they have acquired new experiences. These additional data collections will permit comparison of actual behaviors with earlier predicted behaviors based upon the high school surveys. They will also provide insights into the effects of different experiences on the attitudes of youth toward the military. These experiences will include military service, college attendance, jobs, and marriage.

The Military as a Social Institution

Recent research on the nature of public opinion toward the military and on the consequences of the Vietnam war for attitudes toward the military has quite consistently shown that *as a social institution*, the military is highly respected. It has shown either equal or less decline in public favor compared with other American social institutions. In addition, most Americans directed wrath over the Vietnam war at the federal government and not at the military. They based antiwar sentiments primarily on pragmatic rather than moralistic reasoning and thus did not perceive that the military was involved in an *immoral* war. They held the government responsible for involvement in an *unwon* war.[1]

However, young college graduates have been particularly skeptical about the military and its role in society. This skepticism appears to reflect neither age nor college education alone; it apparently stems from experiences on college campuses during the period of massive antiwar and antimilitary activities.[2]

Since our sample is high school seniors, we cannot give much importance to variations in age or in levels of education. We suspect that differences may increase as these seniors are exposed to the life experiences mentioned above. Hence, much of our focus on youth attitudes toward the military as a social institution is essentially descriptive; that is, we observe the broad picture rather than attempt to explain variations among young people's attitudes.

In examining attitudes toward the military as a social institution, we also evaluate the military in relation to other social institutions with formal organizational components. For example, the family does not have a formal organizational structure like that of religious, legal, or governmental institutions. In this discussion, we present a comparative analysis of American social institutions based on several criteria of evaluation: their contribution to the country as a whole, their influence on American society, problems of dishonesty and immorality, and major changes and reforms needed.

Figure 1 shows the mean scores for twelve social organizations on a response scale ranging from "very poor" to "very good." The most

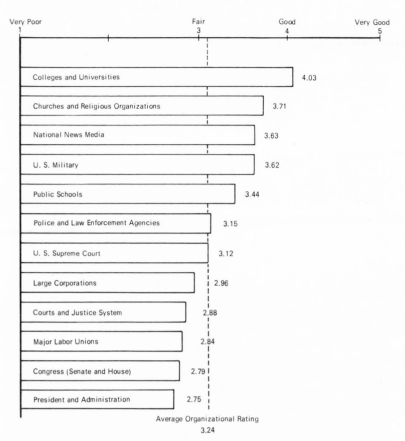

Figure 1. Average Rating of Social Institutions on Their Overall Performance for the Country

favorably evaluated organizations are listed at the top, and the most unfavorably evaluated organizations are listed at the bottom. In addition to the "absolute" placement of each organization in terms of mean score, we also added a vertical, dashed line indicating the average rating of all the organizations.

The military fares quite well in Figure 1, both in the sense that it performs its job closer to "good" than to "fair" and in that it received a rating considerably above average; therefore, it ranks in the top third of the organizations evaluated by the respondents. The military is clearly perceived as a valuable social institution that performs its task well. Since it is an organ of the federal government, its ranking compared with that of Congress and the president and his administration is particularly noteworthy.

In view of the widespread concern with the "military-industrial complex" and the presumed role of the military in furthering militarism

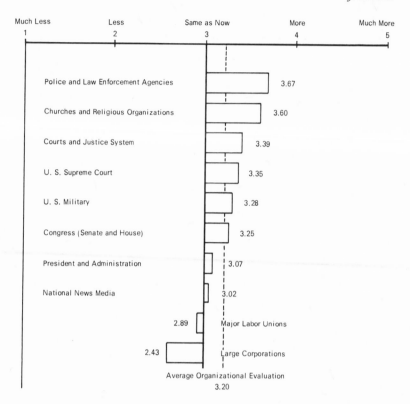

Figure 2. Average Evaluation of How Much Influence an Organization Should Have in American Society

rather than social programs, the findings in Figure 2 concerning the opinions of young people may be surprising. Nevertheless, they are consistent with other research on public opinion regarding the military.[3] In general, people express contentment with the influence of the military and indicate little desire to increase or decrease it. However, in expressing their views of several other institutions, the respondents indicated that they favor expansion or contraction of their organizational influence. If these young people are concerned with a "military-industrial complex," they appear to direct their concern against the industrial portion of the complex.

These data were collected after the Watergate scandal in the executive branch but before the "sex scandals" in Congress. Interestingly, Figure 3 shows that high school seniors evaluated both federal bodies negatively in 1975. Again, the findings indicate that the military has few problems in the area of dishonest or immoral leadership, particularly in comparison with other institutions. The military rating compares favorably with other organizations generally considered to have honest and moral

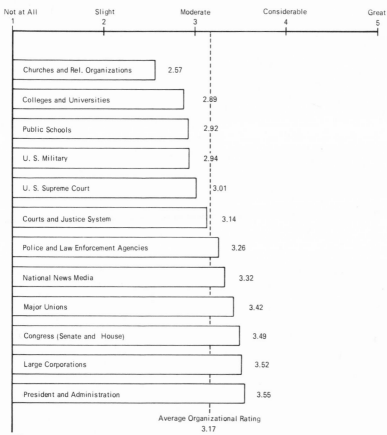

Figure 3. Average Estimation of Problems of Dishonesty and Immorality in Leadership of Organizations

leadership, such as churches, colleges, the public schools, and the Supreme Court.

However, one should perhaps be somewhat concerned that these young people believe that even the most favorably evaluated institutions have "moderate" problems of dishonesty and immorality among their leaders. Unfortunately, we cannot compare these findings with the situation among high school seniors ten years ago to determine whether these views represent a general shift. The findings do provide a baseline for future cohorts. In any case, the military also fares quite well in comparison with other parts of the federal government along this dimension.

The final analysis of the evaluations of American institutions concerns whether young people perceive that these institutions require major changes or reforms. Figure 4 shows that the military is essentially tied with churches and religious organizations for "first place" as the organization needing the least major change or reform. The positive evaluation of the

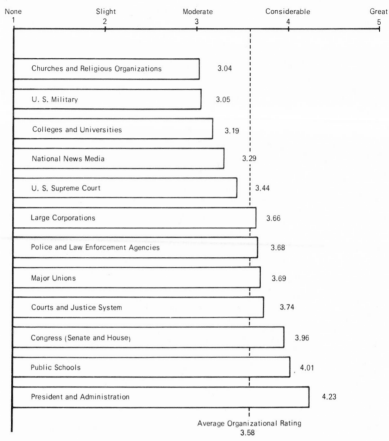

Figure 4. Average Rating of Major Changes or Reforms Needed in Organizations

military contrasts sharply with the evaluation of Congress and the president and his administration. Again, one cannot conclude from the data whether these views of American institutions needing reform or change reflect growing pessimism among young people about the suitability of all institutions in their present form.

These findings are consistent with the general contention that the military as an institution does not suffer from any unique "problem of legitimacy." On another question in the study, 63.8 percent of the respondents indicated that the role of the military services in U.S. society was either "strongly positive" or "mostly positive" during the period since World War II.

An area of general decline in support for the military concerns the proper amount of military spending. The 1975 sample in "Monitoring the Future" continued to show a desire to reduce military spending: 35 percent of the males indicated that military spending is too high; 23.9 percent supported more military spending; and the rest believed that it is generally satisfactory. In the 1969 study, "Youth in Transition" (males only), 42.2 percent indicated too much spending and 18 percent supported more spending.[4] Thus, there may be either a slight increase in support—or a decrease in opposition among youth in 1975 compared with youth six years earlier, but the data still point primarily toward less spending and hence toward a desired restriction of an important resource for the military.

The Military as an Instrument of Foreign Policy

Our past research in this area reveals a general rejection of military force for purposes of intervention, except in a clear case of national defense. This view was expressed by the public as a whole and, to a greater extent, by young people in general and young college graduates in particular. However, there was more support for U.S. military supremacy over other countries, particularly the Soviet Union. Again, this seemed to reflect a concern for national defense rather than for military intervention in other areas of the world.[5]

Table 1 shows the percentages of young people who indicated that they "agree" or "strongly agree"—as opposed to "disagree" or "strongly disagree"—to a series of statements. It includes findings for three groups: males and females from "Monitoring the Future" and males from the (male only) 1969 "Youth in Transition." There is relatively consistent evidence that male high school seniors in 1975 were less supportive of the use of military force and war in general than their counterparts in 1969. For example, they were *less* willing to risk war to stop communism, to concede that the U.S. must go to war at times, and to risk civilian lives in the struggle against communism. They were *more* willing to state that they could not morally participate in any war and kill others and that war, not communism, is the real enemy. They were also less likely to view antiwar protests against military targets as harmful. Nevertheless, they were not inclined to support unilateral disarmament, and they may even be more likely to reject the idea.

Young women in 1975 differ from their male counterparts only in some areas: they are more supportive of disarmament, and they are much more likely to indicate that their moral principles would prevent their participation in war and killing. Other differences are small, inconsistent, and not substantively important.

The overall picture does not indicate that young people have rejected the military as an instrument of national foreign policy. The picture is one of more cautious youth who tend to doubt the overriding importance of the struggle against communism and who view personal moral issues as increasingly relevant in their acceptance of, and participation in, warfare.

TABLE 1

COMPARING YOUTH ATTITUDES TOWARD WAR

Statements in 1969 "Youth in Transition" and 1975 "Monitoring the Future" Studies	Percentage Who Agree or Strongly Agree		
	Males		Females
	1969	1975	1975
The U.S. must be willing to run any risk of war which may be necessary to prevent the spread of Communism	72.5	58.2	62.1
The U.S. should begin a gradual program of disarming, whether other countries do or not	34.5	28.0	38.5
Anti-war protests--such as nonviolent picketing of missile bases or draft boards--are harmful to the best interests of the American people	61.3	42.2	44.0
There may be times when the U.S. must fight a war	91.9	83.0	85.4
The U.S. has a duty to carry on its struggle against Communism, even if it risks the lives of civilians	70.5	51.2	50.7
My moral principles would prevent me from participating in any war and killing other people	26.3	36.0	59.4
The real enemy today is no longer Communism, but rather war itself	57.5	66.2	69.4

This reluctance is evident in a more specific question about participation in "necessary war."

Table 2 shows the distribution of responses to a hypothetical situation concerning whether the sampled youth would volunteer for a war they defined as necessary. The findings in Table 2 are based on responses from the same three groups shown in Table 1. The figures showing the total "probable volunteers" at the bottom of the table were calculated by adding the first three response categories.

Although approximately the same number of American young men in 1975 would volunteer, there is no longer a majority who would volunteer for military service in a war even if *they* defined it as necessary. Increased numbers of young men state that they would "definitely not" volunteer and that there is no such thing as a necessary war.

TABLE 2

YOUTH WILLINGNESS TO FIGHT IN A NECESSARY WAR

Response[a]	Percentage Selecting Each Response		
	Males		Females
	1969	1975	1975
I'm sure that I would volunteer	17.2	17.9	4.2
I would very likely volunteer	12.6	7.4	4.6
I would probably volunteer	32.7	20.6	13.0
I would probably NOT volunteer	19.0	21.3	25.2
I would very likely NOT volunteer	4.5	6.6	11.0
I would definitely NOT volunteer	5.1	14.2	21.8
In my opinion, there is no such thing as a "necessary" war	8.9	12.0	20.3
	100.0	100.0	100.1
Total "probable volunteers"	62.5	45.9	21.8

[a]Question was: "If you felt that it was necessary for the U.S. to fight in some future war, how likely is it that you would volunteer for military service in that war?"

We do not know whether comparable changes have occurred among young women, but, interestingly, the number of young women who reject the idea of a necessary war is approximately the same as the number who could be considered "probable volunteers." On the other hand, one might be surprised that fully one-fifth of the young women indicated a willingness to serve under appropriate conditions. Nevertheless, there is clearly no consensus among young people in 1975 that they should or would serve even in a necessary war. One would expect considerably less enthusiasm for a war considered unnecessary.

This study of young people and their attitudes toward the military would not be complete if one considered only their willingness to serve under wartime conditions. The military is involved only for limited periods in fighting wars, perceived as either necessary or unnecessary, but is a continuing employer of large numbers of men and increasing numbers of women.

The Military as an Organizational Workplace

In the following analyses, the focus shifts from the role of the military in society and in foreign policy to its role as a potential employer of young people. Earlier research shows that the military is perceived as an organization with almost unlimited opportunities, especially by civilians and career military. On the other hand, noncareer military men intending to leave the service are much more negative about available opportunities that their civilian and, particularly, their career-oriented military counterparts.[6]

Figure 5 shows average ratings of the extent to which certain types of opportunities are available within the military; these ratings are ranked according to the types of opportunities perceived as most available and the types perceived as least available. Opportunities for education and promotion are viewed very positively, and opportunities for a fulfilling job and advancement are also viewed as generally available. The least available opportunity is the chance to get one's ideas heard.

Additional questions in the study buttress these findings. For example, young people perceive discrimination against blacks as quite low ($\bar{x} = 2.18$ on the same scale) and against women also as low but not quite nonexistent ($\bar{x} = 2.51$). However, the average rating of "to what extent is it likely that a person in the military can get things changed and set right if he is being treated unjustly by a superior" is even lower ($\bar{x} = 2.48$) than

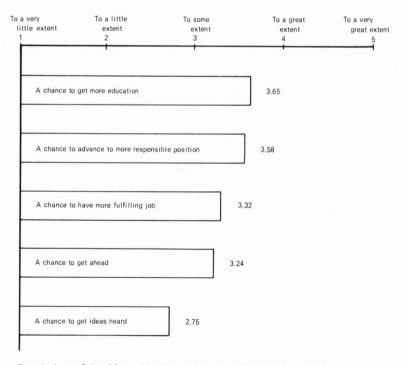

Figure 5. Average Rating of Opportunities Available to People Who Work in the Military Service

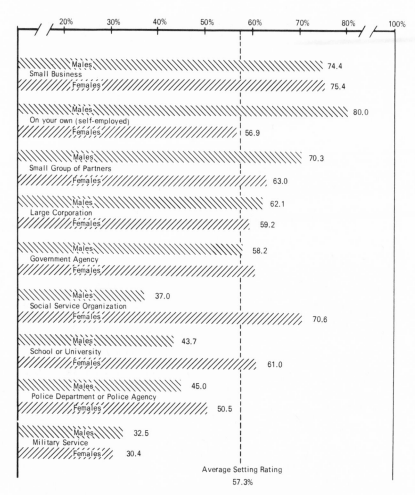

Figure 6. Percent Rating Each Setting As Acceptable or Desirable Place to Work

the chance to get one's ideas heard. Hence, the military is perceived as a workplace with considerable opportunities and little discrimination against particular groups but as an organization with rigidity and arbitrariness.

Although the military rates high in terms of job opportunities, low in racial and sexual discrimination, and lower in individual input and justice, our data, unfortunately, do not include ratings of other potential work settings on these dimensions. However, Figure 6 contains ratings by males and females on the acceptability and desirability of a variety of settings as places to work. In this respect, there are considerable differences between young men and women concerning some work settings.

The most striking aspect displayed in Figure 6 is the extremely low rating of the military as a work setting. All respondents—males and females—perceive the military as the least acceptable or desirable place to work. As indicated above, we do not know whether this low evaluation is based on a comparison of military job opportunities with opportunities in other work settings, but we suspect that the military would rank quite high in terms of most job opportunities. On the other hand, we suspect that the military is perceived as a fine workplace for others—the less fortunate, perhaps—but that its perceived arbitrariness and injustice mean that it has limited appeal as a work setting.

Alternative Post-High School Plans

Since the military is often viewed as a major provider of job training and other educational benefits, we compared it as an alternative to other post-high school training or educational activities in an all-volunteer, peacetime setting. Table 3 presents findings for two interrelated questions. The first two columns show the percentages of young people who indicated that they "probably will" or "definitely will"—as opposed to "probably won't" or "definitely won't"—pursue an alternative post-high school

TABLE 3

YOUTH INTENTIONS VERSUS DESIRES AFTER HIGH SCHOOL

| Possible Future Choice | Percentage Selecting Each Response | | | |
| | Probably/Definitely Will[a] | | Want to Do[b] | |
	Male	Female	Male	Female
Attend a technical or vocational school	27.2	22.1	33.3	28.1
Serve in the armed forces	22.2	8.3	21.6	16.5
Graduate from a two-year college program	28.0	30.8	23.6	30.7
Graduate from college (four-year program)	57.8	47.9	67.1	64.8
Attend graduate or professional school after college	37.5	29.3	52.7	51.2

[a]Response to question: "How likely is it that you will do each of the following things after high school?" (Mark one for each line.)

[b]Response to question: "Suppose you could do just what you'd like and nothing stood in your way. How many of the things above would you WANT to do?" (Mark ALL that apply.)

activity. The first question is stated at the bottom of the table. The second question at the bottom of the table asked the respondents to mark what they would *want* to do after they had indicated the likelihood that they would pursue an activity.

Service in the armed forces appears to be a reasonable alternative for almost one-fourth of the male respondents but for less than one-tenth of the female respondents. Men are almost as likely to consider it as a probable activity as attending a technical or vocational school or graduating from a two-year college program.

However, only one-third as many young women indicated service in the armed forces as a probability when they marked the next most probable activity. In other words, military service is the activity that young people are least likely to engage in after high school when they compared it with civilian educational activities. We do not know how military service would compare with other general *employment* activities, but we do know that it is not favorably evaluated as a workplace.

In addition, service in the armed forces is not a highly desirable activity that young people would *want* to engage in after high school. For men, it is almost as desirable as graduating from a two-year college program, but this comparison probably reflects the respondents' desires to attend four-year, rather than two-year, educational programs, Interestingly, more young women appear interested in military service than are likely to engage in it; similarly, more women also indicate that they would like to attend four-year college programs and, especially, graduate or professional schools, than expect to attend. Military service is still the least desired post-high school activity of those examined.

The racial and socioeconomic composition of the all-volunteer force has been an issue of considerable concern and debate.[7] Rather than review that debate, we present some findings on the reported likelihood of military service for groups of differing backgrounds. Table 4 shows percentages of responses to a question on the likelihood of military service after controlling for both race and sex.[8] The second row from the bottom of the table indicates the percentages of "potential recruits." These figures are simple combinations of the last two categories indicating a probable or definite anticipation of service.

There are major racial differences in addition to the sexual differences already evident in Table 3. Black males are twice as likely as white males to be recruits. Black women are three times as likely as white women to be recruits and actually approximate white males in their expectations to serve.

The bottom row of Table 4 indicates the proportion of young people who would want to serve if they could do whatever they wanted to do and nothing stood in their way. The reality of "economic conscription"[9]

TABLE 4

HIGH SCHOOL CLASSES OF 1976
RACE AND SEX DIFFERENCES IN PERCEIVED LIKELIHOOD OF MILITARY SERVICE

| "How likely is it that you will serve in the armed forces after high school?" | Percentage Selecting Each Response | | | |
| | Males | | Females | |
	White	Black	White	Black
Definitely Won't	40	30	75	59
Probably Won't	41	27	20	23
Probably Will	13	25	4	11
Definitely Will	6	18	1	7
	100	100	100	100
Percentage of "potential recruits"	19	43	5	18
Percent want to do military service if nothing stood in the way	19	31	10	21

for black men is reflected in the considerably smaller number indicating that military service is what they would want to do compared with the proportion expecting to serve. On the other hand, there is some tendency among women to show more desire to serve than expectation that they actually will serve. This may reflect a somewhat untapped market

TABLE 5

PERCENT OF YOUTH WHO PROBABLY WILL OR DEFINITELY WILL SERVE IN
ARMED FORCES COMPARED TO FATHER'S SCHOOLING

| Father's Schooling | Percentage | |
	Male	Female
Completed grade school or less	28.4	13.0
Some high school	30.4	8.8
Completed high school	32.4	10.5
Some college	17.3	3.9
Completed college	11.6	3.5
Graduate or professional school after college	9.0	5.2

currently restricted both by policy and by social attitudes about appropriate roles for women.[10]

These findings reflect very strong variations between young blacks and young whites in the likelihood that they will serve in the military, regardless of the sex of the respondents. This could well be purely a reflection of differences in socioeconomic background between whites and blacks, but as Table 5 shows, no socioeconomic background group (defined by the schooling of the respondent's father) reaches a 43 percent level of expectation of military service, and this includes the respondents from the lower-status social backgrounds.

One should not miss the additional point that there *are* clear socioeconomic background differences in the likelihood of military service. There seems to be a clear demarcation between respondents, male or female, whose fathers have a high school education or less and respondents whose fathers have at least attended college. The latter are much less likely to be "potential recruits." These findings, of course, are very relevant to the ongoing discussion concerning the long-term racial and socioeconomic background of the all-volunteer military.

Another issue of concern is the question of how many young people plan to enter military service soon after high school and how many plan to be in service some years later, either because they expect to make a career of the military after high school or because they plan to enter military service after they acquire further civilian education or work experience. We generated some interesting data by asking the respondents to indicate the kinds of jobs they expect to have when they reach thirty years of age.

Table 6 shows the percentages of young people who indicated they they expect to be in military service—despite a long list of other jobs that

TABLE 6

YOUTH INTENTIONS TO BE IN THE MILITARY AT 30 YEARS OF AGE

Likelihood of Military Service After High School	Percentage	
	Male	Female
Definitely Won't	0.0	0.1
Probably Won't	0.0	0.0
Probably Will	3.7	1.6
Definitely Will	57.2	32.6
Total Indicating Military Service at Age 30	6.6	1.0

they could have chosen. Overall, 6.6 percent of the men and 1 percent of the women indicated that they expect to be in military service at the age of thirty. On the other hand, approximately three-fifths of the males and approximately one-third of the females who "definitely" expect to enter military service after high school also expect to be in the military approximately twelve years later. This indicates that a very high proportion of the young men and a sizable proportion of the young women have career plans and that their plans are consistent with their strong statement of likelihood of military service.

On the other hand, only very small proportions of the other category of "potential recruits" indicate similar career interests. Obviously, this latter group has quite different military career plans, perhaps qualitatively different as to the likelihood of enlisting in the first place; i.e., they are much more likely to remain "potential" recruits only. In addition, Table 6 provides little indication that anyone considers the idea of military service as a deferred option for postcollege (or other training/experience) employment, at least of a career nature.

The literature on the all-volunteer force and recruiting policy has often focused on educational incentives as an important means of meeting recruitment goals of quantity, quality, and broadening the military's racial and socioeconomic base. The argument is that such incentives will provide larger numbers of "in-and-outers" from groups not now expected to enlist and, thus, will make the military more socially representative.[11]

Table 7 shows the percentages of respondents who indicated a probable or definite desire to enter a program that would allow them to exchange

TABLE 7

YOUTH INDICATING DESIRE FOR GOVERNMENT PAID COLLEGE IN
EXCHANGE FOR THREE OR FOUR YEARS' SERVICE

Likelihood of Military Service After High School	College Then Service Male	College Then Service Female	Service Then College Male	Service Then College Female
Definitely Won't	12.9	11.6	10.5	8.6
Probably Won't	24.2	32.9	23.9	26.4
Probably Will	47.2	64.2	42.7	65.6
Definitely Will	55.1	65.2	65.3	50.9
Total Indicating "Probable Desire" to Enter Such a Program	25.6	21.1	24.9	17.1

several years of military service for a college education financed by the government. Two hypothetical programs were presented to the respondents: one called for government-paid education followed by three or four years of military service; the other called for three or four years of military service followed by government-paid education. We have presented the percentages desiring each program, controlling for the sex of the respondents and the likelihood of their military service.

Table 7 shows that large numbers of male and female respondents indicate a desire to participate in such programs and that respondents who indicate a likelihood of serving are the groups most interested in the programs. However, the categories (the "definitely won't" and "probably won't") that were not considered "potential recruits" also include sizable numbers interested in such programs. Approximately one-fourth of the respondents who earlier stated that they "probably won't" serve expressed interest in the proposed arrangement, although none of the respondents in this group had planned to be in the military at the age of thirty. Moreover, as indicated in the top row of the table, significant groups of respondents indicating that they "definitely won't" serve showed interest in such programs. These general findings apply for both males and females. Among those most likely to serve in the miltary, women are more likely to prefer service after college and men more likely to prefer service before college.

Perhaps the most striking conclusion is that the idea of a paid college education in exchange for military service attracts large numbers of young people, including those who are least interested in military service or a military career. This finding should be relevant to policymakers considering the merits of the GI Bill or possible replacements.

Summary of Findings

In general, young people in 1975 reported positive evaluations of the military as a social institution. They perceive that it does a good job for the country, exercises appropriate influence, has minimal dishonesty and immorality in its leadership, and needs only moderate change or reform. They feel that the military has played a predominately positive role in American society since World War II, although they express some concern that it costs too much. Among young people, the U.S. military seems to be one of the most positively evaluated and highly regarded American social institutions.

Young men in 1975 compared with young men in 1969 are generally less supportive of war, the fight against communism, and the risk of civilian lives in future wars. Young women in 1975 are either equally or less supportive of the use of the military as an instrument of foreign policy than young men. The majority of both groups indicate that they would probably not participate voluntarily even in a war defined as necessary. Nevertheless, young people have not generally rejected war and sacrifice, but they appear more cautious in supporting the use of military force and more selective in the price that they are willing to pay.

They perceive that the military offers considerable job opportunities, especially in terms of further education and promotion with little racial or sexual discrimination. But they also believe that the military is arbitrary, unresponsive to individual ideas, and somewhat unjust in the treatment of its employees. Perhaps because of these latter considerations, the military is rated last in a group of potential organizational work settings. It is also generally viewed as the least favored of several alternatives (all educational) to be pursued after high school, especially by women.

The likelihood of serving in the military service is highly linked to the racial and socioeconomic backgrounds of the respondents. Blacks anticipate military service in proportions considerably greater than one would expect on the basis of their socioeconomic status alone. In fact, black women are as likely to expect to go into the military in the same proportions as white men. Large proportions of young people indicating the likelihood of enlisting also plan to be in the military at the age of thirty, especially the young men. There is no indication that high school seniors anticipate military service after college or other training or experience. Educational incentives in the form of government-paid college education in exchange for military service of several years are attractive to large numbers of young people—male and female. This includes sizable numbers of people who otherwise indicate no interest in military service.

Discussion and Analysis

Current evaluations of the future all-volunteer force emphasize dismal recruiting prospects because of three basic factors: changes in the demographic structure, with fewer young people annually entering the recruiting pool after 1979; improvements in the economy, with more competition from civilian jobs; and little prospect of substantial changes in future military pay that would permit faster growth in military compensation in relation to civilian pay. Demographic changes pose particular problems, as indicated by William King in a report prepared for Senator Nunn's Armed Forces Subcommittee on Manpower and Personnel: "by the late 1980's, the military 'total force' will be faced with the problem of recruiting one of every two qualified and available males in the population."[12] The qualified and available pool is "defined as those who are not institutionalized, unqualified, or enrolled in college, but including college dropouts."[13]

The exclusion of college students from the expected pool of candidates may be reasonable based on current experience in recruiting for the all-volunteer force, but it may become a "self-fulfilling prophecy" if advertising, recruiting efforts, and incentive programs ignore this potential segment of the personnel research pool. In addition, current high rates of attrition among first-term volunteers may make the more capable college-bound student with more to lose in terms of future educational benefits an attractive candidate for recruitment and a complete term of service. Given Department of Defense restrictions on the size of the "career force" (beyond four years of service) to 40 percent of the total,[14] a larger proportion of higher-quality "in-and-outers" may be advantageous if they are more likely to complete their term of service and thereby reduce recruiting and training costs.

Policy implications consistent with the research presented in this discussion include the following:

1. The "able and available" pool of candidates could be expanded through educational incentives to include more college-bound and current college students. Expansion would be facilitated by a return to more comprehensive educational benefits or, ideally, by extension of formerly available benefits. As a minimum, such an expansion would require that more of the $100 million annual expenditure on recruit advertising focus on explaining and emphasizing the current contributory educational benefits.

2. The pool of candidates could also include more women, since their basic attitudes toward the military and military job opportunities differ little from men's attitudes, although women are not as likely to expect to serve. Educational incentives appear to have considerable importance for both women and men. However, policymakers should be cautioned not to overestimate the implications of our data or the current waiting lines of women. Waiting lines are more likely when less than 6 percent of the force is drawn from one-half of the potential pool of young people than when more than 94 percent are drawn from the other one-half. In addition, recent follow-up analyses of the Class of 1975 show that after one year out of school, much larger proportions of women who had indicated a high likelihood of military service have changed their minds in comparison with men.[15] Although there may be some additional recruiting potential among women, our data do not indicate massive interest in military service on the part of young American women. Changes in opportunities may generate more interest, but large proportions of American women are not likely to pursue a military career. There will, however, be a stronger interest among black women and black men.

3. These data support the idea that the military will continue to become more racially unrepresentative. Some scholars argue that the growing proportion of blacks will eventually reach a "tipping point," when whites will no longer desire to be part of a given unit or service.[16] Of course, this is an empirical question that may eventually be tested in combat units.

4. On the one hand, the military has no problem of legitimacy among young people in terms of their evaluations of it as a social institution. The same is true to a lesser extent in terms of its use as an instrument of foreign policy, although young people are increasingly cautious of the morality and costs of such use. On the other hand, the military may have a problem of legitimacy among young people in terms of their willingness to commit themselves to service even during a "necessary war." In addition, the probable recruiting base under all-volunteer conditions may have serious consequences for the social representativeness of the military and, hence, for legitimacy as a "citizen force."

Notes

1. Willard L. Rodgers and Lloyd D. Johnston, "Attitudes Toward Business and Other American Institutions" (Paper presented at the annual conference of the American Association for Public Opinion Research, May 31, 1974). See also John D. Blair and Jerald G. Bachman, "The Public View of the Military," in *The Social Psychology of Military Service*, ed. Nancy Goldman and David R. Segal (Beverly Hills, Calif.: Sage, 1976); and David R. Segal and John D. Blair, "Public Confidence in the U.S. Military," *Armed Forces and Society* 3, no. 1 (1976):3-11. Howard Schuman has distinguished between pragmatic and moralistic opposition to the Vietnam war in "Two Sources of Anti-War Sentiment in America," *American Journal of Sociology* 78 (1972): 513-537.

2. Blair and Bachman, "The Public View of the Military"; Schuman, "Two Sources."

3. Rodgers and Johnston, "Attitudes Toward Business"; Blair and Bachman, "The Public View of the Military."

4. These findings and those presented below are taken from the third wave (while they were high school seniors) of a five-way study of high school males and were reported in Jerome Johnston and Jerald G. Bachman, *Young Men Look at Military Service: A Preliminary Report* (Ann Arbor, Mich.: Institute for Social Research, 1971). For a more complete discussion of their findings and the "Youth in Transition" study, see idem, *Youth in Transition*, vol. 5, *Young Men and Military Service* (Ann Arbor, Mich.: Institute for Social Research, 1972).

5. Blair and Bachman, "The Public View of the Military."

6. See Jerald G. Bachman, John D. Blair, and David R. Segal, *The All-Volunteer Force: A Study of Ideology in the Military* (Ann Arbor, Mich.: University of Michigan Press, 1977).

7. See Morris Janowitz and Charles C. Moskos, Jr., "Racial Composition in the All-Volunteer Force: Policy Alternatives," *Armed Forces and Society* 1, no. 1 (1974): 109-123; Alvin J. Schexneider and John S. Butler, "Race and the All-Volunteer System: A Reply to Janowitz and Moskos," *Armed Forces and Society* 2, no. 3 (1976): 421-432; and Morris Janowitz and Charles C. Moskos, Jr., "Comment," *Armed Forces and Society* 2, no. 3 (1976):433-434.

8. Examination of 1976 data to date shows no substantive differences from

the 1975 findings reported here. However, since the sample of blacks is somewhat better in 1976 than in 1975, we present 1976 findings in Table 4.

9. This term has been used by David Cortright, "Economic Conscription," *Society* 12 (May-June 1975): 43-47.

10. For a comparative and longitudinal perspective on women in the military, see Nancy Goldman, "The Utilization of Women in the Armed Forces of Industrialized Nations," *Sociological Symposium* 18 (Spring 1977): 1-23.

11. The importance of educational incentives has been discussed in Johnston and Bachman, Janowitz and Moskos, and Bachman, Blair, and Segal.

12. William R. King, *Achieving America's Goals: National Service or the All-Volunteer Armed Force?* (Washington, D.C.: Government Printing Office, 1977), p. 22.

13. Ibid.

14. Ibid., p. 38.

15. David R. Segal and Jerald G. Bachman, "Post High-School Drop-Outs (and Stayers)" (Paper prepared for the OSD/ONR Conference on First-Term Attrition, Leesburg, Virginia, April 4-7, 1977).

16. Janowitz and Moskos, "Racial Composition."

10

The Military and Higher Education: An Analysis of Factors Affecting the Future of ROTC

Larry W. Reed
L. Anthony Loman

The research reported in this chapter concerns ongoing sociological studies of civilian-military relations. Within this general area, the linkages between the military and civilian society are particularly interesting. Historically, one such linkage has been the concept of the "citizen-soldier." Since the inception of the United States, this idea has been attractive to political leaders and the public in general.[1] Most people viewed a military that included both nonprofessionals and career officers as a means of safeguarding the nation from military dominance of the polity and as a deterrent to politico-military adventurism. As Probert has noted, the framers of the Constitution were well aware of the advantages that could be offered by a "well regulated militia."[2] Although Reserve Officer Training Corps (ROTC) programs did not begin until the mid-nineteenth century, such a source of military officers is well within the general tradition of the "citizen-soldier." Today, however, the future of ROTC as a viable means of staffing the officer corps for the military is open to question.

Significant changes have occurred within ROTC during the past decade, and strong opposition has surfaced in diverse quarters. The difficulties experienced by the program and the subsequent withdrawal of ROTC from many of the country's leading universities and colleges are well known and need not be further recounted.[3] The present research concerns future directions that may be taken by ROTC.

Several investigators have noted existing trends in ROTC enrollments and have made extrapolations as to the future of ROTC. Morris Janowitz has argued that ROTC units will tend to locate primarily in the South and West and that emphasis will be placed on smaller numbers of successful units rather than on the current pattern of large numbers of units scattered across the country, many of which are marginal in terms of officer production. He also indicated that these units would be located at schools in rural areas and at schools with modest academic standards.[4] Janowitz noted that the South has a history of strong military traditions and that many military institutions are located in this general region. As a result, the military has become accepted as an integral part of the local culture.[5]

Yarmolinsky has noted ROTC's continuing appeal to smaller, rural-based universities, which he viewed as representative of the conservative "heartland" of the country.[6] Hauser has characterized the ROTC program as most popular at small schools in rural sections that have traditionally been primary sources of career officers.[7] Karsten has described the shift of ROTC from the Ivy League schools to state colleges and universities in other parts of the country.[8] In his terms, schools located in the "localistic, agrarian South and West" will be the most enthusiastic about ROTC in contrast to leading schools in the Northeast.

An important variable affecting the accuracy of the above statements will be the extent of hostility encountered from the academic community. During the past decade, university students and faculty members have been two principal sources of opposition to ROTC. The willingness of university faculties to oppose ROTC through various means has been widely recognized. Some sources have asserted that faculty members undermine the honor of military service and foster dissent among the student body.[9] Others have argued that opposition to the Vietnam conflict was only a pretense for faculties to manifest their long-standing, latent hostility toward the military.[10]

Tension between faculty members and ROTC staffs is understandable. As Scott has stated, both groups are separated by vast differences in values, structures, styles, and functions.[11] ROTC has been attacked on the grounds that military officers are not qualified to serve on university faculties and that the ROTC curriculum has little or no intellectual content. Others have argued that the constraints imposed by the regimen of military organizations are basically antithetical to free academic inquiry and dissent.[12]

At the same time, other authors recognize that ROTC cannot exist without the cooperation of university facilities and administrators. In 1959, Lyons and Masland, in the first major study of ROTC, pointed out that any program such as ROTC depends on the active support of faculty and administrators.[13] When students enter college, they are often unsure of themselves and of what activities to pursue and organizations to join. If faculty members overtly and implicitly suggest the illegitimacy and lack of worth of a military career, they quickly erode the basis of the ROTC program. Without the support of the institution, including faculty members and administrators, the program can subsist only on the fringe of the academic community without any real voice in the affairs of the institution.[14]

The reactions of the faculties at many of the top schools in the Northeast have been unequivocal during the past decade. They have strongly rejected the ROTC program. The question that remains, however, is the response of faculties at smaller, nonprestigious schools. Karsten has suggested that what happens in Boston and Berkeley generally happens in Mobile and Edwardsville.[15] But this greatly oversimplifies the question. After all, Boston is not Mobile, and this difference bears examination. For example, military traditions have long been closely associated with the South. Thus, to the extent that a school and its personnel reflect prevailing cultural ideologies, one could reasonably assume that this region would have a different pattern of responses to ROTC.

Little contemporary empirical work has addressed the degree to which the faculties of colleges and universities in the United States reflect regional differences. Several studies have examined the extent and location of faculty support for the war in Vietnam. The findings coincide with the hypotheses of writers mentioned earlier that the faculties and students of smaller unranked schools demonstrated the strongest support for the war and that the strongest opposition came from faculties and students in prestigious, highly visible institutions.[16] The extent and type of support and opposition to the military as a whole on U.S. college campuses is itself an empirical question worthy of investigation. As stated above, a general assumption often found in the literature on ROTC is that as a whole, college faculties oppose the military. In a study of several small community colleges in the Midwest, the authors have called this assumption into question, since they found that total opposition to the military in the form of ROTC was practically nonexistent.[17] Thus, a second issue of importance is the degree to which promilitary and antimilitary sentiments among faculty members may be used to predict their attitudes toward ROTC.

Although one might expect a positive relationship between promilitary attitudes and pro-ROTC attitudes, such a relationship will not necessarily be simple. The stress on the *balancing* effect of ROTC as a source of officers, for example, could lead to pro-ROTC reactions from faculty members who were at least partially antimilitary in their orientations. This perspective concerning ROTC has been the subject of research. Several studies have indicated that ROTC training does not inculcate militaristic values among students in the program[18] and that ROTC students consistently manifest less militaristic attitudes than cadets from the various military academies.[19] Furthermore, ROTC officers tend to remain oriented basically toward civilian norms and values even while on active duty and thus to produce what is perhaps a desirable counterbalance to the more absolute value structures of academy officers.[20] These findings have indicated a widespread belief among college faculties that ROTC provides such a balance of civilian, democratic values as opposed to professional military values. Therefore, two sources of support for ROTC have been suggested:

support that stems from promilitary attitudes and support based on the belief that ROTC is a safeguard of democratic values.

The authors collected the data reported in this study to ascertain the general responses of college and university faculties toward the ROTC program as it is presently constituted. Examination of the current literature identified three factors that were consistently mentioned as significantly related to future acceptance of the program: the region of the country in which the host school is located, the academic characteristics of the school, and the type of setting (i.e., rural-urban) in which the school operates. The present research was designed to test empirically the extent to which these factors, treated as independent variables, were related to the future of ROTC. However, in addition to a consideration of these structural variables, the authors developed a second line of analysis. This analysis examined the general attitudes held by faculties toward the military in today's society. We hypothesized that these attitudes would underlie any variation in the responses produced by the above structural variables.

Analysis of the region of the country and type of school is still another issue. Smaller state colleges oriented basically toward teaching will, as organizations, tend to be more closely bound to the local community. Consequently, they will be more likely to share the community's ideologies than will the larger, more prestigious institutions. Similarly, individuals comprising the faculty and administration will usually be more personally and economically committed to the surrounding communities than their counterparts at more prestigious schools. Therefore, these schools may be defined as more *local* in character, and the prestigious institutions as more *cosmopolitan.*[21] Since locally oriented organizations tend to share local ideologies, one might expect that small colleges in the Northeast will reflect, to a great extent, the weaker support for the military that is characteristic of this region.

The Sample

A purposive sample of college faculty was obtained in two stages during the spring semester in 1976. The theoretical criteria used in the selection of the schools were region, rural-urban setting, and type of school. Twenty colleges or universities were selected in the south-southwest and northeast regions of the United States. The number of schools was limited to twenty since the goal was approximately 1,000 faculty responses, or an average of 50 per school. Ten institutions were chosen in the South and Southwest and ten in the Northeast. Within each of these groups, the primary effort was to obtain four small, state-supported colleges devoted mainly to undergraduate instruction, four state-supported universities with a research orientation, and two colleges or universities that clearly ranked higher than the other eight in terms of academic prestige.[22] With one exception (Brown University), the prestigious schools were also state-supported institutions. Student enrollments in the schools in the first category were generally less than 13,000, but enrollments in the other school were generally much larger.

In addition to criteria related to region and type of school, the authors attempted to choose schools from both rural and urban settings. In this regard, a second threefold classification was appropriate. It was not possible to select any schools from a purely rural locale according to current census definitions. Areas identified as "rural" were actually small towns with populations of considerably less than 50,000 people. Schools in these settings comprised the first category. An intermediate category identified as "semiurban" was established to handle schools located in small towns but within or very near standard metropolitan statistical areas. The third category included institutions located directly within urban areas.[23]

The second stage of sampling involved the selection of a probability sample from the faculties of each school. A simple random sample was drawn from faculty lists for the 1974-1975 academic years. This may represent a source of some bias, since the sample did not include faculty members who had moved or retired or new faculty members for the 1974-1975 school year. The sampling was disproportionate in that 100 names were chosen at each school, regardless of the size of the school. Two thousand questionnaires were mailed initially, with two follow-up mailings at approximately three-week intervals. The final return rate exceeded 50 percent, although analysis began when 951 usable questionnaires had been returned. A comparison of selected variables was made across the returns from each mailing. No significant differences were found; thus, nonresponse bias appears minimal.

Characteristics of the Sample

The questionnaire included a number of questions that solicited information on the personal and organizational attributes of the faculties. As indicated in Table 1, most of the respondents were male, a situation that is also a general characteristic in the academic world.[24] The age distribution of the sample is also similar to the distributions reported in other studies of college faculties.[25]

The academic and professional disciplines normally found in the college and university setting were also represented in the sample (see Table 2). The various academic ranks are also distributed throughout the sample. There tended to be fewer instructors in the sample, but this was viewed as a consequence of the distribution of ranks in the schools themselves

TABLE 1

FACULTY CHARACTERISTICS

Sex	Percent
Male	83
Female	17
N =	950

Age	Percent
20 – 30	07
31 – 35	22
36 – 40	18
41 – 45	14
46 – 50	13
51 – 55	12
56 – 60	09
60+	$\frac{05}{100}$
N =	950

TABLE 2

ACADEMIC BACKGROUNDS

Discipline	Percent
Social Sciences	22
Humanities	11
Law	1
Fine Arts	3
Physical Sciences	16
Life Sciences	14
Engineering	5
Education	13
Business	4
Agriculture	5
Military Science	1
Other	5
	100

Academic Rank	Percent
Instructor	6
Assistant Professor	29
Associate Professor	31
Professor	33
Other	1
	100

rather than as a result of sampling biases.

Almost one-half of the sample (47 percent) had prior military experience, and of this group, 20 percent had served as officers. Twenty-five percent of the sample had been enlisted personnel. Only nine subjects out of the total sample had first served in an enlisted status and later become officers. Very few of the subjects (fifteen) were currently members of an active reserve unit. Thirty-six of the respondents indicated that they were currently members of a veterans' organization, such as the American Legion or the Veterans of Foreign Wars.

Since there was also an interest in determining the extent of the closeness of the respondents' ties to their local communities, questions were asked concerning patterns of residence. Before their present employment, most of the respondents (78 percent) had not lived near their present locations. Of the respondents who had lived near their present locations, 44 percent had resided there for less than ten years, and 56 percent had been long-term (ten years or longer) residents.

Analysis of the Sources of Support for ROTC

A six-item summated scale shown in Table 3 measured attitudes toward ROTC.[26] The items summarize several standard arguments for and against the presence of ROTC on campus. Table 3 also shows the proportions of respondents who agreed and disagreed with items, as a rough estimate of the reaction of the total faculty sample to each item. The proportions of anti-ROTC sentiments can be discerned by examining the Percent Disagree column on items 1 and 2 and the Percent Agree column on items 3 to 6. The absence of large proportions of the faculty sample in these cells appears to contradict the notion in much of the literature that faculties as a whole harbor a great deal of latent hostility toward the military and ROTC. Evidently, as indicated in item 4, many faculties feel that many military science courses should not receive academic credit. This response is important in relation to the future of ROTC. As Muhlenfeld has indicated, if credit were removed from military science courses, then ROTC would likely be pushed further toward the fringe of universities and become an even less legitimate program from an academic standpoint.[27]

Table 4 shows the mean scale score for each school. The first ten schools in the table are in the South and Southwest. The predicted regional differences are apparent. Furthermore, the more prestigious schools are generally more anti-ROTC regardless of the region. Negative scale scores indicate anti-ROTC sentiments and positive scores, pro-ROTC sentiments (total mean scale score = 0.001). For purposes of illustration, the range shown in Table 4 (−0.7 to +0.7) is reduced from its original value (range = 4.3, maximum = 1.7, minimum = −2.5).

TABLE 3

ITEMS COMPOSING SCALE OF ATTITUDES TOWARD ROTC

Item	Factor Score	Percent Agree	Don't Know	Percent Disagree
1. ROTC (Reserve Officers Training Corps) provides a desirable point of contact between military teaching staffs and civilian faculties.	-.16	60.2	19.7	20.1
2. The kind of training provided by ROTC (i.e., in terms of discipline and leadership) is needed by college students today.	-.21	43.8	18.2	38.0
3. The military personnel assigned to ROTC units are not academically qualified to teach at the college level.	.17	19.6	43.1	37.3
4. Many military science courses (e.g., map reading, military drill, etc.), because of their content, should not receive academic credit.	.17	43.4	18.5	38.1
5. The techniques of violence taught in military science courses are basically contrary to the traditional philosophy of higher education.	.14	26.8	22.9	50.3
6. ROTC is undesirable because it represents the intrusion of militarism onto the college campus.	.34	15.9	11.9	72.1

A large body of literature concerns attempts to construct attitude scales for the measurement of militarism, pacifism, and "war-mindedness."[28] Although these scales were examined, none seemed appropriate for use with university faculties. Therefore, a set of items designed to tap several sources of promilitary and antimilitary sentiments was created for this study. Respondents were asked to evaluate the positive or negative nature of each item. These items were grouped on the basis of five clusters that appeared through intercorrelational analysis. Table 5 shows these groupings. Each cluster suggested a separate dimension, although, as units, they were themselves somewhat intercorrelated.[29]

In the following analysis, each cluster has been treated as an index allowing a simple dichotomy or trichotomy of the sample in each case. Index I was a set of antimilitary items that dealt with some of the negative economic and social consequences of the military. Indexes II to V were various clusters of promilitary items. As can be seen from the percentage agreeing with the item in Index II, the function of defense from attack by foreign powers brought the strongest positive support (89.2 percent). The question of protecting the foreign economic and diplomatic interests

188

TABLE 4

MEAN ROTC SCALE SCORES FOR SCHOOLS IN SAMPLE

School	Mean	Anti-ROTC –.7 —— 0 —— .7 Pro-ROTC
SOUTH-SOUTHWEST		
1. Appalachian State University	.34	————X
2. Middle Tennessee State University	.31	————X
3. Auburn University	.07	–X
4. Texas A&M University	.33	————X
5. University of South Alabama	.23	———X
6. Tennessee State University	.61	——————————X
7. University of South Carolina	.04	X
8. University of Arizona	–.20	X————
9. University of North Carolina at Chapel Hill	–.02	X
10. University of Texas	–.44	X————————
NORTHEAST		
11. University of New Hampshire	–.29	X————
12. University of Maine – Orano	.16	———X
13. University of Vermont	.01	X
14. University of Rhode Island	.04	X
15. Central Connecticut State College	–.22	X————
16. Millersville State College	–.09	X–
17. SUNY Albany	–.32	X————
18. University of Delaware	–.23	X————
19. Rutgers University	–.67	X————————————
20. Brown University	–.45	X————————

of the United States (Index III) and the positive internal social consequences (Index V) brought less agreement. However, Index IV contains the items most commonly associated with militarism—i.e., anticommunism, linking of the military with patriotism, and consideration of the military as a model for the civic virtues.[30] Each of these indexes was treated as a separate variable affecting the attitudes of the faculties toward ROTC.

The primary goal of this research was simultaneously to analyze the effects of the variables of region, rural-urban setting, and type of school on faculty attitudes toward ROTC. The analysis of these three variables indicated that each, separately, was an important element in the explanation of these attitudes and that, in combination, their effects were additive. This means that faculties at southern schools were more supportive of ROTC than faculties at northeastern schools, that more support existed at less prestigious than at more prestigious institutions, and that more support existed among the faculties of rural than urban institutions. The additive nature of these variables shows, for example, that the greatest support was found at rural, less prestigious institutions in the South-Southwest or that prestigious institutions in the South were generally less supportive than rural, less prestigious institutions in the Northeast, etc.[31]

An exception to the additive effects was the significant interaction of region and type of school. An inspection of means revealed that faculties from the nonprestige schools in the Northeast produced the interaction; that is, there was less support for ROTC at these schools than would have been predicted. As indicated earlier, faculties from these types of schools are likely to be more local in orientation and thus to share in the less positive attitudes toward the military that are characteristic of that region.

A second phase of the analysis was an examination of the three structural variables in the light of the indexes that measured attitudes toward the military (Table 5). Hypothetically, the sets of attitudes toward the military generally were underlying variables explaining sympathy for ROTC in region, locale, and type of school. Analysis indicated this to be true of antimilitary attitudes, attitudes toward national defense, and militarism (Indexes I, IV, and II in Table 5). These attitudinal variables account for the variation in sentiment toward ROTC within the structural variables.[32] The general negative attitudes toward the military explain the negative response to ROTC, but interest in national defense and the more extreme militaristic items account for the positive responses to ROTC. However, one would be incorrect in supposing that this reflects a simple promilitary and antimilitary dichotomy among the faculties

TABLE 5

INDEXES OF ATTITUDES TOWARD THE MILITARY

Index	Items*	Percentage Agreeing with Item	Percentage Disagreeing With All Items in Index
I.	Antimilitary		43.4
	1. Promotes a disregard for the value of human life	23.0	
	2. Leads to a loss of individuality	22.0	
	3. By its very existence increases the probability of war	18.1	
	4. Diverts economic resources from needed civil areas		
	5. Promotes military values such as conformity and authoritarianism which are antithetical to the basic processes of democracy	27.9	
	6. Makes a military coup a real possibility	8.4	
II.	National Defense		10.8
	1. Defends the U.S. against possible foreign military attack	89.2	
III.	Protection of U.S. Foreign Interests		37.0
	1. Protects the diplomatic interests of the U.S.	57.9	
	2. Protects the national economic interests of the U.S. outside its borders	37.2	
	3. Protects the interests of private U.S. based corporation in other countries	18.4	
IV.	Militarism		66.9
	1. Insures democratic government in other countries	5.4	
	2. Provides a concrete example of patriotism for U.S. citizens	15.7	
	3. Protects the free world from further communist inroads	19.5	
	4. Stimulates the virtues of courage, self-sacrifice and discipline in the U.S.	15.9	
V.	Social Consequences		53.0
	1. Serves as an avenue of social mobility	32.2	
	2. Helps stimulate national and local economies	33.0	
	N =	951	

*Respondents were asked to respond to the above items as either negative consequences (Index I) or positive consequences (Indexes II-IV) of the presence of the military in society.

surveyed. As stated earlier, the indexes were intercorrelated. For example, many individuals scored on both national defense and the antimilitary index. About 5.5 percent of the faculties could be scored as purely antimilitary in orientation, and 45.4 percent as promilitary in orientation. The remaining 49.1 percent were ambivalent, expressing both positive and negative attitudes.

An interesting aspect of the present study lies in examining attitudes toward ROTC in terms of the social and academic characteristics of the respondents. Past military experience played an important part in responses toward ROTC (see Table 6). Individuals who had once been part of the military gave significantly more favorable responses to ROTC, and officers were even more strongly supportive. The highest mean scores were obtained for individuals who currently were members of veterans' organizations.

No clear patterns of association existed between academic ranks, although full professors did manifest the strongest support for the program from the four groups considered. Similarly, the correlation between the ages of the faculty members and a favorable response to ROTC was low

TABLE 6

MEAN RESPONSE TO THE ROTC SCALE
BY MILITARY EXPERIENCE

Military Experience	Mean*
Yes (n=435)	.202
No (n=497)	-.173
Military Rank	Mean*
Officer (n=183)	.355
Enlisted (n=233)	.049
Affiliation with Veterans' Organizations	Mean*
Yes (n=35)	.975
No (n=394)	.141

*t-test comparisons for each pair of
means were significant (p < .01).
Negative means indicate overall
anti-ROTC sentiments and positive
means indicate pro-ROTC sentiments
(Range = 4.3, maximum = 1.7,
minimum = 2.5).

TABLE 7

MEAN RESPONSES TO ROTC SCALE BY FIELD

Field	Mean
Military Science	1.434
Agriculture	.616
Business	.321
Education	.217
Physical Sciences	.126
Engineering	-.017
Life Sciences	-.040
Law	-.076
Social Sciences	-.185
Fine Arts	-.458
Humanities	-.492

(r = 0.16); thus, neither rank nor age seems strongly related to attitudes toward ROTC. Furthermore, no significant differences between males and females were found.

However, interesting differences do appear when the faculties are categorized by academic discipline. As Table 7 reveals, faculty members involved in teaching ROTC were naturally the strongest supporters. Within academic fields, faculties in the agricultural sciences and business demonstrated the strongest support for the program. Not surprisingly, faculties in the humanities and fine arts were most opposed to ROTC.[33] A moderate negative response was also reflected by faculties in the social sciences.

Some data were available on the regional origins of the faculties. It was possible to identify faculty members who had been longtime residents of the surrounding area (within a fifty-mile radius of the school) before their employment at the institution. Members who were longtime residents of the South (ten years or more) before their employment were substantially more favorable toward ROTC than members who were short-term residents. Conversely, members who were long-term residents of the Northeast were more opposed to ROTC than short-term residents—which further confirms the proposition of general southern support for ROTC. This finding also has implications for the relation of localism to support for ROTC. Since long-term residents presumably have a local orientation, they should reflect regional differences more strongly. This was found to be the case.

To assess, to some extent, the rationale underlying the subjects' responses to the ROTC items, the questionnaire included an open-ended question on the effects of the disappearance of ROTC.[34] More than one-half of the sample (61.8 percent) responded to this question. Although there was a variety of responses, the majority fell into two well-defined categories. Of those who responded, 42.9 percent referred to a perceived lack of readiness for war and a fear of generally weakening the military. This category of responses was totally concerned with the welfare of the military and national defense. Responses included reference to reduction in the number of officers, reduction in the quality (academic ability, intelligence, etc.) of the officer corps, and consequent reduction in the military's ability to defend the nation.

A second category of responses (40.8 percent) concerned a particular type of negative consequence for both the military and society in general if ROTC were discontinued. These respondents generally viewed ROTC as a means of injecting civilian values into the military system. Responses tended to be detailed and included reference to loss of civilian input and reliance on the military academies for officers, increase in military elitism, ideological separation between the military and the rest of society, and weakened civilian control of the military.

Besides the support that stems from purely promilitary attitudes, therefore, a kind of support also stems from an apprehension of a purely professionalized military. There was marked similarity in the arguments and phrasing of the responses in the second category, but this type of response was not unique to any one institution or set of institutions. There was no significant association between region or type of school and this category of responses, and there was only a small negative association with the rural-urban variable (tau-c = -0.06). Apparently, many faculty members in all the institutions shared a similar ideology. This ideology is similar to Karsten's arguments; that is, support for ROTC does not necessarily indicate unquestioning support for the military but rather for a particular kind of military.[35]

Although faculty members who responded in terms of a weakening of the military (first category) had the most positive mean score on the ROTC scale, both groups were significantly more supportive of ROTC than the portion who failed to respond concerning the future of ROTC. This is very clearly reflected in a separate question about support for ROTC on campus: "if a faculty referendum were held on campus concerning ROTC, how would you vote?" Approximately 90 percent of the members who feared weakening of the military would vote for ROTC; 86 percent of the members concerned with the infusion of civilian values would support ROTC. In contrast, only 64 percent of the members who did not respond in either of these ways would vote for ROTC.

Conclusions

The basic research focus of this study was to determine the extent to which regional variation, type of school, and rural-urban setting affect academic response to ROTC. The effects of several attitudinal variables were also examined during consideration of these three structural variables.

The data analysis revealed several variable relationships. The structural variables were found to fit a theoretical additive model: each of the three (region, rural-urban setting, school type) significantly predicted faculty response and, at the same time, became more strongly predictive in combination. This was an empirical confirmation of the forecasts by Janowitz and others concerning the areas in which ROTC programs are most likely to succeed. However, the problem of accounting for the variation produced by these variables remained.

The present analysis indicates that at least three sets of respondents' attitudes toward the military are important in this regard. These sets center on antimilitary sentiments, a primary concern with national defense, and the pursuit of militaristic ideals.[36] Using regression analysis, the authors found that these attitudinal dimensions accounted for most of the explained variance, but that structural variables contributed very little to explained variance after the effects due to attitudes had been removed. These attitudes seem to underlie and thus explain the differences found in the structural variables. The data indicate that the South is still more promilitary than the Northeast and that attitudes supportive of the military are more likely in the smaller state colleges within this region.

However, an interesting qualification to the above description arose from the analysis of the responses to the open-ended question about the effects of a possible demise of ROTC. The sample could not be dichotomized into simple promilitary and antimilitary groups in terms of the military attitudinal indexes that were constructed. Rather, a large middle group manifested an ambivalent response to the military; namely, they responded primarily to ROTC as an instrument for the infusion of civilian values into the military. This orientation was *not* associated with region or type of school and only weakly with rural-urban settings, but it is a powerful predictor of positive attitudes toward ROTC. This latter group seems to correspond closely to what Cunliff termed the "rifleman" or antiprofessional militarist who lies between the extremes of the "chevalier," or professional militarist, and the "quaker," or anti-militarist.[37] Thus, academic support for ROTC apparently comes from two ideologically diverse sources.

Notes

1. John R. Probert, "The Reserves and National Guard: Their Changing Role

in National Defense," in *New Civil-Military Relations*, ed. John P. Lovell and Philip S. Kronenberg (New Brunswick, N.J.: Transaction, 1974), pp. 131-152.

2. Ibid., pp. 136-137.

3. Peter Karsten, "Anti-ROTC: Response to Vietnam or 'Consciousness III'?," in Lovell and Kronenberg, *New Civil-Military Relations*, pp. 111-127; Joseph W. Scott, "ROTC Retreat," in *The American Military*, ed. Martin Oppenheimer (New Brunswick, N.J.: Transaction, 1971), pp. 54-67.

4. Morris Janowitz, "The Emergent Military," in *Public Opinion and the Military Establishment*, ed. Charles C. Moskos (Beverly Hills, Calif.: Sage, 1971), pp. 255-270; idem, "Strategic Dimensions of an All Volunteer Armed Force," in *The Military-Industrial Complex: A Reassessment*, ed. Sam C. Sarkesian (Beverly Hills, Calif.: Sage, 1972), pp. 127-166; idem, *Military Conflict* (Beverly Hills, Calif.: Sage, 1975), pp. 272-273.

5. Janowitz, *Military Conflict*, p. 273. For analysis of the sources of militarism in the antebellum South, see Samuel P. Huntington, *The Soldier and the State* (Cambridge, Mass.: Belknap Press, 1959); and John H. Franklin, *The Militant South* (Cambridge, Mass.: Belknap Press, 1956).

6. Adam Yarmolinsky, *The Military Establishment* (New York: Harper, 1971), pp. 232-233.

7. William Hauser, *America's Army in Crisis* (Baltimore: Johns Hopkins University Press, 1973), pp. 151-152.

8. Karsten, "Anti-ROTC."

9. For assertions of faculty opposition to ROTC, see William F. Muhlenfeld, "ROTC," in *The Military and American Society* ed. Martin Hickman (Beverly Hills, Calif.: Glencoe, 1971), pp. 188-229; Milton Mayer, "ROTC: The Lower Learning," in ibid., pp. 109-117; Scott, "ROTC Retreat," p. 58; Charles C. Moskos, "The Emergent Military: Civil, Traditional, or Plural?," *Pacific Sociological Review* 16 (April 1973): 274; Yarmolinsky, *The Military Establishment*, p. 232; Hauser, *America's Army in Crisis*, p. 152.

10. Yarmolinsky, *The Military Establishment*, p. 233; Muhlenfeld, "ROTC," p. 121.

11. Scott, "ROTC Retreat."

12. Muhlenfeld, "ROTC."

13. Gene Lyons and John Masland, *Education and Military Leadership* (Westpoint, Conn.: Greenwood Press, 1959), pp. 235-236.

14. Muhlenfeld, "ROTC," p. 129.

15. Karsten, "Anti-ROTC," pp. 121-122.

16. For a review of these studies, see E. M. Schreiber, "Opposition to the Vietnam War among American University Students and Faculty," *British Journal of Sociology* 24 (Summer 1973): 288-302.

17. Larry Reed and L. A. Loman, "The Future of the ROTC on the Small College Campus," *Journal of Political and Military Sociology* 3 (Fall 1973): 229-236.

18. W. A. Lucas, "Anticipatory Socialization and the ROTC," and N. Glazer-Malbin, "The ROTC," both in Moskos, *Public Opinion*.

19. P. Karsten, "Professional and Citizen Officers," in Moskos, *Public Opinion*.

20. Glazer-Malbin, "The ROTC."

21. Our use of these terms corresponds to the definitions developed by Gouldner in his 1957 and 1958 articles: Alvin Gouldner, "Cosmopolitans and Locals: Toward an Analysis of Latent Social Roles—I," *Administrative Science Quarterly* 2 (1957): 281-306; idem, "Cosmopolitans and Locals: Toward an Analysis of Latent Social

Roles—II," ibid., 2 (1958): 444-480. For a review of the further development of the concept, see Andrew Grimes and Philip Berger, "Cosmopolitan-Local: Evaluation of the Construct," ibid., 15 (December 1970): 407-416.

22. In the development of the latter category, a consensual, reputational approach similar to that described by Reece McGee was followed. Reece McGee, *Academic Janus* (San Francisco: Jossey-Bass, 1971), pp. 153-190. As a means of validating this typology, several correlational tests were conducted. Significantly, positive relationships were found between the threefold classification system employed and faculty assessments of the reward structure of the institution (i.e., teaching vs. research), professional goals of the faculty (i.e., teaching and institutional service vs. research and publication), and the actual allocation of time for each of these activities.

23. Table 4 shows the institutions included in the sample.

24. Everett Ladd and S. M. Lipset, *The Divided Academy* (New York: McGraw-Hill, 1975), pp. 179-180. They report that in their national survey, 19 percent of the faculties were female.

25. Ibid.

26. The last four items were drawn from a list of topics found in Muhlenfeld, "ROTC," pp. 118-130. Respondents indicated their reaction by checking one of the five standard Likert responses from "agree strongly" to "disagree strongly." The items were highly intercorrelated, and a factor analysis (principle components with iterations) resulted in one factor. Table 4 shows the factor scores. These were used as weights in a scale composed of summated standard scores. A comparison of the lower and upper quartiles of the scale scores for the sample showed a significant difference between means (Student's t, $p < 0.001$) for each scale item. As a validation, the scale was correlated with the questionnaire item concerning whether the respondent would vote for or against ROTC in a school referendum. The relationship was strong (eta = 0.71).

27. Muhlenfeld, "ROTC," p. 129.

28. For references on earlier work, see H. J. Eysenck, "War and Aggressiveness: A Survey of Social Attitude Studies," in *Psychological Factors of Peace and War,* ed. T. H. Pear (Freeport, N.Y.: Books for Libraries Press, 1971), pp. 49-82. Examples of early scales (pre-1945) are available in M. E. Shaw and Jack M. Wright, *Scales for the Measurement of Attitudes* (New York: McGraw-Hill, 1967), pp. 211-226. A more recent review is W. Eckhardt and T. F. Lentz, "Factors of War/Peace Attitudes," *Peace Research Reviews* 1 (1967).

29. Preliminary attempts at factor analysis also indicated several intercorrelated factors. It is doubtless too simple to treat militarism as a unidimensional phenomenon, as most earlier scales have in practice done. In fact, the history of American attitudes toward the military institution indicates that they are multidimensional. An example might be the coupling of a strong belief in the need for a defense force with an equally strong fear of the military mind.

30. As a sociological term, *militarism* has several different meanings. Some of these are suggested in Stanislav Andreski, *Military Organization and Society* (Berkeley: University of California Press, 1968), pp. 184-186. The term is used here in Andreski's fifth meaning, i.e., an ideology propagating military ideals. The clustering of the anticommunism and patriotism items in this index along with

the item on military virtues (Table 5) conforms with definitions of contemporary U.S. militarism: James A. Donovan, *Militarism, U.S.A.* (New York: Charles Scribner's Sons, 1970), pp. 23-26; Erwin Knoll and Judith News McFadden, *American Militarism 1970* (New York: Viking Press, 1969), pp. 6-7.

31. Analysis of variance showed significant main effects for each of the three variables: region ($F_{2,922} = 33.3$, $p < 0.001$), rural-urban setting ($F_{2,922} = 3.0$, $p < 0.05$), school type ($F_{2,922} = 13.3$, $p < 0.001$). One interaction effect occurred between region and school type ($F_{2,922} = 3.4$, $p < 0.05$).

32. A hierarchical multiple regression analysis was employed. Cf. Jacob and Patricia Cohen, *Applied Multiple Regression/Correlation Analysis for the Behavioral Sciences* (Hillsdale, N.J.: Lawrence Erlbaum Associates, 1975). Attitudinal variables were entered first and setwise followed by the structural variables. Thus, the attitudinal variables had the status of covariates in the analysis. The squared semipartial correlations were significant for only the first three of the attitudinal measures (i.e., Indexes I, IV, and II, in that order, as determined by stepwise regression), indicating that after the variance explained by these three variables has been removed, the structural variables are no longer significant explainers. The variance explained by the structural variables is accounted for by general attitudes toward the military.

33. Ladd and Lipset, *The Divided Academy*, pp. 360-361, also found the strongest opposition to war-related research on campus in the humanities and fine arts. The least opposition came from agriculture, and the social sciences evidenced only moderate disagreement.

34. This question was: "Do you see any consequences for the military in this country if ROTC programs were to be discontinued (please explain)?"

35. Karsten, "Anti-ROTC."

36. See the discussion of *militarism* in note 30.

37. Moskos, *Public Opinion*, p. 289.

11
The Emergent Military: Calling, Profession, or Occupation?

Charles C. Moskos, Jr.

Many chapters in this book discuss the future of the armed forces through a focus on technological developments or global strategy. However, most service members understand and experience the military as a social organization. This chapter applies developmental analysis to the emergent military from a sociological perspective.

Developmental analysis entails historical reconstruction, trend specification, and, most especially, a model of a future state of affairs toward which actual events are heading.[1] It emphasizes the "from here to there" sequence of present and hypothetical events. Stated in slightly different terms, a developmental construct is a "pure type" placed at some future point to ascertain and order the emergent reality of contemporary social phenomena. Models derived from developmental analysis bridge the empirical world of today and the social forms of the future. Or to put it plainly, what is the likely shape of the military in the foreseeable future?

This discussion first considers three models—calling, profession, and occupation—as alternative conceptions of military social organization and then evaluates the models within the context of current empirical indicators. The basic hypothesis is that the all-volunteer U.S. military is moving toward an organizational format that increasingly resembles the occupational model. Second, we specify some expected organizational outcomes in the military system resulting from the shift to an occupational model.

Such terms as *calling, profession,* or *occupation* are frequently used imprecisely in popular and scholarly discussion. Nevertheless, they contain

Support from the U.S. Army Research Institute for the Behavioral and Social Sciences during the writing of this chapter is gratefully acknowledged. The usual caveat that all findings and interpretations are the sole responsibility of the author is especially stressed.

core connotations that distinguish them, particularly in relation to the military.

Alternative Conceptions and Current Trends

A *calling* is legitimated in terms of institutional values: i.e., a purpose transcending individual self-interests in favor of a presumed higher good. A calling usually enjoys high esteem from the larger society because it is associated with notions of self-sacrifice and complete dedication to one's role. Although individuals in a calling do not receive remuneration comparable to what might be expected in the economy of the marketplace, compensation often comes through an array of social benefits associated with the institutional format. Members of a calling generally regard themselves as different or apart from the broader society, and they are so regarded by others. They do not organize themselves into self-interest groups to resolve grievances. Rather they seek redress in the form of "one-on-one" recourse to superiors, which implies trust in the paternalism of the institution to care for its own.

Military service has traditionally had many features of the calling: extended tours abroad; fixed terms of enlistment; liability for twenty-four-hour service; frequent movement of self and family; subjection to military discipline and law; and inability to resign, strike, or negotiate over working conditions. These are features of the military above and beyond the dangers inherent in maneuvers and combat operations.

A paternalistic remuneration system corresponding to the calling model has also evolved in the military: compensation received in noncash form (e.g., food, housing, and uniforms); subsidized consumer facilities on base; payments to service members partly determined by family status; and a major portion of compensation received as deferred pay in the form of retirement benefits.

A *profession* is legitimated in terms of specialized expertise; i.e., a skill level formally accredited after long, intensive, academic training. The prerogatives of the professional center on conditions supportive of skill levels, control of the work situation, and determination of ethical practices by one's peers. The professional often receives compensation in the form of fees for service and individual expertise. There is also the presumption that the practice of one's specialty will be a lifetime career. A profession typically advances group interests through professional associations.

Service members commonly use the term *military professional* to describe themselves, and leading students of the military also use the term to describe career officers.[2] Certainly, the multitiered military educational system for officers, typified by the service academies, command and staff schools, and the war colleges, conforms with the professional model.[3]

Moreover, the various unofficial service associations closely resemble their counterparts in civilian professional associations. Nevertheless, the concept of profession as applied to the military has its limitations. Military compensation is based on rank and seniority and not, strictly speaking, on professional expertise. Interestingly enough, the exception occurs when the military organization permits off-scale compensation for certain professionals with intrinsically nonmilitary skills, such as physicians. In addition, few officers can make the military their entire careers (unlike civilian professionals, whose endeavors are lifetime careers). Moreover, the term *military professional*, in its normal usage, refers to career commissioned officers. Does this imply that others in military service are somehow "nonprofessionals" or, worse, "amateurs"? To complicate matters further, many of the forces eroding the institutional format of the calling also affect the professional model within and outside the military.

An *occupation* is legitimated in terms of the marketplace, i.e., prevailing monetary rewards for equivalent competencies. In a modern industrial society, employees usually have some voice in the determination of appropriate salary and work conditions. Such rights are counterbalanced by responsibilities to meet contractual obligations. The occupational model implies that priority inheres in self-interest rather than in the task or in the employing organization. The trade union is a common medium for articulating self-interest in industrial and, increasingly, governmental occupations.

Traditionally, the military has sought to avoid the organizational outcomes of the occupational model even in the face of repeated recommendations by official commissions that the armed services should adopt a salary system that will incorporate basic pay, allowances, and tax benefits into one cash payment. Tied to elimination of differences in compensation between married and single personnel, this approach would conform to the "equal pay for equal work" principle of civilian occupations. Such a salary system would lead to an employer-employee relationship quite at variance with military tradition. Nevertheless, even the conventional military system has practiced a degree of accommodation to occupational imperatives. For years, the military has recognized the need for special supplements to recruit and retain highly skilled enlisted personnel.

Of course, the models of calling, profession, and occupation are as much caricatures as they are descriptions of reality. But in the military, reality is complicated because the armed forces have elements of all three models and because there are also important differences among the various services, particularly in the greater dominance of technologically sophisticated weapon systems in the air force and navy in contrast with army and marine corps systems. Nevertheless, the heuristic value of the typology allows for a conceptual understanding of the overarching and clearly dominant trends occurring within the contemporary all-volunteer military—the decline of the calling, the limits of professionalism, and the ascendancy of the occupational model.

Although the all-volunteer force that appeared in early 1973 had its antecedents, the end of the draft served as the major thrust to move the military toward the occupational model. In contrast to the all-volunteer force, the selective service system was premised on the notion of the citizen's obligation—with concomitant low salaries for lower enlisted personnel—and the ideal of a broadly representative enlisted force. This ideal was not always realized in practice. The occupational model clearly underpinned the philosophic rationale of the 1970 *Report of the President's Commission on an All-Volunteer Force*.[4] Instead of a military system anchored in the normative values of a calling captured in words such as *duty, honor, country*, the commission explicitly argued that in recruiting, the military should rely primarily on monetary inducements guided by marketplace standards.

Actually, the move toward making military remuneration competitive with the civilian sector preceded the advent of the all-volunteer force. Since 1967, military pay has been formally linked to the civil service, and thus, indirectly, to the civilian labor market. From 1964 to 1974, as average earnings in the private economy rose 52 percent, regular military compensation—basic pay, allowances, tax advantages—rose 76 percent for representative grade levels, such as lieutenant colonels and master sergeants.[5] Even more dramatic, recruit pay from 1964 to 1976 increased 193 percent in constant dollars compared to 10 percent for the average laborer.[6]

Although the army was the only service to rely directly on large numbers of draftees for its manpower needs, all the services were beneficiaries of the selective service system. The draft motivated almost one-half of all voluntary accessions into the military in the peacetime years between the wars in Korea and Vietnam. It was also the major impetus for recruitment into the Reserve Officers Training Corps (ROTC) and Reserve/National Guard units.

Termination of the draft and the rise in military pay have been the most visible changes in the contemporary military system, but other indicators of the trend toward the occupational model can also be noted: (1) proposals to eliminate or reduce a host of military benefits, e.g., subsidies for commissaries, health care for dependents, and major restructuring of the retirement system; (2) the separation of work and residence locales accompanying the growing numbers of single, enlisted men living off base; (3) the incipient resistance of many military wives, at officer and noncom levels, to participating in customary social functions; (4) the unacceptably high rate of attrition and desertion among enlisted personnel in the post-Vietnam military; and (5) the increasing tendency of active-duty service personnel to bring grievances into litigation. The sum of these and related changes confirms the ascendancy of the occupational model in the social organization of the emergent military.

Consequences of the Occupational Model

A shift in the rationale of the military toward the occupational model implies organizational consequences in the structure and, perhaps, the function of the armed forces. This discussion should not be construed as advocacy of such organizational consequences or even of their inevitability. But it does suggest that certain outcomes can be anticipated if the military becomes even more like an occupation. Two changes, in particular, are presently apparent in military social organization: the growing likelihood of unionization and the increasing reliance on contract civilians to perform military tasks. Although seemingly unrelated, both such organizational changes derive from the ascendant occupational model.

Trade Unionism

The possibility that trade unionism might enter the U.S. armed forces was hardly more than a remote thought just a few years ago. Today, there are signs that it could come to pass. The growing militancy of previously quiescent public employees at municipal, state, and federal levels may be a precursor of similar activity within the military system. Many Western European countries, including several members of NATO, have long-standing military trade unions.[7] But the advent of the all-volunteer force made unionization of the U.S. armed forces a stronger possibility. Reliance on monetary incentives to recruit military members is quite consistent with the notion of trade unionism.

In 1975, the National Maritime Union (NMU), a union affiliated with the AFL-CIO, reported that it had considered organizing sailors in the U.S. Navy. For some time, the independent Association of Civilian Technicians (ACT) has been a union for civilians who work full-time for the Reserve and National Guard (almost all of whom are also members of the units employing them). Of the various possibilities for military trade unionism, the most substantial initiatives, by far, are those of the American Federation of Government Employees (AFGE), affiliated with the AFL-CIO. In its 1976 annual convention, the AFGE amended its constitution to extend membership eligibility to military personnel serving on active duty. Most of the AFGE's 325,000 members are civilian employees working on military installations. In mid-1977, the AFGE prepared a referendum to decide whether the union should proceed toward a full-fledged drive to organize military personnel.

Such groups as the AFGE, NMU, and ACT are staunchly patriotic, conservative in their approach to social change, and professed bread-and-butter unions. They have no connection with self-styled servicemen's unions that appeared in the late years of the Vietnam war. But there is a potentially disquieting implication if these established unions succeed in organizing the military: the politicization of the armed forces arising from the usually close working relationship between the AFL-CIO and the Democratic party at national and local levels.

Military unions face several legal obstacles. Current Defense Department directives allow service members to join unions but forbid commanders from negotiating with them. In addition, legislation was introduced in the Ninety-fourth Congress to prohibit unionization of the armed forces (including Reserve/National Guard as well as active-duty personnel). Congress took no action on the measure in that session, but similar bills were introduced in the next Congress. Even if Congress passed a law prohibiting military unions and the president signed the law, its constitutionality would certainly be tested in the courts. Military commanders are already permitted to negotiate with unionized civilian employees on military installations, and since 1975, they have also had explicit authority to sign local labor agreements with civilian personnel.

Undoubtedly, military unions are anathema to the service associations, almost all senior officers, and many civilians. Nevertheless, there is a widespread and quite accurate view among all ranks of military personnel that the institutional qualities of military life are being undermined. This dissatisfaction now focuses on the perceived erosion of military benefits and the job insecurities resulting from periodic reductions in force. Not so well understood is the possibility that the institutional features of the military system may have been traded off for the relatively good salaries enjoyed by career military personnel in the all-volunteer force. A strong potential for unionization exists precisely because military social organization has moved toward the occupational model while many of its members still favor the social supports of the older institutional format. It is also possible that a unionized military would not be accorded the favor that it presently enjoys from the public, which is prone to view the military as the embodiment of a calling.[8] Indeed, society might view a military union in more crass terms than would be anticipated because of the burgeoning reaction against public employee unions in general.

Civilian Technicians

Trends toward military unionization could be incorporated, albeit with some strain, into the structure of the armed forces, but another consequence of the ascendant occupational model departs entirely from the formal military social organization. This is the use of civilians to perform tasks that, by any conventional measure, could be viewed as military in content. The private armies of the Central Intelligence Agency have long been objects of concern within the regular military command. But the anomaly in the emerging order is that the U.S. government increasingly gives contracts directly to civilian firms to perform difficult military tasks at salary levels much higher than comparable military rates. In other words, the very structure of the military system no longer encompasses the full range of military functions.

It is difficult to overstate the extent to which the operational side of the military system now relies on civilian technicians. The large warships of the U.S. Navy are combat-ineffective without the technical skills of contract civilians, the so-called "tech reps," who serve permanently aboard these ships. Major army ordnance centers, including those in combat theaters, require the skills of contract civilians to perform necessary maintenance and assembly. Missile warning systems in Greenland are, in effect, civilian-manned military installations operated by firms responsible to the U.S. Air Force. In Southeast Asia and Saudi Arabia, the U.S. government gave contracts to private companies, such as Air America and Vinnel Corporation, to recruit civilians who performed military activities. In Isfahan, Iran, the Bell Helicopter and Grumman companies established a quasi-military base staffed by former U.S. military personnel who trained Iranian pilots.[9] During the collapse of South Vietnam, the government chartered civilian aircraft to rescue U.S. nationals under virtual combat conditions. The U.S. monitoring force in the Sinai was contracted out to private industry, with the government retaining only policy control.

External political considerations obviously impinge on decisions to use civilian contracts for certain military tasks. The advantage of using overseas civilian technicians may be that these people do not symbolize a national commitment to the same extent as uniformed personnel. Apparently, in certain roles requiring high levels of technical sophistication, civilians are simply more cost-effective than military personnel. Nevertheless, if task efficiency is the issue, a more nagging implication is that military personnel cannot or will not perform arduous long-term duty as well as contract civilians. If this becomes the norm, the whole notion of military legitimacy becomes untenable, since it violates some fundamental beliefs conducive to organizational integrity and societal respect. The trend toward the employment of contract civilians to perform military tasks could be the culmination of occupational ascendancy in the military purpose.

The Need for Understanding

Developmental analysis applied to military social organization reveals the impetus and probable outcomes of present trends in the all-volunteer military. The hypothesis that the occupational model is ascendant in the military system alerts one to, and makes sense of, organizational changes. The logical outcome of an occupational ethic in the armed services is military trade unionism. Concurrently, functions hitherto the province of armed forces personnel will increasingly be performed through civilian contracts.

The identification of observable trends in military organization does not mean that further changes are inevitable. If current developments are major concerns (i.e., the possibility of trade unionism, excessive reliance on contract civilians, service morale, and others), then attention should focus on the fundamental cause—the ascendancy of the occupational model—and not merely on the overt symptoms. Most important, an understanding of these developments can serve to direct organizational change toward desirable ends.

Notes

1. Heinz Eulau, "H. D. Lasswell's Developmental Analysis," *Western Political Quarterly* 2 (June 1958): 229-242.

2. Morris Janowitz, *The Professional Soldier* (New York: Free Press, 1960); Samuel P. Huntington, *The Soldier and the State* (Cambridge, Mass.: Harvard University Press, 1957).

3. Lawrence J. Korb, ed., *The System for Educating Military Officers in the U.S.* (Pittsburgh: International Studies Association, 1976).

4. *U.S. President's Commission on an All-Volunteer Force Report* (Washington, D.C.: Government Printing Office, 1970).

5. Steven L. Canby and Robert A. Butler, "The Military Manpower Question," in *Arms, Men, and Military Budgets*, ed. William Schneider, Jr. and Francis P. Hoeber (New York: Crane, Russak & Co., 1976), pp. 186-187.

6. Tulay Demirles, "Adjusted Consumer Price Index for Military Personnel and a Comparison of Real Civilian and Military Earnings, 1964-1973," *Technical Memorandum, TM-1200* (Washington, D.C.: George Washington University, 1974), p. 9.

7. A survey of the precedents and potentialities of military unionization is Ezra S. Krendel and Bernard Samoff, *Unionizing the Armed Forces* (Philadelphia: University of Pennsylvania Press, 1977).

8. John D. Blair and Jerald G. Bachman, "The Public View of the Military," in *The Social Psychology of Military Service,* ed. Nancy L. Goldman and David R. Segal (Beverly Hills, Calif.: Sage, 1976), pp. 215-236.

9. U.S., Congress, Senate, Committee on Foreign Relations, Staff Report to the Subcommittee on Foreign Assistance, *U.S. Military Sales to Iran*, 94th Cong., 2d sess. (Washington, D.C.: Government Printing Office, 1976).

12

The Military Family and the Changing Military Profession

Hamilton I. McCubbin
Martha A. Marsden

The U.S. military has recently witnessed termination of the selective service system, significant salary increases to make military salaries more competitive with civilian salaries, and efforts to eliminate or reduce a host of military benefits to active-duty personnel, veterans, retirees, and military families. These policies suggest the development of a professional military with the characteristics of an occupation. In applying developmental analysis to the emergent military establishment in American society, Moskos has concluded that the overriding and clearly dominant trend in contemporary military social organization is the decline of the institutional model and the corresponding ascendancy of the occupational model.[1]

Essentially, this trend represents a shift in philosophy from the traditional military model, which is legitimated by values and norms that underscore a "purpose" transcending individual and family self-interests in favor of a presumed good—the defense of the country. In the traditional view, military members and their families are guided by principles of self-sacrifice and dedication. They receive compensation for their efforts from an array of social supports that underscore the intent of the institution to "take care of its own" and set it apart from the general society. In contrast, the occupational model is legitimated by a marketplace that provides monetary rewards for equivalent skills. A dominant characteristic of this ascending model is that members and their families exercise some influence in the determination of appropriate salary and working con-

The authors acknowledge the contributions of Professor Reuben Hill (Regents Professor of Family Sociology), Professor Robert Leik (director, Family Study Center), and the comments by Phyllis Moen, Lance Wilson, and the doctoral students in the Family Impact Trainee Program of the University of Minnesota. We also appreciate the efforts of Drs. Edna J. Hunter and Kathy Durning on an earlier version of this chapter.

ditions. Concomitantly, rights are counterbalanced by responsibilities to meet contractual obligations. Of greatest importance, the occupational model implies first priority to self-interest rather than to the employing organization and its objectives.

A shift from an institutional to an occupational rationale implies not only such organizational consequences as trade unionism and the greater use of civilian technicians but also a gradual but distinct shift in the role of the military family from a passive "dependent" to a prominent and influential social role. The occupational model gives legitimacy to the expression and consideration of family concerns and priorities that were often suppressed as part of the military tradition and norms. Contractual arrangements encourage the development of family rights and benefits that may be commensurate with the demands of life in the military. The enigmatic aspects of military life, such as separations, deployments, force relocations, fluctuating benefits and programs, and family isolation, are taken for granted in the traditional military model. In the occupational format, they may well become negotiable contract items subject to some family influence. Within this framework, the military family can no longer be taken for granted.

This discussion advocates such organizational developments and even predicts their inevitability. More important, it argues for a greater awareness of other potent social forces that emphasize the need for more complementary relationships between the family and military policy. It also suggests that the military should examine and possibly modify its basic assumptions regarding the family, understand the changing role of women and the family in the military, become more sensitive to the impact of military policies on the health and stability of the family, and view the family as an objective of military actions and planning.

Assumptions Underlying Military Policy and the Family

We have not had a serious examination of military policy and the family since Reuben Hill's classic study of war-induced separations and reunions appealed for a "national policy which deals with American families as a precious national resource."[2] No one has made a systematic, comprehensive examination of the assumptions, issues, and policies that impinge significantly on the lives of career-motivated officer and enlisted personnel. Apparently, such an effort must be made in the light of increasing evidence that the family influences the well-being and performance of the military system.

Although family assistance programs are useful in partially alleviating the more obvious stresses of military life, many of these programs have not always been based on thoughtful, consistent, and stable policies that affirm the importance of the military family. Instead, they are apparently based on a number of assumptions deeply rooted in the historical development of the institutional model, but they may not be appropriate today. Some of these assumptions may have been slightly modified over a period of time, but they are, nevertheless, highly influential factors in determining the policies that govern today's military family. The following list summarizes these common assumptions or beliefs:

1. The primary mission of the military is the defense of the United States; family concerns of service members are always subordinate to this mission.
2. The military profession is far more than a job; it is a way of life for both the service member and his or her family. Thus, the concerns of dependents (spouse and children) are clearly secondary to the professional requirements of their sponsor (service member); the family is expected to accept willingly the stresses of military life, which include extended family separations and frequent relocations.
3. The traditional, supportive, but subordinate role of the military wife, which has been strictly and comprehensively defined by the system, must be maintained.
4. The tradition of the military to "care for its own" means that the programs and benefits for family members are a reflection of the military's interest in them, but these benefits should not be considered guaranteed rights.
5. Relative to civilian standards, military pay scales, allowances, and benefits are fair, generous, and conducive to a comfortable standard of living for the family. These benefits are designed to compensate for the unique demands of life in the military.
6. Except in extreme cases, family influences are not significant factors in the recruitment, health, performance, morale, and retention of career military personnel.
7. Because of immense logistical problems, family considerations in job assignments, career planning, relocations, and separations cannot be taken into account, except in rare hardship cases.
8. Family problems are outside the domain of military policy; if they occur, they can and should be handled within the family, with limited help from existing military and community resources when necessary. Difficulties within an individual family, particularly with regard to deviant behavior of the wife or children, reflect negatively upon the service member.
9. It is improper for the family to challenge the military system publicly on policy issues. Family considerations are always considered in the formulation of military policy.

10. Any data about the family needed to formulate and evaluate policies affecting the serviceman, servicewoman, or military family are readily available to policymakers.

A review of relevant research findings casts considerable doubt on the soundness of some of the preceding assumptions and suggests that policies based on them may be undesirably costly to the system. Such costs as the impaired functioning of military wives, children, and families may defy exact computation, but they are nonetheless real and they are documented.[3]

The Changing Role of Women in Society and in the Military

The women's liberation movement in the past few years has provided the impetus for reevaluation of the sex-role definitions, policies, and attitudes that have previously limited the social options available to women.[4] Consequently, many of the economic, legal, educational, and occupational barriers commonly encountered by women are beginning to crumble. Growing numbers of women, as well as men, are critically examining the institutions of marriage and the family with their traditional, strictly defined sex roles. The movement is a strong social force that legitimizes women's interests outside the home and, by extension, men's interests within the home.[5] Stereotyped, traditional, and inflexible sex roles are gradually being modified, and the effects of these changes within the family and society are likely to be substantial.

In attempting to keep pace with the move toward equal opportunity for both sexes, the military establishment has recently begun to recruit more women and to develop more diverse career options for them.[6] However, legal restrictions and social resistance still limit the integration and full use of women in the armed forces.[7] Nevertheless, one may hypothesize that as the military system incorporates women more fully, sex-role stereotypes will tend to erode as men and women engage in a variety of superior-equal-subordinate job relationships. One may also hypothesize that service members will begin to relate to their spouses and children in patterns that are less sex-stereotyped. Double standards of sexual behavior may fade, and the military system could gradually cease to be a "cult of masculinity."

The changing roles of women in society, in the military, and in the family are likely to have profound effects on the quality of military life. For policymakers, a host of family-related issues comes to mind. What is the expected role of the "dependent" husband whose wife is a service member? What is the role of the "dependent" military wife who has a career of her own? What if both spouses are service members? How will these changing situations affect military job assignments, family relocations, and extended separations? Will members of military families become less dependent on the system, more assertive of their personal and family needs, and less willing to subordinate their lives to the orders of the military establishment? Are family problems and divorces in the military community likely to increase? How difficult will it be to recruit, socialize, and retain high-quality military personnel in the light of current and projected social change?

The Changing Role of the Military Family

Many military family members, especially wives, are gradually and often painfully breaking the bonds of military traditions and stereotyped sex roles to develop themselves more according to their own wishes, abilities, and potentials. The contemporary egalitarian family pattern contrasts dramatically with the traditional "companionate" pattern in which the military community molded family life to the requirements of the profession. Until fairly recently, the young serviceman often postponed marriage because of his low salary. When he did marry, the ceremony was often conducted with full military ritual, and the new bride was dramatically introduced into a closed community that would become the center of her life. In his classic study of the military profession, Janowitz was struck "by the extent to which women internalized the values of military honor and military ceremony."[8] Apparently, the strains of military life were less disruptive in earlier times because the family was enveloped in a strictly defined, internally consistent style of life.

The present military family does not always fit into this traditional framework. Today, a service member often marries and begins his career simultaneously; his spouse is far less likely to be actively socialized into the military community. The conflict between two social institutions—the military and the family—over the same resource, the service member, produces strains and dilemmas for all concerned. The power of the family in this conflict is probably most evident in retention studies of enlisted personnel and West Point graduates. These studies reveal that family influences, especially wives' attitudes toward the military, are crucial in determining whether service members remain in the military.

During the late 1960s and early 1970s, the Vietnam war highlighted dramatically the strength and changing role of the military family. One of the most significant developments was the emergence of the National League of Families of American Servicemen Missing in Action or Prisoners of War in Southeast Asia, an organization composed of parents, wives, and other relatives of U.S. servicemen declared prisoners of war or missing in action.[9] This highly visible and articulate group demanded that the government understand the psychological and social hardships experienced by families during prolonged separation, provide families with a full accounting of their missing husbands and sons, end the war as quickly as possible, pressure enemy governments to negotiate for peace, and insure humane treatment to U.S. prisoners, as guaranteed under the Geneva conventions. Backed by extensive publicity from the media and direct communication with the secretary of defense, members of Congress, the secretary of state, and the president, the National League of Families had an important impact on the military establishment and the government. Family services and benefits were developed; legal supports and tax benefits were provided; and, perhaps more important, military families were represented, heard, and respected.[10]

The Impact of Existing Military Policies on Family Life

Relocation

Probably no aspect of military life reflects more clearly the plight of families, particularly the families of enlisted personnel, than forced relocations and the associated financial stresses. Because of the needs of the system, the military routinely orders service members and their families to make major changes in their residences approximately every two years. All but the lowest grades of enlisted personnel receive allowances for moving household furnishings and transporting family members to new locations. In most cases, however, this allowance is highly inadequate, and the families must absorb not only the extra costs of moving but also totally nonreimbursable expenses, such as losses due to buying and selling homes on short notice, temporary family lodging, extraordinary transportation outlays (e.g., automobile repairs), and replacement purchases of household furnishings at new locations.[11] As for the argument that the military family enjoys unique compensating fringe benefits (commissaries, free medical care, housing) unavailable to the civil service family, the present value of these services is highly questionable because of their limited accessibility and quality and congressional efforts to curtail them.

The existence of benevolent organizations, such as the Navy Relief Society, Army Community Services, and the Air Force Aid Society, bear further witness to the financial plight of many military families. In many instances, married servicemen must "moonlight" to meet family expenses. Later, when they must give up their second jobs because of unit or ship deployments or family relocations, the resulting financial strains, coupled with prolonged separation, are often devastating problems for family units. Poverty in the armed forces is more common than many people realize.

In addition to the high costs of frequent relocations, the military family pays social-psychological costs associated with a nomadic life-style. When they are isolated from the traditional supports of extended family, close friends, and stable community relationships, members of military families often experience emotional and interpersonal difficulties apparently related to their "rootlessness." For military children, problems in school, with friends, and at home have been noted and correlated with separations and relocations.[12] And frequent relocations make serious educational or career ambitions practically impossible for the military wife.[13]

Admittedly, military families may enjoy the benefits of a highly mobile life-style, such as travel, excitement, a broadening of values, and camaraderie with other military families. But the financial and psychological difficulties involved in frequent forced family relocations, coupled with escalating costs to the military system, are sufficiently serious to deserve closer examination.[14]

Family Isolation

Because of the needs of the system, the military sometimes gives service families the option, or orders them, to live in foreign countries or in relatively remote areas within the United States. In such situations, families frequently live close together in enclaves of military quarters and become isolated, to some extent, from the nonmilitary community. Even when they are scattered throughout a civilian community, military families frequently isolate themselves from their civilian neighbors. They probably then become encapsulated and satisfy almost all physical and social needs within the closed military community. Extreme dependence on the military system, parochial views of the world, and somewhat distorted environmental influences for children are notable disadvantages of this "ghetto-ization."[15] Although some families may view such situations as assets and may prefer these living arrangements for reasons of safety, convenience, and financial savings, policymakers may well benefit from a thorough review of such family problems as child abuse and school difficulties associated with social-cultural isolation.[16]

Since U.S. military personnel are assigned in many parts of the world, many of them marry foreign-born spouses. In most military communities, a notable proportion of servicemen have European, Japanese, Korean, or Vietnamese wives. Moreover, because of special circumstances permitting Filipinos to serve in the U.S. Navy, entire families may be part of a culture quite different from the culture in which they presently live. For these foreign-born spouses and families, the "double culture shock" of adjusting to military, as well as American, life is indeed difficult.[17] Although very little is known about the children of mixed cultural families in the military, they, too, probably experience unusual difficulties because of the dual heritage and differential treatment by parents, teachers, and peers. In general, mixed cultural families appear to constitute a special and relatively unknown group, but they represent a considerable potential for adjustment difficulties and supportive military programs.

Family Separation

Another major stress experienced by the military family is periodic family separation due to needs of the system for service members to serve aboard ships at sea, in "hardship" duty abroad, on special assignments, or in actual combat. Although the nature, frequency, and length of these separations vary, studies have revealed common threads regarding impaired family functioning. The military wife assumes the particularly difficult role of an "independent dependent." When her husband is gone, she must wear the hats of mother, father, handyman, decision maker, and all-around mainstay of family stability. When her husband returns, she dons her clearly subordinate cap of dutiful military wife. Such dramatic role conflict, particularly the relinquishing of independence and control, may be highly stressful for her and for the rest of the family when the husband-father returns.[18]

The impact of the father's absence on the children's adjustment is highly complex and is related to a host of intervening variables, such as the nature of the separation (wartime or peacetime, prolonged or routine), the age and sex of the child, the mother's attitude toward the separation, the quality of mother-father and child relationships, and the availability of father surrogates during the separation.[19] Despite differences in circumstances and coping responses, forced family separations apparently produce considerable stresses for the military child.

Although today's military family may display resourcefulness and resilience in adapting to the strains of separation and reunion, the longitudinal effects of family functioning under stress appear to be harmful to the wife, children, and the stability of the family unit.[20] What effects does prolonged separation have on military personnel? How do family separations and associated hardships affect the health and performance of the service member? What effect do family life stresses have on the health of career servicemen? What policies may be considered to strengthen the family and minimize the disruptive effects of separation? Should the military actively encourage wives to develop their own interests, skills, and independence so that they may become more confident and effective coleaders of their families? What can be done to facilitate role adjustments following family reunions?

War and Family Life

In addition to the stresses of frequent relocation and periodic separation, the military family must also adapt to the stresses of war. The fear and reality of injury, captivity, prolonged separations, and death may contribute to a number of marital and family difficulties; this is evident from research studies made on military families during and following World War II and the Vietnam war.[21] The deleterious effects of war and prolonged separation on children's emotional and social development are also evident from similar studies done on World War II, the Vietnam war, and the Arab-Israeli conflicts.[22]

The Legitimacy of Family Social Policy

Should family considerations receive higher priority and become an integral part of the military's policymaking process? The traditional argument is no, that increased emphasis on the military role in meeting family social and psychological needs would conflict with federal and state responsibilities for social planning and community programs. In this argument, military involvement in social problems can be justified only when military families face extreme hardships. And even in hardship situations, social services or programs sponsored by the military should be limited in scope. In addition, public and congressional elements question the legitimacy of government intervention in individual and family functions. This line of reasoning and this shuffling of responsibility have contributed, in part, to the piecemeal development of family supports and benefits that are vulnerable to cutbacks, policy changes, and political renegotiation, particularly during this period of economic instability.

In contrast, ample evidence supports a sustained effort to create a significant role for the family in policy development and review. The recent congressional hearings on children and youth emphasized the importance of family health and stability in the United States.[23] Research findings on the military family, the education and training of family specialists, and a positive emphasis on the changing role of women in the military herald a trend toward understanding and clarifying the relationship among military policy, legislation, and the family. An immediate example is the House Committee on Prisoners of War and the Missing in Action. This compassionate committee struggled with the desire to establish policies and actions that reflect an end to the Vietnam conflict. On the other hand, it faced a competing need to respond to the desires of families who have waited years for some final word on their sons or husbands.

The underlying argument for these efforts appears obvious. The military family will emerge as a collective body capable of influencing and challenging policies, regulations, and statutes. Concomitantly, if the military expects to maintain an all-volunteer force with a select group of motivated and skilled professional soldiers, it cannot ignore the potent influence of the military family. Neither can it fail to shape and project the kinds of policies needed to develop a military community that will support the new military. Policies that focus on the superior soldier, the cohesive and effective unit, and the military mission but that subordinate the family unit can only hamper the military's effort to achieve its mission and will ultimately lead to losses in valuable manpower, training, and equipment.

The issue of establishing a partnership between the family and military policy is not a matter of black or white. It is apparently one of degree; that is, how broadly or how narrowly should the family be considered in policy matters? The authors believe that consideration of the family as an integral part of the military policymaking formula is a prerequisite to the development of long-term and short-term personnel policies and social programs.

Restatement of Assumptions

A substantial move toward family partnership in the policymaking process inevitably involves a basic modification of traditional assumptions regarding the family in the military. The authors resolve that these assumptions should be restated as follows:

1. General policies related to the primary mission of the military implicitly and explicitly involve the assumption that the health, development, and stability of the military family is vital to the accomplishment of the military mission.
2. Military policies will have their greatest long-range impact and will be more efficiently implemented if they are made in consideration of the military family.
3. If a high level of personnel competence and effectiveness is attained and maintained, military policies on personnel, their health, morale, performance, and retention must also reflect an emphasis on the supporting role of the military family.
4. Policies on pay scales, allowances, and financial benefits will take into account the hardships and financial demands of military life and their impact on the family; these policies will be consistent with the policies for federal civil service personnel.
5. Policies that offer social programs and medical benefits to the family are not only reflections of the military commitment to strengthening the family unit but are also basic and fundamental rights of these families.
6. Family considerations are natural and realistic aspects of personnel management and are not viewed as dysfunctional or failures in the service member's personal life. These considerations will be sys-

tematically and consistently incorporated into the decision-making formula regarding personnel policies of assignments, career planning, relocations, and separation.

7. Family difficulties and adjustments are, in part, the responsibility of the military system, and policies on the management of these situations will reflect the military commitment to prevent as well as treat them.

8. The family has the responsibility to challenge and/or seek changes in policies that undermine the stability and health of the family unit. Fulfillment of this responsibility is essential to the accomplishment of the military mission.

9. The military system is responsible for systematic investigations to gain knowledge of the military family, to determine the effects of military policies on the family, and to determine the effects of the family on the military. These investigations are essential to the policymaking and policy review process.

Institutionalizing Family Policy in the Military

These assumptions are based on the premise that it is necessary to sharpen the focus on the family, both as an object of military planning and as a primary consideration in the formulation of military policies. Furthermore, the evidence indicates that policies at every level of the military inevitably have consequences for the military family. Since deliberate policy is obviously better than ambiguity and since continuity in policy is better than fragmentation, the authors propose more systematic attention to the military family. To accomplish this objective, the military should adopt one of M. Stanton's proposals; namely, the establishment of a family impact commission or task force within its policymaking and review organization.[24]

Such a commission would be an adaptation of existing programs at national and international levels of government. The purpose of these programs is to develop a policy review process and, ultimately, a set of impact statements that will reflect potential or present consequences of proposed or existing military policies for the family. Other countries have explicit family policies that express a common concern for the consequences of governmental actions on families and society. In Austria, a quasi-governmental advisory committee on family affairs reviews all pending legislation to identify bills that have potential consequences for families. In Sweden, special commissions study controversial or sensitive issues and, on the basis of their studies, recommend new or supplementary legislation. This activity is part of the overall planning process in Sweden; it includes both policy analysis and policy research on specific legislative proposals. In Hungary, concern about unanticipated consequences of certain governmental policies has led to retrospective analyses of legislation and evaluation of its impact on other governmental policies and programs.[25]

The proposed military commission would focus on policy analysis and research and the formulation of family impact statements comparable to the existing environmental impact statement mandated in the Environmental Policy Act of 1971.[26] Simply stated, the ultimate goal of the military commission would be to improve conditions for military families. It would do so by influencing decision making regarding public and military policy for families and children. As in Kamerman's guidelines for the development of a family impact statement, the immediate goal of the commission would be to increase military consciousness regarding policies that affect military families, particularly children. It would make the consequences of military policies more explicit and assist in the modification or development of more complementary policies that contribute to family health and stability.

A continuing effort to improve the well-being of the military family must include the reformulation of basic assumptions underlying military policy family considerations as a criterion of policy, and the creation of a special commission to institutionalize the relationship between the family and military policy. The major task is the formulation of policies that will strengthen the military family and, at the same time, insure support of the military mission. Indeed, well-conceived policies concerning the military family would probably be a major contribution to the service member's health and performance and would facilitate his contribution to the military mission. Such efforts could ultimately result in the complementary relationships envisioned by Reuben Hill: "Two institutions . . . coexist to achieve a level of collaboration that is more rewarding than what is seen by some as the present state of antagonist cooperation."[27]

Notes

1. See Charles C. Moskos, Jr., "The Emergent Military: Calling, Profession, or Occupation?," Chapter 11, this volume.

2. R. Hill, *Families Under Stress: Adjustment to the Crises of War, Separation and Reunion* (New York: Harper and Brothers, 1949), p. 361. See also W. Bennett et al., *Army Families* (U.S. Army War College, Carlisle Barracks, Pa., 1974); and R. Little, "The Military Family," in *Handbook of Military Institutions*, ed. R. Little (Beverly Hills, Calif.: Sage, 1971), pp. 247-270.

3. H. McCubbin, B. Dahl, and E. Hunter, "Research on the Military Family: A Review," in *Families in the Military System*, ed. H. McCubbin, B. Dahl and E. Hunter (Beverly Hills, Calif.: Sage, 1976), pp. 291-319. See also W. Dickerson and R. Arthur, "Navy Families in Distress," *Military Medicine* 130 (1965): 894-898; V. Gonzalez, *Psychiatry and the Army Brat* (Springfield, Ill.: C. C. Thomas, 1970);

E. Hillenbrand, "Father Absence in Military Families" (Ph.D. diss., George Washington University, 1970); R. Isay, "The Submariners' Wives Syndrome," *Psychiatric Quarterly* 42 (1968): 647-652.

4. C. Safilios-Rothschild, *Women and Social Policy* (Englewood Cliffs, N.J.: Prentice-Hall, 1974).

5. S. Bem, "Sex Role Adaptability: One Consequence of Psychological Androgyny," *Journal of Personality and Social Psychology* 31, no. 4 (1975): 634-643. See also J. Burgess, "An Explorative Analysis of Role Alternatives for Men in American Society"; J. Defrain, "Socioeconomic and Personal Factors Influencing Androgynous and Conventional Parenting Modes"; E. Gronseth, "Work-sharing Families: Adaptations of Pioneering Families with Husband and Wife in Part-time Employment"—all papers presented at the Biennial Conference, International Society for the Study of Behavioral Development, University of Surrey, Guildford, England, July 1975.

6. P. Thomas, "Utilization of Enlisted Women in the Military" (Paper presented at the Rand Conference on Defense Manpower, Santa Monica, Calif., February 1976).

7. P. Thomas and K. Durning, "Military Woman and the Navy Wife" (Paper presented at the 84th Annual American Psychological Association Convention, Washington, D.C., September 1976).

8. M. Janowitz, *The Professional Soldier: A Social and Political Portrait* (New York: Free Press, 1960), p. 89.

9. I. Powers, "National League of Families and the Development of Family Service," in *Family Separation and Reunion*, ed. H. McCubbin et al. (Washington, D.C.: U.S. Government Printing Office, 1974), pp. 1-10.

10. E. Hunter and J. Plag, "An Assessment of the Needs of POW/MIA Wives Residing in the San Diego Metropolitan Area: A Proposal for the Establishment of Family Services," Report no. 73-39 (San Diego, Calif.: Naval Health Research Center, 1973). See also H. McCubbin and B. Dahl, "Social and Mental Health Services to Families of Servicemen Missing in Action or Returned Prisoners of War," in McCubbin et al., *Family Separation and Reunion*, pp. 191-198; and R. Nelson, "The Legal Plight of the PW/MIA Family," in ibid., pp. 49-64.

11. R. Marsh, "Mobility in the Military: Its Effect on the Family System," in McCubbin et al., *Families in the Military System*, pp. 92-111. See also D. Saunders, "Poverty in the Army," *Social Service Review* 49 (1969): 396-405; and J. McKain, "Alienation: A Function of Geographical Mobility Among Families," in McCubbin et al., *Families in the Military System*, pp. 69-91.

12. F. Montalvo, "Family Separation in the Army: A Study of the Problems Encountered and the Caretaking Resources Used by Career Army Families Undergoing Military Separation," in McCubbin et al., *Families in the Military System*, pp. 147-173. See also B. Dahl and H. McCubbin, "Children of Returned Prisoners of War: The Effects of Long-Term Father Absence" (Paper presented at the annual meeting of the American Psychological Association, Chicago, Illinois, August 1975); and T. Trunnell, "A Review of Studies of the Psycho-social Significance of Father Absence" (Paper presented at the meeting of the Western American Psychiatric Association, Seattle, Washington, August 1968).

13. E. Finlayson, "A Study of the Wife of the Army Officer: Her Academic and

Career Preparation, Her Current Employment and Volunteer Services," in McCubbin et al., *Families in the Military System*, pp. 19-44.

14. P. Darnauer, "The Adolescent Experience in Career Army Families," in ibid., pp. 42-44.

15. E. Bower, "American Children and Families in Overseas Communities," *American Journal of Orthopsychiatry* 37 (1967): 787-796; and G. Wiley, "Is the Military Family in Trouble?," *Family*, October 1974, pp. 19-24.

16. C. Blochberger, Jr., "Military Families: Differential Lifestyles" (Ph.D. diss., University of California, Berkeley, 1970). See also S. Stumpf and W. Kieckhaefer, "Department of Defense Family Housing Preference Survey: Attitudes and Preferences of Military Personnel and Spouses Concerning Housing and Basic Allowance for Quarters," Technical Report 76-20 (Naval Personnel Research and Development Center, San Diego, Calif., 1975); and D. Satting and J. Miller, "The Ecology of Child Abuse Within a Military Community," *American Journal of Orthopsychiatry* 41 (1971): 675-678.

17. R. Druss, "Foreign Marriages in the Military," *Psychiatric Quarterly* 39 (1965): 220-226; and Y. Kimura, "War Brides in Hawaii and Their In-Laws," *American Journal of Sociology* 63 (1957): 70-76.

18. H. McCubbin and B. Dahl, "Prolonged Family Separation in the Military: A Longitudinal Study," in McCubbin et al., *Families in the Military System*, pp. 112-114. See also L. Stolz, *Father Relations of War-Born Children: The Effect of Postwar Adjustment of Fathers on the Behavior and Personality of First Children Born While Fathers Were at War* (Palo Alto, Calif.: Stanford University Press, 1954); S. Baker, L. Cove, S. Fagen, E. Fischer, and E. Janda, "Impact of Father Absence: Problems of Family Reintegration Following Prolonged Father Absence," *American Journal of Orthopsychiatry* 38 (1968): 347 (abstract); H. McCubbin, B. Dahl, G. Lester, and B. Ross, "The Returned Prisoner of War: Factors in Family Reintegration," *Journal of Marriage and the Family* 37 (1975): 471-478; and P. Metres, Jr., H. McCubbin, and E. Hunter, "Families of Returned Prisoners of War: Some Impressions on Their Initial Reintegration," in McCubbin et al., *Family Separation and Reunion*, pp. 147-156.

19. B. Dahl, H. McCubbin, and K. Ross, "Second-Generational Effects of War-Induced Separations: Comparing the Adjustment of Children in Reunited and Non-Reunited Families," *Military Medicine* (in press); and H. McCubbin, B. Dahl, G. Lester, D. Benson, and M. Robertson, "Coping Repertoires of Families Adapting to Prolonged War-Induced Separations," *Journal of Marriage and the Family* 38, no. 3 (August 1976): 461-471.

20. H. McCubbin, B. Dahl, G. Lester, and T. Hammond, "Fathers at Sea: Characteristics of Navy Families Vulnerable to the Stresses of Separation," *Symposium Proceedings: Fifth Symposium on Psychology in the Air Force* (Department of Behavioral Sciences and Leadership, U.S. Air Force Academy, April 1976), pp. 20-24.

21. H. McCubbin, E. Hunter, and B. Dahl, "Residuals of War: Families of Prisoners of War and Servicemen Missing in Action," *Journal of Social Issues* 31, no. 4 (1975): 95-109.

22. A. Freud and D. Burlingham, *War and Children* (New York: International University Press, 1943). See also H. McCubbin, E. Hunter, and P. Metres, "Children in Limbo," in H. McCubbin et al., *Family Separation and Reunion*, pp. 65-76; P.

Kedem, R. Gelman, and L. Blum, "The Effect of the Yom Kippur War on the Attitudes, Values, and Focus of Control of Young Adolescents"; L. Kristal, "The Effects of Wartime Environment upon the Psychological Development of Children in Border Settlements"; M. Kifshitz, D. Berman, A. Galili, and D. Gilad, "Bereaved Children: The Effect of Mother's Perception and Social System Organization of the Adjustment"; and R. Milgram and N. Milgram, "The Effects of the Yom Kippur War on Anxiety Level and Israeli Children"—all papers presented at the International Conference on Psychological Stress and Adjustment in Time of War and Peace, Tel Aviv, Israel, January 1975.

23. U.S., Senate, Committee on Labor and Public Welfare, Subcommittee on Children and Youth, *American Families: Trends and Pressures, 1973* (Washington, D.C.: Government Printing Office, 1974); S. Kamerman and A. Kahn, "Explorations in Family Policy," *Social Work* 21, no. 3 (1976): 181-187; and R. Hill, "A Program for Training Family Impact Analysts," University of Minnesota Institutional Grant (Department of Health, Education and Welfare, Public Health Service, 1976).

24. M. Stanton, "The Military Family: Its Future in the All-Volunteer Context," in *The Social Psychology of Military Service*, ed. N. Goldman and D. Segal (Beverly Hills, Calif.: Sage, 1976), pp. 135-149.

25. S. Kamerman, *Developing a Family Impact Statement* (New York: Foundation for Child Development, 1976).

26. R. Burchell and D. Listokin, *The Environmental Impact Handbook* (New Brunswick, N.J.: Center for Urban Policy Research, 1975).

27. R. Hill, "Foreword," in McCubbin et al., *Families in the Military System*, p. 15.

13
Worker Representation in Military Organization

David R. Segal

The commitment of individuals to organizations largely depends on the degree to which organizational and individual needs are complementary. That is, individuals increase their commitment to an organization to the extent that they fulfill their own needs while they behave in support of the organization. Conversely, they minimize their commitments when organizational and personal needs are not complementary.[1]

This relationship poses a potential problem for the military organization. Because of its unique social function—the legitimate management of violence—the military requires more personal commitment than other organizations require.[2] Unlike their civilian counterparts, military personnel enter into a contract of unlimited liability with their employer. They cannot unilaterally terminate their employment at any time. They may have to move to, and work in, any environment where the service needs them. They must place the needs of the service above the needs of their families, and they must frequently endure long periods of separation. They are often called upon to work more than an eight-hour day, and they receive no additional compensation for working overtime. In time of war, they face prolonged danger and may even forfeit their lives. Obviously, the man on the firing line must make a commitment of a different order from that of a worker on the assembly line.[3]

There has been considerable debate on whether the military can structurally resemble civilian organizations in modern society and still fulfill its combat function.[4] The military experiences an inherent conflict between its requirements to maintain combat effectiveness and societal pressures to develop a socially representative and responsive military establishment. If the military organization must differ from civilian organization in its structure and processes, it is likely to differ also in its ability to fulfill individual needs insofar as the needs of military personnel are similar to those of civilians.

The Convergence Theme

Military sociology in the 1950s and early 1960s suggested that military organization had become increasingly similar to industrial organization.[5] By the late 1960s and early 1970s, however, scholars had recognized limits in the concept of structural convergence.[6] Moskos, for example, moved from a position of "convergence" to posit a "segmented" model of the military; that is, combat formations diverge structurally from civilian institutions, and noncombat agencies converge.[7]

Some analysts take as dogma the assumption that military organization or some elements of it must be authoritarian, hierarchical, disciplined, and austere. Hauser, for example, feels that this is true for the combat formations of the army. He recognizes that these values are not emphasized in the mainstream of contemporary American life; thus, he feels that military convergence with civilian institutions must be prevented. He envisages that the U.S. Army of the future will consist of combat formations relatively isolated from the civilian sector and protected from such civilian turbulence as racial tension, drug abuse, and lack of discipline. Support army units would remain in contact with civilian society and serve as buffers between society and the combat forces. Only in this way can an authoritarian force survive in a libertarian society.[8] Hauser is not alone in the view that the military must be structurally different and insulated from other enterprises. Huntington takes the same stance regarding the conditions necessary for maintaining civilian control over the military.[9]

Other theorists take an opposite view. Janowitz, for example, feels that military and civilian organizational forms cannot converge completely. Nevertheless, he does not view social isolation of the military as supportive of civilian control and as functional for military operations; he views it as a threat to civilian control and to the social legitimacy of the military institution.[10] To maintain the viability of the U.S. military, he feels that the boundary between military and civilian sectors of society must be permeable and that military personnel must be broadly representative of the civilian population.[11] The goals of extensive civilian-military contacts and social representativeness of the armed forces can be viewed as functional in the sense that they minimize the ideological distance between civilian and military sectors and mitigate against the development of a "military mind." However, they are potentially dysfunctional in another sense. If civilian and military personnel recognize similar values, particularly in relation to job environments, and if the military and the civilian job environments differ because of the military mission, a discrepancy is likely to exist between work values and work situations in at least one of the environments. This poor correlation between individual and organizational needs, in turn, can have negative consequences for organizational commitment and functioning.

The Industrial Model and the Quality of Life

Civilian industry has increasingly accommodated itself to worker desires.

The most traditional manifestation of worker representation has been the routinization of the adversary relationship between labor and management through unionization and collective bargaining.[12] The impetus for labor organization and an institutionalized labor-management relationship came largely from worker demands for improved compensation and working conditions, although management has increasingly recognized the union as a mechanism for social control.

More recently, a broader societal concern with the quality of American life has led to efforts by industry to improve the lot of the worker. The belief was not only that happy workers would be more productive but, to a lesser extent, that improved quality of life is a worthwhile end in itself, even if it does not yield greater productivity. In the mid-1960s, the U.S. government initiated discussions on the development of a social accounting system parallel to the economic accounts that are regularly monitored. These discussions stimulated the development of social indicators[13] for potential inclusion in a social report summarizing nonmonetary characteristics of society—much as the annual Economic Report summarizes fiscal trends.[14] Quality of life in the workplace is one area in which indicators have been developed.

Modern managerial psychology has become increasingly concerned with the effect of organizations on the comfort of workers.[15] One way to increase the comfort of people in organizations is to increase their access to the tangible or abstract resources valued in society. One of the resources valued in the United States and other Western countries is democracy itself, and a report sponsored by the Department of Health, Education and Welfare (HEW) has urged the United States to resolve "a contradiction in our nation between democracy in society and authoritarianism in the work place."[16]

Historically, the military has been structurally very different from civilian industrial organization. Many jobs in the military did not have counterparts in the civilian labor force. The world of work was not distinct from the world of leisure: both worlds were integrated on the military installation where personnel played, worked, shopped, and lived.[17] The organization of work was communal or fraternal rather than industrial.

Moskos has pointed out that, in characterizing the military, the concepts of *profession*, *calling*, and *occupation* have been used in various contexts.[18] The professional model, applying at best only to the officer corps, implies legitimation through expertise based on specialized training, certification as a professional, occupational autonomy, and a service orientation. These characteristics differentiate the profession from other occupational groups. Although career officers have been regarded as professionals,[19] the military has never accorded this status to the junior enlisted ranks and has only rarely accorded it to senior noncommissioned officers. The argument, advanced by Abrams in the mid-1960s, that the officer corps no longer comprises a profession in Britain may now apply to the U.S. armed forces.[20]

The concept of a calling, which suggests voluntarism and excludes conscripts, does not necessarily involve training and expertise and thus is not restricted to officers. It does imply a sacred mission, legitimation through institutional values, a high level of devotion to the tasks of office, communion with others in the calling, and a system of reward based not so much on salary as on the definition of a life-style appropriate to the social position of the calling, i.e., on deference rather than remuneration.[21]

Although military sociology has repeatedly suggested that armies do not fight for ideological reasons,[22] the model of a calling has been appropriate in years past for volunteers in the enlisted grades. The mission of the soldier was to defend his country—as sacred a mission as a secular institution could perform. Indeed, military service became a hallmark of participation in the democratic policy of the Western world.[23] As noted above, the basic organization of the army was fraternal and communal. And the system of compensation was defined not so much in terms of salary; indeed, military pay was rather low. Rather, the reward system was defined in terms of life-styles differentiated by status (the size of military housing units varied with rank, for example) and manifestations of social honor, such as medals and parades. These characteristics differentiated the military calling from industrial and commercial occupations, which based their legitimacy on a direct exchange of labor for remuneration. Of equal importance, remuneration on the civilian job has been based on an explicit contractual relationship specifying work to be done and compensation, including fringe benefits, to be received. The compensation of military personnel has been rooted in an implied contract, although it is defined by statute at a specific point in time. On the basis of norm rather than law, this contract suggested the indefinite continuation of personal and family benefits, including health care, access to commissaries and post exchanges, and housing facilities or allowances. There was an understanding that once the individual successfully completed an initial period of service, he was guaranteed retention until he became eligible for a pension after twenty years of service.

Three interrelated trends are transforming the military calling into a secular occupation. The first trend is a changing technology of warfare that makes civilian populations as vulnerable as front-line troops. Technology has socialized the danger of war and reduced the unique liability and sacrifice of armed forces personnel.[24]

Second, as the technology of warfare has become both more destructive and more complex, the nature, not the distribution, of military jobs has come to approximate the nature of jobs performed in civilian enterprise.[25] Thus, the uniqueness of the tasks performed within the military organization has decreased as the unique liability of the organization in wartime has decreased.

The third factor transferring soldiering to a civilian job is the progressive acceptance of this definition by those who make military personnel policy.[26]

Occupational Orientation and Worker Representation

If voluntary military service were regarded as a calling distinct from industrial and commercial occupations, the issue of whether worker representation should replace authoritarianism in the military organization might have been forestalled. Since the transition to an all-volunteer force, however, civilian policymakers have increasingly acted as though military occupations were equivalent to civilian occupations. Indeed, the President's Commission on an All-Volunteer Armed Force recommended that military compensation should be based on a "salary" system similar to the system used in civilian industry, that lateral hiring of trained personnel from the civilian labor force should be increased, and that, in general, the all-volunteer services should compete with industry for quality personnel as similar, although not identical, entities.[27]

Before the transition to an all-volunteer force, military pay lagged behind civilian pay in the United States. Between 1951 and 1966, for example, military pay increased 60 percent. During the same period, general-schedule civil service pay, which is adjusted to salary levels in private industry, increased more than 70 percent. Moreover, first-term military personnel received no pay increase in the period from 1951 to 1964. During the transition to an all-volunteer force, however, military pay became more competitive with civilian pay. Between 1967 and 1975, regular military compensation (RMC)—the sum of base pay, quarters and subsistence allowances, and tax advantage—increased 87 percent while general-schedule civil service salaries increased 55 percent. In 1971, the first-term soldier received a large pay increase. Pay for military personnel (RMC) is now roughly equivalent to the pay of civil service personnel at comparable grade levels. In 1974, a survey of conditions of military service in the Western countries reported that although these countries had structured their military pay "in relationship to civilian employment," only the United States, Canada, and the United Kingdom indicated that their service pay scales were comparable to civilian pay scales.[28]

In the years before military and civil service pay levels were made equivalent, the economic disadvantages of military service were partially offset by fringe benefits that were viewed as part of the compensation package in the implied contract. These benefits included housing or housing allowances, health care for dependents, educational benefits, commissaries, and post exchanges. Among the latent functions of this pattern of compensation were support of the military occupation as a calling, maintenance of the military installation as a community, enhancement of the fraternal nature of military organization, and legitimation of the military as a social institution.

With the move toward equation of civilian and military pay and attendant increases in direct personnel costs, changes in the structure of benefits
have modified the terms of the implied contract. These changes include
decreases in the availability of medical care to military dependents and
retirees and cutbacks in travel and in the shipment of household goods.
Postgraduate education has been cut back; appropriated fund support for
military commissaries has been under attack; and junior officers with good
service records have been separated through reductions in force before they
achieved eligibility for retired pay. In short, working conditions for
members of the armed forces increasingly resemble working conditions
in a civilian occupation. When one recalls that similar trends influenced
unionization of European armed forces, we can identify conditions leading
to increased demands for worker representation in the U.S. armed forces.[29]

The Quality of Life

As noted earlier, the corporate sector has recently attempted to improve
the quality of organizational life—to "humanize work"—as a worthwhile
end in itself.[30] Indeed, this has been a very active area of technology transfer.
American business has sought to learn lessons from experiments in worker
representation in Scandinavia,[31] and the armed forces have sought to
learn lessons from the experiences of industry.[32] The U.S. armed forces
are not unique among military establishments in their concern for the
quality of work life. As a Canadian study published in 1972 reported:

> an understanding of the sources of satisfaction and dissatisfaction will help
> make it possible for the Forces to improve the general well-being of its
> servicemen. In recent times, the demands placed upon large organizations
> by the pressure of rapid social change has [sic] caused management to view
> the study of employee attitudes, feelings, and general welfare not only as
> a means of increasing organizational effectiveness, but also as a major concern
> it its own right.[33]

Similarly, the Danish armed forces have been concerned for some time
with the thoughts and attitudes of their personnel about their military
service.[34] In emphasizing parallel movements for worker representation in
industry and military service, a British observer noted: "Every effort
is made to trace similarities between human behavior in army and in
civilian life, and in Denmark there appears to be considerable common
ground—for example, a trade union exists for NCOs and regular soldiers,
and consultation channels, in the conference form, are afforded to national
service conscripts."[35]

In view of these trends in industry and world military systems, the rest of this chapter addresses four key questions about the organizational climate that currently prevails in the U.S. military. First, what do military personnel seek from their jobs? Second, to what extent do their jobs provide these characteristics? Third, is this fit between personal values and job characteristics similar in civilian and military organizations? Fourth, what does this fit imply for demands for worker representation?

Reconnaissance Research

The first two of these questions are addressed in reconnaissance research aimed at identifying factors affecting the quality of life in the U.S. Army.[36] In 1973, a series of seventy-six in-depth interviews at an army installation on the east coast sought to identify the significant dimensions of army life.[37] Sixteen dimensions were defined on the basis of these interviews, and in a second reconnaissance effort, they were included in a survey instrument administered to a sample of first-term personnel (n = 1, 193) at two geographically separated installations. On a scale ranging from 0 to 100, the respondents were asked to rate the importance of these dimensions to them and their degree of satisfaction with conditions in the army on each dimension. Table 1 presents the sixteen dimensions and their mean ratings for importance and satisfaction. Obviously, there is a less than perfect fit between importance and satisfaction. The correlation (rho) between the two rankings is 0.2471. Research across the armed services and across nations shows a fairly stable set of irritants that might serve as bases for demands for worker representation. Among

TABLE 1

IMPORTANCE AND SATISFACTION OF JOB CHARACTERISTICS TO ARMY PERSONNEL

Characteristic	Importance		Satisfaction	
	x	Rank	x	Rank
Pay	80.81	1	34.93	11
Personal Freedom	78.19	2	43.93	7
Meaningful Work	75.68	3	46.51	5
Medical and Dental Care	75.39	4	62.10	1
Opportunity to Get Ahead	74.77	5	42.29	8
Location and Length of Duty Tour	74.26	6	33.80	12
Equal Treatment	71.49	7	38.63	10
Education Opportunity	70.40	8	59.94	2
Housing	70.30	9	28.69	14
Leadership	70.08	10	45.05	6
Rules and Regulations	69.51	11	32.24	13
Treated Like an Individual	69.43	12	46.92	4
Getting Things Done	65.49	13	25.72	15
Post Facilities	64.73	14	53.12	3
Haircut Regulations	63.31	15	20.87	16
Food	55.61	16	40.63	9

these irritants are pay, domestic problems, change of station, and military rules and regulations.[38]

Preferred Job Characteristics

Such standardized survey instruments as the Survey of Organizations were used to test whether the relationship between job satisfaction and importance in one organization can be generalized and compared with other organizations.[39] The Survey of Organizations has been widely used in civilian organizations, and data are also available for the U.S. Navy.[40] These large civilian and navy data bases are compared with a 1975 survey of a representative sample of the U.S. Army (*n* = 2,286).[41]

TABLE 2

MOST AND LEAST IMPORTANT FEATURES OF A PREFERRED JOB

Overall Rank	Enlisted Army	Employed Civilian Men	Enlisted Navy
Most Important			
1	Good Pay	Opportunity to Control Personal Life	Opportunity to Control Personal Life
2	Fringe Benefits	Good Pay	Good Pay
3	Opportunity to Control Personal Life	Friendly People	Avoiding Bureaucracy
4	Avoiding Bureaucracy	Fringe Benefits	Fringe Benefits
5	Steady Work	Avoiding Bureaucracy	Challenging Work
10	Opportunity to Serve My Country	Opportunity to Serve My Country	Opportunity to Serve My Country
11	Prestigious Job	No One to Boss Me	Lots of Free Time
12	No One to Boss Me	Clean Job	No One to Boss Me
13	Lots of Free Time	Lots of Free Time	Prestigious Job
14	Clean Job	Prestigious Job	Clean Job
Least Important			

Fourteen measures pertaining to preferred job characteristics were examined for potential differences among army, navy, and civilian samples. Table 2 reflects a high level of consistency across the three samples. In all three work environments, personnel wanted good pay, good fringe benefits, an opportunity to control their personal lives, and avoidance of bureaucracy. On the other hand, such factors as prestige, job cleanliness, availability of free time, not being "bossed," and opportunity to serve the country were relatively less important in all three environments.

Paired to each preference measure was a "perception" item, which appeared in another section of the questionnaire. In these items, respondents were asked to describe the extent to which they felt that their present jobs provided the characteristic in question. Consideration of all possibilities (preference and perception measures for army enlisted personnel, navy enlisted personnel, and employed civilian men) resulted in a 5 x 5 matrix shown in Table 3.

The matrix presents the following pattern:

1. Perceived army and perceived navy profiles correlate significantly with each other; neither correlates significantly with the perceived civilian job characteristic profile. The incumbents of the respective jobs view civilian jobs as distinctly different from military jobs.

2. Preferences are common to all three groups; however, they suggest that what people *want* from jobs is societally, rather than organizationally, determined.

3. Civilian preferences are significantly related to civilian perceived

TABLE 3

RANK-ORDER (RHO) PROFILE INTERCORRELATIONS OF PERCEIVED AND PREFERRED JOB CHARACTERISTICS FOR ARMY ENLISTED MEN, NAVY ENLISTED MEN, AND EMPLOYED CIVILIAN MEN

	Navy Perceived	Civilian Perceived	Army Preferred	Navy Preferred	Civilian Preferred
Army Perceived	.92*	.58	.61	.52	.55
Navy Perceived		.32	.50	.41	.50
Civilian Perceived			.58	.64	.72*
Army Preferred				.96*	.88*
Navy Preferred					.91*

*Significant at or beyond the .05 level of confidence

TABLE 4

AIR FORCE QUALITY-OF-LIFE FACTORS: IMPORTANCE AND SATISFACTION

Factor	Importance Rank	Satisfaction Rank
Equity	1	6
Health	2	2
Work	3	8
Economic Standard	4	4
Personal Growth	5	1
Economic Security	6	3
Personal Standing	7	5
Leadership	8	9
Free Time	9	7

experience, but military perceptions do *not* match preferences. Taken together with the preceding finding, this suggests that preferences are indeed set by civilian socialization and are relatively resistant to change. In brief, military enlisted personnel would like their jobs to be more like civilian jobs.

Although directly comparable data were not available for the air force, research on the quality of life reveals similarities to army and navy data based on the Survey of Organizations.[42] In 1975, a survey of 10,996 air force personnel in grades E-1 to O-6 elicited ratings of the importance of nine quality-of-life factors and the degree to which personnel were satisfied with each factor. Table 4 presents these rank orderings. Again, a poor fit between importance and satisfaction is evident. Moreover, although the items are not identical, there are similarities to the army, navy, and civilian data. Opportunity (equity), fringe benefits (health), job satisfaction, and economic standard of living rank high in the ordering; prestige, free time, and leadership are at the bottom of the scale.

Thus, a very clear picture emerges concerning the issue of preferred job characteristics. Americans in the military and in civilian life attach the greatest importance to personal independence (controlling one's personal life and avoiding entangling bureaucracy) and economic success (good pay and fringe benefits). Job characteristics that *least* concern them are cleanliness, prestige, free time, absence of a "boss," and, perhaps surprisingly, an opportunity to serve one's country.

Differences in Perceived Job Characteristics

The areas in which military jobs are perceived as different from civilian jobs may indicate areas in which the functioning of military organization may be impaired. Table 5 presents comparisons of civilian data with army and navy data on twenty-one job characteristics.[43] Although the army and navy samples differ slightly in relation to the civilian data, there is a definite pattern. On a small set of characteristics, no significant differences are apparent between the civilian and military areas. Included in these characteristics are opportunities to learn new skills, avoiding hard work and responsibility, having free time, and, interestingly, having a chance to make the world a better place. On an even smaller set, the military was perceived as more desirable. Included in this set were steady employment, opportunity for advancement, fringe benefits, and a chance to serve one's country.

On all other characteristics, one or both of the services ranked significantly lower than the civilian sample. The military samples indicated greater dissatisfaction with the pay and prestige of their jobs. These factors can obviously contribute to low motivation, low morale, and low job satisfaction and, in turn, to demands for a greater "worker" voice in the management of the military.

Again, a similar pattern appears with regard to the air force. Questionnaires from 16,751 air force civilian employees elicited satisfaction data on the quality-of-life indicators presented in Table 4. This comparison is different from the first comparison because it includes uniformed and nonuniformed employees within the same branch of military service. Table 6 presents percentages of military and civilian air force samples giving "highly dissatisfied" responses regarding the nine factors. On every single factor, military personnel gave more "highly dissatisfied" responses than civilians. Moreover, two of the three largest differences involved factors that ranked among the three most important preferences for uniformed personnel. If one assumes that the major differences between perceived and preferred job characteristics in the military and civilian samples would affect worker commitment and organizational performance, then differences in organizational functioning could also be expected.[44]

The Survey of Organizations indicates the health of an organization at four distinct but interrelated levels of analysis.[45] First, it measures the behavior of supervisors and peers within the work group. This includes the degree to which leaders and peers encourage useful work, encourage cooperative relationships, recognize a job well done, and remove obstacles to doing a good job.

Second, a series of group process measures indicates whether the group works well together collectively. These measures include the degree of planning in the group, the degree to which the group makes sound

TABLE 5

COMPARISONS OF JOB SATISFACTION ON JOB CHARACTERISTICS FOR
ARMY, NAVY, AND INDUSTRIAL CIVILIAN PERSONNEL

Characteristic	Percentage of Respondents Picking Two Lowest "Satisfaction" Categories		
	Army	Civilian	Navy
No one to boss me on the work	67*	56	61
Steady employment	21*	29	11*
Chance to learn new skills	28	25	24
Don't have to work too hard	49	46	47
Clean job	61*	44	47
Chance to get ahead	37*	46	39
Don't have to assume responsibility	73	70	71
Provides a lot of free time	76	71	66
Good pay	43*	29	46*
Prestigious job	57*	47	60*
Uses my skills and abilities	41*	26	45*
Friendly people to work with	24*	11	18*
Don't have to learn new skills	63	58	67*
Allows me to stay in one place	70*	12	75*
Chance to serve my country	24*	38	24*
Chance to make world a better place	42	40	44
Good fringe benefits	14*	20	12*
Can control my personal life	42*	12	52*
Don't get endlessly referred from person to person when I need help	47*	26	42*
Don't have to go through a lot of red tape to get things done	59*	26	61*
Don't get hemmed in by longstanding rules and regulations that no one can explain	61*	26	63*
N =	2282	213	2522

*Significantly different from civilian sample, p < .05

TABLE 6

PERCENTAGES OF HIGHLY DISSATISFIED RESPONSES ON JOBS
OF UNIFORMED AND NON-UNIFORMED AIR FORCE PERSONNEL

Factor	Uniformed	Civilian	Difference
Equity	17.4	16.6	0.8
Health	15.5	5.0	10.5
Work	22.0	10.6	11.4
Economic Standard	15.6	11.1	4.5
Personal Growth	13.7	11.9	1.8
Economic Security	12.2	8.8	3.4
Personal Standing	13.7	5.6	8.1
Leadership	19.2	13.5	5.7
Free Time	16.2	5.3	10.9

decisions, the degree to which group members are perceived to know their jobs, the degree to which members communicate information to one another and desire to meet group goals, the perceived adaptability of the group, and the degree of confidence and trust that members have in the group.

Third, there is a series of indicators of the general work climate of the organization, that is, of the organizational ethos within which the group functions. These measures include the degree to which people are regarded as a major organizational asset, the mode of organizational decision making, the effectiveness of communication flow, the degree to which organizational conditions encourage effective work, the degree to which organizational resources are up to date and well maintained, and the perceived influence of lowest-level personnel on group functions.

Fourth, there are organizational outcomes. These should include both the effectiveness of the group in performing its mission and the overall satisfaction of the group members. Reliable measures of actual effectiveness were not available for the present analysis. We do have measures of individual satisfaction across a variety of dimensions.

On the basis of the reported differences between the military and civilian data, one could anticipate that the organizational climates of the army and navy would be similar to each other and lower than the civilian climate. This same expectation would hold true for satisfaction as well. The data give no basis for assuming that evaluations of leadership will be lower in the military than in the civilian environment, although the low evaluation of workmates in the military context may reflect a lack of peer team-building and support. There is no a priori basis for anticipating the effects of organizational climate, group leaders, and group peers on the group process measures. We can speculate that if all of these

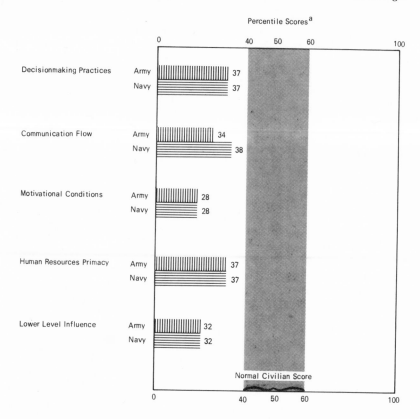

Figure 1. Comparison of Army and Navy Scores to Civilian Organizational Climate Scores

[a]Percentiles based on deciles from a ten percent random sample of 22,000 people from
32 business organizations

antecedents of group functioning are indeed lower in military than in civilian settings, the group process will also be low.

Figure 1 presents percentile scores on the measures of organizational climate for the army and navy calculated against a random sample of the 22,000 civilians who completed the Survey of Organizations questionnaire. With the exception of communication flow, on which the navy scored higher than the army, the data showed a remarkable similarity between the two armed services and a considerable discrepancy between military scores and civilian norms. This confirms the earlier finding that military personnel seek the same characteristics from their jobs as civilians, but they do not perceive that their jobs provide them.

As Figure 2 shows, the services fare better in the areas of supervisory and peer leadership. With the exception of the navy score on leadership

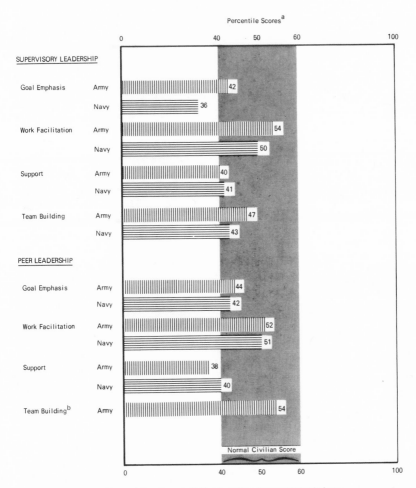

Figure 2. Comparison of Army and Navy Scores to Civilian Supervisory and Peer Leadership Scores

[a]Percentiles based on deciles from a ten percent random sample of
22,000 people from 32 business organizations

[b]One item missing from the Navy data set

goal emphasis and the army score on peer support, the percentile rankings fall within the "normal" range for civilian organizations, albeit at the low end of the range in general. Although the armed services do not compare favorably with civilian employers at the level of the total organization, they fare far better when the emphasis is placed on the individual work group. This raises an empirical question as to whether the positive aspects of the small unit can overcome the dysfunctional elements in the larger structure.

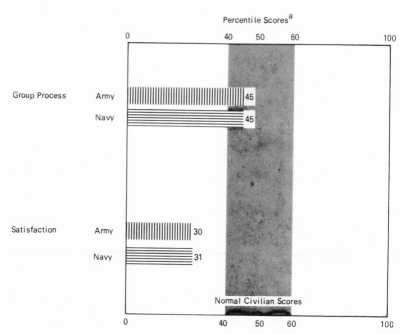

Figure 3. Comparison of Army and Navy Scores to Civilian Group Process and Satisfaction Scores

ᵃPercentiles based on deciles from a ten percent random sample of 22,000 people from 32 business organizations

The results in Figure 3 summarizing the group process and satisfaction measures are not surprising in the light of previous results. Both armed services fall within the normal range as defined by civilians in terms of group process measures. This is consistent with the findings on supervisory and peer leadership. Satisfaction measures for the services, on the other hand, are a decile below civilian workplaces. However, service personnel perceive that the total organizational environment in the military is not as effective as civilian organizations. Although causal influence has not been demonstrated, this poor organizational climate may well contribute to the relatively low level of satisfaction expressed by army and navy personnel.

The data in Figure 3 are consistent with a large body of literature in industrial sociology and psychology showing no clear-cut relationship between job satisfaction and performance when performance is narrowly defined.[46] When the definition of performance is expanded to include work-related accidents, turnover, and absenteeism, however, the correlation with work-related attitudes becomes significant.[47] In the current data, military workgroups perceive that they function as effectively as civilian workgroups, although their level of satisfaction is lower. As indicated earlier, actual job performance measures are not included in the present data. However, the navy data are supplemented with data on retention rates for twenty ships and two air groups.[48] In these data, satisfaction was not significantly related to reenlistment. Group process, however, was significantly related both to first-term reenlistment rates ($r = 0.51$) and to total reenlistment rates ($r = 0.51$).

Three of the measures of organizational climate on which the armed forces samples scored below civilian organization norms were significantly related both to first-term reenlistment rates and total reenlistment rates for the navy sample: decision-making practices (0.46, 0.47); communication flow (0.48, 0.52); and lower-level influence (0.51, 0.55). Most of the supervisory leadership measures were unrelated to reenlistment, although peer goal emphasis was related to both reenlistment measures (0.46, 0.53) and peer work facilitation was related to total reenlistment rate (0.47).

In general, then, neither measures of supervisory leadership nor satisfaction seem to be related to retention. Organizational climate has some impact on retention. Peer relations seem to have the greatest impact on performance—a fact that has long been recognized in military sociology.[49]

Attempts to Improve Organizational Climate

Organizational climate in the navy was related to personnel retention. This knowledge that low morale (and drug abuse) are related to organizational climate[50] and general recognition of the low level of work-related attitudes of military personnel have led to attempts to improve the climate in military units. Research conducted at one army post suggested that evaluation of leadership accounted for almost 40 percent of the variance in perceived organizational climate.[51] In an effort to deal with personnel attitudes within the chain of command, the armed forces have launched a program of leadership-oriented experiments. In one experiment, three social intervention programs were conducted in the army's 101st Airborne Division at Fort Campbell in an effort to improve the organizational climate.[52]

The three programs were an action planning workshop (modeled after a program at the San Diego Naval Training Center),[53] a management development workshop (modeled after a program at Ft. Ord, California),[54] and a feedback skills workshop.[55] These three approaches are only samplings of the organization development strategies used in industrial settings.[56] Judging by industrial experience, the feedback skills workshop probably had the highest odds for success.[57]

The research population was drawn from four battalions from two brigades of the 101st Airborne Division. The platoons within the three rifle companies of the battalions either were assigned to one of the three intervention programs or served as a control group. The experiment was conducted in October 1974. A questionnaire derived in large measure from the Survey of Organizations was administered two weeks before the interventions in September 1974. During October, training in the appropriate intervention strategies was given to company commanders, first sergeants, and platoon sergeants in the experimental units. A second questionnaire was administered six to seven weeks after the training. The survey included all enlisted personnel available for duty on the days that the questionnaires were administered. Table 7 presents mean change scores between pretest and posttest for four measures of organizational climate.

Both the action planning and feedback skills approaches produced changes that were consistently in the proper direction, but only one-half of the changes were statistically significant at $p < 0.05$, using paired t-tests. The management development approach produced results that were statistically insignificant and inconsistent in direction. However, data

TABLE 7

CHANGES IN ORGANIZATIONAL CLIMATE SCORES AFTER EXTERNAL INTERVENTIONS

Index	Treatment		
	Action Planning	Management Development	Feedback Skills
Decisionmaking Practices	.132	.019	.239*
Communication Flow	.200*	-.046	.105
Motivational Conditions	.187*	-.066	.176
Lower-level Influence	.137	.047	.516*

*p < .05, paired t test

were available for the units undergoing management development on absences without leave, arrests, sick calls, or hospitalization. All of these rates declined during the period of the experiment. In the absence of similar data for the other experimental treatments or for the control group, there is no way of knowing whether this improvement reflects the intervention or a general improvement in the entire division. The data do suggest that different intervention programs may produce incremental improvements in some attitudes or behaviors, but there is no universally applicable tool for improving organizational climate or organizational effectiveness. These findings are consistent with Bowers and Hauser's analysis of ten intervention strategies in 1,140 civilian groups.[58] As shown in the Fort Campbell study, they found that management development is an ineffective strategy. They also found that survey feedback is effective in groups at intermediate levels of organizational functioning. Over 60 percent of the 200 navy groups in their study fell in the intermediate range. On the basis of the organizational similarity between the army and navy described above, the author anticipates that this would also be true for most army units.

Discussion

Since the advent of the all-volunteer force, changing military policies and organization have stressed the similarities rather than the differences between uniformed and nonuniformed federal employment. Data from civilian and military samples used in this study show that military personnel seek the same characteristics in their jobs as employed civilians. However, civilians find a good fit between preferred and perceived job characteristics, but military personnel do not. In the absence of conscription, this can obviously put the military at a disadvantage in competition with industry for quality personnel.

Given the poor fit between preferred and perceived job characteristics in military and in civilian organizations, one is not surprised that both organizational climate indicators and satisfaction scores were lower for military personnel. Thus, many young people will opt for civilian employment rather than military service when they finish their education; those who enlist in the military will be likely to return to the civilian environment at the end of their service obligation; and those who remain in the military will seek means to improve their working conditions.

Data from the navy suggest a potential relationship between organizational climate and personnel retention. Leadership has an impact on organizational climate; therefore, leadership-oriented programs seem to have some potential for improving work-related attitudes in the army and navy. Of the techniques attempted to date, survey feedback seems the most promising.

Any change achieved through organizational interventions, however, is likely to be incremental and probably will not resolve the discrepancy between the characteristics that military personnel prefer in their jobs and the characteristics that they perceive. If the initial assumptions based on this study are correct, this discrepancy will result in lower levels of commitment in military than in civilian organizations, ceteris paribus. But determinants of commitment are difficult to identify because other things are not equal.

Most important, organizational interventions cannot address many sources of dissatisfaction with military employment, such as low pay and erosion of benefits. These factors are matters of national policy. Although organizational intervention may address such job characteristics as opportunity to control one's own life and ability to avoid bureaucracy, the magnitude of incremental change in the hierarchical and bureaucratic culture of the military probably will not be sufficient to overcome personnel dissatisfaction. In recent years, when civilian employees in the public sector have faced perceived economic deprivation vis-à-vis those in the private sector, they have unionized on a broad scale to gain some control over the conditions of their employment.[59] And many U.S. allies have already witnessed the formation of unions or personnel associations within their military institutions.[60] Unionization of the U.S. armed forces has become a matter of national debate in recognition that conditions exist for the evolution of this form of military worker representation.

If the U.S. armed forces unionize, management will immediately confront two policy issues. The first issue is the extent to which the military union or public sector unions should be allowed to extend their influence beyond the conditions of work and into the sphere of organizational management. When professionals in public employment have unionized, they have quickly turned their attention to the broad policies that dictate the operation of the agencies that employ them.[61] If military unionism acts as a basis for the professionalization of the enlisted ranks, as has occurred in some police departments,[62] it may be very difficult to limit the intervention of unions in the debate on military policy.

The second issue is the extent to which unionization can take place on a nonpartisan basis. The experience of Western industrial countries has been that the trade union movement has affiliated itself with left-of-center political parties; in the United States, major unions and the Democratic party have maintained at least an informal alliance. U.S. military personnel have historically leaned in a conservative direction, but they have assumed a traditional posture of nonpartisanship. If unionization leads the military to shift its leanings and adopt a new stance regarding partisanship, new models of civil-military relations, in general, and civilian control of the military, in particular, will be necessary. Military policy-makers have behaved in ways that change the definition of the military institution in the United States, but they have not yet sufficiently addressed the consequences of their choices.

Notes

1. See Rosabeth Moss Kanter, "Commitment and Social Organization," *American Sociological Review* 33 (August 1968): 499-517.

2. David R. Segal, "Convergence, Commitment and Military Compensation" (Paper presented at the 70th Annual Meeting, American Sociological Association, San Francisco, California, August 25-29, 1975).

3. No sexist slur is intended by the choice of words here. At this writing, women are excluded by statute from service on warships and combat aircraft, and the U.S. Army and Marine Corps have also excluded them from land combat, by interpretation of that statute.

4. Charles C. Moskos, "The Emergent Military," *Pacific Sociological Review* 16 (April 1973): 255-280; David R. Segal et al., "Convergence, Isomorphism and Inter-dependence at the Civil-Military Interface," *Journal of Political and Military Sociology* 2 (1974): 157-172.

5. Kurt Lang, "Technology and Career Management in the Military," and Oscar Grusky, "The Effects of Succession," in *The New Military*, ed. Morris Janowitz (New York: Russell Sage Foundation, 1964).

6. Morris Janowitz, "The Emergent Military," in *Public Opinion and the Military Establishment*, ed. Charles C. Moskos (Beverly Hills, Calif.: Sage, 1971), pp. 255-270.

7. Moskos, "The Emergent Military."

8. William L. Hauser, *America's Army in Crisis* (Baltimore: Johns Hopkins University Press, 1973).

9. Samuel P. Huntington, *The Soldier and the State* (Cambridge, Mass.: Belknap Press, 1957).

10. Morris Janowitz, *The U.S. Forces and the Zero Draft*, Adelphi Papers 94 (London: International Institute for Strategic Studies, 1973).

11. Morris Janowitz, "The All-Volunteer Military as a 'Socio-Political' Problem," *Social Problems* 22 (February 1975): 432-449.

12. See Eric Trist, "Work Improvement and Industrial Democracy" (Paper presented to the Conference of the Commission of European Communities on Work Organization, Technical Development, and Motivation of the Individual, Brussels, Belgium, 1974).

13. Eleanor Bernert Sheldon and Wilbert E. Moore, eds., *Indicators of Social Change* (New York: Russell Sage Foundation, 1968).

14. See Daniel Bell, "The Idea of a Social Report," *The Public Interest* 15 (Spring 1969): 72-84. The first major government report on the quality of life was in fact the Office of Management and Budget report, *Social Indicators 1973* (Washington, D.C.: Government Printing Office, 1973).

15. Harold J. Leavitt, *Managerial Psychology* (Chicago: University of Chicago Press, 1958).

16. U.S., Department of Health, Education and Welfare, *Work in America* (Cambridge, Mass.: MIT Press, 1973), p. 104.

17. Charles H. Coates and Roland J. Pellegrin, *Military Sociology* (University Park, Md.: Social Science Press, 1965), pp. 374 ff.

18. Charles C. Moskos, Jr., "The Emergent Military: Calling, Profession, or Occupation?," Chapter 11, this volume. For an alternative typology, see David R. Segal, "Entrepreneurial, Bureaucratic and Professional Models of the Military," in *Leadership and Management Appraisal*, ed. K. W. Tilley (London: English Universities Press, 1974), pp. 33-40.

19. Morris Janowitz, *The Professional Soldier* (New York: Free Press, 1960).

20. Philip Abrams, "The Late Profession of Arms," *European Journal of Sociology* 6 (1965): 238-261.

21. See Talcott Parsons's treatment of the concept in *The Structure of Social Action* (New York: Free Press, 1949).

22. Edward A. Shils and Morris Janowitz, "Cohesion and Disintegration in the Wehrmacht in World War II," *Public Opinion Quarterly* 12 (Summer 1948): 280-315.

23. Morris Janowitz, *Military Conflict* (Beverly Hills, Calif.: Sage, 1975).

24. Harold D. Lasswell, "The Garrison State," *American Journal of Sociology* 46 (January 1941). At an organizational level, the differentiation of military and civilian organization on the basis of degree of exposure to violence is discussed in Thomas Spence Smith and R. Danforth Ross, "On Cultural and Demographic Sources of Organizational Structure" (Unpublished paper, University of Rochester, 1976).

25. See Albert D. Biderman, "What Is Military?" in *The Draft*, ed. Sol Tax (Chicago: University of Chicago Press, 1967).

26. For a discussion of this "deinstitutionalization" of the U.S. military, see Charles C. Moskos, Jr., "Social Control of the Military" (Paper presented at the annual meeting of the American Sociological Association, San Francisco, California, August 25-29, 1975).

27. *Report of the President's Commission on an All-Volunteer Armed Force* (Washington, D.C.: U.S. Government Printing Office, February 1970).

28. Assembly of Western European Union, *Conditions of Service in the Armed Forces*, Document 650, 1974.

29. See Victor Werner, "Syndicalism in the Belgian Armed Force," *Armed Forces and Society* 2, no. 4 (Summer 1976): 477-494.

30. Neal Q. Herrick and Michael Maccoby, "Humanizing Work: A Priority Goal of the 1970s," in *The Quality of Working Life*, 2 vols., ed. Louis E. Davis and Albert B. Cherns (New York: Free Press, 1975), 1: 63-77.

31. George Ritzer, "Work-linked Democracy in Sweden: Policy Implications for America," in *Income, Equity and Change*, ed. Irving Louis Horowitz (New York: Praeger, forthcoming).

32. There is in fact little hard evidence from industry that experiments in worker representation have the desired effects. At the end of World War II, Samuel A. Stouffer noted that "in the Army no one would think of adopting a new type of

weapon without trying it out exhaustively on the firing range. But a new idea about personnel fared very differently. The last thing anybody ever thought about was trying out the idea experimentally. . . . Usually one of two things would happen: the idea would be rejected as stupid without a tryout . . . or it would be seized on and applied generally and at once." *Social Research to Test Ideas* (New York: Free Press, 1962), pp. 291-292. The situation has changed somewhat, but not drastically.

33. M. G. Chorney, *Canadian Forces Job Satisfaction Study (Men)*, Report 72-2, Canadian Forces Personnel Applied Research Unit, CFB (Toronto, Downsview, Ontario), p. 1.

34. Steen Borup-Nielsen, Erik Kousgaard, and Bent Rieneck, *Measurement of Attitudes within the Danish Armed Forces* (Copenhagen: Danish Armed Forces Psychological Service, August 1974).

35. Richard Lowndes, "Supervisory Training and Development in Holland and Denmark," mimeographed (Department of Manpower Studies, Anglian Regional Management Centre, 1974).

36. *Reconnaissance research* refers to small-scale research efforts aimed at identifying the research problem in terms of the phenomenology of the research population. See David R. Segal and Joel M. Savell, "Research on Race Relations in the US Army," in *Perspectives on Attitude Assessment*, ed. H. Wallace Sinaiko and Laurie A. Broedling (Washington, D.C.: Smithsonian Institution, 1975).

37. Robert F. Holz and A. George Gitter, *Assessing the Quality of Life in the U.S. Army*, U.S. Army Research Institute for the Behavioral and Social Sciences, Technical Paper 256 (Arlington, Va., September 1974).

38. Nancy Guinn, *Identification of Service Irritants,* AFHRL-TR-75-52 (Brooks Air Force Base, Texas, Air Force Systems Command, 1973).

39. J. C. Taylor and D. G. Bowers, *Survey of Organizations* (Ann Arbor, Mich.: Institute for Social Research, August 1971).

40. David G. Bowers, *Navy Manpower: Values, Practices and Human Resources Requirements* (Ann Arbor, Mich.: Institute for Social Research, June 1975).

41. David G. Bowers, *Work Values and Preferences of Officers and Enlisteds in the U.S. Army* (Ann Arbor, Mich.: Institute for Social Research, September 1975).

42. T. Roger Manley, Robert A. Gregory, and Charles W. McNichols, *Quality of Life in the U.S. Air Force* (Paper presented at the Military Testing Association Conference, Indianapolis, Indiana, September 17, 1975).

43. David G. Bowers and Jerome L. Franklin, *The Navy as a Functioning Organization* (Ann Arbor, Mich.: Institute for Social Research, University of Michigan, June 1973); E. S. Wessner and J. L. Franklin, *The Army as a Functioning Organization* (Ann Arbor, Mich.: Institute for Social Research, University of Michigan, September 1975).

44. See David R. Segal, "Personal Values and Organizational Diagnosis in Military and Civilian Organizations" (Paper presented to the 36th Military Operations Research Symposium, Quantico, Virginia, December 16-18, 1975).

45. Bowers and Franklin, *The Navy as a Functioning Organization*; Wessner and Franklin, *The Army as a Functioning Organization*.

46. A. H. Brayfield and W. H. Crockett, "Employee Attitudes and Employee Performance," *Psychological Bulletin* 42 (1955): 396-424.

47. F. Herzberg, F. Mausner, R. O. Peterson, and D. F. Capwell, *Job Attitudes*

(Pittsburgh: Psychological Service of Pittsburgh, 1959).

48. John A. Drexler, Jr. and David G. Bowers, *Navy Retention Rates and Human Resources Management* (Ann Arbor, Mich.: Institute for Social Research, University of Michigan, May 1973).

49. Shils and Janowitz, "Cohesion and Disintegration."

50. D. G. Walizer, *Social and Organizational Factors Related to Drug Use in the Army* (State College, Pa.: HRB-Singer Co., 1973); W. C. Eckerman et al., *The Role of Company Level Leadership in Preventing Drug Abuse in the Army* (Research Triangle Park, N.C.: Research Triangle Institute, 1974).

51. A. George Gitter et al., *Quality of Army Life: The Effects of Military Leadership* (Boston: Boston Area Academic Consortium, 1975).

52. Donald G. Walizer et al., *An Experimental Evaluation of Three Training Programs Designed to Help Company Level Army Leaders Reduce the Incidence of Social Problems in the Army* (Research Triangle Park, N.C.: Research Triangle Institute, 1975).

53. A. Trygsland et al., *Facilitator's Guide for the Command Action Planning System (CAPS) Workshop* (San Diego: Naval Training Center, n.d.).

54. The Fort Ord Program was based on the principles presented in E. H. Schein and W. G. Bennis, *Personnel and Organizational Change Through Group Methods* (New York: Wiley, 1965).

55. D. G. Bowers and J. L. Franklin, "Survey-Guided Development," *Journal of Contemporary Business* 1 (Summer 1972): 43-55.

56. See Wendell L. French and Cecil H. Bell, Jr., *Organization Development* (Englewood Cliffs, N.J.: Prentice-Hall, 1973).

57. See David G. Bowers, "OD Techniques and Their Results in 23 Organizations," *Journal of Applied Behavioral Science* 9 (1973): 21-43.

58. David G. Bowers and Doris L. Hauser, *Group Types and Intervention Effects in Organizational Development* (Ann Arbor, Mich.: Institute for Social Research, University of Michigan, November 1974).

59. See Everett M. Kassalow, "Trade Unionism Goes Public," *The Public Interest* 14 (1969): 118-129.

60. Gwyn Harries-Jenkins, *Trade Unions in Armed Forces* (Hull University: British Inter-University Seminar on Armed Forces and Society, 1976).

61. Kassalow, "Trade Unionism Goes Public," p. 130.

62. With regard to the police, Peter Feuille and Harvey A. Juris point out that although police unions may well oppose the development of professionalism among law enforcement personnel, these unions will play a role in the future development of policing as an occupation and, to the extent that police professionalism is to be valued, incentives should be found to motivate the unions to participate in professionalization. See "Police Professionalism and Police Unions," *Sociology of Work and Occupations* 3 (February 1976): 88-113.

14
Military Unions

William J. Taylor, Jr.

Times are changing—changing motivations for military service, changing expectations concerning the "terms of employment" for military service, changing aspirations toward personal dignity and "fate control," and changing the size and nature of the "manpower pool" subject to the appeals of service in the U.S. armed forces. These changes have surfaced old and new problems. Some sources suggest that solutions lie in the formation of unions of military personnel—and they are wrong.

The concept of unionizing active-duty military personnel in the United States is new—an outgrowth of the all-volunteer system. An earlier, short-lived American Servicemen's Union (ASU) was one manifestation of the antiwar movement in the late 1960s. Although the ASU was a serious concern for military leadership, it was never seriously considered a "union movement." The end of the Vietnam war and the conscription system removed the raison d'être of both the antiwar movement and the ASU. However, a number of court cases grew out of antiwar protests; they dealt with rights of free speech, assembly, and association under the First Amendment. These cases have a bearing on the constitutionality of the right of servicemen to join unions and engage in union activities.

Certain unions in the United States have involved military Reservists and members of the National Guard—e.g., the Association of Civilian Technicians and the National Maritime Union. Some personnel in the active-duty military are also employed off duty in nonmilitary jobs and hold union membership in a nonmilitary capacity. Such categories of union membership are fundamentally different from the category addressed by this chapter; i.e., membership of active-duty military personnel in unions that purport to represent them through collective bargaining

Editor's note: Reprinted by permission and with significant revision from John E. Endicott and Roy W. Stafford, eds., *American Defense Policy*, 4th ed., Johns Hopkins University Press, © 1977.

with agencies of the federal government. The difference is that *active-duty* servicemen would depend on unions to represent their *collective* interests rather than rely on channels now available to individual members and on the efforts of several nongovernment organizations that lobby on behalf of their collective interests.

Recent Developments in Public Employee Unions

Many people are surprised that systematic union bargaining in the United States has a very short history. Even in the private sector, collective bargaining gained the protection of federal law only four decades ago with the enactment of the Wagner Act. Despite previous efforts, mass unionizing did not succeed until the movement of 1935-1945. In the late 1950s and 1960s, a series of successful constitutional attacks against the authority of states to abridge the right of free speech, assembly, and "association" under the First Amendment led to the recognition of the right of state and local public employees to organize and join labor unions. In early 1962, President John F. Kennedy issued Executive Order 10988, which established the basis for employee-management cooperation in the federal service. Among other provisions, the order recognized employee organizations as bargaining representatives, limited the rights of employees to strike, and authorized advisory arbitration as the final step in a negotiated grievance procedure. Executive Orders 11491 (1969), 11616 (1971), and 11838 (1975) further clarified the rights of labor organizations and federal agency management.

None of these developments in the rights of public employees to join unions touched on the rights of active-duty servicemen to join and engage in union bargaining activities. The simple reason is that Americans considered it "unthinkable" for servicemen to join in union activities that would place them in an adversary role vis-à-vis government authority. Very recently, however, some people have begun to think and do something about the unthinkable. In September 1976, the delegates to the national convention of the American Federation of Government Employees (AFGE) voted to amend the AFGE constitution and to make armed forces personnel eligible for union membership.

Why a Unionized Military Now?

Some sources have argued that the end of military conscription and the creation of an all-volunteer force in the United States has fundamentally altered the principal motivation for people to join and remain in the armed services. According to this argument, the advent of the volunteer force modified the traditional notion that young men have a patriotic duty to serve in the military forces.[1] The antimilitary sentiment that developed as an offshoot of the antiwar movement during the Vietnam era was partially responsible for this change. The end of conscription removed the legal presumption that eligible young males should serve in the armed forces. Finally, increasing numbers of people see no need to maintain large standing armed forces in an era when threats to national security are not widely perceived. In brief, young Americans with alternative employment opportunities prefer "business as usual" to public service in the military.[2]

A relatively healthy economy in the first three years of transition toward a volunteer force (1970-1973) found the armed services in competition with civilian industry for manpower. Military recruitment efforts focused on personal incentives—higher salaries, combat arms bonuses, educational opportunities, and military working and living conditions more commensurate with other walks of life. Military service tended to become more a job opportunity and less a patriotic obligation.

The secretary of defense proclaimed the all-volunteer force a reality in January 1973. Simultaneously, inflation in 1973 took its toll on military personnel costs, which grew rapidly to approximately 56 percent of the defense budget. The critics of heavy military spending and congressional and defense budgeteers interested in holding the line on rapidly escalating personnel expenditures sought ways to cut costs. Many of the measures affected military benefits. Service personnel have long viewed "military entitlements"—such as shopping privileges in post exchanges and commissaries, free medical benefits, active-duty pay scales adjusted for comparability with civilian pay scales, educational opportunities, and adequate retirement pay—as implicit parts of the military contract. Increasingly, these entitlements have been attacked as "benefits" that are not perpetual and certainly not "contractual rights."[3] Although the nongovernmental organizations that lobby on behalf of the military are almost totally opposed to military unionization, they agree that military benefits are being seriously eroded.

Another factor precipitating the fledgling movement to unionize service personnel purportedly has to do with military working and living conditions. The military has supposedly developed a reaction to the reforms and liberalized policies established during the first two or three years of the all-volunteer force.[4] Efforts to hold the line against rising military personnel costs have also resulted in human costs. Manpower reductions without simultaneous reductions in functional requirements mean that fewer people must perform the same job. Greater efficiency results from some reductions, but sometimes people simply must work longer hours for the same pay. "Holding the line" against inflationary increases in other budget categories also has a severe impact on military living conditions, such as construction and repair of military housing and length of overseas tours of duty. Consequently, some sources argue, the everyday facts of military life do not coincide with previous recruitment advertising.[5] Neither the traditional military chain of command nor the inspector general system can readily resolve grievances growing out of such conditions. Military commanders have little impact on decisions about manpower levels and funding levels. They can try to explain the reasons for certain conditions to subordinates; they can exercise leadership to change perceptions and motivations; but they cannot solve the problems that result from inadequate manning or funding.

Thus, two fundamental arguments—that material and individual "rights" have been eroded and that existing mechanisms for promoting "justice" for service personnel are inadequate—have laid the foundation of support for military unions.[6]

Constitutional Issues

The basic constitutional question concerning the right of active-duty personnel to join unions in their principal duty capacity stems from the First Amendment to the Constitution, an amendment that prohibits Congress from enacting legislation that abridges the rights of free speech, free press, and assembly and petition. The U.S. Supreme Court has held that the First Amendment is the cornerstone of the American democratic system of government and has found a "freedom of association" inherent in the amendment.[7] Lower courts have held that public employees have a constitutional right to join labor unions under their First Amendment right to freedom of association.[8] In 1967, the Supreme Court held that Congress cannot pass laws under its "enumerated powers" if those laws place an excessive burden on the rights of federal employees to freedom of association.[9] Thus, both court decisions and the practices of the later 1960s support the right of public employees—federal, state, and local—to join unions, and they also prohibit congressional attempts to abridge that right. Although this precedent includes a wide range of public employees, some of whom may be termed "paramilitary" (i.e., police and firemen), it does not deal specifically with the military.

By deferring to Congress, the Supreme Court has consistently avoided entering the realm of authority and rights in the military. The fundamental grant of congressional authority over the military derives from the Constitution: "Congress shall have the power . . . to raise and support armies, but no appropriation of money to that use shall be for a longer term than two years; to provide and maintain a Navy; to make rules for the government and regulation of the land and naval forces."[10] Two cases, one in 1953 and a second in 1974, contained the essence of the Supreme Court's approach to the law applicable to the military and to the rights of service personnel under the First Amendment. In the first case, the Court dismissed a habeas corpus petition for two air force men convicted of rape-murder in Guam:

> Military law, like state law, is a jurisprudence which exists separate and apart from the law which governs in our federal judicial establishment. This court has played no role in its development; we have exerted no supervisory power of the courts which enforce it; the rights of the men in the armed forces must be conditioned to meet certain overriding demands of discipline and duty, and the civil courts are not the agencies which must determine the precise balance to be struck in this adjustment. The Framers expressly entrusted that task to Congress.[11]

In the second case, involving an appeal from a conviction of violating articles 133 and 134 of the *Uniform Code of Military Justice* (UCMJ), the Court observed:

> While the members of the military are not excluded from the protection granted by the First Amendment, the different character of the military community and of the military mission requires a different application of those protections. The fundamental necessity for obedience, and the consequent necessity for imposition of discipline, may render permissible within the military that which would be constitutionally impermissible outside it.[12]

Thus, when the military has had jurisdiction over an individual, the Supreme Court has refused to interfere with the military courts in exercising a grant of authority from Congress to safeguard the rights of service personnel. The congressional grant of authority to military courts is found in the *Uniform Code of Military Justice* (UCMJ), enacted by Congress in 1950 and revised periodically since that time. The UCMJ establishes the framework for criminal jurisdiction and a system for appeals. And the Supreme Court, on appeal, indicated that the rights of armed forces personnel under the First Amendment may be restrained when a deterioration of discipline adversely affects a higher interest. Thus, a critical issue is whether union membership would erode military discipline.

At this juncture, the Supreme Court has not spoken to the issue of military unions and has deferred to Congress on the relevant rights of military personnel under the First Amendment. Neither have executive orders on the right of federal public employees to unionize addressed the matter of unions for military personnel. And Congress has not passed laws relating to unions of military personnel. Thus, one must look elsewhere for legal guidance on the right to trade union membership for military personnel; that is, to the legal precedents established by lower civilian courts and military tribunals. Of course, the First Amendment explicitly prohibits Congress from enacting legislation that abridges the rights of free speech, free press, assembly and petition, and the Supreme Court has extended the principle to freedom of association. The central question is the degree to which any branch of government—federal, state, or local— can restrict military personnel from full exercise of the First Amendment rights that would form the basis of legal union membership by active-duty military personnel in their principal duty capacities.

Court Decisions and Military First Amendment Rights

Military Courts

The Court of Military Appeals had its first opportunity in 1954 to address some of the issues concerning the rights of military personnel under the First Amendment. In *U.S.* v. *Voorhees*, a case involving an army officer's refusal to delete certain references in an article for publication, the court's decision contained three separate opinions, two of which are quoted below. Each of the opinions agreed, grudgingly, that the protections of the First Amendment applied to military personnel. Judge Quinn's opinion noted that First Amendment rights are restricted by "military necessity." Judge Latimer elaborated on limitations to the First Amendment in the case of military personnel:

> I believe it ill-advised and unwise to apply the civilian concepts of freedom of speech and press to the military service unless they are compressed within limits so narrow they become almost unrecognizable. Undoubtedly, we should not deny to servicemen any right that can be given reasonably. But in measuring reasonableness, we should bear in mind that military units have one major purpose justifying their existence: to prepare themselves for war and to wage it successfully. That purpose must never be overlooked in weighing the conflicting interest between the right of the servicemen to express his views on any subject at any time and the right of the Government to prepare for and pursue a war to a successful conclusion. Embraced in success is sacrifice of life and personal liberties; secrecy of plans and movement of personnel; security; discipline and morale; and the faith of the public in the officers and men and the cause they represent. In connection with this litigation, it is to be remembered that while we can discuss the principles involved in a time of temporary peace, that is the period during which we must prepare for war or other eventualities. A principle which interferes with preparing for war may interfere with its successful prosecution; and a privilege given unwittingly in peace may be a death knell in war.[13]

Again, in 1967, the Court of Military Appeals addressed the issue in reviewing *U.S.* v. *Howe*, a case involving an officer who carried antigovernment signs in protest marches against the Vietnam war while he was off duty in civilian clothes off post:

> We need not determine whether a state of war presently exists. We do judicially know that hundreds of thousands of members of our military forces are committed to combat in Vietnam, casualties among our forces are heavy, and thousands are being recruited, or drafted, into our armed forces. That in present times and circumstances such conduct by an officer constitutes a clear and present danger to discipline within our armed services, under the [civilian] precedents established by the Supreme Court, seems to require no argument.[14]

These and subsequent cases decided by the Court of Military Appeals establish a rather consistent approach to the rights of military personnel under the First Amendment; that is, military personnel have such rights, but they must be balanced by the unique requirements of "military necessity," loosely defined as the military good order and discipline required for national security.

Civilian Courts

Lower federal courts have ruled on First Amendment rights for military personnel in a number of cases that grew out of the protest movement against the Vietnam war. In *Dash* v.*Commanding General, Fort Jackson, South Carolina* (1969), a district court examined the authority of the post commander to restrict distribution of publications on post and to refuse a request to hold an open meeting on post to discuss the Vietnam war. The court first addressed the right of federal courts to decide such questions: "however hesitant they may be to 'intrude,' Courts will be available to determine whether there is a reasonable basis for such restrictions as may be placed on the serviceman's right of free speech by the military establishment."[15] As to the basic issues, the court stated:

> in those cases where this is a reasonable basis for the conclusion that the distribution (of published materials) represents a "clear danger to the loyalty, discipline or morale of his troops" [the Post Commander may] prohibit the distribution. . . . Can training for participation in a war be carried on simultaneously with lectures on the immorality or injustice of such war? In my opinion, the denial of the right for open, public meetings at advertised meetings [sic] on post for discussion of the propriety of the political decision to participate in the Vietnam war was justified "by reason of the peculiar circumstances of the military" and represented no infringement of the constitutional rights of the plaintiffs or others similarly situated.[16]

In 1971, a federal court of appeals reversed a district court decision in *Cortright* v. *Resor*, which had held that the army had violated a soldier's rights

under the First Amendment when it transferred him to another post because
of his anti-Vietnam war activities:

> As stated at the outset, we are far from holding that under no circumstances
> could a civilian court interfere with a transfer order or prescribe other
> relief if that were needed to prevent abridgement of a soldier's First Amend-
> ment rights. We hold only that the Army has a large scope in striking a
> proper balance between servicemen's assertions of the right of protest and
> the maintenance of the effectiveness of military units to perform their
> assigned tasks.[17]

Like the military courts, civilian courts have been relatively consistent
in restricting the First Amendment rights of military personnel when the
exercise of those rights was prejudicial to military good order and discipline
or to the accomplishment of assigned military missions. The requirements
of military necessity must be balanced against First Amendment rights.

The Current Political Climate for Military Unions

Understandably, the American Federation of Government Employees
(AFGE), the National Maritime Union, and the American Association of
Technicians favor unions for military personnel in the United States for two
fundamental reasons. The AFGE and others claim that military benefits
are being eroded and that no one represents the just cause of military
personnel. The AFGE also points to its own success in acquiring pay comparability for federal employees, including the military.[18] The AFGE,
approximately 360,000 strong, sees in two million active-duty military
personnel a significant increment to its power: union members who pay
annual dues of approximately $90 per person and the potential of becoming
the largest and strongest AFL-CIO union in the United States.[19]

Equally understandable is the opposition to military unions by nongovernment organizations that lobby on behalf of the military. To the
extent that unions gain control in representing the interests of military
personnel, the nongovernment lobbying organizations lose their membership, dues, and raison d'être. Members of these organizations tend to
be senior noncommissioned officers, commissioned officers, and retired
military personnel who represent rather traditional and conservative
views generally at odds with the basic philosophical tenets and operational
approaches of unions.

The leadership of the military services and managers in the Department
of Defense tend to view unions as a threat to traditional military good
order and discipline and, consequently, as liabilities to mission accomplishment in the vital arena of national security. Although there is no legal
barrier at present to prohibit active-duty personnel from joining unions,

directives prohibit military commanders from bargaining with them.

The position of Congress is now unknown. In previous years, one might have anticipated strong opposition from older and senior senators and congressmen, many of whom were veterans of World War II or the Korean conflict and some of whom could carry large voting blocs in their hip pockets. Several bills to prohibit armed forces personnel from joining unions were introduced in the Congress. None got out of committee. By mid-January 1977, twelve new bills had been introduced, eleven in the House (H.R. nos. 51, 120, 384, 624, 675, 693, 1105, 1381, 1478, 1623, and 2230) and one in the Senate (S.B. 274) with thirty-four cosponsors.

The views of the target population for union membership—two million active-duty military personnel and 700,000 members of the National Guard and Reserves—are unknown.[20] Few survey results have been released. However, a 1976 sample of 936 air force personnel may be instructive. Forty percent would not join a military union, and 30 percent were undecided, but the remaining 30 percent agreed that they would join. Enlisted personnel were much more prounion than were officers (37 percent versus 16 percent). On balance, the respondents to this survey perceived the environment as adverse for military personnel in the all-volunteer force, and they apparently believed that unions could represent their interests effectively. But many believed that military unions would adversely affect air force effectiveness (49 percent), military discipline (55 percent), and supervisor-subordinate relations (45 percent).[21]

The views of the public on military unionization per se are also unknown. One opinion survey based on a sample of 1,529 people across the country asked two questions simultaneously: "Do you favor or oppose members of the U.S. Armed Forces being organized into unions?" and "Do you believe members of the Armed Forces should be permitted to go on strike?" Eighty-two percent opposed military unions. The strongest opposition came from people over forty-five years old, people with some education beyond high school, and nonunion government employees. The major support for military unions came from people between eighteen and twenty-four years of age (33 percent) and from racial minorities (31 percent).[22]

Unsound Arguments against Military Unions

Some of the popular arguments in the United States against unions of active-duty military personnel are sound; others are not. The argument is well taken that union bargaining and representation of grievances would be prejudicial to military good order and discipline and, by extension, to capability for mission accomplishment. First, not all military personnel would join unions. In any given command, basic interests and organizational loyalties would be split between union and nonunion members of the command. This would undercut esprit de corps, a basic tenet of military good order and discipline. Thus, irrespective of rather common debates over the commander-union relationship, union members in the chain of command would in fact be placed in a relationship different from that of others in the command. This would be divisive. Second, what might begin only as a union representation of the interests (pay and allowances) of military personnel could and probably would grow into direct interference and conflict with command prerogatives. In fact, the late AFGE president, Clyde Webber, has stated that "even if our membership votes to bring servicemen into the union movement, our goal will be to get into contract bargaining and a regular grievance system eventually."[23] Erosion of the chain of command would indeed impair readiness for mission accomplishment.

Would unions involving active-duty military personnel strike? There are no precise precedents for such contingencies, but there are sound analogies. Unions of public employees in the United States generally are prohibited from striking at both the federal and state levels. But the postal unions struck in 1970, and they were successful in their demands.[24] Police and firemen's unions are prohibited from striking in all fifty states, but many have struck, in effect, through work stoppages, such as "sick outs," lasting as long as five days.[25] Obviously, strike prohibitions in executive orders or statutes are not ironclad deterrents to strikes by strong unions of public employees. Can a union prevent its membership or part of its membership from striking? An AFGE president has stated:

> There isn't any way to stop those things. They don't ask me to go on strike. They don't ask their national vice president to go on strike. . . . But the thing about it is that you cannot control individual elements of an organization whether it happens to be the United States Army as has been demonstrated a couple of times in the last three or four years, or the Navy or the Air Force or the AFGE. People take into their own hands what they think they have to.[26]

In view of the clear, if not yet present, danger of military unionization, opponents of military unionization should make their arguments along the lines suggested above.

Some other popular arguments against military unions are unsound; e.g., attempts to relate unionization of U.S. military personnel to the European experience with military unions. Such arguments are full of logical traps. One cannot argue that unionized U.S. military personnel will strike when the European analogies show that the unionized military do not strike. One cannot argue that standards of appearance related to discipline degenerated when European military personnel unionized; such an argument would require proof that mission capability degenerated. This would be a difficult and probably counterproductive undertaking.

European unions have grown largely as part of governing establishments. For example, the governing social democratic parties in the Netherlands and, until 1976, in Sweden came to power largely because of the strength marshaled by trade unions. To the contrary, U.S. unions have grown not only as adversaries to private management but also as political adversaries of federal, state, and local governments over issues related to the rights of American labor. In the European case, where strikes by military unions are prohibited, except in Sweden, a military union "bargains" or consults with elements of its own power base in government, with which its interests are closely identified. In the U.S. case, military unions would bargain in an adversary relationship with government managers whose political power base rests on a span of interests that include organized labor as only one.

The major "rights" enjoyed by unionized armed forces personnel in Western European countries are *not* rights secured by military unions through collective bargaining. In the main, they are rights secured by social legislation under social democratic governments in countries with strong socialist traditions. For example, the Social Democrats legislated the forty-hour work week in Sweden for *all* Swedish citizen, not simply as a collective bargaining agreement with one or more trade unions representing one or more of the Swedish military unions. Furthermore, the right of married couples in the Swedish military to decide whether the civilian working wife or the military husband will stay at home to care for a newborn child for the first six months is the legislated right of *all* Swedish couples. Although it may appear ludicrous to many Americans that a soldier could simply inform his commanding officer, "My wife just had a baby; see you in around six months," this right was important and "just" to the Swedish parliament that passed such legislation.

No one has argued persuasively that European military unions do not serve both their constituencies and their societies well. The point is that the societal context of such unions is simply different from that of the United States. There is no sign that the American people are prepared to support trade unionism of the European variety. Nor is there any sign that Congress is ready to enact the sweeping social legislation typical of countries with stronger socialist traditions.

Arguments against military unions in the United States should be divorced from analogies to continental Europe—simply because there are few real analogies. They should instead treat the American case as unique. The differences are especially marked in patterns of collective bargaining.[27]

Direct Steps in the Right Direction

Those who are opposed to unions of active-duty military personnel should develop their better arguments fully. The latter should become the basis of public debate, and they should be publicized. Most Americans probably recognize the fundamentals of "military necessity"; in any case, "free collective bargaining and the right to strike are increasingly unacceptable to broad sectors of public and political opinion; indeed, many workers, and some union leaders share these views."[28] Recent surveys of American opinion concerning institutions in which people have confidence place military leadership second and labor unions last.[29]

Congress probably has the constitutional authority to prohibit unions by active-duty military personnel in their principal duty capacities. In a court test, a law prohibiting such unions would probably be upheld. The link between the prevailing political climate and court decisions is important. Many leading scholars of the U.S. court system concur that the legal subculture in the United States increasingly reflects society's power structure and that judges are not immune to its influence.[30] The potential economic, social, political, and military impact of a court decision on unions of military personnel and their rights to bargain would be enormous. Courts would probably be loathe to nullify a broadly supported, congressional statute to prohibit a phenomenon that has such important implications for national security.

Simultaneously, the erosion of military benefits should be stopped in order to remove the major basis for union claims to legitimacy in representing the interests of active-duty military personnel. The nongovernment organizations that lobby on behalf of the military should pool their resources to press the case *for* military benefits and, therefore, *against* military unionization.

The institutions and procedures for permitting participative management and for processing grievances in the active-duty military should be reexamined. There is no manifest reason why in-service functional equivalents to union bargaining cannot be developed. Recent studies by sociologists and psychologists, studies partially confirmed by survey data taken in the armed services, suggest that armed forces personnel are just as interested in the conditions of their work as in their pay and benefits. They want not only productive jobs but also the personal dignity that flows from involvement in shaping their own futures. Few are willing to mortgage their futures to the impersonal workings of the "system."[31] Obviously, this is a major challenge for military leadership and management.

Finally, if Charles Moskos, David Segal, Laurie Broedling, and others are correct, the social trends that have given birth to a movement toward unionization are likely to gather momentum. The U.S. military has been based on the twin pillars of "profession" and "calling." Each, in its own way, has legitimized the personal sense of duty and self-sacrifice for a higher public good. Short of the direct compulsion of the draft, the most equitable and efficacious route to restoring the "sense of calling" is a voluntary national service program, without exemptions, under which military service is one of several options.[32] Such a program deserves serious study within the Department of Defense and by Congress. Public debate of such a proposal is the sine qua non for public acceptance.

Any one of the above approaches probably cannot itself stop a movement replete with dangers to national security. A viable policy must incorporate several approaches. Such a policy best assures both justice and dignity for the active-duty service member and the reasonable balance in First Amendment rights that court tests have found within the meaning of the Constitution and the Bill of Rights.

Notes

1. See, for example, David Cortright, "The Union Wants to Join You," *The Nation*, February 21, 1976, pp. 206-209; see also Tod Ensign and Michael Uhl, "Soldiers as Workers," *The Progressive*, April 1976, p. 37.

2. See the AFGE arguments cited by Gary R. Ballard, "Big Labor Pushing for Unionization of Armed Services," *Human Events Magazine*, November 8, 1975, p. 8. Charles C. Moskos has alluded to the possibilities for such attitudinal changes. See his "Social Control of the Military" (Paper presented at the meeting of the American Sociological Association in San Francisco, California, August 25-29, 1975), pp. 10-12; and "The Emergent Military: Calling, Profession, or Occupation?," Chapter 11, this volume.

3. Major General Herbert C. Sparrow, USA (Ret.), "The Promises Men Live By," *Armed Forces Journal International* 112, no. 9 (May 1975): 21-22.

4. See, for example, Colonel Richard M. Jennings, USA (Ret.), "The Military and Social Adaptation," *Strategic Survey* 4, no. 1 (Winter 1976): 73.

5. Cortright, "The Union Wants to Join You," p. 207.

6. Ibid. See also "Congressional Hearings," *Naval Affairs*, March 1976, p. 11; and Sparrow, "The Promises Men Live By," p. 2.

7. *United States* v. *Robel*, 88 S. Ct. 423 (1967); for other cases and related analysis, see Major James A. Badami, "Servicemen's Unions: Constitutional, Desirable, Practical" (Thesis presented to the U.S. Judge Advocate General's School, March 1973).

8. For example, *Atkins* v. *City of Charlotte*, 296 F. Supp. 1068, D.C.N.C. (1969).

9. *United States* v. *Robel*.

10. United States Constitution, sec. 8, cls. 12, 13, 14.

11. *Burns* v. *Wilson*, 346 U.S. 140 (1953).

12. *Parker, Warden, et al.* v. *Levy*, 417 *U.S. Reports* 758 (1974).

13. *U.S.* v. *Voorhees*, 4 U.S.C.M.A. 509, 16 C.M.R. 105 (1954).

14. *U.S.* v. *Howe*, 17 U.S.C.M.A. 165, 37 C.M.R. 437 (1967).

15. *Dash* v. *Commanding General, Fort Jackson, South Carolina*, 307 F. Supp. 854, D.S.C. (1969).

16. Ibid., at 856.

17. *Cortright* v. *Resor*, 447 F. 2d 254 (2d Cir. 1971).

18. "Unionizing: An Interview with Clyde M. Webber, National President of the American Federation of Government Employees," *The Times Magazine*, September 24, 1975, pp. 22-23.

19. "Military Unions? A Look at the Consequences," *The Officer*, December 1975, p. 17.

20. See note 6 above. In fact, however, no one has referenced any definitive data to support such a conclusion.

21. *Federal News*, February 28, 1977, p. 5.

22. "Ditto on Right to Strike," *Army Times*, June 21, 1976, p. 23.

23. Walter Mossberg and Richard J. Levine, "Union Plans '76 Drive to Represent Servicemen: Legalities are Explored, and Pentagon Shudders," *The Wall Street Journal*, June 27, 1975, p. 30.

24. The postal strike of March 1970 resulted in an 8 percent pay raise for postal employees (PL91-375). It should be recalled that the U.S. Army was called in to operate some post offices during this strike. What would have happened had the army personnel been members of a union of federal employees?

25. See Ezra S. Krendel et al., "The Implications of Industrial Democracy for the United States Navy," Technical Report No. NKG-10, prepared under the Navy Manpower R&D Program of the Office of Naval Research, January 1975, pp. 147, 152.

26. "Unionizing: An Interview," p. 43.

27. Adolph Sturmthal, *Comparative Labor Movements: Ideological Roots and Institutional Development* (Belmont, Calif.: Wadsworth Publishing Co., 1972), pp. 50-52.

28. Sumner Rosen, "The United States: A Time for Reassessment," in *Worker Militancy and Its Consequences, 1965-1975*, ed. Solomon Barkin (New York: Praeger 1975), p. 351.

29. *International Herald Tribune*, January 8, 1977.

30. R. S. Lockwood, "The Costs of Military Union Strikes" (Paper presented to the Military Operations Research Society, 39th Annual Symposium, United States Naval Academy, Annapolis, Maryland, June 28-30, 1977), pp. 3-4.

31. See, for example, Nancy L. Goldman and David R. Segal, eds., *The Social Psychology of Military Service* (Beverly Hills, Calif.: Sage, 1976); Laurie A. Broedling, "Industrial Democracy and the Future Management of the United States Armed Forces" (Paper presented at the International Studies Association Convention, St. Louis, Mo., March 16-20, 1977); and the chapters by Moskos and Segal in this volume.

32. Latent support for universal national service appears to exist. See Moskos, "The Emergent Military," pp. 13-14; "Worse Than the Draft?" *New York Times*, January 26, 1977; "Return to Draft in a 'Few Years' Urged by Stennis," *The Washington Post*, December 30, 1976; and "Rethinking the Draft," *The Washington Post* January 25, 1977, p. 1.

Part 4

Organizational Dynamics and Change

15
Military Leadership: The Implications of Advanced Technology

John C. Toomay
Richard H. Hartke
Howard L. Elman

The modern military leader performs in an environment of such rapid technological progress that it has been described as "explosive." The *technology explosion*, the *information explosion*, and the *education explosion* are terms frequently used in the mass media in recent years. Does the military profession need a "leadership explosion" to match these developments? Probably not, for two reasons. First, the effect of technology on military leadership has been to change emphasis, styles, and problems but not the basic jobs of leadership—organizing, focusing, and motivating people. Second, the qualities of an effective leader are still elusive, psychological, and, perhaps, mystical.

The changes brought by technology imply that the air force leader today and tomorrow must master a broader spectrum of leadership techniques, but they do not alter the most central fact of military leadership: the military leader must accomplish his particular mission by using people as his primary resource. While speaking to the students of the Industrial College of the Armed Forces, General Earle G. Wheeler, army chief of staff, succinctly placed in perspective the effects of advancing technology on leadership. "Do not make leadership dependent upon technology," he said, "for technology can fail, but leadership must not fail."[1]

This principle must be applied not only in considering the demands of existing leadership but also in developing future leaders, who can expect even more rapid technological advances. Of particular importance is the obligation of present leaders to keep their successors in mind as they perform their everyday jobs. When the Duke of Wellington remarked that "the Battle of Waterloo was won on the playing fields of Eton," he was reminding us that society must provide more than "warm bodies" or "cannon fodder." Military interest in the field of education is a measure of this concern. When a military leader neglects the training of his successors, he fails to continue the job begun by his nation in its educational system. Trained manpower is probably the military's longest "lead-time" item. As the rate of technological change increases, the military leader must assure that his successor appreciates not only today's technology but also the trends and implications of the technology he will face when he holds a command position.

Although the requirements of military leadership are much the same as those of the past, both obvious and subtle implications of technology require changes in emphasis. That is, changes in leadership result not only from such obvious facts as the increased velocity of weapons but also from the subtle effects of technology on society—its mores, attitudes, and perspectives. The military leader must learn to shape his leadership approach to include the changing technological and sociological environment in addition to the more traditional leadership requirements.

A Definition of Leadership

The basic traits of a military leader have not changed. A leader organizes a group, acts as its spokesman, directs it, and, in so doing, accomplishes things. But functioning as a leader does not imply leadership. Leadership is something more; it connotes success and effectiveness. In this view, then, leadership becomes whatever makes a leader effective, and this varies with the situation. Even in the Boy Scout organization, the *Patrol Leader's Handbook* defines leadership as "a process of getting things done through people" and avoiding simple "school solutions" because varied situations require varied approaches. In his classic work on management, *The Human Side of Enterprise*, Douglas McGregor introduced two philosophies of human nature (Theory X and Theory Y), which produce two extreme leadership styles, one authoritarian and the other motivational. Textbooks frequently present exaggerated examples of these opposing styles because neither style alone is practical in the real world. However, they serve as good starting points in considering the effect of technology on leadership.

The authoritarian approach is useful primarily in teaching discipline, and since it is often cited as the best approach for evoking rapid response in combat, many people assume that it is the sole method used by the military. If the leader is concerned primarily with simple tasks and simple character traits, he may well use this approach coupled with the perfect self-discipline necessary for him to serve as a good example. In such instances, the activities are programmed, and the responses are reflexive.

When the leader works on more complex tasks or on tasks that are not deterministic, this approach alone is not sufficient, particularly if he is concerned with training his successors. He relies more on a motivational approach to provide flexible learning situations and to assure his successors of his confidence in them.

The effective leader seldom can use either of these leadership styles in its simplest form. The normal leadership situation involves people with varying levels of job competence in a variety of work settings. The leader evaluates information, makes appropriate decisions, and directs and controls the execution of the decisions. Since these tasks require unique leadership skills, they may partially account for the varied and overlapping definitions of leadership found in the literature. Regardless of the leadership styles used by military leaders of the past (one cannot imagine Eisenhower, Marshall, or Washington as martinets, nor Napoleon and Genghis Khan as beneficent), the strict application of Theory X is no longer practical in our modern environment. In the first place, the military has become more dependent on a wide industrial base, the military officer has become more aware of the leadership process in civilian industry, and this awareness has led to the development of broader concepts of leadership. In the second place, society's standards concerning the rights and privileges of individuals have changed drastically.

Modern leadership involves a combination of approaches that may include assertion of authority; motivation by example; demonstration of mutual respect; motivation by exhortation, threat, or inducement; and simple, logical persuasion. All of these techniques can be and are used, depending on the situation. Some are normally more prevalent and appropriate to the military situation than others because military leaders differ from nonmilitary leaders in certain important respects.

The military leader's initial leadership experiences usually involve purely military situations in which the presence of visible rank carries persuasive power backed by law and custom. At a similar level of supervision, the civilian leader has much less clout. The civilian leader usually has only a psychological contract (a tacit understanding between the leader and his followers concerning prerogatives), but the military leader has more options. Society has given him firm legal authority because he may confront life-and-death decisions and, in extreme instances, has life-and-death authority. His visible rank and the orders appointing him to a given position are not merely the trappings of office; they are a means of establishing the climate of obedience. Military discipline is an adjunct to military leadership. A military unit is not just a group of people; it is a disciplined group of people. This distinction affects the leadership options available to the military leader. This has been true throughout history, but technology has brought certain significant modifications.

Changes in the Leadership Environment

Technology has changed the military leader's environment in at least four ways. Weapons have changed enormously; people have changed; the military system itself has changed; and interactions with other organizations have become more complex.

As recently as 200 years ago, the sword was the major personal weapon of the military commander, but it is now an anachronism, carried very occasionally in parades. Although this trend has been continuous since the introduction of gunpowder, one should remember that Japanese officers, as late as World War II, still led their troops with drawn swords. Today, the major personal weapon of an air force officer may be a fighter aircraft armed with a nuclear device. One may argue that reference to an F-15 as a "personal" weapon is somewhat loose, but after all, a fighter pilot "wears" his aircraft and takes it into combat alone.

Even a conventional modern automatic weapon has immense firepower. One M-16 has as much firepower as the entire English complement of archers at Agincourt. One AC-130 gunship fires a broadside more destructive than the full firepower directed against Pickett's charge at Gettysburg. Even the rockets launched by a fighter aircraft in the Korean War had greater destructive power than the gunfire of a light cruiser in World War II. None of these examples includes the immense power of nuclear weapons. They stress that the concentration of destructive power has now made the individual or small crew-served weapon the equal of entire mass weapon systems of the past. Because the individual combatant has the major responsibility for the proper use of this immense power, he must be carefully selected and trained, even though he may or may not face a similarly armed foe.

This focus of responsibility explains the military need for centralized control. It is not merely the temptation of more rapid communications or the corruption and self-indulgence nurtured by power that causes major concern with command and control systems and the tendency to make targeting decisions at high levels. A single warship 150 years ago could inflict only so much damage. The increased firepower that allows one aircraft to inflict as much damage as an entire earlier fleet or army implies a need for control at a more responsible governmental level. Accompanying the increased firepower are immense increases in range and decreases in the time scale. A military action is no longer a point effect; it extends over an area large enough to blur the line between tactical and strategic thinking. The decreased time scale also forces the commander to make rapid decisions. The traditional need to "look at the big picture" has not disappeared; it has intensified, but cannot be an excuse for delaying decisions. These factors imply that the on-scene commander must be more responsible; after all, higher authority must observe the situation through his eyes and his judgment. They also imply that the commander must be more obedient to remote authority than commanders of the past. Thus, modern command and control developments symbolize a two-edged sword: they require military leaders who are capable of swift, independent judgment but who are unlikely to abuse their independence.

Two hundred years ago, the major military weapon was the same musket the average colonist used to provide meat for his table, and military enlistments were limited to ninety days. After all, requirement for military training was nil, and three months in service was sufficient to complete a reasonable combat campaign. Today, trained personnel are the longest lead-time items in the military. The modern military leader receives such tremendous benefits from the education and culture provided by society that he would find it almost impossible to operate without it. Centuries ago, England patterned its educational system in a manner that indoctrinated its youth with the traits and basic lore of the Royal Navy. Today, military members recognize the significance of education and culture when they offer advice to the military of developing countries and discover immense cultural gaps concerning such common items as screwdrivers and screws.

The air force no longer has jobs at any level that do not require some formal training. Although on-the-job training is still necessary, all air force personnel must meet specific requirements in formal education and training. College graduates comprise approximately 94 percent of the air force officer corps. A college degree is now mandatory for commissioning in all line areas, and thousands of officers have advanced degrees. A college education is a primary requirement for commissioning not simply because it enables the air force to point proudly to the statistics or because the air force needs professionals in accounting, engineering, or law. The air force has found that college experience broadens the military leader and teaches him to think—not what to think but *how* to think.

The task of leading educated people is more difficult than that of leading uneducated people, but the results are better. A technologically based military requires a totally literate, mechanically proficient, and technically oriented manpower base. The trend is that educational requirements for a military career will increase. The modern military leader must remember that he leads educated people, and he must structure his leadership style accordingly. Educated people need to know organizational goals and the methods that will be used in achieving the goals. "Because I say so" is an acceptable answer only when the leader has earned the trust of his people and when they function as a team.

The process of building a technical society requires teamwork because technical complexity requires division of labor—specialization. A specialist is only as good as the team that he supports; the team, in turn, must support him. Fortunately, teamwork is a basic concept of American society.

Since complete military operations depend on teamwork, the military profession would find it difficult to teach the concept if American society had not laid the groundwork. Any military is a reflection of its society; our military has benefited because the American tradition of teamwork is so strong.

A small, all-volunteer standing army backed by a citizen militia is another long-standing American tradition. With the end of the draft, the United States has returned to a variant of this tradition. The profession must be more selective of its personnel, and the military manager must be sure that he properly motivates his volunteer force.

What motivates? Individuals have usually been motivated by what they perceive to be their own best interests. Before the age of technology, the fighting man was motivated almost entirely by material considerations. Although war leaders have always appealed to religion or ethnic unity, xenophobia on the field of battle was usually reinforced by the hope of booty for the winner and the dread of slavery for the loser. Fear of death and injury has always been present, but this is a negative incentive. What was the major positive incentive? It was the "captives home to Rome whose ransoms did the general coffers fill," as Shakespeare described it in *Julius Caesar*. As late as the Civil War, Admiralty Prize Courts awarded money to naval crews for the capture of enemy ships and their merchandise.[2]

There is not much war booty after a napalm blast. What is the incentive for today's military man? Appeals to patriotism are too general and over-worked in contemporary society. Proper career opportunities offer one inducement, particularly in peacetime, but how can the military leader motivate his people beyond career considerations? One would be grossly cynical and unrealistic if he claimed that men fight only for money. In his book entitled *Motivation and Personality*, Dr. A. H. Maslow states that as a technological society fulfills man's basic materialistic motivations, such self-actualization motivators as prestige and job satisfaction become increasingly important. Self-esteem has been unmistakably linked to bravery, loyalty, and steadfastness in the face of adversity. Thus, the military must maintain and improve its inherent integrity and the image that it provides a valuable service to the country; this, in turn, will generate the respect that will enable it to motivate people. When the commander demonstrates the relationship between one's mission and national objectives and the manner in which those objectives benefit one's family and neighbors, he will motivate an all-volunteer force. Leadership has obviously become more complex and less definable.

Weapons developed since the Industrial Revolution have completely changed the traditional military system. Short-term staff planning has changed from tomorrow morning's assault to a response in the next five seconds to a new radar sighting. Long-term staff planning is no longer next summer's campaign; such planning now involves estimates of the national economy twenty years hence. The prime mission of the military is still that of providing a first-line fighting force capable of winning any conflict, but the effect of technology has been to emphasize preplanning and pre-positioning of resources. Therefore, the support functions have become much more critical and more complex, and the military cannot afford (if it ever could) to place second-rate leadership in this area. The modern military leader must be equally at home commanding a combat unit or managing a support activity. The leadership requirements may appear different, but the two assignments are complementary and equally vital.

Although its share of the gross national product is declining, the military is a centralized and visible force perceived as one of the larger users of national resources. The size of the business (defense is the United States' biggest "company") requires a professional force, whether one considers a fighter squadron or a military laboratory.

The technologically driven growth in support functions generates specialization, and the specialist views himself as a professional. Although career professionalism is desirable, it must not degenerate into parochialism. The specialist must resist the temptation to become an advocate of only the requirements of his specialty, and he must encourage innovation. The charge that the military is too bureaucratic stems both from the need to handle large numbers of people efficiently and from the need to recognize the views of diverse supporting specialties.

What sorts of support functions are there, what is their origin, and how does technology change them in today's military? Although technology has affected all these functions, let us look only at the three largest. Logistics is the oldest military support function. Everyone is familiar with the baggage trains and camp followers that accompanied the armies of antiquity, and everyone remembers Napoleon's quip, "An army marches on its stomach." But how many people realize that Napoleon's comment launched the modern food-processing industry? The art of canning and vacuum packing food originated with Napoleon's requirement for more portable field rations.[3] As a member of the Military Committee of the Continental Congress, John Adams encouraged the establishment of a widespread logistics base when he encouraged the wives left at home in Massachusetts to organize "the making of saltpetre for gunpowder."[4] Today, the logistics base of the air force requires stockpiling literally millions of different items—from rations to munitions to spare parts. Only by computer can the air force manage such supplies. Merely to transport them requires major military forces, such as the familiar Military Airlift Command with its aircraft fleet. The scheduling of such a tremendous transportation system has itself become a major technological task.

Maintenance is another support function that can be traced to the earliest military organizations. Two hundred years ago, the higher-paid enlisted men on U.S. frigates were maintenance specialists—carpenters, sailmakers, coopers, and blacksmiths. One hundred years ago, the power politics of the major world powers revolved around the establishment of overseas naval bases not only for reprovisioning but also for major repairs that could not be made in ports equipped for repair of incidental damage to the merchant fleet.[5] In World War II, the RAF's major aircraft overhaul depots in Egypt were both an objective in Rommel's drives and a major military resource of the Allies in Africa and along the supply line to China.[6] Today, one of the largest air commands—the Air Force Logistics Command—regards its air logistic centers and its depot maintenance function as top priority assignments. But the maintenance of a field-repairable wooden cannon mount is a far cry from depot repair of a jet engine or the return of a computer mainframe to the manufacturer.

Research and development (R&D) is often viewed as a modern military development. This is far from true. When the Hittites first developed iron swords in place of the bronze swords used by their foes, they neglected to preserve the name of the first deputy chief of staff for R&D! Formal military support of applied research is evident in the works of Leonardo da Vinci, Benvenuto Cellini, and other Renaissance figures. The development of modern stellar navigation can be traced to the large monetary prize offered by the British Board of Admiralty 200 years ago for the first practical clock adequate for round-the-world cruises by the Royal Navy.[7] The major differences between modern and ancient R&D functions are differences of size and breadth. Today, the military, like society as a whole, is more likely to support pure scientific inquiry in the hope of achieving applicable results. To make certain that the results are applied— to get more "bang for the buck"—the military today has a higher percentage of officers with the training needed to evaluate technological advances. As technology advances on a broad spectrum, these officers must assure that the military is not caught by technological surprise.

The growth in the size and breadth of military resources obviously increases the number and kind of organizations—military, government, and private—with which any military leader must interact. This interaction can best be analyzed in terms of the increase in information that the modern military leader must consider in reaching his decisions. It is no exaggeration to state that the information available and relevant to decision making has increased a million times over. Far more raw data are now available to the decision maker than he can possibly absorb. He need no longer suffer from a thirst for information; instead he must guard against inundation by information. The problem is to sift the data and preserve the really important factors.

A few hundred years ago, the military leader concerned himself almost exclusively with things in his actual line of sight. Reinforcements farther away than the horizon were seldom capable of arriving in time to influence events. At that time, staff functions were small; the highest commander needed only a staff large enough to act as couriers to subordinate commanders. The display of relevant information was simple: it consisted of a single map or drawings in the sand.

By World War II, factors of importance usually involved an entire theater of operations; only the top governmental level required a world view. Staffs had grown not only because of specialties but also because each staff officer predigested the information in some area to aid in the commander's evaluation. By then, a map was not sufficient. In the play *Command Decision*, by W. W. Haines, the map of Europe in the general's inner office was complemented by status boards on resources—aircraft and crews.[8]

Many military leaders today must retain a global view of their mission, and a global view requires a global information base. The operational commander may face rapidly deployed forces totally outside his normal area of concern. His staff must be knowledgeable on more factors, and it must predigest a larger data base. The information display process is now often computer-driven because the staff cannot process the information fast enough nor can the commander evaluate a situation properly with less information. Does this read like a description of the Joint Chiefs' Situation Room? It could actually describe a situation at wing or brigade level. It is also accurate for the military laboratory commander who tries to remain cognizant of a broad spectrum of technological developments.

Today, both the operational commander and the support commander must evaluate information faster from a broader spectrum of sources than ever before. Both commanders must use automated processing to help in sifting the information, and they must be painfully aware of the limitations of automated data displays. Both require their staffs to decide constantly what data are reasonable and relevant, how the data must be presented, and whether the data provide adequate alternative courses of action.

The Modern Military Leader

As stated earlier, technology has not changed the tasks and intent of military leadership, but it has brought changes in the environment—the weapons, people, military system, and interactions with other organizations. How must the military leader of today modify traditional leadership methods and techniques?

The air force officer of today is inundated with exhortations to "manage"—to manage his resources, manage his men, and manage himself. He faces this challenge as a direct result of technological forces, but at the same time he cannot neglect the traditional military emphasis on leadership. To many people, "management" implies a motivational, gentle, nonauthoritarian approach to supervision, and "military leadership" implies a strict, authoritarian, no-nonsense approach. The well-informed officer recognizes the fallacy of both views. The good manager and military leader recognizes that the situation determines the appropriate leadership style and that he may need to shift rapidly between various styles.

For example, a pro football coach uses a variety of leadership styles as he prepares his team for the next game. On Monday, the team meets for practice and perhaps discusses, in seminar fashion, the opponents of an upcoming game. At this stage, the coach "manages" the team. By Wednesday, some plays have been selected and tried out, and the coach assumes a stricter role. By Friday, emphasis shifts to teamwork, and the coach does not *request*—he *orders*. But when the team meets the opponent during the weekend, the coach expects his players to think and analyze. He does not expect them to depart from pregame plans, if possible, but if the opponent introduces an unexpected play or formation, he expects his players to use judgment and some innovation.

One of the air force's historic advantages is its application of this concept. Every fighter pilot is carefully trained to react instinctively to orders: when his earphones bark, "Yellow Two, break right," he breaks right! But a remark from a former Messerschmitt pilot also underscores the American tradition of innovation. During a panel discussion of fighter tactics in World War II, Ernst Schendel stated:

> The British pilot—We think they were very disciplined, in a way more so than the American pilot. It was much easier to fly against the British pilot. He was much more predictable. The American pilot—we just were never quite sure. . . . He was not at all predictable. You never quite knew what to do or how to handle it. The British—you could almost think with them. When they went into a certain maneuver, you just knew the next thing they would do and if you knew that, you could do the opposite. And it worked many times. . . . It was very unlikely that an American pilot would have done that.[9]

The military leader of today must know when it is "Monday" for his team, when it is "Friday," when he must give the order to "break right," and when he can innovate. The judgment needed to choose among these alternatives justifies his paycheck. The subject of judgment in choosing alternatives is too extensive to cover in this discussion, but in determining the applicable leadership style, the effective military leader must consider the time scale of the response and the level of subordinate experience or skill as it relates to the mission.

In terms of the time scale of the response, the closer one gets to crisis operation (the football game or combat), the less one can allow subordinates to exercise freedom of choice. The relationship of subordinate skill levels to mission requirements should be equally obvious: the leader "back seat drives" when he teaches his son to drive a car, but he does not assume this role as a member of a car pool in heavy traffic. These observations may seem irrelevant to technology, but they are not. An operational commander employing a complicated piece of equipment works at one end of the scale on both the time and skill guidelines; a laboratory commander developing new hardware works at the other end. The modern military leader must be capable of fulfilling both of these jobs, and he may move from one to the other on short notice. The differences between the jobs can be measured by the commander's attitudes toward innovation. Because successful innovations increase the commander's capabilities, the leader must be particularly aware of the capabilities of the two dissimilar organizations.

The operational area offers relatively little obvious opportunity for innovation. Rapid force deployment implies that the commander must follow the book so that all parts of his unit will operate predictably. This does not mean that he allows *no* innovation in operations, but it does mean that he must place severe limitations on the type and degree of innovation. This requirement is as much a consequence of advancing technology as is the need for innovation in the support role. The operational unit usually does not have the time to explore all the ramifications of operating a high-technology device outside the guidelines of the manual. In such cases, however, coordination with the support area can provide important evolutionary developments.

For example, in the Southwest Pacific in 1942, Colonel "Pappy" Gunn saw that the load-carrying capability and maneuverability of the B-25 could provide enhanced close air support.[10] Rather than employ the B-25 as a medium bomber in the conventional level delivery mode, he mounted heavy machine gun packs and adapted cannons for it. His innovation proved quite successful, but it created technical problems. Weapons recoil damaged the aircraft structure; ventilation was inadequate for the cordite fumes; and reloading presented crew problems. Colonel Gunn called in the people at Wright Field and solved the problem temporarily. All problems were solved some months later with the arrival of production-line B-25s armed with cannons.

Almost twenty-five years later, coordination between operational innovators and support specialists once again brought a close air support weapon to deployment. The AC-47 gunship used in Vietnam was operationally deployed quite rapidly during the development of the AC-130. In this case, a relatively evolutionary weapon incorporated new technology to improve on older systems and tactics.

The laser-guided bomb is still another example of rapid deployment of a technically advanced weapon developed through close cooperation between operations and support personnel. Operational personnel were not completely knowledgeable about laser theory, and laser theorists did not have bomb mission experience in Southeast Asia. But proper military leadership enhanced close coordination and brought rapid and successful deployment of a technologically new weapon.

Some significant points stand out in all of these examples. By complicating weapons and compressing the time frame, advancing technology inhibits the operational commander's freedom to innovate. At the same time, it forces him to place premiums on technical knowledge in his command—on the person who can communicate his needs to support functions and on the people on his staff who can coordinate these areas. As Dr. Malcolm R. Currie, director of defense research and engineering, recently summed up this evolutionary trend in weapons development, "I am less concerned about the appearance of unforeseen new weapons, per se, than with innovative uses of technology based on a superior understanding of technology's ultimate significance to future warfare."[11] Made in the context of antisubmarine warfare during World War II, this remark underscores a major improvement that resulted not from revolutionary technology but from evolutionary changes brought through coordination between combat leaders and the scientists in operations research. As Currie points out, advanced technologists do not merely search for a perpetual motion machine or the ultimate weapon; they also make new applications practical for existing systems. They symbolize man's most important natural resource—brainpower.

Does innovation in a technical military system mean complexity? Not necessarily, but technology means division of labor—specialization. The goal for a combat force should be simplicity in the field. Therefore, specialists modularize a system and favor a "remove and replace" concept. But to be effective, this approach requires someone who knows *which* item to remove and replace. This attempt to reduce the technical level required in the field causes the military leader at the lowest level to fulfill an extra requirement. He must create an environment in which his technicians become skilled analysts. Social scientists and management consultants have given a great deal of attention to the campus atmosphere that stimulates invention and creativity. They have also shown how to improve the "by-rote" production line. But they have given inadequate attention to the in-between situation that limits innovation but requires skilled analysis. The operational commander may be constrained from an innovative use of his complex machines, but he must be innovative in his leadership techniques.

The operational squadron commander has well-developed managment information tools available. He is judged on statistical performance, and he is likely to deal with statistics—flying hours, AWOL rates (absent without leave), NORS rates (not operationally ready because of supplies), availability of personnel and equipment, man-hours expended in repair of each subsystem—the list seems endless. Each statistic has a well-defined desirable range and reasonably obvious corrective actions. The most difficult task for this leader is to deal with items that cannot be quantified; for example, how does he measure morale? In the squadron commander's view, good management is generally strict management.

At the opposite extreme, what is his viewpoint when he becomes a laboratory commander? The management information tools are probably even more prominent but less developed. The statistics now include number of technical reports, number of projects on or ahead of schedule, and how close he is to budget. Sound simple? Now his most difficult problem is to show why quantified items do not tell the complete story. A larger number of aircraft available for operations is normally desirable because the definitions and the quality control make the number easily comprehensible and meaningful. A larger number of technical reports is desirable only if the quality of all reports is good in some measurable way. In other words, the lab commander deals day to day with qualitative rather than quantitative measurements. This will force him into a more participative management style of leadership, even if he has not already decided that the need to produce an innovative environment dictates such a style.

Do these two commanders perform widely different jobs? Not really. Both lead by example, both enforce rules, and both rely on their subordinates to provide information for decision making. When the lab commander confronts an airman arrested in town for drunk driving, he probably handles the case just as strictly as his operational counterpart. When the operational commander directs a young lieutenant to prepare plans for the unit open house, he will not necessarily be any more restrictive of the young man's ideas than the lab commander. The two commanders fit their individual styles to the situation at hand, but technology has widened the spectrum of their leadership methods. The belief in American industry that a retired military commander makes a good manager rests on the knowledge that a colonel or general officer has been forced throughout his career to develop the flexibility and judgment to deal effectively with complex situations created by technological advance.

The discussion of leadership methods in operational and support functions oversimplifies the real situation at higher levels of management. For example, an operational wing commander deals with both functions. Although the conventional view of a bomb wing commander may place him in the category of an operational commander, he actually operates through a large staff of experienced assistants. Any student of military history quickly recognizes that a commander of an operating unit large enough to have a well-defined separate staff is likely to deal with more than simple operational problems. Dealing with such a staff requires somewhat unique leadership skills. The commander must encourage free thinking and honest advice, but he must be willing to replace unsatisfactory personnel on the staff. He must be willing to trust the staff so that he can rely on its judgment in processing or filtering information. He must be able to use his staff as a sounding board to test his ideas. He cannot afford anyone whom he does not trust; therefore, he must be willing to rearrange his people. But he must be open-minded enough that this implied threat does not inhibit his most trustworthy people.

One excellent example of leadership-staff failure in the face of advancing technology involves Hitler's firing of General Galland (Fighter Command) and Field Marshall Milch (Inspector General), two of his staff officers.[12] There were many controversies: the Me 262 fighter-bomber story is well known, but this example concerns the V-1 and the V-2 strategic weapons. Both weapons represented admirable technological advances. Both carried the same explosive payload to the same target. The V-2 rocket cost almost ten times as much as the V-1 aerodynamic vehicle in resources and man-hours. The decision to emphasize the V-2 over the V-1 was based on the total lack of defense that could be employed against the V-2. It was a pure terror weapon. If Hitler had encouraged a freethinking staff, Milch and Galland could have pointed out that such a weapon was actually a liability. The V-1 campaign not only forced diversion of Eighth Air Force bombers but also prevented significant numbers of fighters from escorting the undiverted bombers. If one assumes a V-1 penetration rate of only 10 percent (a rate lower than anticipated and achieved), the same resource/manhour investment in either the V-1 or the V-2 would cause equal explosive tonnage on target. But the V-1 would also divert large numbers of Allied fighters. Fortunately, this argument was never properly presented to Hitler because his leadership technique was not appropriate to the commander-staff situation.

Technology has produced other effects on everyone who works at managing, not only commanders. The growth in communications is a multifaceted blessing—and a curse. For many years, the telephone and the radio have provided knowledge of activities in remote locations. Television and the teleprinter enable people to avoid face-to-face meetings. Some meetings are not necessary, but others are. Does the leader have more impact on his personnel in person or over the closed circuit TV monitor?

Appropriateness and relevance are always major concerns in this era of communications glut. The "information explosion" can be all noise. Too often, the manager has so much information that he cannot find the facts. How often does he receive a computer-prepared bibliography only to find that it is a garbage dump? The manager should not cease to use such services, but he must use them with care. And he must remember that information is not necessarily correct merely because a computer prints it. Computers do not make mistakes, but the people who provide the input are quite capable of mistakes (the computer always does what it is told to do, and this may not be what the manager wants it to do.)

In World War II, the services could assume that most recruits understood driving and operating an automobile. Today we can almost make that assumption regarding television sets, electronics, computers, and a whole array of devices that enable people to use avionics with less pretraining. But this increase in technical knowledge does not simply make the recruit more adaptable; it makes him more questioning, and his questions challenge his leaders to manage better. No longer does the leader explain his unit goals only to higher headquarters and his immediate deputy. The entire force now wants to know management's goals and the reasons for them. The leader now operates in a fishbowl. The need for fair and impartial discipline has always been recognized; but discipline in the modern context must not only be fair and impartial—it must also be explainable. Commander's Call is not a propaganda device; it has become an information exchange. The relation of each task to the larger plan must now be communicated to the lowest worker.

As mentioned earlier, the military leader must train and inspire his successor, and he must show sincere concern for outstanding subordinates. The Air Service in World War I began an air force tradition in this area. Major Raoul Lufberry, formerly an ace with the Lafayette Escadrille, flew with the First Pursuit Group and trained Eddie Rickenbacker, Reed Chambers, Alan Winslow, and others. These younger pilots fondly remembered and carefully emulated Major Lufberry's practice of escorting them until they could fend for themselves.[13] His concern led to a firm U.S. policy in World War II of returning leading aces to the states to serve as instructors. The combat superiority of U.S. fighter forces in World War II, Korea, and Vietnam was not due solely to U.S. technology; the protégé system multiplied the effectiveness of the American aces.

Obviously, this concern for subordinates was not confined solely to aircrews. In the development of air power doctrine, people like General Curtis LeMay and General Hoyt Vandenberg were disciples of General "Hap" Arnold and General Carl Spaatz, who, in turn, were disciples of Billy Mitchell. When the air force became the manager of the nation's largest technological force during the 1950s and 1960s, military leaders extended this concern for development of subordinates to systems management, a blend of technology and leadership theory. The commanders of Air Force Systems Command—Generals Ferguson and Phillips—were products of General Schriever's attention to subordinate development. Although these military leaders benefited from the air force's protégé tradition, each was a distinct innovator, philosopher, and leader in his own right.

In the field of science, Edward Teller, associated with the Manhattan Project during World War II and more recently with the Lawrence Livermore Laboratory of the Energy Research and Development Administration, expressed this same concern for the development of his subordinates. John Foster and Harold Brown, major figures in the development of technology for defense, worked closely under Teller and absorbed his philosophy. Teller frequently stressed that he did not want narrow technologists. To be useful, the scientist must temper his much-needed technical specialization with an awareness and ability to *apply* his results.[14] Teller required his doctoral candidates to demonstrate an ability to apply their results practically. His prescription for a good scientist included at least three ingredients: (1) high-quality, possibly narrow, technical expertise characterized by an original dissertation on the forefront of the discipline, (2) the ability to communicate effectively as demonstrated in a successful defense of his dissertation, and (3) the ability to apply the results practically. These ingredients are quite descriptive of the traits needed in an effective military leader. It is not surprising that so many of Teller's protégés rose to management eminence in the Defense Department.

The leader trained in a technical specialty and skilled in the methods of translating this specialty into practice must be capable of adapting to change, devising new tactics, using new technology, and innovating when required. This description is as true for the squadron commander who becomes a major air commander as it is for the military laboratory director who advances in his specialty. At the general-officer level, the question cannot be whether a man's background is operational or support, because he must lead people from both backgrounds and speak the language of both functions. He must effectively use the modern management tools available to him, and he must be capable of using the planning-programming budgeting-system (PPBS) and its reports. He must thoroughly understand the activities of the SPOs (systems project offices). He must be able to use the technical advice of his staff in a manner that will enable him to translate the activities of our technology-intensive defense organizations into clear decisions and support by congressmen and taxpayers.

This picture of today's leader confirms the thesis that technology has not changed the qualities of leadership. But by expanding the situations confronting the military leader and multiplying the tools available to him, technology has made his job more critical, more challenging, and more far-reaching. Technology strengthens his need to vary his leadership approach to fit the conditions. It has increased the educational level of his subordinates, and it has increased their range of competence. The traditional requirement that the commander must train his successor has expanded to a requirement that he must broaden the outlook of all his best people and assure their understanding of the trends for the future. Above all, technology provides opportunities for a better understanding of leadership; as this understanding increases, the American people should be assured of a steady stream of competent leaders for their armed forces and their country.

Notes

1. General Earle G. Wheeler, Graduation Address to the Industrial College of the Armed Forces, Washington, D.C., June 11, 1963.

2. *Encyclopedia Americana*, 1974 ed., s.v. "Prize Courts and Prize Jurisdiction," by Oliver J. Lissitzyn.

3. *Encyclopedia Brittanica*, 1973 ed., s.v. "Canning, Commercial."

4. Peter Stone and Sherman Edwards, *1776, A Musical Play* (New York: Viking Press, 1970), p. 163. Authors indicate quotes in correspondence between John Adams and his wife.

5. Captain A. T. Mahan, *Naval Strategy* (Boston: Little, Brown, 1919), Chapter 6.

6. Winston S. Churchill, *The Second World War*, vol. 4, *The Hinge of Fate* (Boston: Houghton Mifflin, 1948), p. 521.

7. George Daniels, *English and American Watches* (London: Abelard-Schuman, 1967), p. 28.

8. William W. Haines, *Command Decision* (New York: Random House, 1948), Act 2, Prologue, Stage Direction.

9. Connecticut Aeronautical Historical Association, World War II Fighter Pilot Symposium, East Hartford, Conn., December 3, 1971.

10. Carroll R. Anderson, "Mission to Kavieng," *American Aviation Historical Society Journal* 10 (Summer 1965): 88.

11. Norman Polmar, "Thinking About Soviet ASW," *United States Naval Institute Proceedings* 102 (May 1976).

12. David Irving, *The Rise and Fall of the Luftwaffe* (Boston: Little, Brown 1974), pp. 219-221; and Adolf Galland, *The First and the Last* (New York: Henry Holt and Co., 1954), pp. 302-303.

13. Edward V. Rickenbacker, *Fighting the Flying Circus* (Englewood Cliffs, N.J.: Prentice-Hall, 1965), pp. 2-8.

14. Edward Teller, lectures to students and military research associates at Lawrence Radiation Laboratory, Livermore, Calif., 1965-1968.

16
Organization Challenge and Response by 1985

Frank R. Hunsicker

"The idea of organization persists even though the form of organization changes."[1] In an earlier chapter, Toomay, Hartke, and Elman described major challenges to traditional military leadership styles posed by advanced military technology. This chapter further develops an important area that those authors could only briefly mention. The very structure of military organization must be as adaptive as leadership techniques because of important organizational dynamics. A rapidly changing social, cultural, and economic environment determines the expressed purposes of military organizations because they depend on this environment for their resources. Thus, past trends in the external environment provide the foundation for future developments in military organizations. These trends and other environmental factors will force changes in military organizations through 1985 and beyond.

This chapter does not consider the objectives and purposes of military forces, nor does it attempt to predict technological changes in warfare. Instead, it focuses on the changing internal process, behavior, and structure of military organizations through 1985. As suggested in the opening quotation, the form of an organization can be expected to change; however, new organizational shapes and processes depend on a multitude of past, current, and future conditions. For one thing, resources are rationally allocated and directed through organizational processes to accomplish prescribed purposes. Since the nature and quantity of available resources change, one can logically expect a wide and diverse variety of organized actions to accomplish military objectives in the mid-1980s. Although the complete rational development of an organization depends on the situation existing at any given time, reasonable extrapolations can be based on present knowledge of organizational theory.

Officers who will command the forces through 1985 must prepare to cope with significant changes during the next few years. This chapter should provide some insights into the challenges they will face, and it may help them to identify personal goals that will improve their ability to meet those challenges.

Current Organizational Approach

The military services are classical examples of organizations that rely heavily on bureaucratic criteria of hierarchy, standardization, rules, and positional authority. They have been relatively successful applications of the bureaucratic model. This model is not pure, since the services have made some adaptations to overcome perceived weaknesses or to react to measured needs. Thus, the resulting military model is a practical example of adapting a classical bureaucratic model to current needs.

The staff concept is one of the modifications that enables military commanders to retain some measure of centralized control over resources,. Civilian organizations that have adapted the staff concept have often encountered conflicts because they do not possess other bureaucratic characteristics apparently needed to cope with line-staff conflicts. Military organizations usually have fewer line-staff conflicts than their corporate counterparts, partially because of a stronger personal commitment to the mission. This commitment is often a result of the linkage between profession and organization, which is usually not prevalent in civilian organizations. The authority inherent in higher-level military positions is also available to resolve these strains within military organizations.

Although the military services profess highly efficient bureaucratic methods of selection for promotion and job assignment, strong evidence indicates that the process is more personalized at higher ranks in the structure. General Eisenhower's selection to command the combined forces in Europe is a historic example and represents the norm rather than the exception. This deviation from the strict, bureaucratic model represents a realistic attempt to make the bureaucratic model flex to meet the needs of the services. The bureaucratic selection system provides large pools of well-qualified people when it selects the top 50 or 80 percent for promotion, but it is not as adept at choosing the best-qualified 5 percent for top management. To overcome this flaw, the services have developed an informal, personalized system in an attempt to supplement the bureaucratic system.

Because of the growing concern for personal needs and rights, the services have made realistic attempts to humanize the impersonal bureaucratic assignment process. Ten years ago, all negotiation for assignments was informal, and direct intervention with the personnel process was discouraged. In recent years, the system has encouraged contact about the career and personal needs of the individual in the assignment process. This is one more attempt to adapt the military bureaucratic model to current situations.

The most significant attempt to cope with large, complex bureaucratic organizations has been the application of the systems approach. As a method of viewing a whole organization rather than separate parts, the systems approach has been pioneered in military activities and has been successfully adapted by industry and government. It has been used to manage specific programs on both a micro and a macro basis.

The project organization used under the systems concept is one example that contradicts some of the premises of classical organizational structure by establishing temporary organizations. Furthermore, the project organization brought a new perspective to the division of labor by focusing an organization on a single objective rather than on functional outputs; this concept encouraged allocation of resources for producing an attack submarine instead of focusing on suboptimal goals, such as developing a revised standard for armor plates.[2] Systems management has been used to integrate diverse functions and stages of weapon system development, focusing on the single goal of researching, developing, and deploying a weapon system. Thus, the system evolves to meet specific needs without destroying the underlying bureaucratic structure of the total service.

The services also applied the full force of systems thinking, in a macro sense, to functional areas of personnel, finance, supply, and maintenance. Through computers and communications, total functional systems now cross organizational hierarchies with ease. In aircraft engine management systems, one of the oldest and best examples, the application of systems thinking reduced spare-engine inventories by 75 percent. Systems for financial management, as well as supply systems, are now designed to cross service structures. A centralized activity rather than a local supply officer may establish and control inventory levels for mission performance. Centralized bureaucratic rules and standards are incorporated in the computer program, and local supervisors have little discretion in inventory management. Cost savings have resulted in most of these areas.

The declining power of local commanders and supervisors has been one negative result of the systems approach. Deferring decisions to higher echelons has created a new kind of "computerocracy," in which local management is constrained by the computer's inability to incorporate nonprogrammed inputs. This challenge of the future recurs throughout this discussion.

The growth of these giant systems has fostered, and has been supported by, a parallel growth of highly trained specialists whose allegiance is affected by two objectives—one established by their local command and the other by their functional area. For example, supply, maintenance, and club officers are often responsible to both the local commander and their specialist counterparts at higher echelons. The logistics command may set one criterion for using pre-positioned spare parts, and the local commander may feel that another criterion best serves the needs of his unit. The specialist often experiences conflict between two bosses, which violates fundamental management principles. To date, these conflicts apparently have been resolved to the benefit of the total organization; however, as systems become more sophisticated and specialized, the local commander's authority may erode further and bring increased conflict.

The services have been relatively successful in managing large, complex organizations by judiciously applying the bureaucratic model while they attempt to meet human and military needs. The computer has played a major role in this accomplishment. Still, one can visualize military leaders who prefer the bureaucratic organizational approach and incrementally modify the model when it does not perform effectively.

Even with its basic flaws and problems, the model has rarely failed, and there is no real underlying desire on the part of participants, political executives, or legislative bodies to introduce radical changes in this organizational philosophy. Therefore, future changes will be reactions to situations that occur between now and 1985 rather than planned attempts to modify the approach to organizing resources.

Trends That Challenge Future Military Organization

Many trends will affect military organization in the 1980s. Several have been selected here because they pose major challenges to structure, process, and behavior. The roots of the trends are deep; thus, it will be almost impossible to reverse them. Future military leaders will have to cope with these large forces and attempt to alter outcomes.

A continuing conflict and an almost "unholy alliance" between two basic principles of organization will continue with a vengeance into the 1980s. The first principle is centralization of control and direction, a major concern in military organizations because it is an effective way to manage the forces. The advantages and disadvantages of this principle are well documented. The conflict in Southeast Asia presented many examples of tactical and strategic management and control from command centers in Washington, while the decentralized command structure for the Pacific Theatre had little discretion in the decision-making process. Furthermore, the National Military Command Center, a basic concept for control of crises and of nuclear forces, will be strengthened, not weakened, in the future. The proliferation of nuclear powers, increased communication capability, and political imperatives almost dictate central control.

Centralization is not only practiced in the control of operational forces; it has also grown rapidly in support areas. These concepts are rapidly expanding in such areas as logistics and personnel. Logistics centers at the DOD level were only minor considerations ten years ago, but they are now major suppliers for all services. Centralized personnel and pay centers have acquired control and direction of personnel actions formerly decentralized to lower echelons.

Decisions on operational control and command of the forces flow through one structure, but decisions on functional support flow through an alternative structure. A local command often faces the dilemma of responding to the decisions and standards of two systems of authority. Functional areas, such as logistics and personnel, may provide standards and guidance that conflict with the goals and guidance provided by operating commands.

Centralized management of the two basic resource flows of men and matériel is more feasible today because of significant technological improvements in computerization and communication techniques. Some sources suggest that the information revolution has ended and that future changes will be minor, but this may be a false conclusion. The changes brought by the technological explosion of the 1960s have not been completely assimilated, and they may not reach fruition until the 1970s. For example, automated hospitals, already delayed several times, will not appear for several years. As the strengths and weaknesses of advanced systems become apparent, concepts of management may further modify traditional systems. Why cannot pay and personnel systems be combined? Why cannot personnel staffing and training be combined in one structure? Why do we measure manpower standards in one structure and fill the vacancies through another? Computer systems might be geographically centralized, and operating levels would need only remote terminals. Technical feasibility is no longer a barrier to the changes, but behavioral barriers may remain.

The second basic principle of organization—division of labor—often works at counterpoint to centralization, but it has recently joined centralized control in a strange alliance. The traditional military officer was characterized as a generalist, but this stereotype has changed rapidly since World War II. The need for a broad range of specialists is widespread in modern military forces. For example, approximately 75 percent of the colonel positions in the air force support nonoperational functions.[3] This does not mean that top-level military managers are non-operational specialists; instead, aggressive personnel programs have forced operational specialists to gain experience in other specialized fields and thus broaden their ability to manage. The operational specialist has promotional advantages only if he broadens himself through additional specialization. Some specialists in the air force have expanding opportunities for promotion to brigadier general, since approximately 10 to 20 percent of current brigadier selections are not pilot specialists. Furthermore, women entering the forces are not now considered for major combat roles, but they will assume roles as specialists and may rightfully demand roles at higher levels in the organizational process.

Division of labor began as a simpler way to do things, and it resulted in higher efficiency. In *Wealth of Nations*, Adam Smith cited the tremendous efficiency of division of labor in a pin factory. Today and in the future, specialization is more a function of the knowledge explosion than of simple concerns for efficiency. One person does not have the mental capability to deal with all the situations or variables affecting decisions. Legal, financial, and engineering specialists have been joined by maintenance, security, and logistics specialists. The educational process has fostered the concept of division of labor. Twenty years ago, a college graduate in business administration was just that, a business major; today, he has at least four or five specializations from which to choose.

The division of labor has encouraged the development of career ladders for specialists, but these ladders can exist only in a formal organizational structure that requires higher-ranking specialists. Specialists, therefore, may advocate centralized functional control as a means of enhancing their specialization. This drive for independence is possibly a contributing factor in the development of centralized structures for logistics, security, maintenance, and personnel.

A first impression may suggest that principles of centralization and division of labor work together. This is the "unholy alliance" mentioned earlier. It involves a lateral shift of authority through division of labor into specialized areas, while, at higher echelons, commanders straddle vertically parallel structures in a number of specialized areas, such as logistics, personnel, and operations, in an attempt to centralize authority and power. Thus, the conditions are right for a conflict of objectives and, more important, of the means to accomplish objectives.

This continuing development gives rise to two weaknesses. It creates the possibility of function-to-function conflict throughout an organization. Operations and maintenance people may spend unnecessary time in attempts to assign blame for a problem rather than to resolve it. Functional representatives are responsible to two masters—their commander and the functional hierarchy. Furthermore, commanders at lower levels in the mission organization have very limited authority over their functional representatives, since centralized control of personnel, money, and matériel reduces their command flexibility. One observer suggests that local commanders may spend 90 percent of their time dealing with the 10 percent of resources that they have authority to manage. One can easily understand why they might become more concerned with superfluous matters instead of the mission. A basic flaw in the arrangement is that lower-echelon commanders bear heavy responsibility for basic mission accomplishment without adequate authority over the functions assigned to them. Coping with the continued movement toward centralization and division of labor will be a major organizational challenge to leaders of the future.

The changing character of the enlisted force may present another significant challenge. The population eighteen to twenty-five years old, now more than 90 percent of the forces, will decline as a proportion of the labor force after 1980. Competition for the services of young men and women will be intense; therefore, incentive programs to draw and retain qualified individuals will require reevaluation. The current escalation of manpower costs to approximately 60 percent of the defense dollar will probably not be reversed in the 1980s unless there is drastic reduction in force levels or reinstitution of the draft. Alternative courses of action may be necessary to extend the service pattern beyond twenty to twenty-five years and offer variable benefit programs to increase incentive values.

Extension of service careers may be practical, but it will foster changes in the present rank status system to compensate for lower promotion opportunity. Status in rank is a tradition that might be modified to retain qualified people. Variable benefit programs represent attempts to increase the value of reward systems without increased cost. Life insurance has little value for eighteen-year-olds, but it has more and more value as they grow older. As people's basic expectations change, benefit and reward programs should also change.

Egalitarianism, a new expectation, suggests an equal right to rewards, income, and benefits, regardless of work input. This is a rapid extension of the thinking and actions of American society with long-term implications. The pay gap between enlisted men and officers has been closing for years, and the special benefits accruing to senior officers have eroded significantly in recent years. Today, newspapers list and criticize the aide positions assigned to specific officers.[4] In other words, rights of rank are slowly disappearing. Future egalitarian demands could result in additional costs and changes in service traditions. Day-care centers, housing based on family size, and elimination of separate clubs are possible directions of change resulting from egalitarian movements. Although these changes may increase the satisfaction of some service members, they probably will cause dissatisfaction among members who lose the rights and privileges.

Developing new skills required to lead the force will be another significant challenge. Currently, many people suggest that there is a leadership crisis, one they attribute to the increasing complexity and inclusiveness of organizations that sap the power of leaders.[5] However this changing pattern of authority has affected leaders for years. In 1959 Morris Janowitz described the crisis as a shift from discipline by domination to discipline by manipulation.[6] His conclusion may not be as appropriate for 1985, but it illustrates the dynamics of the situation. His "fraternal authority" may be replaced by a more complex kind of "earned authority."

William G. Scott provided one of the best characterizations of future dilemmas facing organizations when he suggested that the value structure of organizations may be moving along three continua: growth to stability/decay; abundance to scarcity; and consensus to conflict.[7] How applicable is the model to military organizations? Which positions do the organizations occupy on the continua? There has been little growth in military forces or hardware in recent years, and the changes in firepower are debatable. The navy emphasizes the decline of ships in service to pre-World War II levels. Current budget conflicts and a lack of earlier popular support suggest stability or decay instead of real growth as a more likely future possibility.

A closely related issue is that of abundance or scarcity. Fewer natural and human resources are likely to be available in the future for national defense; therefore, the organization needs to cope with scarcity, in a real sense, as a major constraint on decision making.

Finally, consensus is giving way to conflict. The traditional consensus of support in organizations based on faith in institutions has been a corner-stone of military authority systems, but declining faith in all institutions, including the military, will result in relatively higher levels of organiza-tional conflict. Working with consensus is much less demanding than working with conflict. Organizations of the future will deal more frequently with conflict, and the tools used for resolving conflict are different from the tools used for managing consensus. One should remember that most methods of resolving conflict seldom completely satisfy all the participants.

The future military leader may well face a major challenge of meeting mission requirements with a relatively stable or decaying organization hampered by a growing scarcity of resources and internal conflict. These trends may seem pessimistic because they portray conditions different from current conditions. Although the pessimism may be overstated, the truth lies somewhere on the pessimistic side of the continua. The conditions cited are challenges, not barriers, to effective organization in the 1980s. Similar scenarios developed in the 1960s to predict contemporary conditions probably seemed pessimistic at the time. Current challenges will result in future organization changes, and, quite likely, a modified systems approach will become the major instrument for coping with the changes.

Military Organizations of 1985

Past structures are major determinants of future organizations, and these structures are usually subject to only incremental changes. Fifty to 60 percent of the tanks, ships, and planes that will be used in 1986 are currently in service. Although changes will occur in organizational behavior, structure, and processes, the bureaucratic model should still be recognizable.

Theorists have suggested the collapse of bureaucracy in the 1960s, the 1970s, and the 1980s.[8] But there will be no collapse. In reality, organizational thinking is shifting from the classical approach with fixed principles to the contingency design, a shift that does not deny the underlying bureaucratic model. Classical organizations will not disappear because of the inherent advantages of standardized procedures and structures. Furthermore, incumbent and future military leadership is, and probably will be, more comfortable with the classical approach; thus, efforts to satisfy people will make only incremental changes. The contingency approach to organization is the current fad, but, at best, it will only aid evolutionary changes in organization.[9]

Robert J. Mockler has suggested that traditional patterns cannot resolve current or future problems; therefore, the contingency approach will develop as an alternative. The common thread that unifies practical and theoretical management is the contingency-situational approach, which suggests that organizational process and structure should be the rational resource that is altered, depending on the situation.[10] History fairly well supports the contention that the bureaucratic model best suits military situations; therefore, one can reasonably expect some incremental changes in the military-bureaucratic model through 1985.

Organizational Structure

Simulated decentralization will probably predominate through 1985. This form of decentralization treats a subunit as a separate entity with accounting costs and budgets focused on the organizational entity and computers assisting in the effort.[11] It may be a diluted form of decentralization because an overlay of powerful functional systems of personnel, logistics, and operations support provides little real authority to decentralized entities. These simulated decentralizations may be a result of the aforementioned unholy alliance between the principles of centralization and division of labor. In this future scenario, the unit commander has cost center responsibility with extremely limited decision-making authority regarding resources; higher levels make decisions on the allocation of resources and direction of activity, and local commanders act as monitors.

This synthetic decentralization could seriously limit the experience and training of future top military commanders. High-level commanders might assume major positions of authority without practical decision-making experience at lower ranks and levels. This dangerous trade-off should be seriously analyzed, since there are few substitutes for progressively higher levels of practical decision-making experience.

To avoid this form of decentralization, a conscious effort would be necessary to shift emphasis toward real decentralization of authority and responsibility. The same tools, computers, and communications that facilitate centralization of controls could improve decentralized decision making. The challenge is to find ways to encourage genuine decentralization.

Leadership

New techniques might be developed to recapture the power necessary for effective leadership. Collective leadership, such as an office of the commander, is one technique that could apply group effort to replace one-man leadership.[12] Various forms of chief executive offices have been developed in the corporate sector to deal with large, complex organizations. An individual would still be designated as commander, but he would depend on a small, loyal staff of generalists-specialists to manage the information necessary for effective leadership; this, in effect, would institutionalize the office of commander. At top levels, the office of commander might resolve conflicts and bargain with the centers of specialist power, such as operations, logistics, and personnel. At lower levels involved in simulated decentralization, the office might gather and analyze information for the commander and thus gain power by controlling communications. The office will earn power primarily through bargaining with subordinates, superiors, and lateral activities; the politics of organizations, in a positive sense, would finally be recognized as the actual way of life.

Human Relations

The satisfaction of personal needs will become a major challenge in the 1980s. Management will extensively use attitude surveys and organizational analysis to determine the health of organizations. New indicators will supplement the court martial, Article 15, and AWOL statistics, and "people" programs might become rights instead of privileges. The commander's efficiency reports may include data on the health of his organization, and "people" management will be the key to promotion. This should not mean that only "nice guys" will succeed as managers; ample research indicates that successful management of human resources depends on a practical understanding of actions, people, tasks, and situations.[13]

Skills

What kind of program for developing personal skills will prepare leaders to meet the challenges of 1985? Future personal development programs should consider six significant areas in any effort to improve management skills.

First, there will be a continuing need to develop basic communication skills. People with the ability to listen, talk, and write effectively will be required more than ever. Growing interdependence accentuates the need for this skill, although little effort is now being made to improve it.[14]

Second, human relations skills should be further developed. Leaders must have the ability to evaluate the quality of human relations in organizations, and they should also take every opportunity to improve their understanding of, and empathy for, their people. Furthermore, they must develop practical skills in designing jobs, in considering the man and the task, and in applying techniques that will improve human relations and job satisfaction.

Third, managerial skills must be improved. Leaders of the future should improve their understanding and ability to use the decision-making process.[15] They must understand, evaluate, and use behavioral processes. Another managerial skill deserving special attention is the design of organizations. Rapid environmental changes may force changes in formal structures. Leaders should sharpen their skills to identify objectives and define the structure that will permit the most effective use of people and processes.

Fourth, technical and administrative competencies must be updated. Leaders at higher levels may be required to rely more on their competence in order to fulfill their roles as leaders.

Fifth, leadership skills must be updated. Leaders in the 1980s must improve their understanding and ability to use power relationships. Traditional power relationships based on coercion, reward, and position have been eroded and should be used discreetly; thus, expert and earned power will increase in significance through 1985. Expert power refers to the competence mentioned earlier, and earned power refers to the leader's ability to bargain implicitly and explicitly with leaders, subordinates, and coworkers and thereby develop a relationship of mutual trust and respect.

Sixth, leaders must develop basic judgmental skills. Textbooks and classrooms are tools for presenting concepts, but experience usually improves judgmental skills. Experiential learning through the use of computerized and noncomputerized simulations might be one method of compressing practical experience. Although the rapidly changing environment presents fewer opportunities for on-the-job experience, repeated use of intense simulations shows promise of compressing this vital learning. Economies of scale, available to the services, provide excellent opportunities to pursue this learning option. Decision practice simulations could be loaded on a central computer to serve participants all over the world. Schools of business are successfully using this concept on a limited basis, with annual competitions between schools to sharpen the decision-making skills of their students. The services might incorporate the concept into professional development programming.

The challenges through 1985 are not insurmountable. Although the scenario presented in this discussion does not show a future environment materially different from the contemporary environment, one should not construe this as justification for complacency. A recent study prepared by the Library of Congress suggests that both quantitative and qualitative factors determine military balance. Qualitative factors include leadership, motivation, organization, command and control, and several others.[16] The quantitative balance may favor several potential enemies of the United States in 1985; therefore, a concentrated effort must be made to insure that U.S. military leaders possess superior qualities.

Notes

1. William G. Scott and Terrence R. Mitchell, *Organization Theory* (Homewood, Ill.: Richard D. Irwin, 1976).

2. David I. Cleland, "Understanding Project Authority," *Business Horizons* 10, no. 1 (Spring 1967):63-70.

3. Several sources were used for this paragraph, but the major source was "Making It in the Air Force: Officers' Perceptions of Career Progression" (Paper presented by Lieutenant Colonel Franklin D. Margiotta at the 1975 annual meeting of the Inter-University Seminar on Armed Forces and Society, Chicago, Ill., October 1, 1975.)

4. "Which Generals Have How Many Aides, and Where?" *Air Force Times* 36, no. 47 (June 21, 1975):401.

5. Warren Bennis, *The Unconscious Conspiracy* (New York: AMACOM, 1976), p. 158.

6. Morris Janowitz, "Changing Patterns of Organizational Authority," *Administrative Science Quarterly* 3, no. 4 (March 3, 1957):473-93.

7. William G. Scott, "Organization Theory; A Reassessment," *Academy of Management Journal* 17, no. 2 (June 1974):242-253.

8. Alvin Toffler, *Future Shock* (New York: Bantam Books, 1970), pp. 124-126.

9. Keith Davis, "Trends in Organizational Design," *Proceedings of Academy of Management*, August 1973, pp. 1-6.

10. Robert J. Mockler, "Situational Theory of Management," *Harvard Business Review* 49, no. 3 (May-June 1971):146.

11. Peter F. Drucker, "New Templates for Today's Organizations," *Harvard Business Review* 52, no. 1 (January-February 1974):45-53.

12. Bennis, *The Unconscious Conspiracy*, p. 159.

13. Victor H. Vroom and Phillip W. Yetton, *Leadership and Decision Making* (Pittsburgh: University of Pittsburgh Press, 1973), pp. 1-32.

14. Frank R. Hunsicker, "Some Needs of the Whole Manager, Some Suggestions for Curriculum Improvement," *Academy of Management Proceedings*, August 1975, p.33.

15. Victor H. Vroom, "Can Leaders Learn to Lead?," *Organizational Dynamics* 4, no. 3 (June 1976):17-25.

16. As quoted in Air Force Policy Letter for Commanders, dated May 1, 1976. AFRP 190-1, 9-76.

17

The Military as a Bureaucracy: The Super Activity Trap

George S. Odiorne

The year 1976 was the bicentennial of a book as well as of a nation. In 1776, Adam Smith wrote his *Inquiry into the Nature and Causes of the Wealth of Nations*, which became the handbook and theoretical guide to an industrial society. For a long time, Smith's work was viewed as the "handbook of capitalism," but in many ways, it was more because it described the basis for industrialization, particularly the development of the bureaucratic organization that made so much of the industrial society possible. The description of the division of labor in the opening chapter of *The Wealth of Nations* is one of the major underpinnings of current organizational theory.

Division of Labor

Smith stated that "the greatest improvement in the productive powers of labor, and the greatest art of the skill, dexterity and judgment which is anywhere directed or applied seems to have been the effects of the division of labor."[1] Although his most frequently cited example was the pin factory where the division of labor could enhance productivity by a thousandfold, he was explicit in suggesting that the division of labor would have its effect in the general business of society, not just in manufacturing. "In every art," he suggested, "there is a proportionable increase in the productive powers of labor which can be attributed to the division of labor." Not only does it improve skill and dexterity; it also saves time and makes possible the application of machines and technology. Furthermore, it does not limit such gains to physical things but even includes machine makers and philosophers.[2]

Division of labor creates a host of highly desired effects and some unintended effects. The desired effect is that it substantially increases the yield from the same amount of resources. Efficiency and effectiveness are the aims and, indeed, demonstrable results. The new specialization of people, the ease of training new entrants into the organization, the possibility of reasonable personnel replacements, and uniformity of quality and quantity of output are demonstrable results of the division of labor.

This form of organization has been identified as a bureaucracy. In its simplest form, a bureaucracy is a group of people working together; one of them holds authority, and the others occupy subordinate positions. Each person handles a different and specialized segment of the divided labor of the group.

The Nature of Bureaucracy

Bureaucracy calls for persons to do different work within the same organizational group. This demands both specialized training and widespread ignorance on the part of each job incumbent; that is, in-depth knowledge of his own work and in-depth ignorance of what most of the other people do. To make the system work, the superior must have *authority*, the power to remove or to issue sanctions on the people below him in rank. The system tends toward authoritarianism and autocratic methods of management, however deftly they may be disguised.

There is a pressure in the bureaucracy to select persons with similar modes of communication, and this tends to make bureaucracies, among other things, ethnocentric. The nature of communication seems to imply behavior that produces an exchange of meaning. Thus, except at the very lowest levels of the organization, life becomes hospitable only to persons with similar social and cultural modes of behaving. This is not necessarily conscious snobbism nor racism in purpose, but it has that effect in practice.

The bureaucracy produces leaders whose most heartfelt assumptions resemble the assumptions of Douglas McGregor's Theory X.[3] Such leaders assume that the average subordinate must be treated as though he dislikes work, avoids it when he can, and, at heart, is probably lazy and, perhaps, a bit dishonest. Thus, he must be directed, coerced, intimidated, or controlled if the organization expects to achieve its purposes. These assumptions, in turn, comprise a self-fulfilling prophecy, and the people behave according to the expectations that the organization holds for them.

Control through system, supervision, and training produces instrumental persons whose major qualities and attributes are contained within their occupations. Such persons disappear into their job descriptions each day and, even in their personal lives, become instrumental. Their recreation and life-style adapt to the bureaucratic mode. As the division of labor piles up on itself, the numerous bureaucratic levels increase the significance of the organization and create occupational phobias in trivial work.

Some Questionable Side Effects

The promised efficiency of bureaucracy has indeed been realized. It has permeated American society, including the military. Even in 1977, much of the military culture reflects times when conflict was tribal, when the individual soldier or officer owned his own weapon, and when the army was a means for the landed aristocracy to maintain its political position against possible peasant rebellions. Today, however, the military is mainly bureaucratic.

The bureaucratization has had the same unintended side effects in the military as in other bureaucracies, including corporations, universities, and government bureaus. The following four major effects have apparently intensified in recent years.

1. *Angry clients.* They are angry against the powerlessness they feel and the depersonalized character with which they are treated in their contacts with bureaucratic organizations. It has become politically profitable to kick the military.

2. *Apathy.* Among its members, including the middle ranks, listlessness, demoralization, and indifference, the shrugging of the organization's shoulders to its purposes and its results, the attitude of "go away, you do your thing and I'll do mine," and the "I don't give a damn" attitude are apparently natural products of bureaucratic organizations. This apathy is often reflected in the organization's contacts with its clientele, and this angers the clients even more. In a business, this means bored clerks producing furious customers, and so on; in the military, it riles civilians and angers lower-ranking people seeking help, information, or action.

3. *Alienation.* The turning away from the organization and its goals, the shirking of responsibility, the avoidance of concern over the consequences of failure to do one's job, and a general retreat from the entire culture—all these can be bureaucratic effects.

A counterculture is often a product of some or all of the three major side effects of the bureaucratic form, particularly among the young, the educated, the successful, and children of the middle class. Communes, drugs, and long hair are natural evidences of the counterculture. This is a paradox. Society organizes for efficiency and, in the process, dehumanizes and depersonalizes organizations; this in turn produces counterforces that diminish efficiency.

4. *The absurd*, as an underlying condition of life, becomes normal in a bureaucracy. *Catch 22* is a preeminent model of a believable overstatement of the military bureaucracy in one moment of time. For Yossarian, starting out in a rubber raft paddling for Sweden from an island in the Mediterranean seemed not only logical but also the only sensible alternative in the light of events described in the book. For most people, however, a sense of

humor, a keen skill for the devious, or a vast apathy will suffice. Only a few actually make concrete moves in rebellion, and the moves usually take the form of malicious obedience.

Changes in the Language and Operation of Bureaucracy

Today, the traditional language of bureaucracies has been supplanted by a new language based on the systems approach and goal displacement.

1. The systems approach, with its simple and completely plausible explanation of everything, joins Hegel's dialectic and other ultimate explanations with numerous applications.

2. It takes disparate parts and their relationships and views them as an integrated whole.

3. It requires three elements: input, activity, and output, with some feedback to tie the first to the third.

4. It is organismic rather than mechanistic in logical presumption, which is suitable for clarifying that which has already been clarified.

Of the numerous kinds of "systems" that could fall within the general systems theory, the cybernetic or feedback system is usually identified as the most typical. The economics of the organization is one application of this type of system. Figure 1 depicts the elements of a cybernetic system.[4]

Inputs are the resources committed to an idea to make it a tangible, going concern. They include capital (fixed, working, cash, receivables, inventories), labor, and materials. *Activities* are the designing, making, selling, keeping books, engineering, bargaining, and other things that *add value*, presumably, to the inputs. *Outputs* are the goods and services, hardware, and software that come out of the system. These outputs are

Figure 1. Schematic of a Cybernetic System:

The Most Commonly Used of the Systems Approaches

Feedback

INPUTS	ACTIVITY	OUTPUT
		Value Added
Resources	Work	Goals
Factors of Production	Procedures	Objectives
Capital	Efforts	Results
Labor	Means	Ends
Materials		

more valuable than all of the inputs used in their making; thus, a *value added* can be computed.

The *value added* is the profit, the need that is filled, the *purpose for committing the input*, and *the activity carried out*. There are two customary methods of disposing of this surplus value: input back into the system or distribution to beneficiaries of the system as dividends, learning, satisfactions, benefits, needs met, and the like. Although this mini-course in the systems approach is somewhat instructive as a map, it is also a diagram of traps for managers and other people who are part of the system.

The easy trap for one involved in a system is to become emotionally overattached to one element of what must be a three-element system.

1. Some people become obsessed with *input* and spend their time in preventing expenditures (for example, the man who disapproves your expense account).

2. Others become *output* fanatics and bearishly resist considering whether the inputs and resources are adequate or whether the activities are possible (the desk pounder and the "I demand results not alibis" type).

3. Far more prevalent, however, is the *activity*-obsessed person. He is competent, professional, often dedicated, but he has lost sight of the inputs used up or even the results sought.

Thus, in system terms, management is a system that begins by defining outputs and then applies these output statements as criteria to judge the quality of activity (behavior) and to govern the release and effectiveness of the inputs.[5]

Even the most noble, exciting, and important objective is forgotten as people engage in the activity initiated to achieve the objective. What begins as a momentary lapse become a habit, then a procedure, and, finally, a religion. Meanwhile, this activity consumes inputs related only to activity and not to output.

The consequences, however, are not limited to material input losses, which are real; they also affect human beings. The organization that locks fanatically into the input-activity loop produces a new dimension of bureaucrat. The superior is often hostile, exacting, judgmental, and primitive; the subordinates become professionally irresponsible. He becomes so enamored of his profession that he resists the very idea of making commitments to output of either a tangible or an intangible character. "Give me resources continually, but don't ask me to commit in return to a specific output."

The only recourse of the providers of inputs is to reduce or eliminate inputs and observe the losses that might occur. This is almost certainly a painful way to learn, but it is a prevalent approach, in part, because mature persons are sometimes unwilling to behave in a responsible and committed fashion. Bosses fail to define their goals, to provide help in achieving them, to leave people alone while they work, to inform them of their progress through self-control systems, and to regard them according to their accomplishments.

Strategic Effects of the Activity Trap

The military organization today is composed mainly of people who are not engaged in primary combat operational units or occupations. Approximately 15 percent of the army are foot soldiers, tankers, or members of other combat occupations, and a lower percentage of airmen are engaged in flying or other combat operations. Most persons in the military are mechanics, systems people, computer programmers, and other noncombatants. If the people counted as involved with the military included Department of Defense civilians and the employees of mainly military contractors, the ratio of combat to noncombat personnel would shrink even further. This condition is perfectly understandable in the sense that the miltary is a highly technological business, but it allows the phenomenon of the activity trap to become even more pervasive and, perhaps, deadly.

The Activity Trap raises the costs of the simplest operation by complicating it, and it makes the complicator more respected and revered than the simplifier. The Naval Air Rework Facility, a marvel of sophistication, has one defect—it cannot take in an airplane, repair it, and return it to its squadron or carrier on time to save its soul. When this happens, the answer is to add more systems people to improve upon the defective systems that previously caused the backlog.

Furthermore, this approach raises military spending to multibillion dollar levels that have an inflationary impact on the economy. Inflation then becomes the basis for justifying ever-increasing expenditures. This inflationary cycle of deficit spending and government expenditure feeds on itself.

The growth of sophisticated systems approaches requires more highly educated and sophisticated people to man them. Such people have immense capacities to resist traditional military discipline. In time, it becomes impossible for the command structure to command its own organization by the methods that it knows best.

Towns, cities, states, and even regions become wholly dependent on the flow of military funds into their economies. They know the risks and addictive effects of seeking more funds, but they resort endlessly to such tactics as protecting unnecessary military bases, make-work projects funded through defense budgets, and similar quasi-welfare programs. Similarly, many industrial concerns build their organizations around defense contracts and then, to preserve their identity and existence, resort to political and other methods that make little or no contribution to military goals. As a result, the Activity Trap becomes tightly bound in place by money.

These well-known and familiar tactics produce a sense of inevitability and powerlessness among command officials and civilian leaders, who learn to narcotize themselves against the situation. Old-fashioned military autocracies and commands continue their activities in areas that are unimportant, and they are totally impotent to deal with important strategic questions.

Although the Activity Trap apparently weakens military effectiveness and fails to achieve missions, it has an equally dangerous side effect on people: they *shrink* personally and professionally. Almost any superior and one of his subordinates can serve as an example of the shrinking process. One can ask the employee to write down the specific work objectives expected by his boss during the next quarter. One can also ask the boss: "What results would you like to see that man produce next quarter?" The average manager and subordinate will not agree on work objectives, but they will be reasonably close on activities to be conducted. Essentially, the differences in answer will cause the subordinate to shrink in his potential. Research shows that on regular, ongoing responsibilities, the average boss and subordinate caught in the Activity Trap will fail to agree on expected outputs at a level of 25 percent. If they fail to agree on regular responsibilities, they will disagree at a level of 50 percent on the subordinate's major problems. The worst gap is the failure of boss and subordinate to agree on methods of improving the subordinate's job. On this count, they will fail to agree at a level of 90 percent.[6]

As a result, nothing really changes in the way things are done. The environment changes, expectations change, and employee values change. But methods remain static, and outdated employee activities cripple the organization.

The organization drains its people of their zap, and it becomes an employer of pygmies. The pygmies resemble real people, wear neckties and uniforms, drive cars, and pay taxes, but they are performance midgets. They nod their heads when the boss chastises them, but they know that they have been cheated. They are stabbed daily as unwitting antagonists in duels. Trees fall on them, and *then* somebody yells "timber." And what is their defensive recourse? They keep *active!*

They redouble their energy when they have lost sight of their goals. They may be chastised or even fired for doing something "wrong" when they do not know what is "right" in the first place. They run a race without knowing the length of the track. They wonder if it is time to sprint for the wire, but they cannot guess when to sprint because the race may be a 100-yard dash or the Boston Marathon.

The effect is cumulative. Since the employees do not know the ordinary objectives of their jobs, they are hit for failures that result from not knowing the requirements for success. The prospect of failure produces a reluctance to discover problems, for the problems may be attributed to their shortcomings. Suggesting something new in such an environment is risky; continuing the old activity insures survival. In other words, appearing busy is safer than being productive. This tendency toward activity is not inevitable if top people try to circumvent it. The law of gravity is always with us, but some people build bridges.

The Antidotes for a Military Activity Trap

Two different movements could possibly overcome the worst effects of the lamentable Activity Trap. Legislative supervision and the scrutiny of public interest groups independent of the military for funding support have become increasingly popular pressures. These groups include the press and other media that consider the military beyond popular control. The results of this movement are self-evident.

On the other hand, the military has proved in the past that it is capable of self-reform. The following examples show how a new thrust in the administration of the military could possibly overcome Activity Trap management styles:

1. more demanding attention by top management to missions, purposes, and strategies and their use in evaluating subordinate missions and strategies
2. a major shift in emphasis from *adding* resources to *movement* of resources from goals of less contribution to goals of higher contribution
3. focus of inspectors general on audits against objectives rather than audits against some of the more traditional inspection modes
4. major efforts to obtain commitments to objectives at all levels of organization, with accountability of responsible people to explicit commitments

Any further attempt to define the nature of self-reform in the military must come from within the military, but the idea of self-reform is important. Obviously, there are people who serve that function now, all too often to their own peril. Increased emphasis on self-reform of military management is not inevitable. It is always possible that reform could begin outside the military establishment, and such reform could have many unfortunate effects on the organization and the nation.

Notes

1. Adam Smith, *An Inquiry Into the Nature and Causes of the Wealth of Nations* (Chicago: University of Chicago Press, 1977).

2. Ibid.

3. Douglas McGregor, *The Human Side of Enterprise* (New York: McGraw-Hill, 1960).

4. Norbert Weiner, *The Human Use of Human Beings: Cybernetics and Society*, 2d ed. rev. (Garden City, N.Y.: Doubleday, 1954).

5. George S. Odiorne, *Management and the Activity Trap* (New York: Harper and Row, 1974).

6. Ibid.

Part 5

Developments at the Academies

18
Modernization and Growth at the Service Academies: Some Organizational Consequences

John P. Lovell

The admission of women is only the most recent and highly publicized in a series of important changes at the U.S. service academies. Despite their strong commitment to tradition, each of the academies has undergone a profound metamorphosis since World War II. By the 1970s, they could boast of achieving what academy officials on various occasions have viewed as a "revolution" in their programs. In only two decades, faculty members have vastly improved their academic qualifications, and "lock-step" curricula have been abandoned in favor of electives and expanded academic programs. Educational facilities and resources have been modernized and expanded, and professional military training has reflected the latest in technological developments. Procedures for indoctrinating new cadets and midshipmen have tended to emphasize positive leadership and minimize traditional harassment. The recruitment base has been broadened to include sizable percentages of minorities and women.

However, unmitigated triumph has not been a consistent pattern at the academies. High levels of student attrition, rising operational costs, honor scandals, and other indications of widespread student and, perhaps, faculty malaise have brought criticism and scrutiny by the press, the Pentagon, Congress, and the General Accounting Office (GAO).

Paradoxically, many of the actions initiated by academy officials during recent decades to adapt to changing external demands exacerbated internal tensions and created problems that reached acute proportions in the 1970s. One can unravel this paradox of change at the academies only through a detailed analysis similar to that provided in the author's forthcoming book-length study.[1] However, this chapter does contain significant findings that should provide the clues necessary to understand the dynamics and the paradoxical consequences of change.

The Pattern

Reform and innovation at the academies tend to reflect a combination of external stimuli and internal initiatives. As distinguished from trivial or cosmetic changes, the most important changes have occurred when the external climate has encouraged change and when academy leaders have held office long enough to develop an interest in new programs. In Figure 1, the name of each superintendent who served for at least three years during the post-World War II period is listed above an arrow spanning his tenure in office. Commandants of cadets or midshipmen who served at least two years concurrently with a superintendent are listed below the arrows to the left of the diagonals. Academic deans who served at least two years concurrently with a given superintendent are listed below the arrows to the right of the diagonals. Because of this three-year tenure requirement, Figure 1 includes the names of only sixteen of the thirty-one postwar superintendents who had completed tours by mid-1977. But all sixteen of them were associated with major changes at the academies, with the possible exception of Rear Admiral Charles Melson, superintendent of the Naval Academy from 1958 to 1960. Although the process of internal ferment and program evaluation began at the Naval Academy under Melson, the changes actually initiated during his tenure were extremely modest. Sweeping changes were not implemented until Read Admiral James Calvert became superintendent for a four-year tour beginning in mid-1968.

Major General Maxwell Taylor initiated key reforms at West Point during the early postwar years. The status quo was largely maintained until Lieutenant General Garrison Davidson became superintendent in mid-1956. Internal studies by Davidson on virtually all facets of academy life—from military training to academics—resulted in important reforms. However, many of these reforms did not become effective until Major General William Westmoreland succeeded General Davidson. Thereafter, reform at West Point continued at a decidedly incremental pace until Lieutenant General William Knowlton and his successor, Lieutenant General Sidney Berry, confronted a period of organizational turbulence (honor scandals and court litigation) and initiated almost continuous adjustments in their efforts to quell the turbulence.

Only the Air Force Academy has had a consistent pattern of relatively long leadership tours. Undoubtedly, such tours were essential for the innovation that characterized the Air Force Academy throughout its first decade. The tenure of the single most influential innovator during that period, the dean, Brigadier General Robert McDermott, included service under each of the academy's first five superintendents.

External influence was also an important element in the process of change. The periodic ebb and flow of innovation and reform at the academies reflects, in part, a pattern of changing cues from the Defense Department, the parent arms of the service, Congress, academic accrediting

307

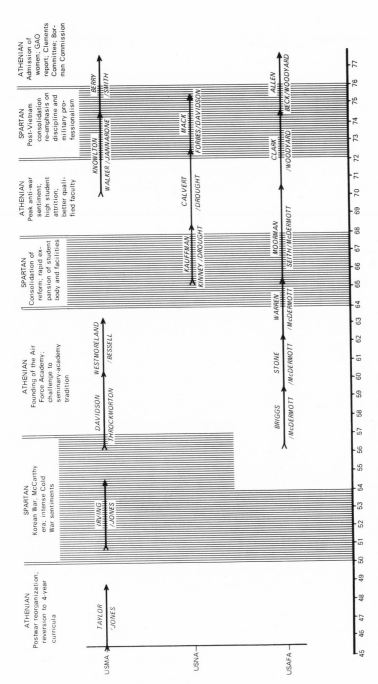

Figure 1. The "Climate" of the Task Environment and terms of Office of Academy Hierarchy

agencies, boards of visitors, alumni, and the press. Collectively, these institutions comprise the organizational task environment on which the academies depend for their resources and legitimation.[2]

Cues from the various components of the task environment have rarely been totally consistent with one another. Academy leaders tend to respond more readily to explicit demands from the task environment than to vague cues, and they respond to cues according to the potential influence that the source of a cue can exert on organizational resources. The different components of the task environment have varied in their actual influence, depending, in part, on the formal authority of each element, on circumstances, such as a scandal at an academy, and on the force of a personality, such as that of Vice Admiral Hyman Rickover, a Naval Academy alumnus and persistent critic of the academies.

Despite these important caveats, one can detect, in general terms, the impact of discernible shifts in the dominant "climate" of cues from the task environment. Thus, Figure 1 depicts fluctuations between cues in an "Athenian" climate that encourages modification, expansion, and improvements and cues in a "Spartan" climate that cautions against experimentation and emphasizes discipline and the cultivation of the traditional martial virtues. Of course, the divisions that mark the shift from an Athenian to a Spartan climate are imprecise, and they are not necessarily identical from one service to the next. However, graphic representation of these fluctuations suggests a pattern of changing cues explainable not merely as random swings of a pendulum but, rather, as understandable modifications in the response of national leaders to changing policy needs.

Cues to the academies from their task environment span a variety of procedural, structural, and programmatic matters that are broader than the Athenian-Spartan realms of concern. But cues that have been translatable into a relative emphasis on Athenian or Spartan concerns are especially interesting analytically because of the Spartan-Athenian duality of the service academy mission. On the one hand, the goal of the academies is to provide prospective military officers with discipline, training, and professional socialization, which includes the development of pride and career commitment. On the other hand, they serve as institutions of higher education committed, as a minimum, to academic accreditation and, optimally, to the status that accrues to institutions of recognized academic excellence.

Especially since World War II, the duality of mission has generated internal tensions at the academies. Throughout the nineteenth century, officials at West Point and at Annapolis found little reason to question the primacy of the goal of discipline and character building. Certainly, the prospective officer needed to acquire an education, but there was little if any conflict between the provision of such training and the cultivation of the martial virtues. In short, the academies could aspire to be both Sparta and Athens because they perceived the Athenian commitment as comfortably subordinate to the Spartan commitment.

Even on the eve of World War II, West Point remained essentially a military seminary, its program and its organizational ethos still faithfully patterned along the lines drawn by Superintendent Sylvanus Thayer more than one hundred years earlier. Annapolis also had seminary qualities, but it was first and foremost a trade school. It concentrated on providing Naval Academy graduates with practical skills for use on board ship and with the discipline associated with "running a tight ship."

In the years since World War II, however, the armed services have become increasingly aware of the need for greater breadth and depth in the education of its officers, and this awareness has led to greater emphasis on academics. The result has been a heightening of "Spartan-Athenian" tensions reflected organizationally in competition for the time of cadets and midshipmen and for the allocation of resources.

The pattern has not been a linear increase in the demands for academic reform, however. As Figure 1 suggests, notable fluctuations have occurred. At the end of World War II, for example, leaders of the armed services felt the need to assimilate wartime experiences and the accompanying strategic, tactical, and technological changes into military education and training. The result was a highly favorable climate for innovation at the academies.

During World War II, West Point and Annapolis adopted accelerated, three-year programs of instruction. At the end of the war, both institutions, encouraged by their respective service headquarters to assimilate the lessons of the war and to update curricula and procedures, undertook a re-examination of their program. Under General Maxwell Taylor, organizational ferment was evident, especially at West Point, with expansion of the social sciences and the introduction of military psychology and leadership. Both academies retained curricula that were prescribed for all students, except for their choice of foreign languages. However, West Point undertook some limited experimentation in permitting certain advanced students to validate basic courses and enroll in specially developed advanced courses. Both academies modified academic coursework and military training to incorporate new developments in technology and to reflect the heightened concern with interservice cooperation that resulted from the war.

In 1949, at the direction of the first secretary of defense, James Forrestal, a board headed by Robert L. Stearns and General of the Army Dwight D. Eisenhower launched a comprehensive study of service academy education. The board rejected a variety of alternatives to the existing four-year undergraduate programs, which had specific service identities. This served as an endorsement of most of the key assumptions underlying the existing programs, such as the rationale for prescribed curricula, rather than as a stimulus to radical change.[3]

The onset of war in Korea further reduced the incentive for experimentation. Instead, the academies emphasized the traditional Spartan component of producing capable combat leaders. In such a climate of low external support for academic experimentation, a relatively long term of office for such top academy leaders as Major General Frederick Irving at West Point from 1951 to 1954 was, in itself, no stimulus for change. Under such circumstances, a long term for a superintendent may well assure continuation of the status quo.

With the end of the Korean War, the climate of the academy task environment became less hostile to change, although the shift was not nearly as marked as it had been at the end of World War II. The cold war remained intense in the mid-1950s, and military officials continued their preoccupation with the Spartan component of the academy mission.

The Service Academy Board recommended the creation of a separate Air Force Academy in 1950, but Congress took no action to implement the recommendation until 1954. Once charged with the development of a new institution, the founders of the Air Force Academy had a good deal of license to engage in experimentation irrespective of continuing Spartan emphases and cold war concerns in Washington. But they did not have total license. Most of the founders of the academy were not predisposed to depart radically from the traditional seminary-academy model. Almost all of the officers who held key command, staff, and faculty positions from the founding of the academy through the crucial early years were West Point graduates. Many of these officers believed that the new academy should have a distinct identity and reputation, but they also were sufficiently steeped in West Point tradition to adapt much of it to the Colorado setting.

The service academies compete with one another for essentially the same pool of young men and women with the necessary qualifications and motivation. Thus, under the leadership of the second dean, Brigadier General McDermott, the Air Force Academy became innovative, and the other services found it difficult to ignore the air force example. Organizational ferment had begun at West Point under General Davidson, largely independent of the Air Force Academy example. But the "enrichment program," academic majors, and graduate course credits introduced at the Air Force Academy provided a catalyst for further reform at West Point and at Annapolis.

By the late 1950s, the external climate was conducive to reform at the Naval Academy. The Melson years (1958-1960) mark the beginning of a period of incremental reform that continued into the mid-1960s. During this period, the task environment not only encouraged but sometimes insisted on change; for example, a directive from Secretary of the Navy Fred Korth in 1963 mandated the hiring of a civilian academic dean and called for an increase in the ratio of civilians to military officers on the faculty. However, no Naval Academy superintendent served more than two years during this period.

By mid-1965, when Draper Kauffman assumed command at the Naval Academy for a three-year tour, external support for academic reform had waned. The other academies had shifted from a period of major academic changes, such as the introduction of electives, to a period of consolidating and evaluating the new programs. A major honor scandal at the Air Force Academy in 1965 led some persons to charge publicly that academics had been overemphasized during the era of experimentation. Moreover, military officials had become preoccupied with the escalation of U.S. involvement in Vietnam. As in the past, the test of combat led military professionals to reconsider the priorities that had been assigned to the various dimensions of military education and training, and they sought to give more weight to Spartan rather than Athenian values.

By the late 1960s, however, popular support for U.S. involvement in Southeast Asia had begun to wane. Vocal opposition to the war, especially among college youth, had increased. U.S. military institutions in general and the academies in particular had come under pressure to be less authoritarian and more in tune with the rest of society. Finding it difficult to attract enough qualified applicants for existing vacancies, academy officials sought ways to make the academies more attractive. These external pressures came at a time when internal links to the civilian sector, especially to civilian higher education, had increased. Decisions to upgrade the qualifications of faculty members in the late 1950s to the mid-1960s led to a far higher percentage of faculty members who had spent extended periods of study at civilian graduate schools. An influx of Reservists to replace regular officers assigned to Southeast Asia further augmented the number of faculty members with links to the civilian sector. During this period, Rear Admiral James Calvert assumed command at the Naval Academy and instituted major reforms. The external climate was especially conducive to change at Annapolis, which had not only experienced the conditions described above but also had borne the brunt of Vice Admiral Rickover's criticisms of service academy education. Moreover, the aspirations of civilian faculty members for reform at the Naval Academy provided compelling incentive for change.

By the early 1970s, the academies apparently had surmounted the severe problem of attracting qualified applicants. Moreover, the "winding down" of the war in Vietnam and the end of conscription helped to relieve the pressures on the services to "civilianize," and this, in turn, alleviated the pressures on the academies for modeling their programs more closely on the programs of civilian institutions of higher education.[4] Changes continued during the period of Spartan emphasis, but, ironically, many of the changes had the effect of reversing earlier initiatives and led to reductions in electives, termination of programs for immediate civilian graduate schooling, and reemphasis on engineering and professional military studies.

By 1976, however, a variety of pressures had been building for further reform at the service academies. Congress imposed one of the most dramatic changes with legislation mandating the admission of women to the academies. The admission of women, in turn, required academy officials to reexamine their various programs, requirements, and facilities to determine the need for further modifications. Similarly, the GAO studies, released in 1975 and 1976, had required internal assessment and action by academy officials. A concurrent review of the academies by a DOD Committee on Excellence in Education (Clements Committee) also called for reforms in the structure and content of education and training.[5] Because of revelations of widespread cheating in 1976, West Point was the most vulnerable of the three academies to external monitoring and control; thus, it was subjected to further review by a commission headed by former astronaut and West Point graduate Frank Borman.[6] Following the commission's report, the army created three additional committees early in 1977 to identify actions necessary to remedy the organizational deficiencies highlighted in the report.[7] General Andrew Jackson Goodpaster was called from retirement to assume the superintendent's post and oversee needed changes.

Growth and Bureaucratization

During the post-World War II evolution of the academies, increased emphasis on academics confounded by periodic fluctuations in Spartan and Athenian cues from the task environment has occurred within a context of significant growth. The pattern of growth has been distinctive at each of the academies: the Naval Academy experienced most of its postwar growth in the 1940s and 1950s; the Military Academy expanded its numbers dramatically in the late 1960s and early 1970s; and the Air Force Academy has experienced rapid growth since the first class entered in 1955.

By the 1970s, each of the academies had graduated classes of 800 to 900 young men from student bodies of approximately 4,000. These figures may seem small in relation to the student populations of most state universities in the 1970s; nevertheless, the growth of the academies during modernization introduced structural complexity and bureaucratization to a degree that brought qualitative changes in the life of each institution. Organizational cohesion and shared values in the earlier "seminary-academy" era had been made possible by intimacy. With growth has come the specialization of roles, the introduction of new layers of authority, the proliferation of formal rules and regulations, and the codification of customs.

Specialization makes it more difficult for academy staff and faculty members to play multiple roles (academic instructor *and* company tactical officer) and to move freely from one domain to another. The modern superintendent is no longer merely a father figure; he is a manager who must coordinate the efforts of, and arbitrate disputes among, a galaxy of functionally specialized subordinates. Moreover, layers of authority have gradually been introduced between officials who make the rules governing academy life and the cadets and midshipmen who, typically, are most directly affected by the rules. Thus, organizational cohesion has weakened as academy life has become more complex and as cadets and midshipmen have become more remote from officials at the top of the hierarchy. Consequently, ties to subgroups—the company or squadron, the athletic team or extracurricular club, the graduating class—have assumed proportionately more importance, and they have created loyalties that academy officials paradoxically both cultivate and fear.

Life at the service academies has always been regimented. Earlier, relatively limited written regulations, supplemented by verbal injunctions at the discretion of officers in positions of authority, were sufficient guideposts of permissible behavior. However, the trend has been to expand ad infinitum the list of formal regulations. Over the decades, less and less has been left to chance or to the discretion of academy personnel. New articles, paragraphs, and subparagraphs have been written to anticipate each contingency and, progressively, to reduce the list of excuses that inventive cadets and midshipmen may offer to justify behavior contrary to official expectations. Similarly, such practices as plebe indoctrination and the maintenance of an honor code were once handled informally through procedures passed along from one generation of cadets or midshipmen to the next generation. These practices are now codified and, thus, rigidified.

Although the recent governmental studies of the academies (the GAO reports, the reports of the Clements Committee, and the Borman Commission report) have identified many manifestations of bureaucratization in academy life, they have been curiously inattentive to the postwar growth that contributed to the bureaucratization. Particularly astonishing in a study that purports to analyze trends is the GAO attrition study's insensitivity to growth. Since the GAO study began with the graduating classes of 1964, its representation of attrition trends for the three academies suggests a rather stable pattern through the Class of 1970. Thereafter, attrition increases at the Air Force Academy and the Military Academy, and a possible reversal of the upward trend begins with the Class of 1975 at West Point.

However, in Figures 2, 3, and 4, standardized attrition data are plotted against standardized enrollment data for each academy for a much longer period than the period examined by the GAO. These figures cover the entire period since the end of World War II for West Point and Annapolis and the period since the first class entered the Air Force Academy in 1955.[8] As suggested by Figures 2, 3, and 4 and confirmed by statistical analysis, there has been a high correlation between growth and attrition at each of the academies.[9]

Moreover, when the growth and attrition data are superimposed on Figure 1, which shows the phases in the evolution of the academies, the result suggests some probable limitations in efforts already under way to reverse the attrition trend. Over the years since World War II, there have been periods of declining attrition and sudden increases in attrition. Some of these fluctuations may be explained in terms of responses to internal reform, such as the decline in attrition at West Point after General Davidson's reforms, or to changes in the external climate, such as the sharp rise in attrition at the Military and Air Force academies during the mounting antiwar protests in the late 1960s. Over the span of approximately thirty years, however, the trend at each academy is increased attrition paralleling the enrollment trend.

Viewed in this broader perspective, attrition trends are attributable neither to failures in short-term leadership nor to ephemeral moods among the post-Vietnam generation of American youth. Rather, the long-term rise in attrition is a symptom of malaise in institutions where bureaucratized regimentation has replaced the Spartan but intimate seminary existence of an earlier era. Although the ostensible reasons for attrition vary from voluntary resignation to academic failure and disciplinary dismissal, surveys of students who remain at the academies indicate that alienation is the underlying problem.[10]

The need for military officers probably will not require an increase in the size of the service academies in the near future. Thus, attrition may have peaked. As a minimum over the next several years, the academies may avoid the eruption of severe organizational crises stemming from student disaffection, such as the honor scandal at West Point in 1976. Optimally, imaginative and energetic academy leaders may improve morale, and this could lead to a reduction in attrition by several percentage points.

However, it seems unlikely that significant, sustained reduction in

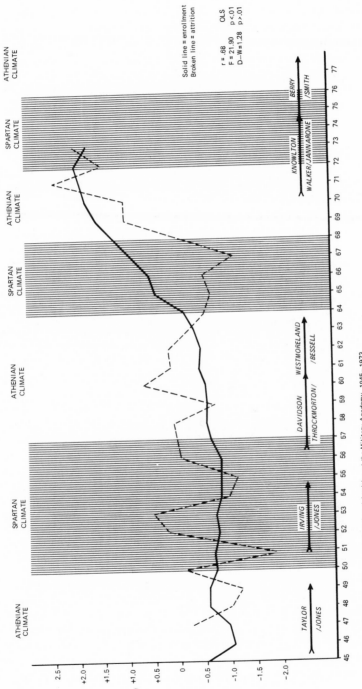

Figure 2. Standardized Measures of Growth and Attrition at the Military Academy, 1945–1973

316

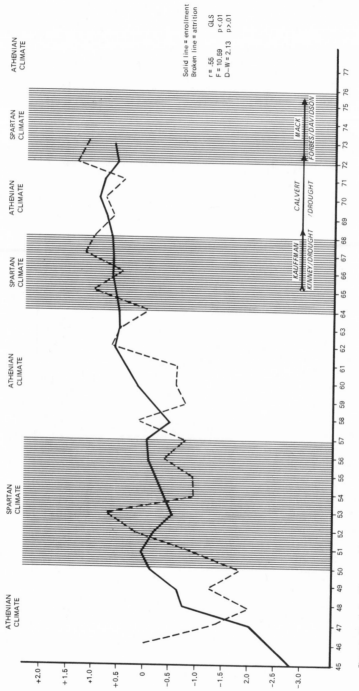

Figure 3. Standardized Measures of Growth and Attrition at the Naval Academy, 1945–1973

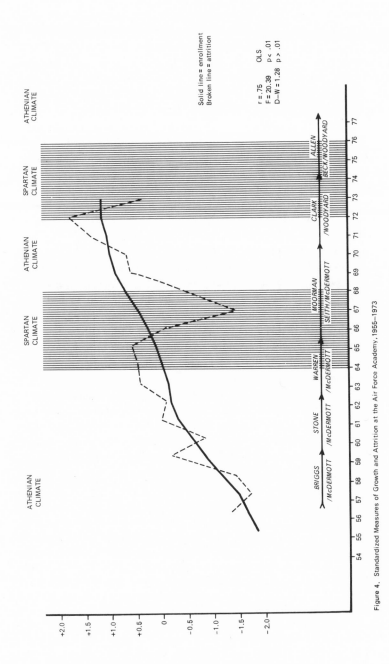

Figure 4. Standardized Measures of Growth and Attrition at the Air Force Academy, 1955–1973

organizational malaise and thus in student attrition can be achieved through incremental reforms. Tinkering with the curriculum (reducing the course load and providing more attractive electives), with the system of discipline (granting more privileges and giving more opportunities for leadership), and with methods of indoctrination (more hours of instruction in ethics and more emphasis on "positive leadership") may elicit the approval of cadets and midshipmen and reduce discontent. But no amount of tinkering can eliminate the stresses inherent in the duality of the academy mission.

In the final analysis, the service academies cannot be justified merely as educational institutions. Their raison d'être lies in their claim to uniqueness as institutions designed not only to educate but also to provide career motivation, discipline, military training, and character development. In short, the process of professional socialization lies at the heart of the academy mission. If this process could be completed without the requirement for a college education, it would require no more than a year or eighteen months. But modern military officers *require* college education, and the socialization process stretches over a four-year period. Thus, in his senior year at the academy, the cadet or midshipman still "learns" how to shine his shoes, keep his belt buckle polished, and go to bed by an appointed hour each evening. Because of the increased emphasis on the academic role, these demands of "in loco parentis with a vengeance" seem more incongruous and thus more onerous to contemporary cadets and midshipmen than to their predecessors, who also did their share of complaining.

The service academies could be both Spartan and Athenian in an era when they assumed that the Athenian commitment should be comfortably subordinated to the Spartan commitment. Now that Athens and Sparta make equal claims on the identity of the academies and its members, reconciliation of these claims has become a challenge that would tax the wisdom of Thucydides and the patience of Sisyphus.

Notes

1. The study, tentatively entitled *Neither Athens nor Sparta? The Service Academies in Transition*, focuses on organizational change at the Military, Naval, Air Force, and Coast Guard academies, with emphasis on the period since World War II. The Coast Guard Academy shares many organizational characteristics with the DOD academies, but in other respects, its evolution has been distinctive. For reasons of space, the present discussion is restricted to the three DOD academies.

2. The concept of "task environment" was developed by William R. Dill, "Environment as an Influence on Managerial Autonomy," *Administrative Science Quarterly* 2 (March 1958):409-443; and further refined by James D. Thompson, *Organizations in Action* (New York: McGraw-Hill, 1967).

3. U.S., Secretary of Defense, *A Report and Recommendation to the Secretary of Defense by the Service Academy Board*, prepared by Robert L. Stearns, chairman, et al. (Washington, D.C.: Department of Defense, January 1950). See also the discussion in John W. Masland and Laurence I. Radway, *Soldiers and Scholars: Military Education and National Policy* (Princeton, N.J.: Princeton University Press, 1957), pp. 117-121.

4. Charles C. Moskos, Jr., notes the tendency of military studies in the late 1960s to identify a growing convergence of U.S. military and civilian institutions; by the early 1970s, however, several observers had identified a halt or reversal of the trend toward convergence. Moskos, "The Military," *Annual Review of Sociology* 2 (1976):55-77; see also David R. Segal et al., "Convergence, Isomorphism and Interdependence at the Civil-Military Interface," *Journal of Political and Military Sociology* 2 (1974): 157-172.

5. U.S., Deputy Secretary of Defense, "The Service Academies: Conclusions and Initiatives" (Ten-page mimeographed memorandum to the Departments of Army, Navy, and Air Force, April 28, 1975); also U.S., Deputy Secretary of Defense, "Assessing Levels of Achievement at the Service Academies" (Mimeographed memorandum to the secretaries of the army, navy, and air force, December 12, 1975). Some of the similarities and differences in the findings of the GAO and the Clements Committee, respectively, are evident in the testimony of key personnel reported in U.S., Congress, House of Representatives, Committee on Government Operations, Legislation and National Security Subcommittee, *Hearings: Problems in Administration of the Military Service Academies*, 94th Cong., 2d sess., March 17, 1976.

6. U.S., Secretary of the Army, Special Commission on the United States Military Academy, *Report*, prepared by Colonel Frank Borman et al., December 15, 1976.

7. Collectively, the three committees were termed the "West Point Study Group."

8. The term *growth*, as used in this chapter, refers to the pattern defined by net student enrollment figures at an academy from year to year. Necessarily, the figure for a given year must be an average because month-to-month changes occur with attrition. We are able to get a good approximation of enrollment at an academy for a given year by combining the figures for the size of the freshman class at entry with figures for the sophomore, junior, and senior class, respectively, at graduation. The method exaggerates the size of the freshman class, where substantial attrition will already have occurred even after two months, and underestimates the size of the sophomore and junior classes, which will be larger in the estimate-year than at graduation. A cross-check of this method of calculation with actual reported enrollments for various years revealed its reliability. Enrollment figures on a year-by-year basis are not conveniently available for all three academies. However, since matriculation and graduation figures are regularly reported, this method of estimation provides a reliable common basis of comparison.

The term *attrition* refers to losses from the student body of an academy, either voluntary or involuntary losses. In explaining attrition in terms of events or trends by year, it would be most helpful to know the total attrition that occurred for the four classes in attendance for a given year. Since such data are not available for the present analysis, we use instead data on total four-year attrition for each graduating class, plotting the attrition at the end of the first year after entry of the class because at least half of the attrition for a class typically will have occurred by then. The following analysis describes attrition as symptomatic of mounting cadet and midshipman alienation and discontent, which are found to be related to growth and attendant bureaucratization and to Spartan-Athenian tensions in the academy milieu. The author recognizes that many factors contribute to attrition. The present interpretation is likely to be less relevant to an explanation of attrition that occurs during the cadet or midshipman's first summer than to attrition that occurs subsequently.

9. The author is indebted to his colleague, Francis W. Hoole, for advice and assistance in the statistical analysis. For further information, see Lovell, *Neither Athens nor Sparta* (forthcoming); and J. Johnston, *Econometric Methods*, 2d ed. (Tokyo: McGraw-Hill Koyakusha Ltd., 1972).

10. For example, see USMA, Office of the Director of Institutional Research, *The First Class Questionnaire, Class of 1975* (West Point, N.Y.: USMA, June 1975); and idem, *The First Class Questionnaire, Class of 1976* (West Point, N.Y.: USMA, August 1976). In response to the question, "If you could reconsider your decision, would you now come to the U.S. Military Academy?," there was an almost linear decline in "yes" responses from 88.2 percent of the Class of 1957 to 47.3 percent of the Class of 1971. "Yes" responses increased somewhat thereafter, peaking at 66.3 percent of the Class of 1975 and then falling to 54.7 percent of the Class of 1976.

19

Making It at the Air Force Academy: Who Stays? Who Succeeds?

Ronald F. Schloemer
Gus E. Myers

Many sociological studies have been written about the U.S. military, but little public information is available on service academy cadets, particularly cadets attending the U.S. Air Force Academy (USAFA). USAFA cadets have either been neglected, or assumptions about them have been based on studies of West Point cadets. Information on their own distinctive attitudes, performance, and social characteristics has been scanty, or it has been based on untested hypotheses and outdated assumptions.[1]

This problem was partially considered in a recent study of successful air force officers attending professional military colleges at Air University.[2] Margiotta's analysis updates earlier social portraits of military elites and provides a description of the next generation of air force leaders. But his study did not fill the information void surrounding the cadets at Colorado Springs.

A two-man Air Command and Staff College research study group was formed to add data on Air Force Academy cadets to earlier sociological portraits of the military elite and to complement similar studies of West Point and Annapolis cadets. In general, previous studies of academy cadets describe a relatively high degree of social representation at these institutions and show little hint of overrepresentation by social class or geographic region. The Air Force Academy is no exception; its recruit-

This research was done at the Air Command and Staff College (ACSC) with the cooperation of the United States Air Force Academy (USAFA). We thank Lieutenant Colonel Franklin D. Margiotta, our research adviser; his encouragement and constructive criticism helped to shape and direct our ideas. We are especially indebted to Mr. Risdon J. Westen and Major Michael J. O'Connell, USAFA; their suggestions and assistance with computer analysis simplified our efforts. We are also grateful to Brigadier General Stanley C. Beck, commandant of cadets. Of course, only the authors are responsible for any errors.

ment and selection processes attract cadets socially and statistically similar to those found at sister academies.

A New Approach

A second purpose of this study was to experiment and improve on previous methods of studying military elites. Much of the literature appears to assume that graduation from a service academy is a necessary and sufficient "punch" in the ticket to general officer promotion.[3] Degrees of success *before* commissioning are ignored or are treated as irrelevant to future military success. Such studies rarely go beyond the annual recruitment patterns of the academies, and they assume that all graduates have equal chances of getting ahead. The social composition of entering freshmen classes supports implied predictions about the future elite. The assumption is that the raw material enters the academy and comes out four years later with little discrimination concerning the potential of individual graduating seniors.[4]

Since we spent a combined period of six years at the USAFA, we recognize that significant academic and motivational attrition in the first two years decreases the size of entering classes. Our objective was to determine whether the backgrounds of the upper classes are relatively the same as the backgrounds of freshman classes.[5]

This loss to attrition, especially to involuntary attrition, could indicate a process of socialization and selection that occurs after the individual enters the academy. It might also duplicate similar processes that we have witnessed in the officer corps—e.g., reductions in force, being passed over for promotion, and competition for promotion.

Decreased promotion opportunities in a peacetime military are not unique to the 1970s. The difference today is that even a regular academy commission no longer assures the security of previous years. For the first time, significant numbers of Air Force Academy graduates are passed over for promotion to the rank of permanent regular captain. To "make it" in today's air force officer corps, one must demonstrate outstanding performance, regardless of the source of his commission, or face decelerated promotion or involuntary separation.[6]

These factors prompted us to try a new approach in our study of USAFA cadets. We desired to push the frontiers of understanding further than previous studies. By analyzing the biographical and attitudinal factors that might affect a cadet's performance, we wanted to determine who stays and who succeeds at the academy.

We targeted the cadets in the Classes of 1976 and 1977 for a number of reasons. Our sample would include cadets who have virtually committed themselves to remain at the academy.[7] Furthermore, performance data on upperclassmen are more reliable than preliminary rankings of freshmen.

Finally, we recognized that the Class of 1977 was the first draft-free class and felt that a comparison with the Class of 1976 might be interesting.

We relied heavily on three sources of comparative data. The first was Morris Janowitz's classic work, *The Professional Soldier*.[8] In his book, Janowitz portrayed the officer elite recruited in the 1920s and 1930s as predominately southern, rural, aristocratic, and Protestant, but he also predicted more representativeness over a period of time. In order to test Janowitz's predictions, we gathered new data.

A second source was the annual study by the American Council on Education (ACE) on entering college freshmen.[9] This study permits comparisons with civilian college peers and with West Point and Annapolis classes. The Air Force Academy's input to the ACE studies allowed us to observe changes in the Classes of 1976 and 1977 from the time they entered the academy.

A third source was Margiotta's study of air force officers attending the Air War College (AWC) and the Air Command and Staff College (ACSC). His analysis of a potential 1980-1990 generation of air force elites encouraged comparisons between cadets and successful officers currently on active duty.

We constructed a twenty-question survey, administered it to the two classes in January 1976, and achieved a response rate of 55 percent. The cadets identified themselves by a computer-readable number that permitted us to match our survey against stored academy performance data. We then performed cross-tabulations to test hypotheses about the type of cadet who stays and who succeeds militarily at the academy.

Like civilian colleges, the service academies use grade point averages as a measure of academic performance, but each academy defines "military success" or performance somewhat differently. The Air Force Academy may have the most elaborate system of the three academies, since the Military Order of Merit (MOM) amalgamates peer ratings, Air Officer Commanding (AOC) ratings, conduct and discipline records, military training grades, and cadet performance reports similar to air force officer effectiveness reports. Cadets are evaluated by classmates and upperclassmen, the AOC, and officer instructors. Twice each year, these evaluations are combined to rank each cadet with other cadets in his class. Each input is weighted differently in each class year. Peer ratings weigh more heavily for fourth classmen (freshmen) than for first classmen, and AOC ratings always weigh heavier than other factors. These weights are best illustrated in Figure 1.

Each area is rarely evaluated in isolation. Because of necessarily limited contact with new cadets, the AOC may be influenced by peer ratings and discipline records, especially if they indicate extremes in interpersonal behavior or conduct.

The MOM is a quantified cumulation of a cadet's attitude, aptitude,

Figure 1. Weights Assigned to MOM Inputs

	Class	AOC	Peer	Perform-ance Report	Military Studies	Wing Trng	Conduct and Discipline
(Freshmen)	4th	40%	20%	5%	15%	5%	15%
	3rd	45%	15%	10%	15%	5%	10%
	2nd	45%	10%	20%	10%	5%	10%
	1st	45%	5%	35%	0%	5%	10%

Source: Commandant's Operating Instruction 537-1, Administration of the Cadet Military Rating and Cadet Performance Report (U.S. Air Force Academy, August 1974)

interpersonal skills, acceptance of discipline and authority, and demonstrated performance of military duties.[10] Cadets who score high in the MOM enjoy more privileges and leadership opportunities than cadets who rank near the bottom. Like a high grade-point average and a place on the academy dean's list, a high MOM and a place on the commandant's list is a measure of cadet success.

Since reported officer performance is critical for promotion, our study focused on the cadet's military performance and linkages to the social variables identified in our research. To the extent that certain attitudes, orientations, or segments of society may be overrepresented in the extremes of measured performance, we hoped to clarify conceptions about officers who may comprise the future elite.

To test our hypotheses, we first tabulated the responses to each question and then divided those who chose any particular response according to their quartile standing in the MOM. If the variable had few predictive qualities, we expected to find an even distribution of respondents over the four quartiles of the MOM. The example below illustrates this method.

Political Identification	Responding	% in Top Q	% in 2d Q	% in 3rd Q	% in Bottom Q
"Middle of the road"	29	24	32	21	32

n = 729   (Expected value = 25% in each)

In the example, 29 percent of the responding cadets identified themselves politically as "middle of the road." Of these 221 cadets, 24 percent rank in the top quartile of the MOM, 32 percent in the second quartile, etc. In other words, "middle of the road" political self-identification does not seem very important to MOM rankings.

Using these methods, we attempted to answer some key questions about cadet performance and success. For example, how strong are the correlations between attitudes and MOM? Is a strong and positive desire for later rewards linked to success at USAFA? Does a cadet's political orientation have any bearing on his ranking within the class? Is there a connection between academic achievement and military success? Finally, we sought to determine linkages between socioeconomic and demographic factors and the MOM. Is there a correlation, for example, between a high MOM and a cadet's social origin, race, or religious practices? If such linkages exist, why are they present?

The rest of this discussion focuses on the three dimensions of attitudes, academic performance, and social background. When we found strong correlations, we tried to analyze or explain why they existed.

Attitudes and Orientations

The cadet military rating system evaluates the attributes and qualities considered desirable for air force officers. On the basis of our observations of cadets, we believed that cadets who aspired to higher rank in the air force, expressed positive career intentions, and perceived themselves as politically conservative would be overrepresented in the upper quartiles of the MOM.[11]

We found significant correlations between future rank aspirations and career intentions, but we were wrong about conservative political identification. As shown in Table 1, the higher the aspirations for rank, the more likely that a cadet would have a higher MOM. The opposite is also true. Of the 10 percent who stated that they realistically aspire to the rank of major general or higher, more than one-half ranked in the top quartile of the MOM. Of those who felt that they could rise to the rank of brigadier general, fully two-thirds ranked in the upper half of the MOM.

We do not argue that high expectations for promotion cause higher MOMs; in fact, the reverse may be more likely. Cadets who perceive themselves as militarily successful at the academy may believe that they are more likely to continue their success on active duty in the air force.

Because of our observations of a competitive AF officer promotion system, we were surprised that two-thirds of our cadet respondents thought that they would at least achieve the rank of colonel or higher, and that another 15 percent believed that they would achieve a retirement career grade of lieutenant colonel. The academy obviously creates high career expectations.

This same relationship was also evident in career intentions. The more positive a cadet's commitment to an air force career, the more likely

TABLE 1

CADET CAREER ATTITUDES AND MOM

	Respond-ing %	Top Q (%)	2nd Q (%)	3rd Q (%)	Bottom Q (%)
"To what rank do you realistically aspire?"					
Captain	12	18	18	29	35
Major	7	18	18	38	26
Lieutenant Colonel	15	15	31	23	31
Colonel	44	23	30	27	20
Brigadier General	10	31	36	19	14
Major General or higher	12	54	18	16	12
N =	756				
"What is your current military career interest?"					
Plan to get out	8	16	20	33	31
Look, then make up mind	37	22	27	23	27
More than one tour, but no career	7	21	27	34	18
Plan 20 year career	32	23	31	25	20
Plan 30 year career	16	42	24	19	15
N =	747				

that he would rank in a higher quartile of the MOM. Table 1 shows that 42 percent of the cadets planning thirty-year careers rank in the top quartile. The distribution of cadets planning to leave the air force after their initial five-year commitment reinforces this pattern. Two-thirds of this group rank in the bottom half of the MOM.[12]

We tested an unproven contention that academy cadets achieved higher levels of success in the air force because they had earlier career commitments than officers from other commissioning sources. As shown in Table 2, the academy cadets are firmer in their plans to make the air force a career than were older air force officers at the time of their initial recruitment. One should recall that academy cadets graduate with regular commissions and that this makes career status a more logical and realistic aspiration. Only 14 percent of the senior officers surveyed

TABLE 2

COMPARISON OF ATTITUDES TOWARD AIR FORCE CAREER

Military Career Interest	AFA Cadets %	AWC & ACSC Officers %
Plan to get out	8	30
Look, then make up mind	37	40
More than one tour, but no career	7	1
Plan Air Force career	48	28
Other		1
N =	747	680

Sources: Margiotta, 1976, p. 164 (Note: Officers expressed career interest at time of service entry); USAF Academy, 1976.

were academy graduates, and the overwhelming majority entered service with Reserve commissions.[13]

To our surprise, political conservatism was not very helpful in predicting higher scores on the MOM. Cadets characterize themselves politically as more conservative than liberal (Table 3). Only 5 percent regard themselves as "liberal"; but 12 percent view themselves as "conservative" and another third as "somewhat conservative."[14] Interestingly, at the time of their initial entry to the academy, almost one-fourth of each class described themselves as liberal. Part of this conservative shift may have come through the socialization process in the academy environment. We suspect, however, that a greater number of more liberally oriented cadets simply dropped out. This seems to be supported by the attrition study conducted by the General Accounting Office.[15] We can also qualify our findings by noting that college students generally have become more conservative since 1972.[16]

A higher percentage of "liberal" cadets achieve a lower score on the MOM than cadets who view themselves as conservative, but the difference does not statistically support our hypothesis. The distribution by quartile standing shows no marked clustering around any political self-identification; this suggests that political self-perception is not helpful in understanding a cadet's class standing.

We surveyed cadets' perceptions of their fathers' political orientation and expected differences between generations. The results in Table 3 help to explain a conservative identification among cadets. Two-thirds

TABLE 3

POLITICAL IDENTIFICATION VS MOM

	Percent Responding	Top Q (%)	2nd Q (%)	3rd Q (%)	Bottom Q (%)
Cadet's Political Identification					
Conservative	12	26	33	20	21
Somewhat conservative	31	32	24	27	18
Middle-of-the-road	29	24	32	21	23
Somewhat liberal	24	18	24	32	26
Liberal	5	23	23	17	37
N =	762				
Father's Political Identification					
Conservative	30	30	27	24	19
Somewhat conservative	40	28	25	25	22
Middle-of-the-road	16	21	30	24	25
Somewhat liberal	6	19	31	23	27
Liberal	2	8	39	31	23
Don't know	6	9	30	37	24
N =	762				

of the cadets perceived their father as right of center on the political spectrum, and only 2 percent perceived their fathers as liberal. As in the findings for cadet political orientations, we found that cadets who perceive their fathers as conservative fare only slightly better on the MOM. We did find some differences when we compared only the top quartiles. Thirty percent of the cadets who perceive their fathers as conservative rank in the top quartile, compared to only 8 percent of the cadets who view their fathers as liberal. However, because of the small number of respondents in this latter category (2 percent of the sample), we reached no definite conclusions.

Our hypothesis was confirmed that younger cadets would not consider themselves as conservative as older generations of officers. Table 4 compares the cadets with the Janowitz study of air force general officers

TABLE 4

COMPARISONS OF POLITICAL IDENTIFICATION

Political Identification	AFA Cadets %	AWC & ACSC 1974 %	Air Force 1954 %	Army & Navy 1954 %
Conservative	12	23	15	24
Somewhat conservative	31	41	47	45
Middle-of-the-road	29	22	*	*
Somewhat liberal	24	13	32	20
Liberal	5	1	3	6
N =	762	675	157	419

Sources: 1954 data from Janowitz, 1960, p. 237; Margiotta, 1976, p. 169, USAF Academy, 1976.

*Not a response in Janowitz

and with Margiotta's survey of air force field-grade officers in the Air War College and Air Command and Staff College.[17] Unless further research reveals the political orientations of these older elites at the time of their initial recruitment, our comparison is self-evident. Without such evidence, we expect conservatism to increase with age and rank.

Academic Performance

The effect of cadet academic standing on future aptitude, performance, and success is a long-argued and unanswered question. This may be due to a lack of data or to conflicts in existing data. There was no significant relationship between academic standing and military aptitude in a 1968 study of fifty-eight West Point cadets dismissed for lack of military aptitude.[18] In an AFA study of graduates from the classes of 1959 through 1969, however, there was a positive correlation between academic success at the academy and success in the air force. When academic standing was linked to primary and below-the-zone promotions, decorations, least attrition, and the like, graduates with high academic orders of merit fared considerably better.[19] In her study of army generals, Maureen Mylander describes the effect of academic performance as follows: "Contrary to a widespread Army belief and a number of earlier studies showing that academic success at West Point does not correlate with success in attaining general's rank, a survey of the 233 West Pointers among the Army's 491 generals as of August 1, 1973, revealed that 50.2 percent ranked in the top

TABLE 5

ACADEMIC PERFORMANCE VS MOM

Academic Quintile (GPA)	Percent Respond- ing	Top Q (%)	2nd Q (%)	3rd Q (%)	Bottom Q (%)
Top (3.50 - 4.00)	15	50	28	12	9
4th (3.00 - 3.49)	23	34	32	21	13
3rd (2.50 - 2.99)	32	17	29	29	25
2nd (2.10 - 2.49)	25	14	22	28	36
Lowest (0 - 2.09)	6	17	24	33	26

third of their graduating class, 31.3 percent ranked in the middle third, and 18.5 percent finished in the lower third."[20]

Both the AFA study and Mylander's survey sought linkages to military success in the academic environment; we believe that academic standing is also linked to military success at the academy. Our findings in Table 5 strongly support this notion. Of the 15 percent in the top academic quintile (grade-point average 3.5 to 4.0), fully one-half rank in the top quartile of the MOM, and only 9 percent of this group are rated as the lowest military performers. Our findings generally show that the higher the Academic Order of Merit (AOM), the higher the MOM, and vice versa. One deviation appeared when we compared the bottom academic quintile with the next higher academic quintile. The overall military performance of the lowest academic group is slightly higher than the group above it. This is predictable if one understands the tenuous position of cadets holding the minimum academic grade-point average of 2.0. Their prospects of staying at the academy would be jeopardized if they did not have noticeable military qualities in their favor. We were also not surprised that the cadets in the second lowest academic quintile are overrepresented at the bottom of the MOM.

The MOM supposedly measures military qualities without conscious regard for a cadet's academic standing, but reasonable explanation can be given for the academic-military performance linkage. Two of the smaller MOM inputs relate directly to academic potential. The military studies grade and the wing training scores are quantified and entered into the MOM evaluation system; this favors the more intelligent cadet.[21]

Other explanations are more indirect. A high grade-point average is its own reward in this highly competitive arena of relatively bright students. Coupled with an acceptable personality, a high grade-point average often generates respect from peers. Respect for intelligence can then translate into favorable peer ratings, which heavily affect the MOM.[22]

Finally, negative feedback from the faculty to the AOC can affect the AOC evaluation. If the classroom instructor highlights what seems to be an attitude problem, the cadet may be rated low in the military order of merit. In such cases, academics may be viewed as a military duty, although "academic performance" is not evaluated on any rating form currently in use.

Social Characteristics

Our study also focuses on demographic, socioeconomic, and family characteristics that may influence cadet success.[23] We were particularly interested in comparing our cadets to officer elites of older generations and to one another, since the Class of 1977 was the first class to enter under the all-volunteer concept. We describe only the significant differences in responses between the Classes of 1976 and 1977. To determine whether particular social groups were selecting themselves out by academic and motivational attrition, we compared our data with ACE data compiled when these classes entered the academy two and three years ago.

Social Origins

In his 1976 study of air force future elites, Margiotta confirmed Janowitz's predictions that officer regional affiliations would be more representative of the U.S. population.[24] Considering the Air Force Academy's active recruitment program and the congressional appointment system, we hypothesized that our sample would closely correspond to the U.S. population distribution. However, our findings indicate that regions of past overrepresentation among general officers are underrepresented at the academy. Table 6 shows that 22 percent of the cadets come from the South, an area that held 31 percent of the 1970 population. The Northeast is still somewhat underrepresented. Twenty-six percent of the cadets come from the West, although this region accounted for only 17 percent of the population.

We could determine no single reason for overrepresentation or underrepresentation, nor did this variable significantly affect cadet standings in military performance. Overrepresentation of the West may be attributed to nothing more complex than the location of the academy and its academic visibility to intelligent high school students from that region.[25] Another factor may be the concentration of air force bases from which sons of military fathers would seek a disproportionate number of competitive appointments.[26] Despite the attractiveness of the academy to high school

TABLE 6

COMPARISON OF GEOGRAPHIC ORIGINS

	Past Elite[a] %	Current AF Elite[b] %	AWC & ACSC[b] %	Pop. 1950[a] %	AFA Cadets %	Pop. 1970 %
Regional Affiliation						
North East	25	20	22	26	19	24
South	25	40	32	31	22	31
North Central	43	27	30	30	27	28
West	7	13	15	13	26	17
Other	–	–	–	–	7[c]	–
N =	106	341	630	151M	775	205M
Rural/Urban						
Rural (under 2,500)	67	*	36	41	17	26
Urban (2,500 +)	30	*	62	59	72	74
Military site	3	*	2	–	11	–
N =	105		678	132M	774	203M

Sources: a – Janowitz, 1960, pp. 59-106.
b – Margiotta, 1976, pp. 158-160.
c – Seven percent indicating "other" for geographic origin may reflect the mobility of a military upbringing.
* – Not reported.

boys from the West, they do not perform any better than cadets from New England, an area traditionally underrepresented at the service academies.

We next examined the size of the communities where the cadets were reared. We validated the Janowitz and Margiotta findings and predictions that military elites would become more representative of the population and would lose their rural flavor. Only 19 percent of the Class of 1976 reported a rural or small town background. The Class of 1977 is even less rural; only 15 percent were reared in small communities, and a greater number come from larger cities and suburbs. ACE data did not report this variable at the time the cadets in our sample were freshmen. We cross-tabulated this factor with the order of merit list, but we found that our original hypothesis was invalid. Cadets from a rural background did not achieve a higher MOM because of a factor that Janowitz calls the "military sense of honor" and "simpler kind of patriotism" that flourishes in rural areas.[27] Rural or urban rearing made no statistical difference in the success of our sample. A more homogeneous culture brought by mass communications and a highly mobile society may have rendered these variables less meaningful.

A breakdown of cadet religious affiliations shows that the cadets are generally representative of the U.S. college population, except for cadets of the Jewish faith. Approximately 1 percent of the cadets are Jewish, compared with 4 percent of American four-year college freshmen.[28] One-third of the cadets are Catholic, and the majority remain Protestant. A sizable number (11 percent) consider themselves nondenominational Christians, and another 10 percent either have no religious preference or consider themselves atheists or agnostics.[29]

When we cross-tabulated religious denominations with the MOM, we found no significant relationships, with the minor exception of cadets who chose atheism or agnosticism. In this case, we found a slight tendency toward a lower MOM, but the size of the cell samples was too small to consider it statistically significant.

We did find an interesting connection between church *attendance* and the order of merit. As shown in Table 7, church attendance produces a near mirror image in the MOM. Thirty-four percent of the cadets who are church members and attend regularly rank in the top quartile of the MOM, and 32 percent who do not regularly attend rank in the bottom quartile. Regular church attendance is greater for the Class of 1977 than for the Class of 1976.

Since freshman data are unavailable, we cannot verify whether the differences between classes carried over from initial recruitment. We can only speculate about the effects of church membership and attendance, since evaluators are probably not biased against nonchurchgoers. More likely, church membership coupled with attendance indicates a more

TABLE 7

CADET RELIGIOUS INTEREST VS MOM

"What best describes your current religious interest?"	Percent Respond- ing	Top Q (%)	2nd Q (%)	3rd Q (%)	Bottom Q (%)
Church member; attend regularly	34	34	26	22	18
Church member; no regular attendance	35	22	30	27	21
Not a church member, but attend anyway	6	19	33	29	19
Not a church member; no regular attendance	25	18	24	26	32
N =	753				

favorable orientation to authority, conformity, and socially approved values. This speculation is suggested by recent studies that demonstrate the significance of "religious interest" as the single best predictor of conservative attitudes.[30]

We intended to determine whether racial or minority backgrounds correlated with particular MOM quartiles. Although blacks make up approximately 10 percent of the U.S. college population, less than 3 percent of the upper classes at the academy were blacks. Authors and researchers differ in explaining this underrepresentation, but a common theme surfaces. Years of formal segregation and handicaps in education prevented blacks from making significant inroads into the upper ranks of the military profession. Today, opportunities in the civilian market for college-educated blacks lure them away from military officership, a profession with which few educated blacks identify.[31] Nonwhite minority respondents were too few to provide any statistical measurement of performance factors by race or ethnic group.

Socioeconomic Factors

As indicated in Table 8, past and future air force elites perceive their family origins as primarily lower-middle-class. Margiotta argues that this factor supports predictions of a more socially representative officer corps.[32] Cadets, on the other hand, perceive themselves as primarily *upper* middle-class; this factor is confirmed by parental occupation and estimated parental income. Sixty-two percent claim white-collar family back-grounds, and 26 percent reported their father's occupation as blue-collar. When we compared recent figures of parental income with data collected

TABLE 8

COMPARISON OF SOCIOECONOMIC CLASS

	AF General Officers (1950) %	AWC & ACSC %	AFA Cadets %
Family's Socioeconomic			
Upper	–	–	2
Upper-middle	30	24	55
Lower-middle	62	64	39
Upper-lower	8	11	4
Lower-lower	–	1	–
N =	60	671	773
Principal Wage Earner's Occupation			
Professional/Managerial	38	31	30
Military	–	4	22
Other	42	10	10
Total white collar	80	45	62
Skilled worker	not	27	22
Unskilled worker	given	9	4
Total blue collar		36	26
Farm owner/manager	15	12	3
Other	–	7	9
N =	60	680	773
Parent's Combined Income			
$30,000 - more			13
$20,000 - 29,999			27
$12,000 - 19,999			39
Less than $12,000			19

Sources: 1950 Generals: Janowitz, 1960, pp. 86, 90, 91;
Margiotta, 1976, p. 160; USAF Academy, 1976

when these cadets were freshmen, we found that more cadets from *lower* socioeconomic family backgrounds had dropped out. Only 19 percent of the remaining Classes of 1976 and 1977 estimated a parental income less than $12,000 when they entered the academy. This is less than the 30 percent who reported this income when they were selected to attend the academy. Only 8 percent of the entering freshmen estimated parental income above $30,000, but 13 percent of the cadets who remain reported their family income above $30,000 when they were entering freshmen.

TABLE 9

FAMILY CONSTELLATIONS VS MOM

	Percent Respond-ing	Top Q (%)	2nd Q (%)	3rd Q (%)	Bottom Q (%)
Birth Order/Family Configuration					
Only child	4	4	59	19	19
Oldest child (with one or more siblings)	46	27	29	22	22
Youngest (with one more older)	17	33	22	24	21
Middle child (two or more brothers)	7	20	28	32	20
Middle child (two or more sisters)	4	29	24	24	24
Middle child (two or more siblings both sexes)	23	20	25	31	25
N =	767				
Parent's Status					
Both alive, married to each other	91	26	27	25	22
Both alive, divorced	5	21	28	23	30
Both alive, separated	1	14	43	43	0
One parent deceased	2	13	50	19	19
Both parents deceased	–	–	–	–	–
N =	769				

We next sought to determine whether social class origins affected cadet performance. Since earlier studies had shown the father's occupation to be the single best indicator of socioeconomic status, we cross-tabulated this variable with the MOM.[33] Sons of military officer fathers had the highest MOMs of all occupational groups listed in our survey. Sons of unskilled workers were slightly overrepresented in the bottom half, but the number of respondents in this category was too small to be statistically significant.

Family Constellation

Because of previous research on early socialization, we anticipated that

TABLE 10

COMPARISON OF GENERATIONS OF NATIVITY

Nativity	West Point '59-'60 %	AWC & ACSC '74 %	AFA Cadets '76-'77 %
Foreign born	1	1	3
First generation (one or both parents foreign born)	8	10	6
Second generation (parents or grand- parents native born)	91	89	91
N =	1448	679	768

Sources: West Point: Janowitz, 1960, p. 84; AWC and ACSC: Margiotta, 1976; USAF Academy, 1976.

family configuration and stability would make a significant difference in cadet performance. This was not the case. Table 9 shows the birth orders and family stability that characterize the upper-class cadet. One-half of our sample are the eldest sons in their families.[34] They come from highly stable and atypical American family backgrounds: *91 percent have parents who are both alive and still married to each other.* When we tested these findings against the MOM list, we found no reportable differences in relative success.

Our study supports past findings that air force elites in the next century will continue to be overwhelmingly native-born. As noted in Table 10, 91 percent of the cadets are at least second-generation Americans; that is, the cadet and his parents were born in the United States. The small percentage of cadets who reported that they were "foreign-born" were born at military sites overseas. The nativity of the cadets closely approximates samplings of West Point cadets and air force officers in the Classes of 1974 at Air War College and Air Command and Staff College. The contrast between these native-born Americans and the varying ethnicity of the U.S. population remains.

An interesting dimension explored in social science literature is the effect of an individual's military heritage. The contention is that the services may be leaning toward self-recruitment of the sons of military career fathers.[35] We were interested in determining whether military heritage affected success at the academy. Table 11 shows that almost

TABLE 11

MILITARY HERITAGE VS MOM

Family Military Heritage	Percent Respond- ing	Top Q (%)	2nd Q (%)	3rd Q (%)	Bottom Q (%)
Grandfather career military	2	29	21	21	29
Father career military	23	31	29	21	19
Both of the above	3	29	24	24	24
Father and/or grand- father noncareer military	47	25	28	25	22
None of the above	25	20	26	29	25
No family military heritage	13	20	29	26	25
Father career officer	16	36	30	17	17
Father career enlisted	11	25	24	29	22
Father noncareer officer	14	26	27	29	18
Father noncareer enlisted	46	23	27	25	25
N =	769				

one-fourth of the cadets said that their fathers were career military; these military sons did slightly better in military performance. Our only significant finding is that sons of career *officers* are most likely to achieve higher scores on the MOM. Although other cadets were fairly evenly distributed through all quartiles of the MOM, two-thirds of the sons of officers rank in the upper one-half of the class. Sons of general officers represent less than 1 percent of our sample. This figure is not statistically significant, but interestingly, five of these six cadets rank in the top one-half of the class.

We were not surprised that one-fourth of our respondents came from career military families, since Lovell reported the number of West Point cadets from military families as relatively constant, approximating 20 percent over a fifteen-year period.[36] Upon entry, these same classes reported 15 percent of their fathers as "military." After two or three years, the proportion had climbed to more than 25 percent. These figures support Marron's conclusion that sons of military fathers have lower motivational attrition than sons of most other occupational groups.[37]

TABLE 12

COMPARISON OF FAMILY MILITARY HERITAGE

Family Military Heritage	AWC & ACSC %	AFA Cadets &
No family military heritage	70	13
Father career officer	3	16
Father career enlisted	2	11
Father noncareer officer	6	14
Father noncareer enlisted	24	46
N =	674	769

Sources: Margiotta, 1976; USAF Academy, 1976.

There was a striking contrast between the cadets and the AWC and ACSC officers (Table 12). Only 3 percent of these majors, lieutenant colonels, and colonels had career officer fathers, but 16 percent of the cadet sample reported career officer fathers. Eleven percent of the cadet's fathers are enlisted career individuals compared with only 1 percent of the officers in the 1974 study. Eleven percent is the average figure between the Classes of 1976 and 1977, since the Class of 1977 actually had a 4 percent increase in career enlisted fathers. Although this is not a major difference, it may indicate a trend in recruitment that could be verified in future studies. Finally, only 13 percent of the cadets reported that their fathers had "no military experience," but 70 percent of the field-grade officers are listed in this category.

The recruitment patterns of our cadets and the older generation of officers are clearly different. Cadet fathers were eligible for the draft during World War II and the Korean War. The field-graders generally came from a generation of fathers who were too old to participate in these two wars. We thus expect these academy recruitment trends to continue. The percentage of cadets reporting fathers with no military experience may shrink even further as children of Vietnam veterans apply for entry to the academy. Unless future studies indicate a marked increase in numbers of sons of *career* military fathers, we cannot validate the formation of a military "caste" in American society.

Implications: Who Stays? Who Succeeds?

Is it important that there are major differences in the military backgrounds of the fathers of several generations of air force officers? Since military heritage affected cadet attrition and military performance rankings, we believe that these differences are meaningful. More importantly, however, we think these heretofore unverified differences are suggestive of broader questions that must be asked of research into the military. Do the data on Air Force Academy cadets suggest it is time to rethink many earlier assumptions about the military elite?

This study permits us to begin generalizing about the potential air force elite who will assume leadership roles in the next century. Janowitz was more or less correct in his predictions about the next generations of the U.S. officer corps. Future air force elite will not come from southern rural origins; in fact, they will be overwhelmingly urban and nonsouthern. They will not come from humble surroundings and be seeking upward mobility, but they will have backgrounds normally associated with other careers and professions. In general, they are intelligent, white, Protestant, native Americans drawn from the suburban West and Midwest, and there are more Catholics than before. They tend to be firstborn sons of conservative, upper-middle-class, white-collar fathers who, if not career men themselves, have served in the military. Cadet rearing is marked by a high degree of family stability in which church membership was probably the norm. The cadets still identify with some denomination, but more than one-half no longer attend church regularly.

We found the cadets to be somewhat conservative and to have aspirations for high rank and long service. Differences between the Class of 1976 and the Class of 1977 are slight. Race, regional affiliation, and birth order contributed little evidence to predict the success of future elites. The strongest associations clustered around career attitudes, academic performance, church attendance, and family military heritage.

Like most beginning research, this study may lead to several future avenues of research. For the first time, an attempt was made to determine variables that may relate to cadet socialization and attrition at the academy. We also attempted to measure those factors that might affect reported military performance. There indeed appears to be a socialization process at the academy. However, in this study, we can only speculate that this process may mostly reinforce earlier learned values or lead to attrition among those with conflicting values. The evidence shows less attrition among cadets from higher-income families, cadets with conservative identification, and sons of career military fathers. Those cadets who were exposed earlier to military systems and to values consistent with the academy's values do better while they are at the academy. Further research is required to expand and document these tentative conclusions.

Finally, we believe that we have cracked open a door to research methods whose use is long overdue. This is the first large-scale, systematic attempt to determine what social factors might affect the military success of academy cadets. We should no longer assume that graduation from an academy equals rapid advancement and ultimate selection to general officer. We have documented the obvious—that different cadets perform very differently at the Air Force Academy. Our data suggest that earlier studies of officer social origins will no longer describe future elites. The next steps are logical. These research techniques could be expanded to all academies and to other commissioning sources. They could be adopted for senior officer ranks in the services. More rigorous social science statistical techniques could be applied to all collected data.

Rational choice in a democracy requires debate. Informed debate requires information and data. This study has expanded our understanding of future military leaders and of the social variables that seem to affect their success and their choices about a military career. There is still much to be done before our understanding of the military profession is adequate.

Notes

1. This is probably due to the general dearth of systematic data collection from a relatively young academy. Many initial policies and practices were carried over from the U.S. Military Academy. The Air Force Academy's leaders—superintendents, deans of the faculty, and commandants of cadets—have been West Point graduates. We are thus not surprised that researchers so far have made few distinctions between West Point and Colorado Springs.

2. Franklin D. Margiotta, "A Military Elite in Transition: Air Force Leaders in the 1980s," *Armed Forces and Society* 2, no. 2 (Winter 1976): 155-184.

3. The career advantages of West Point graduates, for example, are critically but plausibly discussed in Maureen Mylander's *The Generals* (New York: Dial Press, 1974), p. 60.

4. This may be due to a lack of understanding of how "success" is measured at the academies and to a failure to distinguish among academic, physical, or military success. An understanding of these distinctions is crucial to an understanding of the selection processes at the academies.

5. Comptroller General of the United States, *Report to the Congress: Student Attrition at the Five Federal Service Academies* (Washington, D.C.: General Accounting Office, March 5, 1976) henceforth referred to as the GAO Report. The GAO Report listed several interrelated causes of the high attrition rate (46 percent in the Class of 1975 alone), but it gave no single overriding cause. It called for further study of attrition.

6. According to academy officials, 88 graduates of the late 1960s and early 1970s were passed over for promotion to permanent regular captain. When an officer is twice passed over for a permanent grade, he is forced to leave the service. For an appreciation of the crucial impact of an officer's efficiency report, see Mylander, *The Generals*, pp. 64-70.

7. Fourth-class and third-class cadets who resign are normally excused from further military duty. Second-class and first-class cadets who are separated or whose resignations are accepted retain an active-duty commitment, except for cadets separated for physical disability, unfitness, or unsuitability for further service. First and second classmen are normally transferred to the Air Force Reserve and ordered to active duty in an enlisted status.

8. Morris Janowitz, *The Professional Soldier: A Social and Political Portrait* (Glencoe, Ill.: Free Press, 1960).

9. American Council on Education, *Entering Norms for College Freshmen, Fall 1972* (Washington, D.C., Fall 1972, 1973). Since the ACE data do not break out specific colleges, we relied heavily on the Air Force Academy's input to the annual ACE survey.

10. The cadet performance evaluation report includes ten major categories, such as performance of duty, initiative, judgment, and leadership. These reports are written by fellow cadets higher in the chain of command.

11. Both of the authors recently completed tours of duty at the Air Force Academy. Their hypotheses stem from a review of the literature, personal observations, and interviews of cadets.

12. This coincides with the findings of the GAO report, which correlated low MOMs with increased attrition rates; see p. 36.

13. For a fuller explanation of commission types and impacts on career opportunity, see Mylander, *The Generals*, pp. 60-61.

14. The political orientations of West Point cadets can be found in Laurence I. Radway, "Recent Trends at American Service Academies," in *Public Opinion and the Military Establishment*, ed. Charles C. Moskos (Beverly Hills, Calif.: Sage, 1971). For entering midshipmen at Annapolis, see Charles L. Cochran and Luis R. Luis, "Midshipmen Political Characterization and Academy Socialization," in *Civil Military Relations*, ed. Charles L. Cochran (New York: Free Press, 1974). As in our study, both rely heavily on statistical information provided to the American Council on Education, *National Norms for Entering College Freshmen*.

15. Using the same type of question, the GAO study found that the dropouts tend to perceive themselves as "liberal." See also William C. Lucas, "Anticipatory Socialization and the ROTC," in Moskos, *Public Opinion*. Lucas concludes, for example, that ROTC students develop basic orientations and commitments long before they go to college.

16. Margiotta, "Military Elite in Transition," pp. 170-171.

17. Ibid., p. 169.

18. Ramon A. Nadal, *Characteristics of Cadets Dismissed for Lack of Military Aptitude* (West Point, N.Y.: Office of Military Psychology and Leadership, United States Military Academy, 1968). After screening the records of fifty-eight dismissed cadets of the Classes of 1963 through 1967, Nadal's main conclusions were: (1) cadets eventually declared deficient in military aptitude are identified by the first aptitude rating during the freshman year; (2) some cadets are not discharged as early as they could be; (3) a very close relationship exists between low physical education standing and poor military aptitude; (4) there is no significant relationship between academic standing and military aptitude; and (5) the main failure of cadets dismissed for lack of military aptitude is lack of interpersonal skills.

19. "Officer Performance vs. Cadet Performance" (United States Air Force Academy, Colorado: Office of Cadet Evaluations). This report also correlated MOM and officer performance, with similar results; in every category, officers who had high MOMs as cadets were more successful than officers with low MOMs as cadets.

20. Mylander, *The Generals*, p. 343.

21. The military studies program is not under the dean but under the commandant of cadets. A first classman's grade-point average is unaffected by military studies, since he has only a pass/fail course in the second semester. Second classmen, however, are assigned a letter grade that affects their grade-point average as well as their MOM. Wing training is also administered by the deputy commandant and conducted on Saturday mornings. Quiz scores on strictly military-related subjects are then used as inputs to the MOM.

22. Over 50 percent of the cadets in both classes graduated from high school with an A-minus average or better. ACE statistics indicate that approximately 20 percent of students in civilian four-year colleges graduated with such averages. For comparative statistics on West Point, see Radway, "Recent Trends," p. 5; for the Naval Academy, see Cochran and Luis, "Midshipmen," p. 118.

23. For a study of West Pointers, see Joseph E. Marron, *The Socioeconomic Background and Performance of West Point Graduates* (West Point, N.Y.: Office of Institutional Research, United States Military Academy, 1972).

24. Margiotta, "Military Elite in Transition," p. 157.

25. According to a summary of data on entering freshmen prepared in 1972 by the Air Force Academy for the American Council of Education, 90 percent of the cadets chose "Has a good academic reputation" in response to the statement, "Reasons noted as very important in selecting this college."

26. Lovell cites the competitive appointment system and the clustering of army posts within the Atlantic Coast region to explain the overrepresentation of that area in West Point's Class of 1964. Although this explanation is plausible, we feel that it is only one of many factors affecting recruitment patterns. For a more complete explanation of his rationale, see John P. Lovell, "The Professional Socialization of the West Point Cadet," in *The New Military*, ed. Morris Janowitz (New York: Russell Sage Foundation, 1964).

27. Janowitz, *The Professional Soldier*, p. 85.

28. American Council on Education, *National Norms for Entering College Freshmen, Fall 1973* (Washington, D.C., Fall 1973).

29. The number of cadets professing atheism or agnosticism is considerably higher than in earlier studies of the other academies; our data may reflect the change to noncompulsory chapel attendance effective in 1972.

30. Cochran and Luis, "Midshipmen," p. 134.

31. Edward Bernard Glick, *Soldiers, Scholars and Society: The Social Impact of the American Military* (Pacific Palisades, Calif.: Goodyear, 1971), p. 30. See also Charles C. Moskos, Jr., "Minority Groups in Military Organizations," in *Handbook of Military Institutions*, ed. Roger W. Little (Beverly Hills, Calif.: Sage, 1971).

32. Margiotta, "Military Elite in Transition," p. 159.

33. Marron, *West Point Graduates*, p. 2. In his study, Marron investigated the effect of the father's occupation on a cadet's Aptitude for Service Rating (ASR)—

West Point's equivalent of the MOM. He found little connection to the ASR, but he did conclude that military sons have the lowest motivational attrition rate at West Point and in the army.

34. We could not compare this finding with freshmen ACE data, but the phenomenon of eldest son attraction to the service academies is supported in a 1973 West Point study. See Joseph E. Marron, *Birth Order, Family Configuration and Personal Problems* (West Point, N.Y.: Office of Institutional Research, United States Military Academy, 1973).

35. In 1971, Morris Janowitz warned that the military may be drawn from an ever-narrowing base of self-recruitment. See Janowitz, "The Emergent Military," in Moskos, *Public Opinion*.

36. Lovell, "The West Point Cadet," p. 136.

37. Marron, *West Point Graduates*, p. 11.

20
Who Goes to the United States Naval Academy?

John F. Fitzgerald
Charles L. Cochran

In the previous chapter, Schloemer and Myers described Air Force Academy cadets and identified some of the factors that might affect cadet performance at the academy. Theirs was the first large-scale study of this nature conducted at any military academy; thus, it identified many research possibilities. Using Schloemer and Myers's methods, we administered the same survey at the Naval Academy. Not surprisingly, many of our conclusions parallel the conclusions reached in the air force study, but we also discovered areas for improving the research methods used. On the basis of both research efforts, we suggest that further refinement and study in certain areas would make these analyses more valuable.

To gain a better understanding of midshipmen with high career aspirations, we administered the questionnaire on a voluntary basis to a random sample of 20 percent of the first and second class (seniors and juniors). The sample produced 425 respondents (the number varies slightly from question to question), for a participation rate of almost 100 percent. One major difference between this study and the air force study makes our findings somewhat incompatible with the data gathered at the Air Force Academy. That is, the military performance (MP) grade used by the Naval Academy is computed differently from the military order of merit (MOM) grade used by the Air Force Academy.

Measuring Military Performance at the Naval Academy

Historically, a military aptitude grade measured a midshipman's potential for a naval career. In July 1976, this measuring system was renamed the "military performance grade," but it remained a composite of various ratings. Midshipmen officers in the brigade evaluate other midshipmen within their platoons. The company officer, a naval officer, is ultimately responsible for writing each midshipman's military performance (MP) sheet, and he determines the weights to give these evaluations. He also has access to other information, such as demerits, academic grades, and

345

quality points received by the individual. Faculty members are requested to submit evaluations on midshipmen who perform very well or very poorly in the classroom. Under the system in effect during this study, midshipmen rated their peers within their companies and were, in turn, rated by their peers. The company officer includes these peer evaluations as factors in arriving at military performance grades for midshipmen. He uses all of these sources of information and his own personal evaluation of the whole man in assigning the grades.

The military performance grade differs from the military order of merit used at the Air Force Academy. Rather than division into quartiles, the possible grades for MP are A, B, C, D, and F. In practice, the grades most frequently assigned are A, B, or C. If a midshipman receives an F, he must appear before a brigade aptitude board, where he is either dismissed or assigned a grade of D and placed on probation for one semester. If he fails to improve his grade, he is ordinarily separated at the end of the following semester. A midshipman who receives a D for two consecutive semesters must also appear before a brigade aptitude board. If he is not separated, he is placed on probation for one semester. If he does not improve his grade within one semester, he is separated in most cases.

Only 2 percent of the sample made grades in these categories. Since midshipmen must improve grades of D or F or face separation, this study does not include an analysis of this small group. An equally compelling reason for excluding midshipmen in the D or F category is that this small number would seriously reduce the value of statistical tests, especially the chi-square test of significance.

One should note that a grade of A, B, or C is not a forced distribution of thirds; the distribution of A's, B's, and C's was 40 percent, 29 percent, and 31 percent, respectively. Any significant departure from the mean grade in the cross-tabulation serves as an "analytical flag" marking that relationship for specific analysis. This difference in allocating military performance grades does not give the same demarcations obtained at the Air Force Academy, which uses a rank-ordering system with forced distribution into quartiles.

Professional and Political Characteristics

A major hypothesis tested in this study is that midshipmen who aspire to high rank or to long careers will tend to be overrepresented in the upper ranges of the military performance grades.[1] Unlike the findings at the Air Force Academy, our findings show few strong correlations between midshipmen aspirations for high rank or length of service and military performance grades. Stronger associations appeared when we matched career aspirations with rank aspirations.

TABLE 1

MIDSHIPMEN CAREER ATTITUDES AND MILITARY PERFORMANCE

Aspirations	Responding Percent	Percentage Receiving MP grade of:		
		A	B	C
Rank				
Lieutenant (0-3)	24	40	28	32
Lt Commander (0-4)	7	34	31	34
Commander (0-5)	18	26	31	43
Captain (0-6)	34	44	27	29
Rear Admiral (0-8)	7	42	29	29
Vice Admiral (0-9)	10	51	32	17
Expected Distribution	100	40	29	31
Career				
30 years	8	38	38	24
20 years	28	47	24	29
Less than 20 years	14	33	28	40
Look, then make up mind	39	40	30	29
One tour	11	28	30	41
Expected Distribution	100	40	29	31
N =	408			

For example, as shown in Table 1, 40 percent of the midshipmen aspiring to the relatively low rank of lieutenant (0-3) have MP grades of A, which is almost the expected distribution. The correlation is stronger between a high MP grade and aspirations to the rank of captain (0-6) and above, but even here it is not pronounced. Midshipmen who anticipate flag rank appear to have high self-confidence in the sense that more expect to achieve the rank of vice admiral (forty-one midshipmen) rather than rear admiral (twenty-eight midshipmen). However, in none of these cases is the relationship between MP grade and rank aspiration a significant departure from the mean grade distribution of 40, 29, and 31 percent for grades of A, B, and C. Thus, the hypothesis of a strong relationship between high MP grade and rank aspiration is not uniformly substantiated at the Naval Academy.

Although 31 percent expect to achieve the rank of lieutenant or lieutenant commander, an additional 50 percent expect to retire at the rank of captain or higher. It is not surprising that such a high percentage of midshipmen have such goals. Their backgrounds suggest that they are ambitious, aggressive, intelligent, and, generally, high achievers. Most academy students have done extremely well academically in high school, and they have been unusually well represented in such achievements as election to class president, earning varsity letters, and other scholastic honors.

The next question is whether their aspirations are realistic. The authors argue that the percentage of midshipmen aspiring to the rank of captain or above is not unrealistic. A study by the Center for Naval Analyses found that 27 percent of all Naval Academy graduates actually do achieve the rank of captain or higher when they are placed in the promotion zone. In addition, a few more are promoted to this rank from above and below the zone. A realistic estimate is that 30 percent of all academy graduates will achieve the rank of captain or higher.[2]

A cross-tabulation of military performance grades with the midshipmen's intended length of service yields interesting results. Table 1 indicates that midshipmen receiving A's and B's view themselves as more likely to remain on active duty for thirty years than midshipmen receiving C's. Forty-seven percent of the midshipmen indicating an intention of staying for twenty years had A's and 41 percent of those indicating their intention to leave the navy following their obligatory service received C's. These results and the direction of the tendencies are hardly surprising. Individuals being rewarded by the system can be expected to look more favorably on the prospects of a long association with the organization conferring the rewards.

The relationship between anticipated length of active service and anticipated rank is perhaps the most revealing relationship in the area of career aspiration. Table 2 shows clearly that a majority of midshipmen intending to remain in service for twenty years expect to reach the rank of captain (0-6), and a majority of those anticipating thirty-year careers expect to achieve the rank of admiral (0-7 to 0-9). In contrast, midshipmen planning to serve only their required tours of duty realistically expect only to reach the rank of lieutenant. The correlation between envisioned length of service and anticipated rank achievement is statistically quite strong (tau = 0.423).

Our study of the Naval Academy midshipmen thus closely parallels the findings at the Air Force Academy in regard to career intentions.

TABLE 2

CAREER ASPIRATIONS BY RANK ASPIRATIONS

Career Aspirations	Responding Percent	Percentage Aspiring to Each Rank by Career Aspiration					
		Lt	Lt Cmdr	Cmdr	Capt	RAdm	VAdm
30 years	8	0	0	0	27	23	50
20 years	28	1	2	13	62	12	10
Less than 20 years	14	9	20	44	22	2	3
Look, then make up mind	39	35	8	19	28	4	7
One tour	11	81	9	4	4	0	2
N =	417						

Approximately the same proportion at each academy are uncertain of their long-range career intentions; this seems realistic. We might note that midshipmen who are uncertain about their career intentions signal their uncertainty by unexpectedly high rank aspirations. For example, of the 160 midshipmen who expect to look at the service before they make up their minds about long careers, fully 40 percent expect to become captains or admirals. This suggests that these cautious young men lean in the direction of serving and that their first or second assignments will be important elements in their final career decisions.

This preliminary research suggests further important research in the area of career intentions. For example, it would be interesting to test the correlation between a midshipman's military performance grade and his career intentions during his experience at the academy. If his career intentions closely shadowed his aptitude grade, this would indicate something about positive and negative incentives. It would also indicate whether career intentions were primarily the cause or the effect of the grade received.

Political Attitudes and MP

One might hypothesize that midshipmen with conservative social and political attitudes would naturally be more compatible with the military style and would receive higher aptitude grades than midshipmen with liberal attitudes.[3] Midshipmen in the sample were asked to identify themselves on a five-point scale that included the following categories: liberal, somewhat liberal, middle-of-the-road, somewhat conservative, and

TABLE 3

POLITICAL IDENTIFICATION AND MILITARY PERFORMANCE

Political Identification	Responding Percent	Percentage Receiving MP grade of:		
		A	B	C
Conservative	11	30	34	36
Somewhat conservative	34	46	27	28
Middle-of-the-road	26	40	28	32
Somewhat liberal	22	42	29	29
Liberal	7	19	39	42
Expected distribution	100	40	29	31
N =	415			

conservative. As Table 3 shows, midshipmen who identify themselves as either liberal or conservative are more likely to receive C's than any other grades, and those who describe themselves as somewhat liberal, somewhat conservative, or middle-of-the-road receive more A's than any other grades.

Only 19 percent of the midshipmen who described themselves as liberal received A's—as opposed to 40 percent that would normally be expected. At the same time, 42 percent of those who described themselves as liberal received C's when only 31 percent would be expected. This showing may reflect the compatibility of certain personality traits with MP or, conversely, a bias in the determination of the MP grade in favor of conservatives. Nevertheless, the overall results indicated in Table 3 are not statistically significant. Naval Academy findings are surprisingly congruent with Air Force Academy findings. The upper classes at both institutions are approximately the same in political identification, a variable that seems to have little effect on reported success at both academies.

In exploring further, we cross-tabulated political identification with career intentions and formed no significant relationship. In short, there is no support for the working hypothesis that politically conservative individuals would adapt and flourish in the conservative environment of the academy. They do not perform markedly better than individuals with liberal orientations, nor do they express significantly higher intentions for long naval careers.

TABLE 4

FATHERS' IDEOLOGY AND MIDSHIPMEN MILITARY PERFORMANCE

Fathers' Ideology	Responding Percent	Percentage Receiving MP grade of:		
		A	B	C
Conservative	33	46	23	31
Somewhat conservative	40	35	33	32
Middle-of-the-road	13	38	34	28
Somewhat liberal	5	33	19	48
Liberal	2	44	44	11
Did not know	7	41	24	35
Expected distribution	100	40	29	31
N =	416			

Father's Ideology and MP

Another method of determining whether the early socialization environment relates to MP is to cross-tabulate the father's perceived ideology with midshipman MP. As indicated in Table 4, midshipmen see themselves as coming from families that tend to be overwhelmingly conservative. Again, there is no evidence that individuals from more conservative families score higher on MP grades (X^2 = 10.983, $p > 0.50$). Unfortunately, the questionnaire was concerned only with determining the ideological predispositions of parents; it did not probe the father's participatory activities. Perhaps a valid working hypothesis is that parents with strong participatory orientations evidenced by voting, family discussions of political issues, subscriptions to periodicals, working for political causes, and campaigning for candidates would suggest stronger political socialization and a more profound impact on the attitudes of offspring. It would be interesting to examine the relationship between the MP of midshipmen whose parents are strongly participatory and that of other midshipmen and to analyze the results across the political spectrum.

In exploring the question of ideology still further, we examined the relationship between the fathers' ideologies and midshipmen ideologies.

Various studies have verified a correlation between the political identification of offspring and parents.[4] For example, similarity in party preference
between parent and child is much higher than support by a parent and
child for specific social issues or attitudes.[5] In this study, midshipmen were
asked to indicate their perception of their fathers' political positions on
the same five-point scale ranging from liberal to conservative. They could
also indicate that they did not know their fathers' political attitudes.[6]
Table 5 shows the midshipmen's perception of their fathers' ideologies
and their correlation with their own attitudes. The correlation is relatively
strong (X^2 = 38.21, $p > 0.01$). This finding confirms other studies that
have suggested a median correlation at approximately 0.6 for party
identification between parent and offspring.[7]

This questionnaire did not request party identification, but, presumably,
conservative and somewhat conservative can be equated with the
Republican party, somewhat liberal and liberal with the Democratic party,
and middle-of-the-road with independent or no preference.[8] In a study
of the 1952 election, the Survey Research Center found that only 10 percent
of the adults had a party identification different from their parents.[9]
Table 5 shows a somewhat higher defection rate by midshipmen toward
the liberal end of the spectrum. This seems to support the findings of
Maccoby[10] and Hyman[11] that the socializing effects of an adolescent's
peer group generally tend to encourage defections from parental ideology
in the direction of broader community standards. Since midshipmen
come from such perceived conservative family backgrounds, they appear
particularly vulnerable to the resocializing effect of peer groups toward
broader standards held by the community. Midshipmen would be ideal
subjects for further research concerning determinants of the relative
strength of parental and peer group influence in political socialization.

Social Origins

Geographic Distribution

Janowitz reported earlier that military elites overrepresented the
South-Southwest and the rural sector; this is no longer a social characteristic
of midshipmen.[12] As shown in Table 6, the South and Southwest, as well
as the North Central region, are slightly underrepresented. The West and
particularly the Northeast are somewhat overrepresented, but the overall
regional distribution of midshipmen is not significantly different from
the national distribution of population. This statistical overrepresentation
in the region where the academy is located is replicated in the Air Force
Academy study.

An examination of community origins reveals that urban areas are
slightly overrepresented and that rural areas are slightly underrepresented.

TABLE 5

FATHERS' IDEOLOGY BY MIDSHIPMEN IDEOLOGY

Fathers' Ideology	Responding Percent	Midshipmen Ideology (by percentage)				
		Conservative	Somewhat Conservative	Middle-of-the-road	Somewhat Liberal	Liberal
Conservative	33	25	51	11	11	3
Somewhat conservative	40	3	36	32	22	6
Middle-of-the road	13	2	7	38	38	14
Somewhat liberal	5	4	9	5	54	27
Liberal	2	22	0	22	11	44
Did not know	7	3	24	41	31	0

N = 422

$X^2 = 38.216$, $p \leq .01$

TABLE 6

GEOGRAPHIC ORIGINS OF MIDSHIPMEN

Origins	1976 USNA	Percentage Population 1974[a]	Past Elite[b]
Region			
Northeast	36	27	27
South/Southwest	25	29	31
North Central	20	28	30
West	19	17	12
N =	421		
Rural/Urban			
Rural (under 2500)	19	27	56
Urban (2500+)	75	73	44
Military site	6	--	--
N =	423		

a = Statistical Abstract of the United States, 1975, GPO, Washington, D.C.

b = Janowitz, 1971, pp. 59-106.

But, as is true of the regional distribution, the differences between the midshipmen sample and the distribution within the larger U.S. population are not statistically significant. We had anticipated that if differences in military performance were associated with geography, those from southern and rural backgrounds would rank higher in MP than those from urban and nonsouthern areas of the country. Such was not the case, however.

In fact, as Table 7 suggests, urbanites appear to score somewhat higher in MP than those from rural areas: that is, the former receive 41 percent A's; the latter, 31 percent. This, of course, results from underrepresentation of the rural contingent in the A category, a deviation from the expected distribution of 9 percent. The relationship is reversed in the B category, however, and the resulting strength of association is weak (tau = 0.02).

TABLE 7

GEOGRAPHIC ORIGINS AND MILITARY PERFORMANCE

Origins	Responding Percent	Percentage Receiving MP grade of:		
		A	B	C
Region				
Northeast	36	42	30	28
South/Southwest	25	43	30	27
North Central	20	32	32	35
West	19	37	24	39
Expected distribution	100	40	29	31
N =	404			
Rural/Urban				
Rural	19	31	43	26
Urban	75	41	26	33
Military site*	6	50	19	31
Expected distribution	100	40	29	31
N =	416			

$X^2 = 9.686$, p $<$ .05

*Omitting the category of military site, $X^2 = 7.911$, p $<$ .02

Thus, the South today is not overrepresented at the Naval Academy, nor do southerners or individuals with rural backgrounds display more talent for military performance than urbanites and nonsoutherners. Any historical relationship that may have once existed between military performance and southern heritage is not apparent in these classes at Annapolis.[13]

Religion

The Naval Academy is disproportionately Protestant in the sense that Protestants comprise 56 percent of the academy population but only 32 percent of the national population (see Table 8). Among Protestants, the Episcopal church is no longer the preferred affiliation, although its adherents at the academy exceed the national proportion (5 percent to 1

TABLE 8

MIDSHIPMEN RELIGIOUS AFFILIATION BY MILITARY PERFORMANCE

Religion	Responding Percent	Percentage Receiving MP grade of:		
		A	B	C
Traditional Protestant	23	49	24	27
Pietistic Protestant	21	34	43	23
Other Protestant	12	40	33	27
Total Protestant	56* Average	42	33	25
Roman Catholic	30	41	24	35
Jewish	1	–	too small	–
Other	6	30	33	37
None	7	23	17	60
Expected distribution	100	40	29	31
N =	420			

*Comparing Protestants to Catholics, X^2 = 5.332, p $>$.05

percent). Moreover, the sects that Janowitz categorized as "traditional"[14] now comprise only 23 percent of the overall sample and 41 percent of the Protestants in the sample. The largest single religious affiliation is Roman Catholicism. There are relatively more Catholics at the academy than in the population at large (30 percent to 23 percent).

Among midshipmen professing adherence to particular religious sects, the traditional Protestant group stands out as relatively high MP achievers. In comparison with the remaining Protestants, however, this difference is not statistically significant (X^2 = 8.003, p > 0.05). In a comparison of Protestants with Catholics, no significant difference is apparent in military performance.

We also asked midshipmen to evaluate their social origins, and we compared their religious affiliations with perceived social class backgrounds. We hypothesized that the relatively large number of Roman Catholics would be linked to the democratization of recruitment suggested by Janowitz and that the Catholic midshipmen would be disproportionately

TABLE 9

MIDSHIPMEN RELIGIOUS AFFILIATION BY SOCIAL CLASS

Religion	Responding Percent		Social Class Percentages		
			Upper	Middle	Working
Protestant					
Traditional Protestant	23		2	75	24
Pietistic Protestant	21		0	44	56
Other Protestant	12		3	43	54
Total Protestant	56	Average	2	56	42
Roman Catholic	30		1	50	49
All others	14		4	49	47
N =	424				

recruited from upwardly mobile blue-collar families.[15] As noted in Table 9, this is not the case. Interestingly, a rather even split occurs between working-class and middle-class origins across religious categories. Moreover, when the Protestants are grouped as traditional, pietistic,[16] and other, the traditional group stands out as disproportionately middle-class in origin.

The strongest statistical difference between midshipmen occurs between those who profess a religious affiliation and those who claim to be nonbelievers (X^2 = 32.282, $p > 0.001$). The difference, summarized in Table 10, is statistically significant, and the relationship is quite strong. The MP grades for the midshipmen professing a religious belief correspond almost exactly to the true distribution of A's, B's, and C's. Among the nonbelievers, the departures from the true distribution are striking; they receive 16 percent fewer A's and 29 percent more C's than would be expected. The indifferent performance of the nonbelievers compared with the performance of the believers is further suggested by the relatively high gamma of 0.57.

Furthermore, a clear relationship exists between military performance and attendance at church services. Midshipmen who attend church services regularly, regardless of whether they adhere to a particular religion, score significantly higher in MP than midshipmen who do not attend church services when the ratio of A's to C's is compared (gamma = 0.31). Although independent evidence is not available to support the notion, we

TABLE 10

RELIGIOUS BELIEF, CHURCH ATTENDANCE AND MILITARY PERFORMANCE

Religious Participation	Responding Percent	Percentage Receiving MP grades of:		
		A	B	C
Believe in God				
Believer	93	41	30	29
Nonbeliever	7	23	17	60
Expected distribution	100	40	29	31
N =	417			
Church Attendance				
Attends	43	46	30	25
Does not attend	57	35	28	36
Expected distribution	100	40	29	31
N =	417			

suggest that midshipmen who manifest adherence to a religious sect and choose to attend church services regularly are more comfortable with accepted notions of traditional authority and, hence, more at home in the highly structured military environment of the academy.

Race

A comparison of the military performance grades of minority mid-shipmen (10 percent of the sample) and those of white midshipmen reveals (Table 11) no statistically significant difference between the two groups ($X^2 = 1.107$, $p > 0.50$). Fifty percent of midshipmen with Spanish surnames fall in the C category in military performance. Orientals are evenly split between the A and C categories. However, in the case of both Oriental and Latino midshipmen, the total is only eight and is entirely too small to warrant generalization. Black midshipmen (5 percent of the sample) also comprise too small a group (twenty-one) to draw conclusions; they are distributed across the A, B, and C range, with the highest single proportion receiving the grade of A in military performance.

TABLE 11

MILITARY PERFORMANCE BY RACE

Race	Responding Percent		Percentage Receiving MP grade of:		
			A	B	C
White	90		40	30	30
Total Minority	10	Average	38	24	38
Black	5		38	29	33
Oriental	2		50	0	50
Spanish	2		25	25	50
Other	1		40	40	20
Expected distribution	100		40	29	31
N =	417				

Socioeconomic Factors

Social Class

There is no statistically significant relationship between military performance and fathers' occupations (Table 12). In every category with the exception of the unskilled and clerical categories, the proportion of A's, B's, and C's is essentially what one would expect in terms of normal distribution. Combined with the skilled worker category, the unskilled and clerical categories were aggregated as working-class/blue-collar; as such, they show lower aptitudes (fewer A's and more C's) than the farm, managerial, and professional groups. But when the data are aggregated in this manner, the sample loses its significance (X^2 = 12.076, $p > 0.50$).

Somewhat surprisingly, the sons of military fathers do not clearly stand out as a high achievement group. They tie with the management and other groups in the A category. In fact, the sons of military fathers place third in a comparison of the A and B grades for these three groups.

Family Constellation

Table 13 indicates the birth order and family stability characteristics of the first and second class midshipmen. The majority (91 percent) come

TABLE 12

FATHERS' OCCUPATION AND MILITARY PERFORMANCE

Fathers' Occupation	Responding Percent	Percentage Receiving MP grade of:		
		A	B	C
Farm	19	42	29	29
Blue collar/working class	32	31	34	35
Manager	20	43	31	26
Professional	19	42	27	31
Other	10	42	26	32
Expected distribution	100	40	29	31
N =	409			

from stable families, and most of them (95 percent) have one or more brothers and sisters. The midshipman who is an only child does somewhat less well in military performance than his peer with siblings, and this difference is especially evident in the A category, where they receive 15 percent fewer A's than would be expected. Viewed as a whole, however, these differences must be dismissed as statistically insignificant ($X^2 = 9.785$, $p > 0.50$).

Finally, midshipmen from one-parent families did not perform in a significantly different way from midshipmen from two-parent families. There is no statistically significant difference between the two groups, although midshipmen who have lost one parent through death deviate from the expected proportion of A's in MP by 13 percent.

Nativity and Self-Recruitment

A large, but not surprising, 93 percent of the midshipmen are second-generation or third-generation Americans. The 2 percent responding as "foreign-born" are either foreign nationals or midshipmen born on overseas military bases; 5 percent have one parent born in a country other than the United States.

Janowitz observed that a large number of service academy students (25 percent in the 1960s) came from career military families.[17] The proportion

TABLE 13

FAMILY CONSTELLATION AND MILITARY PERFORMANCE

Family Constellation	Responding Percent	Percentage Receiving MP grade of:		
		A	B	C
Birth Order				
Only child	5	24	38	28
Oldest child	42	38	30	33
Youngest child	18	42	27	30
Middle child (2 or more brothers)	10	41	19	40
Middle child (2 or more sisters)	3	54	15	31
Middle child (2 or more siblings, both sex)	22	43	34	23
Expected distribution	100	40	29	31
N =	418			
Parent's Status				
Married	91	41	29	30
Divorced	4	35	15	50
Separated	1	40	40	20
One dead	4	18	47	35
Both dead	0	--	--	--
Expected distribution	100	40	29	31
N =	416			

of self-recruited midshipmen was still a relatively high 25 percent in 1976 (Table 14). Eighteen percent of the sample were the sons of career officers, and 7 percent were the sons of career enlisted men. An additional 61 percent of the sample had fathers who had some military experience. Most of this group served as enlisted men, suggesting the pervasive reach

TABLE 14

MILITARY HERITAGE AND MILITARY PERFORMANCE

Father's Military Experience	Responding Percent	Percentage Receiving MP grade of:		
		A	B	C
Career military	25	42	25	33
Some military	61	41	30	29
No military	15	32	32	36
Expected distribution	100	40	29	31
N =	420			

of the draft during the past three and one-half decades. Table 14 gives an initial impression that midshipmen whose fathers have had no military service do somewhat less well in aptitude than the others, but this difference in performance is not statistically significant (X^2 = 5.367, $p > 0.30$).

Who Succeeds at Annapolis?

A comfortable 70 percent of the midshipmen are career-oriented, with 50 percent aspiring to the rank of captain (O-6) or higher. It is not surprising that career-oriented midshipmen also rank higher on military performance.

Ideologically, the upper two classes of midshipmen are recruited from politically conservative families and are themselves slightly to the right of center or middle-of-the-road (45 percent are conservative, and 25 percent are middle-of-the-roaders). But conservative ideology does not relate to career aspirations or to military performance any more than liberal ideology does.

The sectional and community origins of the midshipmen correspond to the national distribution, and they are not associated with military performance. This suggests that the rural and southern predilection for martial performance is a thing of the past.

Most midshipmen are Protestants, and they are represented in a proportion larger than their national strength. But this phenomenon is not so pronounced as in past generations. An interesting post-World War II phenomenon is the relatively large number of Roman Catholics (30 percent) at the academy.

There is a strong association between religious affiliation and MP. In terms of MP grades, midshipmen who profess a religious attachment (93 percent) clearly outperform midshipmen who are nonbelievers. Similarly, midshipmen who regularly attend church services (43 percent) score higher in MP than midshipmen who do not attend church services.

Racial minorities (10 percent of the sample) are well represented at the Naval Academy in comparison with other institutions of higher education, and they achieve as well as their cohorts. There is no significant difference in their military performance and that of Caucasians.

Finally, there is no significant difference in MP across social class lines. Nor do the sons of career military personnel demonstrate a greater aptitude for military performance than those who are not self-recruited.

Comparison of Future Military Elites

In many respects, we found that midshipmen at the Naval Academy closely resemble their compatriots at the Air Force Academy. Apparently, both groups are drawn overwhelmingly from relatively homogeneous middle-class and upper-middle class groups whose parents were born in the United States. Many of the same variables related to successful performance at both academies. We thus found that this pioneering research effort was a good beginning, but, like most first efforts, it may be improved.

Perhaps the most fruitful area lies in reinforcing the cooperative effort symbolized by this research. Continuing cooperation between academies may lead to insights into some of the future problems that will face both the military and the academies. For example, the Naval Academy has experienced considerably less attrition than the other academies, but no one has yet adequately explained the causes. Thus, the research methods begun in these two studies might continue and, in fact, expand.

With more time, a logical follow-up would involve careful analysis and comparison of the data already gathered from the two academies. Sophisticated statistical techniques could perhaps test hypotheses about cause-and-effect relationships. A more detailed analysis might explain similarities and differences between the populations that are drawn to the Air Force Academy or Naval Academy. Obviously, further study is necessary regarding the people who remain at the academies and their reasons for staying or leaving.

The next step would involve development of a broader survey instrument to provide more depth in background and attitude data. This instrument could be administered during the first months of academy attendance, perhaps at the same time that the American Council on Education gathers its data on college freshmen. Such an instrument would permit development of a useful profile of those who leave the academies early in their careers. Early administration of this questionnaire might also permit further analysis of the unexplained career and rank aspirations of upperclassmen.

Current air force and navy studies could not explain whether success at an academy creates expectations of long military careers or whether more complex variables generate expectations of long careers.

These data could be used following graduation to determine whether cadet performance at an academy affects later career success and aspirations. Such information might help to shape both recruitment and academy policies. Greater depth in the survey instrument might also aid in understanding the particular attractiveness of an academy for people who live in the vicinity of that academy.

A final interesting but difficult area for improvement might involve development of a performance weighting or indexing system that would enable researchers to understand more readily the student bodies at each academy. These suggestions are based on the assumptions that underlie this volume. The future appears complex and troubled for the U.S. military. Midshipmen and cadets will face crucial leadership roles as members of the cadre of dedicated professionals who will lead the U.S. military into the twenty-first century. An understanding of the types of people who succeed at the academies is important in recruiting and educating the appropriate young men for this important task.

Notes

1. David E. Drew and Alexander Astin, "Undergraduate Aspirations: A Test of Several Theories," *American Journal of Sociology* 77, no. 6 (1972):1151-1164.

2. This does not take into account the number of officers who take themselves out of the running for these ranks by leaving the service or who, while staying in, consciously decide on a career pattern, for a variety of reasons, that precludes promotion to these ranks.

3. See Charles L. Cochran and Luis R. Luis, "Midshipmen Political Characterization and Academy Socialization," in *Civil-Military Relations*, ed. Charles L. Cochran (New York: Free Press, 1974). A similar observation has been made by Bengt Abrahamsson, *Military Professionalism and Political Power* (Beverly Hills, Calif.: Sage, 1972), pp. 72-75.

4. See Fred I. Greenstein, *Children and Politics* (New Haven: Yale University Press, 1965); R. Middleton and S. Putney, "Student Rebellion Against Parental Political Beliefs," *Social Forces* 41, no. 4 (1963):377-383.

5. R. W. Connell, "Political Socialization in the American Family: The Evidence Re-examined," *The Public Opinion Quarterly* 36 (1972):323-333.

6. Other studies have suggested that children's perceptions of parental attitudes are not highly accurate. Much of the inaccuracy can be attributed to a lack of communication between parent and child. Children also tend to overestimate the level of agreement within a family by suggesting agreement by the parent with the child more frequently than is warranted by about 10 percent. See Richard G. Niemi, "Political Socialization" in *Handbook of Political Psychology*, ed. Jeanne Enutson (San Francisco: Jossey-Bass, 1973).

7. Connell, "Political Socialization."

8. In the 1976 presidential election, 74 percent identifying as liberal voted for Carter and 70 percent identifying as conservative voted for the Republican candidate. Gerald Pomper et al., *The Election of 1976* (New York: McKay, 1977), p. 61.

9. Angus Campbell, Gerald Gurin, and Warren E. Miller, *The Voter Decides* (Evanston, Ill.: Row Peterson, 1954).

10. E. Maccoby, R. E. Matthews, and A. S. Morton, "Youth and Political Change," *Public Opinion Quarterly* 18 (1954):23-29.

11. Herbert Hyman, *Political Socialization* (Glencoe, Ill.: Free Press, 1959).

12. Morris Janowitz, *The Professional Soldier* (New York: Free Press, 1971), pp. 79-103.

13. Samuel P. Huntington, *The Soldier and the State* (New York: Vintage, 1957), pp. 211-221.

14. Traditionalist includes Episcopalian, Presbyterian, Congregationalist, Lutheran, and Evangelical.

15. Janowitz, *The Professional Soldier*, pp. 79-103, xxv-xxix.

16. Pietistic includes Baptists, Methodists, and Disciples of Christ.

17. Janowitz, *The Professional Soldier*, pp. 95-96, xxv-xxvii.

21

Evolutionary vs. Revolutionary Changes in Military Academy Cadets

Robert F. Priest

Who are the West Point cadets? As noted in the earlier chapter on Air Force Academy cadets, West Point cadets have not suffered from a lack of study. Professor Janowitz's classic study of the social origins of the professional soldier[1] drew heavily on institutional research data gathered at the U.S. Military Academy in the late 1950s.[2] Lovell's work on the professional socialization of the West Point cadet reflects the early 1960s.[3] Radway's comments on recent trends at the U.S. service academies reflect the late 1960s.[4] Book-length analyses of West Point, such as the work by Ellis and Moore, usually include a description of the typical West Point cadet.[5] Thus, a considerable body of scholarly information is already available about West Point cadets. But since every institution changes with time, there is always a need for new analyses.

When choosing the topic for this chapter, it was decided not to duplicate precisely the surveys conducted at the other two academies. Rather, this analysis takes advantage of the rich body of data already accumulated at West Point and also provides perspectives on a historic event that will have important effects on both the U.S. Military Academy and the U.S. Army. This chapter thus examines two kinds of changes in the West Point Cadet Corps—evolutionary and revolutionary. It first considers variations in the characteristics of students admitted to West Point. Since the high level of academic aptitude required of service academy cadets is well documented, this discussion describes small but consistent changes in other traits of new cadets. The admission of women to the Military Academy

The opinions expressed in this chapter do not necessarily reflect the official position of the U.S. Military Academy, the U.S. Army, or any other government agency. The author would like to thank the following for helpful suggestions on earlier versions of this chapter: Dr. Nora S. Kinzer, Captain Alan Vitters, Lieutenant Colonel William Taylor, Jr., Captain K. G. Carlson, Dr. Richard P. Butler, Mr. Claude F. Bridges, Colonel G. W. Kirby, and Lieutenant George D. Waters.

represents a sharp discontinuity. Therefore, the latter part of this chapter reviews data on the characteristics of women cadets and the implications of these data for the distinctive cultural milieu of West Point.

Changes in the Characteristics of Entering Male Cadets

The process of recruiting and selecting cadets naturally produces some variables from year to year in the traits of the entering class. Houston has recently reported on trends in admissions variables over a ten-year period from the Class of 1967 to the Class of 1976.[6] By using a statistical model that rules out sampling variation, he identified small but significant changes in the characteristics of entering cadets during this period.[7]

Over the years, West Point has enrolled a fairly constant proportion of senior class presidents, other senior class officers, student body presidents, debate team members, Eagle Scouts, valedictorians, members of high school drama clubs, Bausch & Lomb Science Award winners, and American Legion Award winners. These data reflect the leadership experiences of entering West Point cadets. In addition, they support the image of the Military Academy presented by earlier writers. Several other variables, however, show significant changes during the past decade. For example, West Point has reduced the percentages of cadets who have completed one or more semesters of college, ranked in the upper fifth of their high school class, or belonged to the Boy Scouts.

Somewhat less academically experienced, younger cadets may affect the motivation of the corps in a number of ways. At the same time, West Point has tended to admit more graduates from its preparatory school and more all-conference athletes. Taken together, these trends suggest a slight deemphasis of academic skills and increased emphasis on athletic skills. These changes are *not* necessarily the result of deliberate policy decisions. West Point's recruiting and selection procedures have, over the last ten years, been fairly stable, except for the changes mentioned in this discussion.

The academy does not explicitly select cadets on the basis of religion, political conservatism, or personal values, goals, or expectations. Nevertheless, male cadets at West Point differed from male students at four-year colleges in these characteristics—as shown in the American Council on Education (ACE) survey of entering students at West Point and at more than 200 four-year colleges from 1966 to 1976. This discussion notes the backgrounds and personal values that appear to be changing in West Point's entering classes more than the statistical model of sampling fluctuation allows.[8]

One social characteristic of particular interest is "father's occupation." In a study of an earlier group of cadets, Marron concluded that "there is a strong bias in favor of applicants of military fathers in the admissions process and in perseverance both at West Point and in the Army."[9] The percentage of cadet fathers with "military career" backgrounds has declined over the last ten years from 19 percent in 1968 to 11 percent in 1975.[10] The data suggest that the bias has diminished in recent years.

West Point has increased the percentage of nonwhite cadets from 2 percent to 8 percent since 1966. The change is statistically significant, and it has proceeded in an almost linear fashion during the ten-year period.[11] In part, this change reflects an active program of minority recruitment by the West Point admissions office.[12] The increase in nonwhite representation over the past ten years confirms Janowitz's prediction of a trend toward a more socially representative military.[13] Furthermore, West Point now admits fewer Protestants than it admitted ten years ago. The percentage has declined significantly in an almost linear fashion from 64 percent in 1966 to 55 percent in 1975. During this same period, Protestantism was still the predominant religious preference, and West Point attracted a higher proportion of Protestants than four-year colleges in the ACE survey. In addition, during this period, Roman Catholics increased from 31 percent to 36 percent in an almost linear fashion. In contrast, the four-year college in the ACE survey has attracted approximately 30 percent Roman Catholics for the past ten years. Margiotta noted the increase in Roman Catholics in his sample of air force elites.[14] He also reported increases in pietistic Protestantism at the expense of Episcopalianism, increases that were partially confirmed by the USMA ACE data.

Competition for admission to prestige colleges has affected a number of students. Both at four-year colleges and at West Point, fewer students now submit as many as three applications for college admission in contrast to earlier years. When asked to rate the importance of various reasons for selecting a college, West Point cadets increasingly indicated that the "good academic reputation" of the college was very important. Among students at four-year colleges, in contrast, the importance of "a good academic reputation" was much lower, and it has not increased over the years. Aspirations for graduate degrees have also increased. In 1966, 25 percent of the West Point cadets expected to attain only the bachelor's degrees and, in 1975, only 11 percent. Although the trend was almost linear among West Point cadets, there was no comparable trend among males at four-year colleges.

The political conservatism of military cadets has been well documented in the literature. The ACE data support the general finding that West Point cadets are significantly more conservative than students at four-year colleges. For each class, the degree of difference has been approximately the same. A large proportion of cadets report that they are middle-of-the-road (42 percent); therefore, one must remember that the proconservative bias is only relative.[15] The difference between West Point and the four-year

college on the liberalism-conservatism scale accounts for no more than
3 percent of the variance. There is no evidence of a change in the relative
conservatism of entering cadets, and one may expect this difference to
continue in the future.

The ACE survey includes a series of questions on the goals that
entering students consider essential or very important. In 1966, 57 percent
of the West Point cadets gave such a rating to "becoming a community
leader." They were higher than males at four-year colleges on this goal.
By 1973, West Point entrants had significantly decreased the importance
given to such a goal, and they were approximately equal to students at
four-year colleges. The goal of "keeping up to date with political affairs"
has declined in a linear fashion for both cadets and college students.
"Developing a meaningful philosophy of life" has declined in importance
for both West Point cadets and four-year college students. On the other
hand, the goal of "being very well off financially" has increased in
importance linearly over the last ten years for West Point cadets but not
for males at four-year colleges. Thus, for the years 1966 to 1970, West Point
entrants were less interested in being very well off financially than men
at four-year colleges, but from 1971 to 1974, they were more interested.
In the same vein, the goal of being "an expert in finance" has increased
significantly for West Point cadets but not for male college students in
general. The increased emphasis on financial rewards is consistent with
the higher pay scale in the volunteer army and with a transition to what
Moskos calls the occupational model of a military career.[16]

It would be misleading to portray the West Point cadet as the only
one who has changed in the last ten years. In some dimensions, West Point
cadets have remained relatively the same while students at four-year
colleges have changed. For example, few West Point cadets have considered
it important to succeed in "my own business." In contrast, students at
four-year colleges formerly considered this goal very important, but it has
now decreased significantly in importance. In addition, male West Point
cadets still consider "raising a family" important in spite of the relative
decline of this goal among civilian college males of the same age group.
Furthermore, West Point cadets give relatively higher importance to
influencing "political structures," but this goal has declined in importance
for civilian college students.

Many differences between West Point and the four-year college emerge
when one considers the expectancies of students. During the past decade
15 percent of the students entering four-year colleges considered the
chance "very good" that they would "change major fields." The comparable figure for West Point was 4 percent in 1967, but it increased linearly
to 17 percent in 1975. Clearly, West Point cadets are now more open to
alternative forms of education. Since West Point does not offer academic

majors, a change in majors implies leaving West Point.[17] If the academy introduces academic majors in the future, cadet attrition may decrease. A related change has occurred in student expectations about changing their career choices: West Point cadets have increased in their expectations of "changing careers" from 3 percent to 13 percent over the years; in contrast, the expectations of civilian college students in this respect have decreased from 19 percent to 13 percent. Finally, 33 percent of West Point cadets expect to marry within a year after college, in contrast to 18 percent of civilian college men. Thus, although West Point cadets have become more flexible in regard to college majors and career options, they still maintain a positive orientation to traditional family relationships.[18]

The characteristics of men who entered West Point obviously changed during the period from 1966 to 1976. Society was changing, and in some respects, West Point men changed faster than society—in father's occupation, religion, motives for attending college, goals for financial well-being, and flexibility of career orientation. In many instances, the result was that West Point cadets were more similar to their civilian college contemporaries and to the image predicted by military sociologists. However, the admission of women to the Military Academy was *not* a gradual shift of the type documented for men; it was a hotly debated, deliberate policy change mandated by Congress.

Sex Differences and Institutional Effects

There is significant technical literature on human sex differences.[19] At the same time, there is a body of research on the impact of college on students[20] and on differences between students who attend different types of colleges in the United States.[21] Until recently, these two research traditions were not considered together. However, through a careful analysis of the American Council on Education Student Information Survey,[22] three categories of differences can now be examined simultaneously: differences that strongly characterize a particular institution and distinguish it from other institutions; differences between males and females; and interactions between sex and the institution. For example, 20 percent of males and 40 percent of females may have a certain attitude; therefore, gender is associated with a 20 percent difference in attitude. To continue the example, suppose that 25 percent of USMA cadets and 35 percent of the norm group have a certain attitude; thus, "institution," as an independent variable, is associated with a 10 percent difference in attitude. If there is no interaction between the independent variables in this example, then a 20 percent sex difference is found at the academy and among the norm group. If there is an interaction effect, the sex difference is not consistently of the same size or direction at the academy and the other institution.

West Point is unique in many ways. In the debates over the admission of women as cadets, some sources asserted that coeducation would cause West Point to lose important unique characteristics. This report concludes that West Point demonstrates its continued uniqueness by enrolling cadets of both sexes who differ from other college students without creating a sex × institution interaction effect. Such an interaction indicates a noteworthy reversal—that women cadets at West Point are different in unique ways from men cadets and from students at other schools. Such interactions should provide valuable insights into the unique potential strengths and weaknesses of women cadets in this newly coeducational institution.

Data were collected from 119 women cadets in the USMA Class of 1980 and from 1,366 male cadets. Normative data on students at four-year colleges were collected for freshmen entering college in 1976, based on 99,203 students at 254 four-year colleges.[23] Table 1 presents the results for selected variables.[24] These variables show an institutional effect and no sex × institution interaction; that is, West Point maintains its unique qualities in contrast to the four-year college.

West Point is still distinct from the typical four-year college because it enrolls a relatively high percentage of students whose fathers' occupations were military. As noted earlier, both male and female cadets, in contrast to students at other four-year colleges, are less likely to characterize themselves as middle-of-the-road or liberal. West Point attracts both male and female cadets on the basis of its "special educational programs" to a greater degree than other colleges; cadets are less likely to note that "I wanted to live at home" as a very important reason for selecting their college. In self-ratings, both male and female cadets see themselves as better than average in the following traits: academic ability, drive to achieve, mechanical ability, originality, physical attractiveness, political conservatism, popularity, popularity with the opposite sex, public speaking ability, intellectual self-confidence, social self-confidence, stubbornness, and writing ability.

In attitudes, both male and female West Point cadets *are more likely than other students to believe the following:* they disagree that "as long as people work hard, they should be paid equally, regardless of ability or quality of work"; they agree that "parents should be discouraged from having large families"; they agree that "there is too much concern in the courts for the rights of criminals"; and they disagree that "college grades should be abolished."

In the goals that they consider essential or very important, West Point cadets are higher than others in wanting to "become an authority in my field." Both male and female cadets are different from other college students in their perceptions of various personal probabilities: they see less chance of "transfer to another college before graduating"; they see

TABLE 1

PERCENT OF MEN AND WOMEN WITH EACH CHARACTERISTIC TRAIT

ACE Item	West Point Men	West Point Women	Four-Year College Men	Four-Year College Women
Father's Occupation: Military Service (Career)	14	22	3	2
Middle-of-the-Road or Liberal, politically	64	70	79	85
Academic Ability	92	95	59	57
Drive to Achieve	89	94	66	66
Mechanical Ability	40	25	34	10
Originality	50	52	44	42
Physical Attractiveness	42	40	34	26
Popularity	59	51	39	30
Public Speaking Ability	45	47	29	23
Intellectual Self-Confidence	78	73	54	41
Social Self-confidence	58	61	44	36
Writing Ability	49	54	35	30
Agree: As long as they work hard, people should be paid equally regardless of ability or quality of work	19	14	25	23
Agree: Parents should be discouraged from having large families	66	60	59	50
Goal of becoming an authority in my field	83	82	74	68
Expect to transfer to another college	4	5	13	15
Expect to find a job after graduation in own field	86	84	60	60

TABLE 2

PERCENT OF MEN AND WOMEN WHO HAVE A GIVEN SEX-RELATED TRAIT
AT WEST POINT AND THE FOUR-YEAR COLLEGE

ACE Item	West Point		Four-Year College	
	Men	Women	Men	Women
Goal of Financial Well-being	50	40	55	38
College Representative recruited me for this college	12	3	8	5
Understanding of Others	71	80	65	75
Agree: Discourage large families	66	60	59	50
Agree: Women should receive the same salary and opportunities for advancement as men in comparable positions	92	99	89	96
Agree: To much concern for the rights of criminals	74	55	64	53
Agree: Ban persons with extreme views from speaking on campus	34	22	28	23

a much greater chance of "finding a job after graduation in the field for which you were trained."

Thus, on 79 of the 150 traits examined, USMA females differ from four-year college females to the same extent that USMA males differ from four-year college males. Many of the unique traits are obviously the result of USMA's highly selective admissions policy, which insures that USMA cadets rank above average college students in ability. In other cases, the uniqueness results from the cadet's accurate perception of USMA goals and environmental pressures. In still other cases, such as the political orientation of cadets, the uniqueness is a result neither of selection nor deliberate training; it is a historical accident that has evidently become an informal basis of self-selection by applicants. In general, the results show that the academy still has a number of variables in which its cadets differ from students at four-year colleges, despite the integration of women. Thus, contrary to some predictions, the integration of women into West Point has not erased the unique characteristics of the student body.

Table 2 shows variables on which USMA females differ from USMA males to the same extent and direction as males and females at four-year colleges. As for goals considered essential or very important, women students at the academy and elsewhere cited financial well-being less frequently than men students. In identifying their reasons for selecting "this particular college," women were more attracted to "special education programs" than men. Men were more likely than women to report that "a college representative recruited me." Although the difference is no doubt unintentional, it exists both at the academy and at four-year colleges. In self-ratings of traits, women rated themselves lower in mechanical ability, popularity, political conservatism, and popularity with the opposite sex and higher in understanding of others, writing ability, and artistic ability. Women's attitudes differed from men's attitudes in the following ways: they were less likely to agree that "parents should be discouraged from having large families"; they were more likely to agree that "women should receive the same salary and opportunities for advancement as men in comparable positions"; they agreed less that "there is too much concern in the courts for the rights of criminals"; and they agreed less that "college officials have the right to ban persons with extreme views from speaking on campus."

In general, fifty-five variables with sex differences applied equally at the academy and at other four-year colleges. Of this number, thirty-five variables also showed an institutional effect. Thus, in spite of the fact that West Point selected women who were above average in certain traits (an institutional effect discussed above), the selection process did not eliminate or reduce the ordinary male-female difference on these same traits. Political conservatism and punitive attitudes toward "criminals" are *not* a part of the USMA mission statement. Nevertheless, the results show that USMA cadets have more of these traits than other college students and that women are less punitive and less politically conservative than men. If such an increase in diversity is not at variance with the USMA mission, it could be viewed as a valuable addition to the West Point Corps of Cadets, especially since West Point graduates will supervise more women in the future army. Females rated themselves lower in mechanical ability, and this rating is consistent with data from standardized test of mechanical aptitude. No special tests for mechanical reasoning were used to select female cadets.

Table 3 shows that the typical USMA female is less likely to want a large family than is the male cadet. Other college women generally tended to want more children than college men. The below-average childbearing expectations of USMA women is consistent with the desire for a military career. One thrust of the feminist movement has been to emphasize that "marriage versus career" may be a false dichotomy. From a feminist perspective, the ideal job allows both marriage and a career.[25] The above interaction shows clearly that the first USMA female cadets did *not* think from a feminist perspective but from a more traditional perspective of "marriage versus career."

TABLE 3

PERCENT OF MEN AND WOMEN OF EACH INSTITUTION WHO
HAVE EACH INTERACTIVE TRAIT

ACE Item	West Point Men	Women	Four-Year College Men	Women
Number of children expected: two or less	60	70	67	61
Goal of raising a family	66	38	60	56
Very good chance of: getting married within a year after college	30	15	16	19
Agree: Married women best confined to home	41	5	37	9
Agree: A couple should live together for some time before deciding to get married	31	34	49	38
Agree: If two people really like each other, it's all right for them to have sex even if they've known each other for only a very short time	44	20	59	30
Agree: Students from disadvantaged background should be given preferential treatment in college admissions	24	13	38	34
Agree: Marijuana should be legalized	24	31	47	43
Goal of keeping up with politics	61	69	45	38
Political Liberalism	18	25	23	18
Athletic Ability	77	67	55	27
Leadership Ability	87	86	54	44
Mathematical Ability	82	87	43	28

Additional evidence on the family expectations of female cadets is apparent in their assent to several statements of goals: the female cadets were less likely to consider raising a family as "essential or very important" than *any other group*. In addition, they were *less* likely than male cadets to estimate that they will "get married within a year after college," in contrast to the opposite pattern for other college students. One implication of the results is that male cadets are not likely to consider such women as potential spouses.

The attitudes of the first group of female cadets reflect a surprising mixture. As would be expected, they were far less likely to agree that "the activities of married women are best confined to home and family" than other groups. They agreed more than USMA men that "a couple should live together for some time before deciding to get married," although, consistent with an institutional effect, they agreed less than other college students. USMA female cadets did not agree, as much as other groups, that, "if two people really like each other, it's all right for them to have sex if they've known each other for only a very short time." Thus, in addition to the normal conservatism of women in accepting casual sex based on short acquaintances, USMA women are even more conservative.

USMA female cadets considered the goal of "keeping up with politics" more important than male cadets and college students considered it. They rated themselves higher in political liberalism, reversing traditional male dominance in liberalism at other four-year colleges. Consideration of these two interactions together leads to the conclusion that USMA women were strongly interested in influencing the political process. They were more inclined to favor legalizing marijuana than USMA men, although USMA students were less in favor of the measure than students at four-year colleges. Despite the relatively liberal trend of their opinions, USMA women were least likely to agree that "students from disadvantaged backgrounds should be given preferential treatment in college admissions." Most USMA cadets were opposed to such preferential treatment, but the women were more strongly opposed than the men. This seemed to imply that women did not want preferential treatment for themselves based on the presumed disadvantage that results from being a female. If such an interpretation is correct, female cadets expressed a belief in mobility through individual achievement, which is the antidiscrimination strategy most approved by male cadets.[26]

The perception of athletic ability shows an institutional effect, a sex effect, and an interaction. USMA cadets rated themselves higher than four-year college students in this area. At other colleges, males showed a strong tendency to rate themselves higher than females in athletic ability, but at the academy, the sex difference has diminished considerably in perceived athletic ability. Incidentally, the data show that USMA women probably compared themselves to other students of their own sex, since USMA women score well below USMA men on objective measures of athletic ability. Nevertheless, the results suggest that the academy has been successful in reducing traditional views of sex differences in athletic skills.

As might be expected, women cadets reported less frequently than USMA men that "someone who came here before advised me to come" as a reason for selecting West Point; they thus reversed the pattern of male-female differences at the civilian four-year college. In contrast to USMA men, women were less likely to report "low tuition" as an important influence in selecting West Point.

Two other self-rated personal characteristics also show an institutional effect, sex difference, and sex x institution interaction: leadership ability and mathematical ability. In both traits, male and female cadets were approximately equal and higher than civilian college students, but the college man ranked higher than the college woman. By selection, West Point virtually eliminated a sex difference in these two very important areas.

Thus, seventeen variables are characterized by a sex x institution interaction, alone or in combination with a simple institutional effect or a simple sex difference. For some variables, apparently as a result of selection, West Point eliminated a sex difference that exists at other institutions. For other variables, the sex difference at other colleges was reversed, representing the special characteristics of the female cadets in the Class of 1980.[27]

Evolutionary Changes in Cadet Characteristics

The admission of women to the West Point Corps of Cadets has raised several issues. The results show that there are still significant differences between West Point cadets and students at four-year colleges in family backgrounds, reasons for attending college, perceived abilities, attitudes, goals, and perceived life chances. For several variables, the difference between West Point and other colleges occurs in the absence of sex differences of any kind. For other variables, a sex difference occurs in addition to the typical West Point-other college difference. Thus, West Point women, like women at four-year colleges, were different from their male counterparts in certain self-rated personality traits, goals, and attitudes. But the most interesting findings show that for certain traits, West Point women, unlike women at four-year colleges, are equal to West Point men. Other traits reverse the typical male-female pattern of sex differences; for example, in regard to having children, marrying, or raising a family. In certain social attitudes and in politics, West Point women are unique. In a number of ability variables, West Point women are the equals of West Point men, in striking contrast to the pattern at four-year colleges.

In several instances, West Point apparently has achieved, at least initially, a kind of equality of ability between the sexes not found at typical four-year colleges. In other instances, sex differences remain. Undoubtedly, some of the sex differences that remain after West Point's selection procedure are harmless differences in personal style, differences that do not relate to the USMA mission. But because of West Point's special vocational program, some of the remaining sex differences need to be reduced further by training or selection. In view of the variability in male classes over the past ten years, one may expect a similar pattern of variability in female classes of the future.

According to a commandant of cadets, West Point's role is to be a bridge between a changing society and the relatively unchanging demands imposed by the stresses of warfare. Society has changed, and this report documents a number of specific changes in the cadets who enter West Point.[28] If one accepts the goal of training cadets to reach relatively fixed standards of performance, then the changed characteristics of new cadets should be taken into account in the design of training programs. In such a context, the question "Who are the West Point cadets?" is an important one.

Notes

1. M. Janowitz, *The Professional Soldier: A Social and Political Portrait* (New York: Free Press, 1960).

2. One medical research project of the U.S. Army Hospital at West Point functioned from 1955 to 1958: entering plebes were surveyed every year to identify "characteristics related to leadership." R. Sanderson, W. Hausman, B. West, and R. Keim, "Who Comes to West Point: A Survey of the Personal, Social, and Family Backgrounds of United States Military Academy Cadets" (West Point, N.Y.: U.S. Military Academy, September 1960).

3. See J. Lovell, "The Professional Socialization of the West Point Cadet," in *The New Miltary*, ed. M. Janowitz (New York: Russell Sage, 1964).

4. Radway cites three different institutional research reports based on West Point data. In contrast, only one empirical study of Air Force Academy cadets was cited and no study of Naval Academy cadets. See L. Radway, "Recent Trends at American Service Academies," in *Public Opinion and the Military Establishment*, ed. C. Moskos (Beverly Hills, Calif.: Sage, 1971).

5. Ellis and Moore based their description on a number of institutional research studies conducted by the director of institutional research. See J. Ellis and R. Moore, *School for Soldiers: West Point and the Profession of Arms* (New York: Oxford University Press, 1974), pp. 22-27; a review by K. Galloway and R. Johnson in *West Point: America's Power Fraternity* (New York: Simon and Schuster, 1973), pp. 81-83, offers a somewhat briefer account.

6. J. Houston, "Trends in Admissions Variables through the Class of 1976" (West Point, N.Y.: Office of the Director of Institutional Research, Report 76-017, January 1976).

7. When the statistic reported is a proportion, conventional analysis of variance was used, estimating the mean square error by its upper bound, 0.25. To simplify the analysis, the proportion was assumed to be based on a sample of exactly 989 cases. Although these assumptions sacrifice precision, they result in a conservatively biased statistical test: the results reported as significant at the 0.05 level are probably even more significant. The data are found in Houston and refer to classes from 1968 to 1976, especially Tables 6 and 7.

8. An F-test, $p < 0.05$; see note 7. The N assumed for each class was 1100. The USMA data are based on information supplied by the ACE to the Office of the Director of Institutional Research and on first-time college freshmen. Some of the data are unpublished, but every year the office publishes a report based on the ACE data. The most recent report is J. Houston, "The First Class Questionnaire, Class of 1976" (West Point, N.Y.: Office of the Director of Institutional Research, Report 7T-002, August 1976). There are ten such descriptive reports published by the Office of the Director of Institutional Research.

9. J. Marron, "The Socioeconomic Background and Performance of West Point Graduates" (West Point, N.Y.: Office of the Director of Institutional Research, Report 72-034, May 1972).

10. Note that this reanalysis of the ACE data is selective. Occupational categories other than military were not examined for evidence of change. In addition, the ACE method of asking about the father's occupation may be insensitive. We may have overlooked other variables, such as income, which may also show systematic change over time.

11. All statements about linear trends in this chapter are supported by a statistically significant ($p < 0.05$) product moment correlation between the survey year and the percentage of students in the given response category. Correlation is not causation, of course, but this procedure does rule out pseudotrends based only on sampling fluctuations.

12. Had this analysis gone in the same directions as those reported in Chapters 19 and 20, the same problems might have emerged. As the samples of upperclassmen taken at the Air Force Academy and Naval Academy were broken for statistical analysis, the numbers of minority members in any one cell became too small for generalizations with any statistical validity.

13. Janowitz, *The Professional Soldier*.

14. F. Margiotta, "A Military Elite in Transition: Air Force Leaders in the 1980s," in *Armed Forces and Society* 2, no. 2 (February 1976):155-184.

15. The conclusions about conservatism in the other two academy student bodies support this analysis (see Chapters 19 and 20). There are some comparison problems, since our West Point data are of freshmen and the others' data are of the upper classes. Schloemer and Myers point out (in Chapter 19) that the more liberal cadet may "select out" of an academy during the first two years.

16. See Moskos' analysis in Chapter 11 of this volume.

17. It would be most instructive to compare similar trends at the other two academies, which do have academic majors.

18. This is also supported by a 1975 study of cadet attitudes toward women. See R. Priest, "Cadet Attitudes Toward Women—1975" (West Point, N.Y.: Office of the Director of Institutional Research, May 1976, Report 76-015).

19. E. E. Maccoby and C. N. Jacklin, *The Psychology of Sex Differences* (Stanford, Calif.: Stanford University Press, 1974).

20. K. A. Feldman and T. M. Newcomb, *The Impact of College on Students* (San Francisco: Jossey Bass, 1969).

21. A. Astin, *The College Environment* (Washington, D.C.: The American Council on Education, 1968).

22. A. W. Astin, M. R. King, and G. T. Richardson, *The American Freshman: National Norms for Fall 1976* (Berkeley and Los Angeles: University of California Press, 1977).

23. Ibid., p. 11.

24. The present analysis is an analysis of selected Self-Inventory Form (SIF) items. There were 150 variables selected for analysis in this report. In order to approximate the results of a 2 x 2 analysis of variance, three planned comparisons were made, comparing the four groups: USMA men, USMA women, four-year college men, and four-year college women. Since the four-year college names include data from West Point, the comparisons are not independent. Nevertheless, the size of the normative sample is so much larger than the West Point sample that the effect of this contamination is practically negligible. To test the main effect of institution, contrast weights of 1, 1, -1, and -1 were used; to test the sex difference effect, weights of 1, -1, -1, and -1; and to test the sex x institution, weights of 1, -1, -1 and 1. Since the Ns are unequal, these contrasts are not orthogonal, although they would be in the equal N case. For each variable, the mean square error was estimated by its maximum possible value, 0.25, for any given proportion; as a result, the F-tests reported below are underestimates and are thus biased against finding significant results.

25. C. Bird, "The Androgynous Life," in *Values of the New Feminism*, ed. M.L.T. Thompson (Boston: Beacon Press, 1970).

26. Priest, "Cadet Attitudes Toward Women."

27. In progress at the Office of the Director of Institutional Research are three longitudinal studies of changes in cadet traits. In one, the Rokeach value instrument was given at entrance and just before graduation to the Class of 1975, and it showed significant changes; in a second, the ACE self-evaluation on the SIF was given at entrance and just before graduation to the same group; and in a third, the Personality Research Form was given to new cadets in the Class of 1978 just before and just after Cadet Basic Training, with highly significant differences emerging.

28. It is beyond the scope of this chapter to deal with the argument that modern warfare is significantly changing, as well as society. There is a change in the nature of weapons used, and we have volunteers instead of conscripts to lead. Such arguments only enhance the need for the kind of research in this chapter.

Part 6

Prescriptions for the Future

22
The Future Demands of Military Professionalism: The Views of a Retired Navy Vice Admiral

Gerald E. Miller

The fundamentals of the military profession in the United States will undoubtedly remain unchanged for years to come. They are embodied in the Declaration of Independence, the Constitution of the United States, the commissions awarded to officers by the president, the oaths of acceptance of the commissions, contracts with enlisted personnel, and the oaths of acceptance of the contracts. These documents call for all members of the profession to support and defend the Constitution. This is right and proper because the Constitution is the basic law of the land. American civilization cannot exist without a body of laws, and it will cease to exist unless the laws are viable.

Officer commissions and petty officer appointments are awarded on the basis of "special trust and confidence" in the "patriotism, valor, fidelity, and ability" of the recipients. Commissions require the service member to "perform all manner of things" and to "serve at the pleasure of the President of the United States." For enlisted personnel, the period of service continues for the duration of the contract unless the contract is extended in an emergency. The basic requirements for duty are essentially the same as the requirements for commissioned officers.

One of the most specific statutes pertaining to the fundamentals of the military profession is directed principally toward commanding officers of navy units, but the thrust of the law applies to the entire profession. Among other things, the law states that "commanding officers and others in authority shall take all necessary and proper action . . . to promote and safeguard the morale, physical well-being and general welfare of the officers and enlisted men under their command and charge."[1]

The United States has enjoyed relatively stable conditions of government and 200 years of proof that this system of government is sound. One has no reason to believe that these fundamentals will change in the period from 1980 to 2000. On the contrary, they will probably become more firmly entrenched and will continue to provide the legal basis on which the profession will operate. At least the words will remain the same;

interpretations of the words and methods of implementation will change. These changes, in turn, will modify the demands on people to prepare for, and perform in, the military profession.

Basic Changes

Changes in the military profession will directly reflect changes in society. This is the traditional and logical manner by which the military profession evolves and develops its characteristics. Since the U.S. military includes members from the whole society, the rules and regulations of that society will have a significant impact on the military services. In most instances, changes in the military will lag behind changes in society, especially if they are sociological in nature. On the other hand, if the changes are technical, military changes may well lead in the material and technological improvement of the whole society.

Significant technological development will no doubt continue; consequently, the military will be forced to place increasing emphasis on technical matters. Traditionally, the military profession has been staffed with individuals at least familiar with, and sometimes even expert in, technical areas. The expansion of technical education programs will undoubtedly continue over the years for the military and for society. Officers with postgraduate education are commonplace today, and they may become even more numerous in the future. Various approaches will provide this education, but regardless of the approach, technology will place increasing demands on the ability of the individual if he expects to succeed. The MIT postgraduate, the Rhodes scholar, and others will still have significant voices in the leadership role, and more emphasis on technical training will be required for enlisted personnel. If the military profession does not keep pace with technical changes in society, it will no longer have control of itself. Technical knowledge will be essential in order for leaders to retain a voice in choosing the weapon systems the military will have in the future.

The most significant changes and demands to confront the profession will probably be sociological in nature. Dramatic changes are occurring in social structure throughout the United States and the world, and the military profession will reflect these changes. Those who lag in this field will find themselves behind the profession. The traditions and life-styles of the past were beautiful for some people but not for others. Just as women's liberation, equal opportunity, civil liberties, and other social concepts have become prominent in civilian society, they will likewise be prominent in the military profession.

Many traditionalists have criticized Admiral Elmo Zumwalt for some of his actions as chief of naval operations. During his tour of duty in that position, he instituted many sociological reforms in the navy, reforms that reflected similar alterations in society and responded to pressures from civilian authority to institute such changes. Some circles severely criticized him and others praised him. He made many serious mistakes in his methods of implementing the changes, but at least he attempted to force the navy to catch up with society. I have no intention of endorsing Admiral Zumwalt, his ideas, concepts, and, particularly, his leadership methods, but I applaud his objective of bringing the military profession into closer conformity with social realities.

In view of further changes that will occur during the years 1980 to 2000, the military profession can expect a continuing breakdown of the barriers in its class structure. Traditional lines of demarcation will continue to fade between the commissioned officer corps and the enlisted ranks. This trend is evident even in the uniforms worn by officers and enlisted personnel. The past requirement that "leaders" must be distinguished from "followers," even in the uniforms worn, is diminishing as society modifies its class structure. As society evolves from upper-class, middle-class, and lower-class distinctions to a more homogeneous middle class, the military class structure will also change. This trend may or may not be desirable, but significant changes are inevitable. Those who intend to lead and make the military a career must recognize the trend and incorporate it into the profession.

The term *fraternization* has many connotations, but basically the mixing of commissioned officers and enlisted personnel has been taboo in social life. During the period 1980-2000, this notion will be seriously questioned as a natural reflection of changes in the larger society.

The role of women in the military will increase considerably, just as it will increase in civilian society. Many members of the navy have been appalled at the idea of women aboard ships, but they must eventually come to grips with the problem, just as the service academies have adjusted to women. If civilian society elevates women to leadership roles, the military profession must reflect similar changes, even though numerous mistakes can be expected.

As civilian society resolves problems of race and equal opportunity, the military services will naturally develop solutions to similar problems. One can argue persuasively that the military has been a leader in providing equal opportunity, although it was slow initially in implementing the idea. It still faces a formidable task, but members of minority groups must accept a major share of the responsibility to take advantage of available opportunities and to produce in a competent manner. The military must concentrate on helping members of minority groups to recognize existing opportunities. This can be one of the most satisfying tasks for the profession in the years ahead.

Role of the Military in International Affairs

In addition to the impact of social changes, the military role in international affairs will also contribute greatly to the changing characteristics of the profession. For example, if military force no longer has a viable role in preserving peace and maintaining stability in international affairs, military personnel and their duties will change drastically. Some people feel that political action is the only proper means of achieving stability. If this view prevails and becomes national policy, one can expect the military to degenerate into a relatively weak and second-rate profession.

On the other hand, if peace is achieved through strength and if the United States becomes more involved as a leader in maintaining peace, the military profession will continue to grow in significance, and as a result, it will enjoy high prestige and outstanding leaders. It will be one of the most attractive professions in American society. In my view, the evidence indicates that the latter course will prevail.

In either event, the military role will be more sophisticated than in the past. The Korean and Vietnam wars demonstrated that merely being "firstest with the mostest" and possessing the ability to crush the opponent no longer leads necessarily to a satisfactory military solution. The use of force, either in a subtle display or with an extravagant threat of massive retaliation, has always required an element of sophistication. The difference is that the forces of history, the variety of advanced weapons, communications advances, and the complexity of modern international relations force military professionals to become better technicians and students of diplomacy and to understand the backgrounds and characteristics of many diverse societies. As these societies become more interdependent, they produce pressures that tend to generate a need for military strength to resolve difficulties. Members of the military profession must be more sophisticated and better educated in order to appreciate the complementary role of the military in the conduct of diplomatic affairs. Conversely, diplomatic and political leaders must develop a better understanding of the military profession.

Military Authority

Perhaps the most significant and least understood influence currently at work on the military profession results from the changing nature of the authority reposed in military leaders. Authority—the opportunity to be "in charge"—is the essential, predominant characteristic of the profession. It is the element that attracts and develops leaders. Men and women seek responsibility and opportunities to excel, to contribute, and to make their mark. They may well get the opportunities, but their ultimate ability to accomplish anything will depend largely on their authority to do the job. As the degree of authority varies, other aspects of the profession will likewise undergo alterations. If a great deal of authority is vested in the military, a military career will be stimulating and interesting. On the other hand, if authority is continually taken away, as it has been for the past two decades, the viability and attractiveness of the profession will decrease. A basic tenet of all professions is that the greater the authority bestowed on a profession, the higher the quality of the personnel in the profession. And, of course, the opposite holds true.

Before and during World War II and through the Korean War, the military interpreted "civilian authority and control" only in terms of "policy." It did not involve the details of "what to do" or "how to do" a particular task. It related only to objectives, not means. Senior leaders constantly cautioned military members against going into details with civilian authorities concerning military plans and methods of accomplishing the objectives set forth by civilian authority. That well-established concept is now so foreign to the U.S. military profession that one can only express amazement at the speed with which change was made.

Essentially, the shift in authority began after World War II with the creation of the Office of the Secretary of Defense (OSD) and the appointment of the first secretary of defense, James Forrestal, despite his initial objection and final reluctant concurrence. The transition from his modest, high-level, policy staff to the present-day multibillion-dollar OSD is unbelievable. For thirty years, OSD has had the most significant effect of all institutions on the military profession, and many people view that effect as highly unfortunate. The main effect has been the removal of authority from the military professional. Much of the authority given to him by law now actually rests in the hands of civilian-appointed officials or members of their staffs.

The expansion of the OSD has manifested itself in the creation of such offices as the Defense Communications Agency, the Defense Intelligence Agency, the Defense Supply Agency, and so forth. One of the most recent actions further wresting control from the military has been the creation of the post of a second deputy secretary of defense, whose task has been the revamping of defense intelligence organization and functions. Essentially, this removed the Joint Chiefs of Staff (JCS) from line authority in intelligence matters. Consequently, the JCS now have an intelligence role only in their control of the operating units performing the intelligence function. Tasking and authority for control rest with civilian authority.

Ostensibly, the post of second deputy secretary of defense was established to straighten out the intelligence program, but the new office will probably not be abolished when that mission is completed. On the contrary, it can logically assume supervision of international security affairs, arms sales, intelligence, logistics, and so on, and the original deputy secretary of defense can retain his expanding role in hardware requirements, weapons design, procurement, maintenance, and so on. This process will further remove authority from the military.[2]

A similar situation has been created in the weapons procurement function. Traditionally and logically, the operating forces have defined weapons requirements, and other members of the profession have translated requirements into procurement actions. Now, civilians in the OSD and other civilians in the halls of Congress almost exclusively control weapons definitions and procurement. The principal deputy secretary of defense has recently assumed responsibility as the procurement czar. The complex nature of modern weapon systems may have required many of these changes, but the fact remains that the authority once vested in the military no longer resides there. Ten years have passed since the chief of the bureau of ships and his deputy resigned from the navy because the authority traditionally vested in their offices to design and procure ships was taken away just as they personally reached those positions of responsibility.

Another new and significant action affecting authority has been the centralization of the internal audit function. A recent directive created a Defense Internal Audit Agency headed by a civilian director, who reports to the secretary of defense, with staff supervision by the assistant secretary of defense (comptroller).[3] In signing the memorandum, the deputy secretary of defense stated that he viewed the establishment of the agency "as a step towards a possible goal of total consolidation of DOD internal audit activities."

Anyone familiar with corporate business structure knows that one of the best ways to determine what is happening in an organization is to control the audit. The individual services (the military profession) are losing control of their own audit function—and this is another derogation of authority, the essential element of the profession.

A similar weakening of authority is occurring in other elements of the military profession, such as the procurement of airplanes and tanks, the development of manpower programs, and operations. Secretary McNamara's reversal of a decision by the military on the producer of the F-111 aircraft was a classic example in the early 1960s. A reversal of a decision by the military on the producer of a new tank, the XM-1, is the most recent example. All of these actions have had a deleterious effect on military morale, and they must be viewed with serious concern.

Proposed action by Congress to inject itself more into the details of defense business represents another possible threat to military authority. Proposals have been advanced to make Congress an integral link in determining weapons requirements, in designing weapons to meet the requirements, in determining methods of procurement, and in naming the producers of the weapons. If Congress accepts these proposals, the military will encounter major problems in regaining the authority so essential in keeping the profession viable. The ultimate user of a weapon should have a voice in determining the specifics of the weapon to be procured. We have wandered a long way from this fundamental precept.

An even more significant trend in recent years has been the decline in the military profession's prerogative of choosing its own leaders. Traditionally, the chief of each military service has selected officers for promotion to top management positions. This prerogative was seriously jeopardized during the McNamara era, when the service secretaries assumed an expanded role in selecting officers for promotion to flag and general officer status, for promotion to three-star and four-star positions, and for assignment to key operational and managerial positions. Although officers promoted initially to flag or general officer rank were selected by board action, the service secretaries influenced the criteria used for selection. The promotion of officers to higher ranks (three and four stars) and selection for key positions have now become significant functions of the secretary of defense.

When Melvin Laird was the secretary of defense, one senior official in a position to know reported that Secretary Laird had injected more politics into the military profession than all of his predecessors combined. James Schlesinger continued the trend by injecting himself into the selection process; that is, officers being considered for three-star rank had to appear before Secretary Schlesinger for a personal interview before promotion.

There is no quicker way to gain complete control of any profession than to select its leaders, and there is no quicker way to demoralize a profession than to select leaders whose qualifications are subject to question by the members of the profession. One of the characteristics of any profession is that its practitioners must have a strong voice in selecting their leaders. The selection process evolved by the military over the years has earned the confidence of its members. Actions by temporary civilian political appointees in the Department of Defense and elsewhere during the past decade have done much to destroy that confidence.

The Basic Demand of the Future

Obviously, the military profession must take aggressive action if it expects to recoup some of the authority that it has lost in recent years. Ideally, it should demonstrate better performance as a whole and have the authority returned as a gift. But it would be naive and unrealistic to expect such a step—even if the the profession were to perform in the most exemplary fashion. History shows that authority once lost is rarely returned without some unusual prior action. A strong, intelligent leader, functioning as an individual, might dispense, delegate, or return authority. A bureaucracy such as OSD will, because of its very nature, continually attempt to take more authority.

Senior leaders in the military profession will undoubtedly recognize this fact. As a result, there probably will be a closer bonding together of the services. Unity of thought and concerted action on key issues can do much to strengthen the military position and remove the reasons for civilian authority and control over every aspect of the military decision-making process. Closer union can come through informal agreements implemented on a day-to-day basis by leaders and members of the respective services. But it may be unrealistic to think that such voluntary cooperation will materialize.

A somewhat undesirable but more realistic approach is to form various associations specifically to gain benefits and advantages. For example, many associations currently exist for specific purposes relating to the military profession, often to gain some kind of benefit for the members. Some are officially registered lobbying organizations, such as the Retired Officers Association, aimed at influencing the OSD and Congress. Others, such as the U.S. Navy League, expend energy and funds in trying to educate selected audiences on particular philosophies. Interest in these associations evidently increases as authority diminishes within the services. At least one of several new associations is on the verge of launching an aggressive membership drive in response to queries from the young, active-duty community seeking to unite for the common good.[4]

Another path of action is the enrollment by the military in established trade associations or unions. The idea of unions for military personnel is not new. Military services in several foreign countries are unionized. Policemen and firemen in major cities have joined unions in addition to associations within their respective professions. The motivation for joining a union has generally been to gain more bargaining power for benefits. A key benefit subject to bargaining in the military profession is authority. Restoration of authority downward in the command channel could do much to eliminate the motivation to unionize, but evidence of such restoration is lacking.

One can only speculate as to whether members of the U.S. armed forces will unionize during the period 1980 to 2000. To date, most service leaders have taken a "head in the sand" approach to the subject, but the problem will not go away. Furthermore, interest in the idea of unions exists in both the commissioned and the enlisted ranks.

The American Federation of Government Employees (AFGE) claims that military people are now turning to the AFGE for help in stemming further erosion of benefits and limits on pay increases because the associations that represent them in Washington are doing a poor job. The AFGE is a federation of 300,000 government employees. Whether it would fight for restoration of military authority is debatable, but it could gain power for the members of the profession.

The concept of unions for the armed forces evokes great concern and strong statements from traditional supporters of the military profession. Senator Strom Thurmond and Representative Floyd Spence (South Carolina) have introduced resolutions in the Senate and House that would prohibit unionization of military personnel.[5] According to a recent editorial in *The Retired Officer,* several other congressional leaders support the resolutions. Senator James Eastland of Mississippi states that he is "in perfect agreement supporting such legislation." Senator Sam Nunn of Georgia believes that "unionization could have an adverse impact upon command and authority." Senator Frank Church states that he appreciates concern about unionizing the military and that he would oppose such a move. Representative Olin Teague of Texas says that he is "against any form of unionization of military personnel," and Senator Jesse Helms of North Carolina believes that "such an idea is absolutely absurd."[6]

Despite the protestations of these knowledgeable and longtime supporters of the military profession, the changing nature of society and the erosion of authority are triggering the interest of military members in the union concept. These members will join forces in the years 1980-2000 to gain benefits and restore the authority necessary for a viable profession.

As military people observe their active-duty leaders in uniform, they see less willingness to fight battles for benefits and authority. As authority disappears, the ability to gain a rightful share of benefits for the troops likewise disappears. In reflecting the attitudes of the country at large, members of the military profession believe that their share should equal that of other professions. They are no longer prone to settle for "giving" so that others may "take."

As these people look to OSD for a champion, they confront legislation, proposals, and programs initiated for further derogation of benefits and authority. In many instances, they consider OSD "the enemy." And as they look to Capitol Hill for help, they see the traditional leaders of the armed services committees disappearing from the ranks through retirement, death, and political change. These committees are now being staffed with more liberal, antimilitary elements of society. Military members still view Congress as a solution to many of their problems, but apparently they cannot find the leadership necessary to lobby for them.

One can logically assume that during the next few years, the military profession will give considerable attention to unions, existing and new associations, or any other body that can lead in the fight for benefits and privileges. Most of this interest and action will stem from the diminished authority of the profession. Any further removal of authority will cause further decline in the profession. The most important future demand on the U.S. military profession will be to regain its authority.

Notes

1. Article 5947, Title 10, U.S. Code.

2. As of April 15, 1977, it was the announced intention of the secretary of defense to abolish the newly established post of second deputy secretary of defense. For it, he would substitute three "undersecretaries of defense," inserting them between the deputy secretary and the assistant secretaries, thereby creating a completely new echelon of control in the OSD.

3. Deputy Secretary of Defense Memo dated August 17, 1976, subject: "Organization for Internal Audit in the Department of Defense."

4. M. L. Lien (Lieutenant Colonel, USAF, Ret.), "Military Associations: A Positive Force for Defense," *The Retired Officer*, December 1975.

5. S. 3079 and H.R. 12526, respectively.

6. "Unions Are Alien to Our Defense System," *The Retired Officer*, May 1976.

23

The Future Demands of Military Professionalism: The Views of an Army Major

James R. Golden

The perceived demands of military professionalism have always taken divergent directions. To some sources, professionalism has meant a politically neutral, socially isolated elite, highly skilled in the decisive use of force. Others have stressed the need for a politically sensitive, socially integrated, and responsive organization geared to the measured use of force. Elements of both views of professionalism have always been present, and the degree to which each perspective dominates has varied within different services and organizations at any one period of time. Therefore, the difficulty of defining the current state of military professionalism in any meaningful, comprehensive manner complicates any attempt to forecast the future demands of military professionalism. At a given time, an observer is more apt to find a flow of interactions within the profession more akin to the merger of tide and current in an estuary than to the predictable pattern of a cascade.

Two divergent models of military professionalism provide a useful base for an analysis of the current state of the profession and the future demands that will be placed upon it. The models reappear in the literature under several headings, but the essential distinctions are quite consistent. The basic models are those of Huntington in *The Soldier and the State* and Janowitz in *The Professional Soldier*.[1] Both sought to nurture concepts of military professionalism that would increase internal checks on any potential obstacles to civilian control. The Huntington view emphasizes the development and provision of narrowly focused military skills and advice in a setting of political neutrality. Janowitz argues for a constabulary force that would be prepared to make war but would focus on keeping

The author acknowledges assistance in the development of this chapter by several colleagues in the department of social sciences at the Military Academy: Major Wesley Clark, Major Ralph Hallenbeck, Colonel William Taylor, Jr., and Captain William Sammon.

the peace in situations where the distinctions between military and political actions were imprecise. As Larson summarizes the Janowitz model, "The professional officer would be broadly recruited, educated in political as well as military affairs, possess managerial and technical skills yet retain the 'warrior spirit,' cultivate a broad perspective on civilian and military, as well as domestic and international affairs, and be motivated by professional considerations."[2]

The two models thus call for substantially different professional standards. Larson's description of the Janowitz view as "pragmatic professionalism" is appropriate, but his characterization of the Huntington position as "radical professionalism" is somewhat pejorative and imprecise.[3] Distinctions between "pragmatic professionalism" and "traditional professionalism" may be more useful. Other writings draw similar dichotomies between military "integration" and "isolation," military-civilian "convergence" and "divergence," or "managerial" and "heroic" qualities. ·

Neither the pragmatic nor the traditional models are apt to provide an adequate summary of where the profession has been, where it is, where it is going, or, perhaps most important, where it should go. Yet it can be useful to view the professional norm as an amalgam of views that lie somewhere along a continuum between the two extremes, with a distribution extending from that norm in either direction. Various types of units may hold different views on the ideal professional standard, with line units on the end of the distribution toward traditional professionalism and higher-level staff units on the end toward pragmatic professionalism. When the military has faced a hostile environment that demands small peacetime regular forces, it has tended to respond in the direction of traditional professionalism. This pattern applies to the period of retrenchment in the 1920s and 1930s and may apply to the army in the mid-1950s as well.

However, these periods of retrenchment serve only to highlight a longer trend toward the integration of traditional military values with civilian values and political constraints. This trend has followed from an appreciation of the restraints inherent in limited war, from the evolution of new civilian attitudes on human dignity and civil rights, and from expanded interaction with the civilian community implicit in a large peacetime military establishment. To a considerable extent, pragmatic professionalism has been forced on the military by shifting circumstances beyond its control.

In terms of the two models, the evolution of military professionalism in the 1970s may be described as a gradual shift toward pragmatic professionalism, with emphasis on the controlled use of force and a convergence of military and civilian values, interrupted by periods of retreat to traditional professionalism. Both Janowitz and Moskos forecast a shift toward traditional professionalism in the early 1970s as the military responded to what it perceived as a narrowing officer recruitment base, the prospect of an all-volunteer force, and a return to a conventional public attitude of antimilitarism.[4] Indeed, two army colonels, Bradford and Brown, concluded that "the most pressing threat to military capability is overexposure to rapidly shifting societal values," and they called for "isolation to preserve identity" rather than "immersion to stimulate rapid accommodation."[5]

Some retrenchment toward a traditional view of military professionalism did occur as the Vietnam war wound down. Attention abruptly shifted from potential limited war to the more traditional problems of waging conventional war, particularly in Europe. Adjustments in barracks lifestyles to meet the perceived needs of a volunteer force were not reversed, but any further changes in standards obviously would meet strong opposition. The economic recession in 1974 and 1975 brought an expansion of volunteers, which permitted this reaction to changing standards to take hold. However, the long-term pressures forcing a more complete integration of military and civilian values show little sign of abating.

If the traditional public attitude really has been antimilitary, the current attitude is more accurately "amilitary."[6] The environment is not as hostile as it is apathetic. But the pressures for adapting to new standards of equality and civil liberty in all institutions are very real, and the military will either adjust to them slowly in a way that preserves its essential core values or abruptly in ways that threaten those values. The risk of having new standards imposed by fiat from outside the profession is a danger—not because external control is illegitimate but because such changes tend to be precipitate rather than evolutionary. Any further retreat by the military to preserve traditional values through isolation could have dangerous consequences in the future. This does not imply that many traditional values are not worth preserving; indeed, many are essential to the profession. But if those essential values are preserved, they must be applied intelligently in a shifting institutional setting. This will require a pattern of adaptation that distinguishes between long-term trends and short-term fads and recognizes that the changes required in different types of units will vary with the structure and mission of the units.

Certainly, various units have always adapted to their specific missions, and the military professional has been forced to acquire the skills relevant to a range of professional assignments. But the range is steadily broadening, and individuals find it increasingly difficult to perform effectively in the traditional generalist career pattern. Line assignments remain the best preparation for the command of line units, but they are less adequate preparation for managing sophisticated research and development programs, for interfacing with DOD budget control processes, or for advising on the use of force in a world characterized by expanding economic and military interdependence. The result of these pressures is often frustration with growing civilian oversight within the Department of Defense in particular and within the federal government in general.

But frustration will not reverse these trends, and the pressure for pragmatic adjustment to external pressures will persist. The dilemma is to find ways to preserve the effectiveness of line units and, at the same time, insure that professionals can satisfy increasingly sophisticated management and advisory requirements. Competence in the management of violence will still be the basis for developing a military professional, but adjustments in traditional career patterns and professional education may be required to provide an increasing number of specialists in other, less traditional military skills. The professional may anticipate a series of abrupt adjustments as he moves from units with traditional roles to assignments requiring significantly different skills in much different environments.

If the future demands of the profession lead to more divergent career patterns, what essential core values must be preserved? They must be values that transcend the active combat environment and encompass the full range of the professional experience. There have been many eloquent statements of the essential values of military professionalism, but the motto of the Military Academy expresses them elegantly and simply: "Duty, Honor, Country." Each of these concepts must be defined in terms of the current institutional setting to have any operational meaning. Reverend James D. Ford, chaplain at the Military Academy, expresses this point in these relevant questions: Duty, to whom? Honor, by what standard? Country, to what extent?

Duty, to Whom?

The concept of duty assumes a subordination of personal desires to service directed at some broader objective. The oath of military service defines that objective as the support and defense of the Constitution of the United States. As a member of a service, an individual accepts a series of narrowly defined duties to superiors and subordinates consistent with his responsibilities to uphold that oath. The broad requirements of duty become meaningful through a complex series of interpersonal responsibilities. Most combat studies have concluded that individuals fight to uphold their responsibilities to other members of their group rather than to achieve some national objective. Yet the two concepts are interrelated. Although individual actions are rarely linked directly to the oath of office or national objectives, long-term commitment to those obligations, at least in part, permits an individual to subordinate personal desires and accept responsibilities imposed or required by the organization.

Although duty demands subordination of self-interest, it also requires a commitment to personal excellence. This commitment certainly requires mastery of the physical and technical skills in a combat environment; it also requires an ability to work in an increasingly complex social and technological environment. In this sense, the concept of duty requires more than the execution of responsibilities to superiors and subordinates; it requires each individual to stretch his contribution to the limits of his potential. A commitment to duty thus requires a sense of motivation that goes far beyond personal gain, and it creates an obligation for continuing self-development to improve the extent and quality of one's service.

Motivation

There is perhaps no way to structure a motivational system that does not draw upon individual ambition, and in many respects, ambition can be a healthy attribute in a profession that is ultimately centered on competition. The danger is that personal ambition that translates into careerism can have a damaging impact on the profession. If the individual views each job as a stepping stone to a subsequent job with greater responsibility or to earlier promotion, he may place more emphasis on the appearance of performance than on the substance of service. In some instances, people have not reported or attended to problems to avoid the appearance of failure, or units have attempted tasks beyond their capabilities to avoid any suggestion of weakness. The current system of determining individual advancement in the services imposes a heavy penalty on any appearance of failure, particularly when the number of jobs viewed as critical to career development is limited. In addition, turbulent permanent-change-of-station policies to provide greater access to career-enhancing jobs can have a disastrous impact on the continuity of middle and senior management.

The army response to these latter problems has been to extend the periods of service in key positions, particularly in command assignments. But the result of this shift has been a reduction in the number of people who can serve in the jobs perceived as essential to advancement. In the current army career pattern, successful completion of battalion command is virtually essential for promotion beyond the rank of colonel, but fewer than 10 percent of the officer corps will have the opportunity for such a command. Thus, the limitations on continuing promotion of officers not selected for battalion command will be perceived earlier in the individual's career. Nonselection would have a significant impact under any motivational system, but the consequences are severe in a system that places such stress on competition centered on personal ambition.

There is no way to escape the fact that some individuals will not be able to rise to the top of the organization. But it should be possible to structure the system in a way that provides for forms of career satisfaction other than rapid progression through a narrowly defined career pattern. Specialization in a field of interest can provide significant psychic rewards to an individual and clear benefits to the service if it is viewed as a free choice and not mandated by failure in a principal specialty. The Army Officer Personnel Management System (OPMS) has provided for alternate career patterns, but the alternatives are still perceived as somehow inferior to the primary command-oriented career pattern.

The current retirement system, with its arbitrary requirement for twenty years of service, tends to reinforce exactly the wrong type of career behavior. Since retirement benefits are not vested, the pressure to remain on active service for twenty years is intense, especially as the twenty-year mark approaches. Thus, those not selected for rapid advancement are not really free to resign and seek employment elsewhere. Instead, they must find jobs to perform in the service until retirement, and those jobs are normally in specialty positions out of the mainstream. Such jobs can have a very important impact on service missions, but they are downgraded as retirement positions. In-service retirement is not a new phenomenon, but it poses a serious challenge to professionalism.

Changes that emphasize the importance of each job per se, rather than as pauses in a continuing sequence, would be helpful. The shift toward specialized tracks geared to an individual's unique interests and talents promises some relief in this area. The challenge to service personnel systems is to treat each member more as an individual and less as an interchangeable part. The change in army policy permitting an action officer to follow an action all the way up the chain of command is clearly a move in the right direction. Further adjustments that assign individual responsibility proportionate to individual ability, with less emphasis on rank, are necessary. A promotion policy that accepts the value of each job and a job assignment that is less contingent on a set pattern of preceding jobs would reinforce the concept that outstanding performance of duty in any assignment is important.

Careerism that perceives personal advancement as a major objective is clearly antithetical to the concept of duty. But as other authors in this volume have noted, substantial evidence shows that the military profession has assumed many other characteristics more typical of an occupation than of a calling. There is increasing pressure for comparability with other occupations in terms of compensation and working conditions and, perhaps, less emphasis on the more unique sources of motivation for military service. In facing the prospect of unionized armed forces, national leaders must make a fundamental choice. The options are to reinforce the occupational view by making compensation and working conditions more comparable to alternatives elsewhere or to stress the uniqueness of the military calling and the traditional basis of compensation and motivation.

As a motivating factor, increased emphasis on pay may be linked, in part, to the shift to a volunteer force. Many of the inducements for initial service in a volunteer force focused on the equivalence of military and civilian pay opportunities. The argument that recipients and potential volunteers undervalued traditional military payments "in kind" suggested that increases in base pay should be the major adjustment in the compensation system. The concept of stimulating service through competitive pay in a form most equivalent to civilian compensation marked a fundamental shift from earlier policy. Traditional policy has been to provide compensation that would permit a service member to maintain a life-style consistent with his or her rank. This meant a significant portion of pay "in kind" in the form of housing, medical services, commissary privileges, and so forth. The retirement system provided sufficient pay at the end of service to compensate for the limited opportunity to save during service. But in general, military pay was not the equivalent of civilian pay, either in form or in total, since military service was not the equivalent of civilian employment.

As the emphasis on pay equivalence has increased, the distinction between military service and private employment has become more blurred. The sense of community and unit attachment has declined in the service, and there is an increasing tendency to view military service as just another nine-to-five job. This tendency will undoubtedly increase under the mounting pressure for unionization. In the interest of efficiency, Congress faces considerable pressure to reduce payments "in kind" even further and to make military pay even more equivalent with civilian compensation. But, to some extent, an individual bases his commitment to an institution on the benefits that the institution can offer. "In kind" payments are dispersed through service organizations, but the monthly check goes directly to the individual's bank. Thus, the shift to conventional civilian pay can seriously undermine the rewards available through the service.

This trend has been manifested at the unit level by a general shift toward centralized provision of services. Supplies, promotion, pay, and other services are increasingly provided from central offices rather than administered by individual units. As a result, unit commanders have the same responsibilities but less discretion in applying centrally managed and provided resources. Another result is that one's identification with his or her unit is weaker. The increased level and changed form of military pay may have the same impact on the identification of service members with the military profession.

The motivation of members of the profession is clearly a complex problem, and the issues are not one-sided. The case may certainly be made that attempts to motivate high standards of service by holding out the prospect of personal advancement and improved compensation are perfectly legitimate. However, to the extent that these motivational techniques reduce the emphasis on service and commitment to duty, they pose serious problems for the future of military professionalism.

Self-development

The services tend to view education as a process that takes place in a classroom environment to train individuals for fairly specific future tasks. This view frequently results in the requirement to transmit an established bloc of information or a procedure to be used in solving a specified problem. In service-sponsored civilian education, this takes the form of identifying the specific job that an individual will subsequently perform to "use" the education. Such a narrow view of education fosters the attitude that education occurs only in a formal school environment and that service education is useful only when it focuses on a specific task to be performed. This view also fosters the mistaken impression that one is educated by the passive act of attendance rather than by an active struggle to formulate and organize new concepts.

The fulfillment of the concept of duty does not require continuing education in the limited sense of systematic instruction, but it does require a continuing struggle to reach one's full potential. This type of development demands an attitude of intellectual growth that challenges the past with the realities of the present and the requirements of the future. The central challenge to the profession is most often not the solution of a stated problem but the early perception of a new question that needs to be answered. The major problem is timely adaptation to a changing military environment.

In peacetime, particularly in the army, a limited potential exists for realistic training to test and evaluate new concepts of combat. Since the ultimate test for such ideas is not available, there is a need for an atmosphere of intellectual ferment that challenges traditional questions and searches for new solutions. Service schools foster such approaches, to some extent, but a current misguided attitude is that such reassessments should be limited to periods of formal instruction. Generals Eisenhower, Patton, Marshall, and many others are obvious examples of individuals who used intensive personal study during peacetime to prepare themselves for subsequent responsibilities. There is also a real need for commanders and staff officers to test new concepts and record their observations for others. Intervals between troop duty assignments should be viewed as major growth periods in which individuals can make significant contributions in an area of the service most related to their talents and experience.

Such contributions need not be limited to people with the highest formal education. There is ample room in current doctrine for fundamental contributions that could have a significant impact on the profession. Adaptation to increasing problems of airspace control and improved accuracy of antitank weapons are two such areas that come immediately to mind. Although formal education is not a requirement to contribute to an environment that challenges current wisdom, it should be noted that formal education can be useful in bringing relevant concepts from a variety of disciplines to bear on current problems of the profession. Such programs should not be evaluated solely on the basis of their contributions to specific future tasks; they should be evaluated in the broader context of their contribution to an atmosphere that promotes continuing intellectual development.

The plea is that the talents of people in the profession should be more fully mobilized to address the concerns of the profession. This is not a time for complacent acceptance of current solutions. There is a real need for a challenging environment that does not restrict new ideas because they may be wrong but encourages them because they may be right. The ultimate test must not be the rank of the proponent or the fervor with which he defends a position. The ultimate test short of combat must be the quality of the idea—quality tested through free and open debate.

Duty, to whom? In the final analysis, duty represents a commitment to ourselves—a commitment to subordinate the prospect of short-term personal gain to the long-term interests of the nation. In practical terms, such a commitment takes the form of meeting responsibilities to others in the group. The subordination of personal interest requires confidence in the objectives of the profession and in the ability of the services to provide for basic individual needs. The challenge to military professionalism is to provide an institutional setting that fosters this commitment to duty.

Honor, by What Standard?

Standards of integrity in virtually every profession have been drawn into question by a series of scandals that have attracted public scrutiny. In virtually every instance, the response has been a soul-searching review of the basis for the profession's ethical standards. The military profession has been no exception. The My Lai cover-up was perhaps the most blatant example of unethical conduct, but other instances have raised fundamental questions about the military profession's integrity and ability to enforce acceptable ethical standards.

But is not the military profession simply a reflection of the society from which it is drawn? Can the military expect standards of conduct significantly different from standards demanded by other occupations? If different standards are applied, how should they be defined and how can they be enforced?

Quite probably, the individual's standards are firmly entrenched long before he enters military service. As the ethical norms of society shift, it may become increasingly difficult to gain strict adherence to a military standard that stresses high integrity. But it is perfectly reasonable for those entering the military profession to accept standards of conduct necessary for the successful performance of their duties. From this utilitarian point of view, the profession has every right to maintain standards of honor that may differ from commonly accepted practices elsewhere. But if sanctions are applied to departures from the ethical standard, the standard must be clearly defined in terms of the requirements for the effective performance of duty.

Many of the strongest arguments for high standards of integrity have nothing to do with the military profession. Certainly, there is a broad foundation in a variety of religious faiths for individual standards of honor. Standards of conduct influence the perceptions that we have of ourselves and that others have of us. A demonstrated lack of integrity reflecting a desire for personal gain over other objectives can reduce the trust of others. George Bernard Shaw claimed that he once asked a woman to exchange her favors for one thousand pounds and she accepted. When he lowered the offer to five pounds, she asked indignantly what he thought she was. Shaw replied that they had already established that and that they were now haggling over the price. Once integrity has been sacrificed for personal gain, we only haggle over the price; those for whom and with whom we work will recognize that fact.

Such broad principles cannot be incorporated in a professional standard until they are related to the specific requirements of the profession. Issues of integrity and honor affect the profession at three levels. In ascending order of uniqueness, they are unit effectiveness, leadership, and "official acts."

At the daily working level, an atmosphere of trust and confidence is essential for military organizations to operate effectively. This atmosphere certainly includes "official acts" (discussed below), but it also extends to the "unofficial" relationships among the individuals in a unit. Mutual confidence and esteem are essential to a unit's esprit de corps. Patterns of behavior established through long periods of experience are difficult to change in the face of important decisions, and high standards of personal integrity must be nurtured so that mutual confidence can survive long periods of great stress. Mutual confidence based on personal integrity is essential to insure that difficult tasks requiring joint efforts can be accomplished under the most trying conditions.

Leaders must command a level of respect and confidence proportionate to their responsibility. Such respect may be built on many attributes, but strength of character would certainly be high on any list. When orders imply substantial sacrifice and risk on the part of subordinates, they must have no lingering doubt of the commander's real motivation. To execute the orders effectively, they must accept his personal integrity without question. The commander cannot direct such acceptance by fiat; it must be based on mutual respect and demonstrated professional integrity.

These examples reflect the need for personal attributes that contribute to unit cohesion and professional leadership. Although weaknesses in character may be appropriate targets for efficiency evaluations, more severe sanctions must be reserved for official acts that are clearly in the line of duty. Two areas that deserve special attention are actions relating to combat or readiness reporting and actions relating to the control of public resources.

In the latter area, military professionals must accept the same responsibilities as other public officials. Certainly, they must be strictly accountable for the responsible use of resources that have been placed at their disposal. This responsibility is clearest in the area of property control, but it also extends to the use of other resources. Expending ammunition to avoid laborious turn-in procedures is a case in point. In addition, the interface of military professionals with the defense industry, particularly in matters relating to procurement, is an extremely sensitive area that requires the highest standards of personal integrity.

Of course, the most obvious and perhaps the most unique requirement for high standards of honor in the military profession has to do with the necessity of accurate reporting in combat. The danger of unnecessary loss of life in such situations is too obvious to warrant elaboration. Moreover, there is a compelling need for accurate reports that correctly reflect the current status of forces and their readiness for combat. The advice of the military professional to military or civilian superiors must accurately reflect current situations; otherwise, the consequences for national security decisions can be severe.

Thus, the military has every reason to require standards of integrity necessary for the effective performance of military duties. But the heart of the matter is that a commitment to duty is an empty promise if the individual lacks personal honor. Whom does the profession serve? When integrity is sacrificed to the pressures of the moment, the motivation is invariably personal advantage, not service.

If professionals demand integrity of themselves, can they tolerate dishonesty in others? Obviously, the answer is no, because the profession's ability to perform its vital mission is weakened when individual gain dominates commitment to duty. Moreover, honor in the profession is, to a significant degree, indivisible. If the profession reinforces the requirement for integrity, individual actions tend to conform to the group norm. On the other hand, a pattern of sacrificing integrity on such routine matters as maintenance, training, or readiness reports can easily affect standards of honor in other areas. As John Lovell explains the importance of the group norm, "Virtue may be its own reward; but a person's sense of honor, like his loyalty, is typically maintained in relation to the reference group."[7]

However, a decision not to tolerate dishonorable acts does not necessarily imply judgment without compassion. Everyone has been placed in positions where the consequences of sacrificing personal integrity appeared minimal, especially in comparison to the group norm, where the short-term consequences of an action were very advantageous. One step across the line does not necessarily render an individual dishonorable. Indeed, such an experience can serve as a catharsis to reinforce a commitment to personal honor. But the danger is that such acts can erode standards of honor, and in some cases, even a single act can have severe consequences. A pattern of tolerating individual acts with even minor impacts can erode the atmosphere of trust essential to the military profession.

The services still suffer general schizophrenia on issues of honor. On the one hand, they accept the importance of honor; on the other, they assume that the act of commissioning automatically produces honorable men. Many who lament the failure to maintain higher standards of integrity suggest that such traits are learned long before the service can influence the development of a sense of honor. But these views ignore the group impact on individual behavior. The military should provide an institutional environment that reinforces an individual's sense of honor and isolates violations of integrity as clearly unacceptable acts. The annual conferences on responsibility at the Army Command and General Staff College emphasize small group discussions of realistic challenges to personal integrity. This is one useful mechanism for emphasizing honor in the military profession.

Honor, by what standard? The demands of military professionalism require a sense of honor that encompasses an obligation to reduce pressures for toleration and to encourage mutual trust. This does not suggest a vendetta against people who step over arbitrarily defined lines, but it does suggest that actions must be challenged and openly discussed if they threaten mutual confidence. In some cases, specific acts may be defined as clearly unacceptable, and strong, widely understood sanctions applied. But in most situations requiring moral judgments, no clear lines can be drawn before the fact. In such instances, military professionals must define the standard of honor as they attempt to deal with difficult daily decisions. If those decisions are guided by a sense of personal responsibility that subordinates private gain to the interests of the country and the profession, we will move closer to meeting the future demands of military professionalism.

Country, to What Extent?

Every military professional must be willing to accept risks that may lead to the loss of his life in the nation's defense. As a corollary, he must also be prepared to subordinate the welfare of his unit to the accomplishment of an essential mission. Indeed, the ultimate purpose of military discipline is to train individuals and units to accept such risks and to continue to work effectively under the stress and confusion of combat. But the authority of the military professional to require such sacrifices carries with it a responsibility to insure the legal and judicious use of force and to guarantee the preparation of his unit to execute missions that it may be directed to perform, including deterrence of aggression by an adversary.

Fortunately, the military professional takes his oath to the Constitution rather than to a specific individual or office. Thus, although the president has broad authority over military professionals as commander in chief, his authority to direct military actions is restricted. His orders must lie within the limits of the constitutional process, and the military professional must understand those limits. The Nuremberg Trials confirmed a second restraint on the actions of military professionals. The military professional remains morally responsible for his actions; thus, his commitment to the nation's defense does not give him license to follow any arbitrary order, even if a legally constituted higher authority gives the order. The individual must remain the ultimate arbiter of his actions. This is an awesome responsibility in a profession that places such emphasis on the prompt execution of orders, but it is a responsibility that the military professional must be prepared to accept.

Fortunately, the instances in which an order must be challenged on constitutional or moral grounds are extremely rare. The professional executes his normal duties with confidence in the orders of superiors, a confidence based on a sense of mutual trust and commitment. Perhaps the central characteristic of the military profession is the ultimate commitment of its members to accept extreme hardship and risk in the nation's defense. But such unlimited commitment on the part of subordinates creates unlimited responsibility for superiors. That responsibility extends beyond the requirement to prepare for combat so that losses will in fact be held to minimum levels. The responsibility extends to the point of insuring a level of preparedness that will reduce the probability of actually committing men in combat.

At the highest levels of responsibility in the profession, this natural desire for readiness confronts budgetary restrictions. The result can be frustration with a civilian hierarchy that is perceived to have excessive control not only over detailed decisions on force structure and weapons procurement, but also over operations. Such frustration is perhaps most intense among professionals who have operated primarily in line assignments and who have had little experience with the budgetary process or direct civilian supervision. Thus, the trend toward increased civilian representation in key operational positions within the Department of Defense is a cause for alarm in some quarters.

However, civilian control is legitimate, and the trends that have led to increased oversight show no signs of abating. Concern with the inflationary pressures of high budgets will continue to focus attention on the size and composition of the DOD budget, and the trade-offs between defense and other types of public expenditure will endure. Recent congressional reorganization of the budgetary process provides new mechanisms for detailed examination of the size and composition of defense spending. As concern for the civil liberties of servicemen and servicewomen has expanded and as the legal ramifications of decisions have increased, the trend toward expanded civilian oversight has been reinforced. Moreover, in a world of expanding economic and military interdependence, the pressure for interagency coordination may well create further civilian oversight within the Department of Defense. Recent crisis situations have indicated that civilian guidance, in some instances from the president himself, may be given directly to field commanders at low levels of operational control.

The concept of civilian control, which has always been a central value in the U.S. military profession, clearly follows the constitutional process. That principle is not questioned. The military professional obviously must be able to adapt to forms of control that will frequently involve direct supervision, as well as policy and budgetary review.

Thus, the military professional should acquire skills that will enable him to deal with his civilian counterparts and superiors. Even in areas traditionally reserved for military judgment, the professional must become more proficient in explaining options and justifying decisions. Such skill is essential not only to provide highly competent military advice but also to understand the civilian decision-making process and to present the supporting arguments and analyses most useful in that process.

The adjustment of the three services to the planning, programming, and budgeting system is an example of this process. The services were initially unable to provide the type of analysis needed in the DOD decision process, but in time they developed analysts who could provide useful inputs to the system. The initial reaction was frustration, but once they understood the new process, the services were again able to argue their positions effectively.

The military professional has a clear obligation to explain the capabilities and limitations of military force to civilian leaders in terms that are understandable, realistic, and accurate. When civilian leaders find it politically expedient to press for greater performance with fewer resources, the military professional must make the actual facts very clear, but he must also be as objective as possible. National security arguments that merely serve the parochial interest of a service can be extremely damaging to public confidence in military advice.

Some sources suggest that members of the military profession must be apolitical to insure subordination of the military to civilian authority. This view is correct when applied to partisan political activity, but it is woefully inadequate when one understands that politics is a contest for the allocation of power and resources. In this sense, the profession has a clear political obligation to provide military advice on matters that will insure adequate consideration of national security interests in the allocation of resources and proper evaluation of the capabilities and limitations of the military as an instrument of foreign policy. This requires an understanding of the decision-making process in the federal bureaucracy and the manner by which decisions can be legitimately influenced by the active presentation and defense of ideas.

Country, to what extent? The commitment to country must be tempered by an awareness of individual moral responsibility and guided by an over-riding commitment to the constitutional process. Within these limits, the obligation of the military professional to the country is absolute. Such a commitment extends not only to the execution of legal orders; it also creates the responsibility for maintaining the highest possible levels of military preparedness. The military professional must understand the role of civilian control when deciding on the appropriate levels and forms of readiness, and he must present his views effectively in a decision-making process characterized by increased civilian supervision.

Future Demands of Military Professionalism

Perhaps the classic debate between traditional professionalism and pragmatic professionalism has been somewhat overdrawn. The real alternatives facing the profession are not withdrawal to traditional values on the one hand or rapid accommodation to shifting societal values on the other. The real alternatives concern the pace of accommodation and the maintenance of those traditional values worth preserving in a changing institutional setting. Such decisions cannot be made for the profession as a whole, but they will in fact be made by the ways in which different types of units adjust to new demands placed on them.

Even the general comments that have been heroically applied to the entire profession in this brief chapter suggest simultaneous shifts in the directions of pragmatic and traditional professionalism. The emphasis on commitment to duty and the focus on service as motivational factors may be viewed as a shift toward traditional professionalism. The call for expanded emphasis on matters of honor may be viewed as a retreat to traditional values, but on the other hand, the view of honor as an issue for open debate may be a means of fostering a pragmatic adjustment to a shifting environment. The suggested need for increased appreciation of the civilian decision-making process and the call for a challenging environment of intellectual ferment may clearly be viewed as pragmatic adjustments. There is no contradiction in these conclusions. If the profession expects to meet the demands of the future, it must hold fast to core traditions worth preserving, but at the same time it must adapt to the shifting environment in which it must operate.

The unifying argument in the Huntington and Janowitz positions is that the real checks on the future performance of the military flow from the concepts of professionalism internalized by military professionals. The future will demand a renewed commitment of the professional to the principles of duty, honor, and country and a clear understanding of these principles in terms of personal action. The navy advertising slogan reads: "It's not just another job." To the extent that military service is viewed as just another outlet for personal ambition, the future of the profession will be in doubt. To the extent that each professional interprets duty as a broad commitment to contribute to the limits of his potential; that each contributes to an atmosphere of mutual trust through commitment to personal honor; that each serves the country, not with a blind commitment to its leaders but with complete dedication to its constitutional process, the military profession can meet the demands of the future with confidence.

Notes

1. Samuel P. Huntington, *The Soldier and the State: The Theory and Practice of Civil-Military Relations* (Cambridge, Mass.: Harvard University Press, 1957); Morris Janowitz, *The Professional Soldier: A Social and Political Portrait* (Glencoe, Ill.: Free Press, 1960).

2. Arthur D. Larson, "Military Professionalism and Civil Control: A Comparative Analysis of Two Interpretations," *Journal of Political and Military Sociology* 2 (Spring 1974):62.

3. Ibid., p. 64.

4. Morris Janowitz, "The Emergent Military," and Charles C. Moskos, Jr., "Armed Forces and American Society: Convergence or Divergence?," in *Public Opinion and the Military Establishment*, ed. Charles C. Moskos, Jr. (Beverly Hills, Calif.: Sage, 1971).

5. Zeb B. Bradford and Frederic J. Brown, *The United States Army in Transition* (Beverly Hills, Calif.: Sage, 1973), p. 175.

6. Colonel Richard F. Rosser, "American Civil-Military Relations in the 1980s," *Naval War College Review* 24, no. 10 (June 1972):14-15.

7. John P. Lovell, "Professionalism and the Service Academies," *American Behavioral Scientist* 19, no. 5 (May-June 1976):605-626.

24
Education in the Military:
A Look into the Future

Thomas W. Carr

A major sociological fact of our time is that the United States is running out of eighteen-year-olds. The World War II baby boom has ended, and in proportion to the total population, the age group between seventeen and twenty-two will soon include the smallest number of individuals in recent history.

If one assumes that the United States will need to maintain an active-duty military force of approximately 2.1 million and that women will continue to join the services at approximately the present or at a slightly faster rate,[1] then the military faces an enormously difficult task. By 1984—an appropriately Orwellian year on which to focus—the military must recruit approximately one of every three qualified male eighteen-year-olds annually in order to maintain the current all-volunteer force. *One of three!* If reserve requirements are also considered, the DOD must recruit 1 of every 1.9 males during the period 1985 to 1990.[2]

The Role of Education

In an earlier chapter, John Blair noted that high school seniors are more likely to join the military if educational incentives are provided. How can education be used to improve the odds of succeeding in such a difficult recruiting task? How can the quality of the force be maintained or developed? What new societal role will the armed forces be asked to assume? What will be the impact of this role on a major competitor for high-quality eighteen-year-olds—the education community itself? These and related questions are central issues concerning the future of education in the military.

Not only the military services, but civilian education, too, is affected greatly by demographics. In the five years between 1960 and 1965, the preponderant U.S. age group dropped from 35-40 to 17. To compound the problem, many of these seventeen-year-olds chose to remain in school rather than join the work force. American education responded by accelerating the construction of a vast production line of higher education.

During the 1960s and early 1970s, new campuses by the hundreds sprang up to meet an enormous projected demand. Today, most American homes are located within easy commuting distance of a college, university, community college, or junior college. One of five professionals in the United States works in some facet of education. In short, the machinery was completed just as the raw material began to disappear.

The effect of this development on institutions of higher education has ranged from serious to disastrous. A 1976 study conducted by *Change* magazine revealed that almost one-half of more than 2,000 institutions surveyed were financially unhealthy. Only 11.7 percent of four-year undergraduate colleges fell in the "healthy" category.[3]

Consequently, higher education is now more alert to demographic trends. It recognizes, for example, that within the next ten years, the number of those twenty-five to thirty-four years old in the population will increase by 44 percent. Thus, adult or continuing education is no longer a subsidiary activity of postsecondary institutions. According to the National Advisory Council on Extension and Continuing Education, it represents the fastest growing educational function. This expansion has been so rapid that American education has reached a major turning point— for the first time in history, the majority of students enrolled in post-secondary institutions are adults continuing their education on a part-time basis.[4]

Therefore, one can predict that by 1984 higher education will focus considerably less attention on the teenage learner and considerably more attention on the adult. The phenomenon of high school education followed by four years at the same college is likely to diminish as the predominant pattern. This tradition will be replaced with a number of school/work variations, many involving vocational and technical education, and only a small percentage providing four years of continuous learning at a single institution.

By 1984, the military, too, will have changed further—both in its image and in its substance. As described in this volume, management and hardware systems within the armed forces will be as complex as systems in other sophisticated fields of endeavor. Perhaps 85 to 90 percent of the skills required in the military will relate to civilian occupations, and job transferability will create new problems and new opportunities for military recruitment. As noted earlier, the U.S. labor force will become considerably older. Unless new job opportunities exist, the inexperienced eighteen-year-old will find more intense competition from mature and experienced workers than is true today. Thus, many young people may view the military as an attractive and worthwhile opportunity for training, education, and work experience.

Some Possibilities for the Future: Military Education in 1984

1. The military and higher education may avoid the potential battle over eighteen-year-olds simply by joining together in a series of cooperative ventures. It has been said that the military already represents, in microcosm, the so-called learning society that some educators see in America's future. Long noted for its sponsorship of educational innovations, the military, as much as any other sector of society, encourages the pursuit of education among its people. Approximately one-half million military personnel are involved in various types of education programs costing more than $1 billion annually. At the last count, more than 1,000 civilian institutions provided most of this education, and the demand is not slackening.

The military has a particular interest in recruiting those who are attracted by educational opportunities, for studies show that they score higher on tests of intelligence, occupational ambition, and self-esteem and that they have a higher propensity to enlist. Thus, many recruited people will want to pursue their education during their military service and after discharge from the military. Furthermore, military training programs can help them to gain confidence in their ability to learn, demonstrate the relationship of learning to real life, and sharpen their interest in *more* learning. Many who enter the military service after a somewhat mediocre high school experience will leave with confidence and interest in pursuing their education. By 1984, education will recognize the military not as a villain but as a major user of, preparer for, and motivator toward continuing postsecondary education.[5]

Each year, the military will return several hundred thousand men and women to civilian life after their years in the service. Thus, civilian society will benefit from this national resource of trained personnel, and higher education will also benefit, since many of these people will become full-time and, in most cases, mature and eager students. Most of the others will attend school at least as part-time students at some point during the decade following their release from the military.

2. American young people will increasingly join the military to acquire postsecondary education and training. According to a recent study, the chance to learn a valuable skill is the most important attraction for men sixteen to twenty-one years old to enter the armed forces. (Interestingly, "helps you get a college education while you serve" is rated quite low.) This study also shows that vocational and technical education is perceived as widely available and highly important within the military. Such findings coincide with the recent rise in the perceived importance of vocational/technical education—as opposed to college education—in civilian society.

Civilian workers are frequently concerned that job training will not relate to job performance or that they will not find a job to apply the skills learned. There is little chance of either event after military training. Instead, positive feedback between the trainer and the using command in the military organization limits oversupply and assures sufficient training for effective performance. This feedback is rare in the civilian training establishment.

Military training schools are generally criterion-referenced, and civilian schools are generally norm-referenced. This difference in organization and educational/training philosophies accounts for the superiority of the military school in producing graduates who can perform reliably in their initial assignments.

A major distinction between military and civilian training schools is the manner of testing and interpreting test scores. In civilian training, test scores are compared with other test scores, and evaluation takes the form of comparative scores—letter grades or class rankings. Although such normative evaluation distinguishes between better or faster students, it does not indicate whether mediocre students can perform satisfactorily.

In contrast, military evaluation of students gives less attention to relative performance within a group of students and more attention to a student's ability to perform a task or series of tasks required on the next job. A test score is simply a pass/fail indication; a student's performance on a test is compared only with a standard of performance based on an analysis of what is required to do a particular task. Of course, military schools conduct some normative testing to identify honor graduates and to establish class rankings for assignment preferences. But the underlying philosophy of military training is criterion-referenced. Thus, in a country increasingly concerned with the tangible benefits and substantive uses of education, the military training system represents an efficient and useful model.

3. Because of the large percentage of young people involved in military service, the military will become a more significant instrument for youth socialization by 1984; that is, it will assume an even larger part of the role once dominated by the family, the church, the school, and the civilian work setting. For increasing numbers of American youth, military service will represent a first significant step toward independence and adulthood. Therefore, the Department of Defense may assume a larger role both in exposing young people to their taste of higher education and in remedying deficiencies in their secondary school experience.

If the rate of voluntary enlistment weakens considerably in the future, alternatives to reinstitution of the draft include using more women and civilians in appropriate assignments, intensifying recruitment and reenlistment efforts through extra incentives, changing the nature of some jobs so that they can be performed by people who fail to meet present standards, lowering standards, or, as an added possibility, providing remedial education to individuals who otherwise do not meet enlistment standards.[6]

The Department of Defense might involve itself in screening efforts, with referrals to other agencies; or it could itself conduct programs of basic remedial education.

To date, the defense mission has not included responsibility for remedial education. However, with declining numbers of youth in the population and little likelihood of major reductions in military manpower needs during and beyond the next decade, the DOD may have to assume a major role in helping to induct youth into the U.S. work force—including intensive remedial programs, counseling, basic skill development, and vocational training aimed at filling military job requirements.

4. By 1984, the military and education will enter into a massive new partnership, symbolized by modern learning centers on military bases around the world. These centers will include skilled professional counselors, on-site university representatives, and sophisticated learning equipment. Remote locations will feature video-disk lectures by outstanding authorities for playback on large television screens in classrooms or on individual monitors in barracks. Complete libraries of such materials will supplement courses at the vocational/technical, baccalaureate, and even graduate level, and they will be made available to virtually every military base and major naval vessel by cooperating universities and will be updated in remote areas by satellite transmission.

Educational programs on overseas bases and at sea will receive the same kind of scrutiny now provided by regional accrediting associations in the United States. In all cases, emphasis will be given to high standards of quality.

Education in the military will focus more precisely on job requirements, but the variety and complexity of those jobs will continue to increase. The military will reflect a reemerging university emphasis on general education and the liberal arts. The armed services will continue to emphasize *performance*, but they will also support foundation courses provided by civilian institutions aimed at increased understanding of *man* and *nature*.

5. Education will be the focus of new programs to recruit especially qualified personnel. In one program, undergraduates on campuses not hosting ROTC will be offered commissions after two periods of summer training if they are outstanding students in hard-to-fill specialties and if they have other qualifications. Based on the present Marine Corps Platoon Leaders Class, this program will open commissioning opportunities on virtually every campus in the nation and, at the same time, reduce the lead time required to produce officers.

In another recruiting effort involving education, high school students will be selected to fill critical enlisted specialties. When they complete basic military training during the summer following high school graduation, they will enroll in community or junior colleges on DOD scholarships.

Upon graduation with associate degrees, they will enlist as noncommissioned officers and serve periods of obligated service in their new
specialties.

6. A major thrust to coordinate military training and civilian education
will result in the establishment of the largest postsecondary institution
in the world. Under the genetic title "Community College of the Armed
Forces," this institution will offer programs aimed at upgrading the
technical skills of the enlisted and warrant officer force and will provide
general education for nontechnicians, especially those in combat arms.

A major portion of the college will be based on the program offered
by the present Community College of the Air Force (CCAF), organized
in 1972 to integrate technical military instruction and voluntary education
into meaningful career patterns. The CCAF received authority to grant
the degree of "associate in applied science" to enlisted personnel in
1976, and its program has grown rapidly since then. It offers degrees in
eight general career areas: administration and management, aircraft and
missile maintenance, communications, crafts and trades, distribution
services, electromechanical, health care sciences, and public services. These
areas include ninety-one separate programs ranging from nuclear technology to weather forecasting. These programs are not only associated
with an air force specialty, but also parallel, as closely as possible, the
postsecondary two-year programs at community colleges throughout the
nation. Civilian licensing and certification requirements are incorporated,
when possible, into the design of the programs.

Each program requires from sixty-four to seventy semester hours of
instruction, including a minimum of twenty-seven hours of technical instruction at regionally accredited air force training schools; twenty-seven
hours of related education, such as science, math, and humanities, at
regionally accredited civilian institutions; four hours of physical education
(basic military training); and six hours of management and military
science at a civilian institution, at an NCO academy, or by examination.

The future Community College of the Armed Forces will be open to
enlisted and warrant officer personnel of all military services and will
feature several major programs. The first program, modeled after the
present CCAF, will require a share of credits earned at accredited
military training schools and will provide an opportunity for members
to become recognized masters of their specialties. Under this version,
"associate in applied science" degrees may be awarded either by the
Community College of the Armed Forces or by cooperating civilian
institutions.

A second CCAF program, available at virtually every military base,
will provide postsecondary educational opportunities to individuals in

combat occupations that are not readily translatable to civilian skills or academic programs. This version, similar to the Navy Campus for Achievement and a proposed army counterpart, will rely on a network of cooperating civilian institutions to provide courses and flexible credit transfer arrangements leading to "associate in arts" degrees. Community College of the Armed Forces experts will provide liaison to the academic world and assist colleges and military services as necessary. The program will help to equalize the discrepancy in educational opportunities that has long existed in the military between the technical occupations and occupations involving combat skills. The Community College of the Armed Forces will also feature a single, computerized transcript for all military personnel. Typically, degrees will require five to ten years of part-time academic work and thus will be limited largely to *career* noncommissioned and warrant officers. These efforts will represent the first large-scale attempt to recognize the educational achievement of noncommissioned and warrant officers in a manner that is best understood by the American people—the awarding of a degree.

The Fine Line

This discussion does not imply that the relationship between the armed forces and higher education in 1984 will not involve problems. Far from it! The strains between higher education and the military are real and deep-seated. *Education* implies creativity, improvement of the human condition, and preservation of cherished social values. The *military* stresses obedience, established procedures, and hierarchy; it has only a carefully calculated utilitarian interest in more abstract searches for pure knowledge. The Department of Defense will continue to stress competence and performance regardless of how these qualities are achieved, and it will not insist that learning can only, or even best, be achieved within the formal classroom.

Some people feel deeply that some DOD educational programs make a mockery of higher education standards by allowing college credits simply for passing examinations or by evaluating past experience obtained without the supervision of individuals with proper credentials. In its educational programs, the DOD must walk a fine line between improving performance and enhancing understanding, between teaching replication and fostering innovation, and between increasing the efficiency of the organization and upgrading the health of society. Simply stated, the problem is how to combine the best features of training and education to produce both better performers and better human beings.

Education and the armed forces have come a long way together, and the future looks bright. Dr. Roger Heyns, former president of the American Council on Education, describes the complementary role of education and the armed forces as follows:

> For the military as an organization, the education of its working active-duty population has been a part of its program for at least twenty-five years. With the advent of the volunteer force, the personnel and manpower policies of the military are moving education to a more nearly central role.
>
> Within the military . . . programs are being fashioned that have implications for extending education into the work setting of the broad national society. . . . It is, therefore, a matter of special importance that we seek cooperatively to establish education effectively in the work setting of the Armed Forces. The joint efforts of the Armed Forces and education will then stand as a model . . . in bringing education to the nation's working population, and the lessons that academe and the military have learned together will be of value beyond their importance to the military departments.[7]

Notes

1. 40,000 women per year, on the average, are presently joining the services.

2. The actual percentage needed in FY 1985 is 39 percent of qualified and available males seventeen to twenty-two years old. This eliminates mental and physical ineligibles, those in mental and penal institutions, and full-time college students.

3. Andrew H. Lupton, John Augenblick, and Joseph Heyison, "The Financial State of Higher Education," *Change* 8, no. 8 (September 1976):21-36.

4. National Advisory Council on Extension and Continuing Education, March 31, 1975 (Washington, D.C.: Government Printing Office, 1975), *Equity of Access,* Ninth Annual Report.

5. One might draw an interesting analogy between service-sponsored education and service-sponsored life insurance during World War II. At first, the insurance industry violently opposed service-sponsored life insurance. But the services created a new awareness among millions of people concerning the benefits of life insurance, and it became a boon to the insurance industry.

6. The decision to end the draft was a carefully calculated gamble. Thus far, thanks to massive and skillful recruiting efforts, a faltering economy, and high teenage unemployment, the all-volunteer force is a success in 1977. But the slice of the military budget taken up by manpower costs has risen steadily—from 47 percent in FY 1964 to 58 percent in FY 1977. And there are serious concerns about maintaining the strength and capability of Reserve forces lacking "draft-motivated" enlistments.

7. Roger W. Heyns, "Education in the Armed Forces: Explorations in Cooperation with Postsecondary Education," address before the Armed Forces Education Conference, University of Maryland, December 10, 1974.

Part 7

A Summary Perspective

25
The Changing World of the American Military

Franklin D. Margiotta

Nothing is permanent except change.
—*Heraclitus*

The words spoken in ancient Greece echo through the pages of this volume. Thirty-three contributors viewed the U.S. military from the perspectives of twelve separate academic disciplines, from extensive experience within the military and the government, and from analyses of several bodies of empirical data. Despite their divergent views, there is a unifying, if implicit, theme in their writings—the U.S. military faces a troubled future dominated by rapid and dramatic change.

Furthermore, as Morris Janowitz suggested in the Foreword, the authors imply that we must reexamine some fundamental concepts and theories underlying the study of the military institution and civil-military relations during the past two decades. The authors met their charge to seek new insights and broader understanding of the U.S. military; in fact, several of them produced pioneer research in areas formerly not explored.

Thus, the charter for this summary perspective is to answer Morris Janowitz's challenge and make explicit some of the avenues for research implied by the analyses contained in this volume. The purpose is to encourage the conceptual reassessment currently under way by the "new generation of Fellows in the Inter-University Seminar on Armed Forces and Society." By framing questions worthy of further research or policy study and attention, the chapter focuses on some of the major factors that are apparently shaping the U.S. military. This analysis introduces

Author's note: I am indebted to several individuals for their constructive comments on an earlier version of this chapter: Professors Morris Janowitz, Fred Hartmann, Samuel P. Huntington, Sam Sarkesian, John Fitzgerald, and Charles Cochran; and Lieutenant General Raymond B. Furlong, USAF; Lieutenant General Robert G. Gard, Jr., USA; Major General Robert N. Ginsburgh, USAF, Ret.; and Colonel William J. Taylor, Jr., USA. Of course, only I am responsible for any errors in this chapter. It represents my analysis and is not the policy or position of the Air Command and Staff College, the air force, or any other governmental agency.

potential future problems and new ways of thinking about the military; it makes no attempt to prescribe fully drawn theories, solutions, or policies.

It is obviously impossible to predict the future, but we can outline areas where further research and inquiry might be fruitful. In dealing with the complex issues and the wide range of professional backgrounds represented in this volume, we propose a series of research hypotheses to focus the findings of this research. These hypotheses flow generally from earlier discussions in this volume, but only the writer takes full responsibility for them and for any flaws in the analyses. The reader should remember that these research hypotheses are not "statements of truth," but, rather, they are focusing devices for continued study of these issues. The ultimate answers may just as likely invalidate these hypotheses as substantiate them.

This volume has addressed several major questions that describe important features of the U.S. military's future. What important international and domestic trends will influence the military in the late twentieth century? How will public attitudes, youth attitudes, and attitudes on college campuses affect the recruitment of enlisted and officer personnel? What new social factors might require the attention of the military profession in the future? What are the implications of advanced technology, organizational dynamics, and bureaucratization? Who are the cadets at the military academies, and how well prepared are they for dealing with the uncertain future described in this volume? What are the future demands of military professionalism?

The complex responses to these questions suggest a period of major adjustment for the U.S. military in the next decade. If only one-half of the changes implied by this volume become reality, the U.S. military may be forced to struggle through an identity crisis. A broad research hypothesis summarizes the findings of this book.

Research hypothesis: The U.S. military will experience a period of intense adjustment before a new, broadly accepted identity emerges. The first three chapters suggest that this reevaluation is under way and that traditional dimensions of military professionalism are changing. However, with adjustments to the Vietnam war almost complete, our contributors warn of other changes that will impinge upon the military. Congress, the American public, and the world community appear to restrict the potential direct use of U.S. military force. The growth of congressional power and staffs and the continuing centralization of authority within the civilian and military chains will diminish the options available to all levels of the military hierarchy. There will be shortages of qualified personnel and important resources. The social composition of the forces will change; minorities, women, and families will play greater roles. To what degree will these trends fragment an already diverse military?

Technology will also continue to change the nature and functions of military tasks and make recruits less amenable to guidance without logic. Some chapters contend that behavioral, rather than authoritarian, leadership styles will be the norm and that leadership will become less fixed and more situational. One is not surprised that Admiral Miller and Major Golden wrestle with the problem of reconciling traditional concepts of professionalism with the demands of the future military.

Their difficulties mirror the interesting phenomenon of the military profession as it also wrestles with dramatic and rapid change on so many fronts. Sarkesian's analysis of five major empirical studies points to evidence of this identity problem. Self-doubt seems to trouble the military officer corps despite considerable evidence of support by the civilian community.

There is a divergence of views between civilian perceptions of the military and officer perceptions of the host society and civil-military relations. Almost immediately after the conclusion of U.S. participation in the Vietnam war, the military began a dramatic climb in public opinion polls. Literally dozens of polls have identified military leaders as honest and efficient and the military as a trusted institution as highly regarded as churches and colleges. As an institution, the military is much more respected in public opinion polls than Congress, labor unions, or the federal bureaucracy. But the military feels unappreciated and does not believe that civilian society gives it a fair status. This negative self-concept should be examined further.[1]

One can speculate about causes for this misconception. For one thing, the military may fail to recognize that a large public institution consuming enormous funds is legitimate game for criticism by congressional leaders and the press. Mistakes and cost overruns in the Department of Defense tend to be large-scale; as such, they are ripe for investigative reporting. Many officers often confuse criticism by the media and individual members of Congress with public opinion, which may not share the same views.

Another plausible explanation is that military officers subconsciously perceive that their families and friends do not appreciate or understand the difficulties of military jobs. When they deal with their fathers and uncles—a World War II and Korean generation of servicemen—they often find "Sad Sack" or "Catch 22" views of military service.[2] These personal experiences may partly explain these officers' self-perceptions, but there are also at work broad but subtle international and domestic trends that will shape the future dimensions of the U.S. military.

International and Domestic Influences

The environment of the 1980s appears more complicated than ever before, with international and domestic forces overlapping in an increasingly interdependent world. On the basis of the analyses of several contributors, we conclude that the world will probably continue the trend away from bipolar or superpower domination of events. Their analyses lead to several important implications for future research.

Research hypothesis: The likelihood of the direct use of military force by the Western democracies, including the United States, will decrease. This hypothesis is suggested by growing Soviet power and the diffusion of power based on the importance of resources and the spread of high-technology weapon systems. The continued spread of nuclear weapons could diminish even further the influence of the United States and the Soviet Union. Increasingly complex world conditions present major challenges for new thinking and research in deterrence concepts and theory. Specific research areas might include the concept of deterrence in terms of a relatively stable U.S.-Soviet balance or of a militarily superior USSR, continued arms control and declining force sizes, the emergence of many nuclear armed countries, and improved conventional warfare technologies as capable as nuclear weapons in target destruction.

As weapon technologies become more capable, other interesting research areas impinge on the diminishing possibility that military force will be used directly as an instrument of national power. In the nuclear age of the 1980s, military force may become more important for its political symbology and as a necessary backdrop that makes possible the use of other instruments of national leverage and influence. This may further diminish the possibility of the direct use of force by the major powers. A research focus on economic power and influence based on resources may be particularly fruitful for students of international politics. The apparent growing desire and capacity of the "world community" to restrict conflicts may also be worthy of further investigation.

The international community views unfavorably any relatively large-scale conflicts involving major suppliers, producers, or importers of either resources or industrial goods. Unless the conflicts occur in remote areas of the globe within or between nation-states that have little economic stake in the well-being of the rest of the world, enormous pressures will demand quick resolution of conflicts short of final victories or defeats. Conflict simply is not "good business" for the growing world economy. Will the superpowers pressure each other to restrain client-states through threats to withhold the machinery of advanced warfare? Is there a trend toward general stability? Will conflict be increasingly localized, high-intensity, high-technology, and short-lived without ultimate resolution of the issues faced by either side? Or might the inability or unwillingness of the medium powers and the superpowers to become directly involved in stability operations lead to a more unstable and conflict-ridden Southern Hemisphere? Will the 1980s be characterized by Soviet adventurism?

These intriguing questions are of some import to the U.S. military. Detailed case studies of the politics of certain recent armed conflicts might aid in understanding potential restrictions on future conflicts. The wars in the Middle East, for example, might explain how increasingly overlapping international relationships constrain states from using maximum force even in the first days of an attack. Will these constraints make the United States more likely to exercise its military influence through provision or withholding of munitions rather than through direct commitment of forces? The answer to this question has important implications for U.S. force structures and the ratios of combat and support troops.

In the 1980s, the military faces other difficult questions concerning shortages in international resources, such as the potential scarcity of certain metals for building high-performance aircraft and other advanced war technologies. Most urgent, however, appears to be DOD reliance on petroleum fuels and lubricants. The United States is the largest single consumer of petroleum products. The DOD uses approximately 1.7 percent of this total and is the largest single consumer within the United States; the air force uses more than one-half of the DOD allocation. Although the 1980s may not see critical petroleum shortages, U.S. reliance on external sources of oil for its economic well-being and for its military readiness makes protection of both the sources and the shipping lanes crucial in the event of crises.

The earlier chapters also signal the emergence of civil-military issues that may be as important as the restrictions developing on the international scene. The changing U.S. military scene is merely a reflection of a larger set of shifting relationships that are fundamental to the system by which the United States is governed.

Research hypothesis: The United States is involved in a realignment of the constitutional balance of powers; the relative growth in congressional power will profoundly affect the U.S. military. The analyses in this book imply that this hypothesis is the result of many trends, but primarily of the Vietnam war, Watergate, and increases in social programs and expenditures. The legislative branch has begun to redress the excessive power accrued by the executive since the early days of the Depression. This resurrection of historic congressional strength became evident in the mid-1960s when the growth in the size and competence of congressional staffs signaled increasing interest in foreign policy and national security. Executive control of the budget and the increase in budgetary entitlements not controllable either by Congress or the president are other areas that have excited congressional interest and brought a swing toward a more traditional balance.[3]

Two legislative actions cited in this volume are important symbolic events in the reestablishment of congressional initiatives—the War

Powers Resolution of 1973 and the 1974 Budget and Impoundment Control Act. The resolution is a major potential restraint on the use of military force by the executive branch and is worthy of closer research for its effect on the U.S. armed forces. Essentially, the War Powers Resolution limits the president to a sixty-day commitment of the armed forces before he must seek congressional concurrence and approval. It injects Congress into contingencies below a declaration of war, which is viewed as a limited alternative in the nuclear age.

With the advent of nuclear weapons, foreign policy elites apparently came to a tacit agreement not to generate emotional commitments to wars on the periphery of U.S. interests. They adopted policies calling for constrained use of military force in striving for narrow political objectives. Acting primarily under his constitutional powers as commander in chief, the president committed large-scale U.S. forces to involvement in high-intensity, long-term conflicts without congressional declarations of war. Over the long term, this tactic proved unsatisfactory to Congress and the American public, although it was designed to minimize the potential for democratic overcommitment to any particular war on distant continents. The restrictions of the War Powers Resolution are clear signals that Congress will be more active in the most important national security choices of the future.[4]

The general public is also reluctant to commit U.S. forces abroad. However, strong executive leadership or clearly perceived threats might change these attitudes; the president always retains the capacity to mobilize congressional and public opinion behind his commitments in the national security arena. But passage of the War Powers Resolution apparently codifies the general boundary drawn by the public and described by Trice, Russet, Nincic, and Blair. Currently, the executive branch appears to have less latitude in this area than at any time since the end of World War II. These congressional and public restrictions make the jobs of the president and the military difficult in an age when cataclysmic or dramatic threats to U.S. security are not likely. There will be few Pearl Harbors in the future. Instead, threats to U.S. security and well-being will come in longer-range, more subtle, and more sophisticated forms. Researchers might use polling data to trace public understanding of these more complex security issues.

Similar restrictions in the budget area emerge from the passage of the Congressional Budget and Impoundment Control Act of 1974. Military leadership faces new budgeting procedures and another set of important actors in justifying major program budgets. However, there has been a gradual increase in public support for funding military budgets; this support is reflected in recent congressional votes on important military programs. The prospects for minor real growth in military spending power are mildly optimistic. The public and Congress have apparently put Vietnam and its negative side effects behind them and now seem willing to support a substantial military and its budgetary requirements. This does not mean that individual programs will not be cut back. There seems to be recognition that the military did not modernize during the Vietnam era and that in many areas, the Soviet Union has achieved military parity or, in some cases, substantial numerical superiority.[5]

On the other hand, one must recognize (as noted by Hale and Jordan) that the federal budget is now a more limited resource but is subject to virtually unlimited demands. Many of these demands stem from earlier programs that now require mandatory budget entitlements (although not funded from general taxation, the Social Security program is a major example of future budget problem areas).

And this budgeting takes place within a constrained economy. Growing interdependence in the international economic arena and limitations placed on growth by scarce resources, particularly energy, suggest a national economy that may never again expand at the rapid rates of the post-World War II era. Inflation, a degree of industrial stagnation, and relatively high unemployment face advanced industrial societies as they move into a postindustrial age. Thus, the military may continue to receive a "fair share" of the total federal budget, but it must recognize that this budget will be a portion of a total gross national product that may not expand as rapidly as in the past. All programs will be more carefully scrutinized, and outyear costs will be measured against other military programs and large social programs.

Several chapters thus signal that a major political revamping is under way and that the new balance between executive and congressional power has not yet been drawn. Congress has not only taken a more intense interest in helping to shape national policy and in guiding the executive bureaucracy; it has also taken major implementing steps. It has created its own bureaucracy devoted to researching and preparing approaches to matters involving national security policy. The Department of Defense may be profoundly affected by this important shift in civil-military relations. This changing relationship suggests several potential research areas, since congressional legislation sets budget levels and often provides major policy guidelines.

Indeed, increasing staff capability in the executive and legislative branches may require the military services and the Department of Defense to reexamine their techniques for justifying military programs. A whole series of questions emerges. Can the sheer size and weight of the DOD staffs and the complexity and volume of information continue to overawe other agencies? Will operational skills and a chest full of ribbons be as credible as they were in the past? Capitol Hill will see more intellectual and more detailed debates on military programs. A new chief of staff will face testimony on a narrow issue that he had never before addressed in his military career. His questions will be framed by a congressional staff member with high credentials and years of experience in following a given program.

Will traditional military assignment policies on functional experience and high turnover effectively serve the Pentagon staffs? If valid and legitimate military programs are to be approved, perhaps they must be managed by credible military staffs similar to the increasingly powerful congressional and executive staffs. That is, credentials, experience, and continuity in dealing with Congress may become as valuable as operational experience and rank. Will the DOD find it necessary to create new, elite, continuing staff agencies to handle congressional relations and testimony?

If further research documents the preliminary conclusions of our contributors, there are other important research implications for the selection, education, and career patterns of the military elite. Will a new era of executive-congressional relations alter traditional U.S. civil-military relations so profoundly that the heroic leaders of U.S. combat forces find their interests best represented in Washington by a "military managerial" elite? Has there, in fact, been a subtle shift within the military in these directions?

Military Manpower Issues in a Changing Social Institution

Several chapters in this volume suggest that a very significant problem facing the U.S. military in the future will be the inability to attract sufficient numbers of qualified personnel. Corollary issues emerge when one considers the changing social realities that require adjustment if the military expects to retain quality personnel.

Research hypothesis: Under the all-volunteer force concept in the 1980s, the U.S. military will face greater difficulties in attracting and retaining sufficient quality personnel to maintain the size and social composition of the total force authorized in 1978. The increasing volume of published and staff analyses indicates growing public recognition of this manpower problem.[6] Thomas Carr summarized a major part of the problem when he noted that in 1984, the U.S. military *must recruit one of every two male teenagers* not planning to attend college if it expects to retain the social composition and size of its 1978 active-duty and Reserve force. This area demands research and innovative thinking, because one of every two is a very high goal, given the evidence presented in this volume. These are gloomy but realistic predictions based on a birthrate that began to decline in the late 1950s.

The attitudes and perceptions of recruited youth may be as important to research as attempts to analyze the impact of a declining birthrate.

Based on the chapters by John Blair and David Segal, one can conclude that the military will have continuing difficulties in recruiting because of an image problem. The military does not project favorably about job satisfaction and the treatment of enlisted forces. In fact, however, the military appears neither as bad as the teenage perceptions surveyed by John Blair nor as good as it must eventually become on the basis of David Segal's measurements of job satisfaction. Further research might determine the causes of negative perceptions of the military as a prospective job environment. These perceptions are, in fact, quite different from the much less negative attitudes toward the military job climate reported by enlisted military members. However, these members did not consider the military climate as satisfying as the work climate reported by employees in civilian industry.

The military bears unique burdens, such as family separation, long duty hours, moves on short notice, service overseas, and the ultimate hazard in defense of the nation. With this organizational climate, the military will find it difficult to compete with civilian industry because few civilian jobs require so much unless salaries are exceptionally high. On the other hand, the military offers job security, long-term benefits, responsibility and upward mobility, and, oftentimes, exciting assignments to counterbalance the rather mundane daily existence of most workers in industry.

The armed forces are currently conducting research in job satisfaction and are directing several innovative experiments in job design. All services are experimenting with advanced management techniques and organizational development strategies. Research might discriminate between units or organizations with high retention levels and units or organizations with retention problems. Such research must discriminate between individual leadership, leadership styles, basic missions, geographic locations, job structures, and the like. In a draft-free environment, human beings can no longer be treated as a "free good," whose time is worth very little. This is an era of "human resources," with each individual costing more and requiring more attention. Provision of productive work seems essential to insure any success in recruitment or retention; otherwise, the innovative, high-quality individual may separate.

On the other hand, officer recruitment appears somewhat more promising. The studies in this volume confirm that the military academies are producing quality officers in a rigorous, highly competitive environment. This bodes well for manning military leadership requirements of the future. In addition, the attitudes of college faculties toward the Reserve Officer Training Corps (ROTC) suggest that the ROTC can produce officers to defend the United States and to retain liberalizing and civilianizing influences within the military. These faculty attitudes represent potential only. If the quality of the officer corps is to approximate the quality of academy graduates, then serious efforts must be made to reestablish ROTC units on highly reputed university campuses. In addition, research might determine how to reestablish the legitimacy of military service to outstanding civilian college students.

Thus, in terms of officer quality and quantity, the potential for the 1980s is somewhat brighter than the outlook for recruiting large numbers of enlisted members from a dwindling supply of teenagers. Analysis of the feasibility of recruiting older people at higher enlisted levels may lead to lateral entry as one answer. Further study might examine increased hiring of civilians in "occupational model" forms to perform much of the routine support and maintenance functions.

In his sociological analysis of the military, Charles Moskos suggests that the military is moving toward an occupational model and away from the more traditional modes of viewing the military as a "calling," institution, or profession. Moskos's model seems an accurate surface description of trends within the U.S. armed forces. Although the occupational model is enlightening, it restates, in many respects, Janowitz's forecast that the U.S. military would require increased combinations of administrative and managerial talents with the more traditional attributes of the heroic combat leader.

Moskos's analysis, however, is only the beginning of research into the complexities of the modern military. Moskos provides a precise description of recent trends in the military, but his model deserves further consideration in terms of its depth of analysis, causes of trends, and the effects of an occupational model on the military. In the first case, the model aids understanding of macro trends, but it cannot accurately describe any particular subset of the military. As is necessarily true of most models, it oversimplifies reality.

There are vast differences in functions, missions, and manning within the U.S. military. The author's experiences in the U.S. Air Force lead to the conclusion that there are perhaps thirty or forty air forces. All air force members share the blue uniform and a vague belief that they contribute to national defense. But beyond these two shared values, they may find very little in common. By adding these observations to Moskos's thoughts, one can formulate another research hypothesis by changing the level of analysis.

Research hypothesis: The closer one gets to an organization that will perform in combat, the more institutional that particular organization will be. Bomb squadrons, fighter squadrons, and missile operations have a high institutional character. These organizations consist primarily of officers, and they are normally characterized by high esprit de corps; by commonly shared values and knowledge; and by symbols, such as unique patches and flying scarves, that set them apart. These combat organizations also share unique hard-ships—the potential for overseas missions at any time and the requirement to be always alert and on duty during holidays and nights. There is always the risk of death in combat; but in flying organizations, death may come on a routine training flight. These factors build a unique and all-encompassing life-style for these individuals and organizations. Never-theless, further research may document that these units also share major aspects of Moskos's other categories.

This hypothesis must also be tested against army/marine ground combat units to determine whether it is valid in organizations with high ratios of enlisted personnel. On the other hand, policemen and firemen face similar threats in their daily work, but they join unions and seem concerned with occupational concerns. Are attitudes more important than job characteristics? What role does leadership play in organizations closest to the combat roles?

In units other than combat units, similar elements of the dedication required in operational units are apparent, but the factors of risk diminish. Examples of pseudoinstitutional organizations in the air force include organizations associated with maintaining and guarding aircraft. These organizations are manned overwhelmingly by enlisted members who are also subject to immediate overseas deployment but are in less danger of loss of life. Their duties demand that they perform their tasks at any time of day or on holidays.

As we move further from the flight line toward support areas, the occupational model appears more prevalent. Staff work, for example, is perhaps more bureaucratic than institutional, although the military in many ways has created a unique bureaucracy with distinct characteristics. Functional support areas, such as finance, personnel, supply, procurement, and civil engineering, are more able to organize their activities on the basis of a standard workday and standard workweek. Even further away from the operational units, the occupational model becomes even more prevalent. In the massive logistics complexes, one finds fewer military members and more civilian employees who lead relatively stable lives with normal working hours.

Entirely different and necessarily looser styles of operation are common in the large research and development complexes. These operations are similar in many respects to the operations in any large bureaucratic research system. Rank is often less important than credentials, experience, and scientific know-how. Virtually no research has been conducted on the social organizations that develop among the highly technical services associated with these large support areas. Every organization in the military may thus be more or less vocational, professional, or occupational; the same observation may be made at another level of analysis—the individual.

For a better understanding of the U.S. military in the late twentieth century, one must recognize that every individual carries within him varying traits associated with each of Moskos's descriptive categories. He brings his own set of values, backgrounds, education, and socialization to a particular assignment. During any one day, he may perform several roles or adopt attitudes that might be classified as institutional, professional, or occupational.

Not only does Moskos's model require further qualification in level of analysis, but researchers might also examine the validity of his explanation of causes. Moskos suggests, in general, that the move to an all-volunteer concept based on economic competition in the marketplace has produced an occupational model. This neglects the broad social movements that have led to increased demands by workers and youth for participation in choices and for "fate control." One might deduce from other analyses contained in this volume that several other powerful factors have merely been reinforced by higher pay. These same factors might also explain, in a subtle manner, why an all-volunteer force is based on an economically competitive approach. The field seems open for historians to examine the origins and causes of the trends described by Moskos.

Research hypothesis: The current internal organization and operating style of the U.S. military developed more fully with World War II and was caused by expansion of the size of forces, a shift in officer recruitment patterns to lower social classes, and major organizational and attitudinal changes required by advancements in technology. Of particular importance is further research on the implications of advanced technology for the social organization of the military. From the author's air force perspective, one might argue that technology is the *organizational essence* of the air force. This same phenomenon will grow in all of the services. The air force is not organized around masses of men who deliver firepower; it is, instead, organized around a relatively small number of sophisticated, high-technology war machines. These machines are produced in cooperative ventures with industry at the cutting edges of science and technology. They incorporate a continuously expanding array of improved mechanical, electrical, and aerodynamic devices. The fighting force in the air force is relatively small, and it consists of college-educated officers who have completed significant advanced training within the military. The technology of the equipment requires more intelligent users who combine intellectual and physical skills to make their machines function efficiently. The air force can deliver high volumes of firepower, and it can range the globe at a moment's notice. Indeed, this is a unique fighting force.

The technology of maintaining these machines also requires a different kind of organization and enlisted man. The air force wing exists to support the fighting squadron. Brainpower and training often take precedence over physical stamina in the tasks of a wing. Repairing an advanced airborne radar system or using a computerized supply system to produce the required inventory of parts requires an enlisted technician carefully trained in the classroom and on the job.

Technology ultimately affects organizational and leadership style as well. The bodies of knowledge required to keep high-technology machines operational are diverse and complex. Therefore, functional specialization requires that individuals must learn narrow and specialized tasks in greater depth. Many of these tasks are similar to the tasks performed in civilian occupations related to high-technology areas, such as computers or industrial production.

A wing commander cannot fix his airplanes, although he is able to fly them; an army or marine division commander can field-strip his men's rifles, but he cannot repair his armor or helicopters. Technology has led the military toward an industrial type of scheduling and planning. Machines must be repaired on fixed time schedules; work loads must be planned and programmed months in advance at distant locations. Since work away from combat is relatively scheduled and planned, it is more likely to "create" an occupational mode. The finance travel clerk, required to support frequent overseas travel by operational crews, need not work on Saturday evening. It may be more efficient to have him available during a relatively standard workday in an occupational mode.

In many respects, technology that demands high levels of specialization and relatively high levels of education and training drives the occupational model in all services. Productive research might examine whether the nature of the jobs associated with a high-technology military might be an underlying factor in the adoption of an economic approach to recruitment. If one requires quality computer programmers, inventory specialists, and procurement experts, then one must compete with the private sector. The factors that led to the development of an occupational model present a fertile field for continuing research. This research might also be better informed if it shifts from primary concern with the army, which of necessity has a much higher proportion of its manpower in combat units of a more traditional institutional mode.

Finally, one might consider further research in the areas of Professor Moskos's conclusions. A certain nostalgia for "the good old brown shoe days" is implied in Moskos's analyses. However, both John Blair's and David Segal's massive samples of civilians and military members indicate that the military must compete with the civilian job market.

Research hypothesis: There is no need to assume that all recent organizational trends within the U.S. military are negative. Many social scientists wonder about the relative success of the air force in recruitment, retention, and the low level of such indicators of dissatisfaction as desertion rates, AWOL rates, and disciplinary incidents. Could one reason for this success be that the air force is less traditional and has subconsciously moved toward an occupational style based on its high-technology business? Are fewer air force people in an institutional/vocational role?

Does the inherent risk of flying make air force institutional roles a compelling and invigorating challenge? Are other services burdened by the fact that they can only simulate and exercise their military missions, while flying involves a realistic challenge? Must we not qualify Moskos's model on the basis of Blair's and Segal's data and conclude that the effect of an occupational model may be a positive factor in recruitment and retention of high-quality personnel in certain areas? Further research is necessary to determine the roles, missions, functions, individuals, and organizations directly required to perform primarily in an institutional/vocational mode.

Moskos's recent analysis is one of the more interesting statements of trends in the military to appear during the past fifteen years. But, as in all preliminary models, it suggests more questions than it provides answers. Further research is necessary to deepen the analysis and to question the causes and effects of these trends. Further understanding is also required in several areas that will affect the retention of high-quality personnel.

The social composition of the U.S. military has been dramatically affected by equal rights movements and by the recruiting problems of attracting sufficient volunteers to the all-volunteer force. Both of these pressures have increased the numbers of minorities and women serving in the U.S. military and have opened career opportunities in almost all fields, including the military academies and pilot training.

Research hypothesis: In the 1980s, the concentration of minorities and women will continue to increase in the U.S. military. The military will deal with this trend in a programmatic manner, but it will face problems in the process. As noted in the Introduction, this volume does not deal specifically or precisely with the issues of minorities or women in the military services. In responding to just demands and the social milieu of the late 1960s and early 1970s, the Department of Defense was frequently ahead of society in integrating its forces and in accepting women as equal partners. The history of this process is not appropriate for this volume, but in terms of the future, several research issues are worthy of attention. Of course, we might caution that this is a volatile, rapidly changing situation where research may be quickly overtaken by policy or events.

There is no longer a question of whether women should be members of the military or whether minorities should have equal rights and equal access to jobs. Programmatic approaches have now replaced these older, burning social issues. While engaging in "consciousness raising" and "awareness training," the military developed programs and policies to insure equal opportunity. The issues for the 1980s have been removed from the affective domain and will be in the cognitive domain. The question is not whether blacks and women should be given equal opportunity but whether a commander fairly enforces policies and programs to ensure those opportunities. Future research will be much more concerned with behavior patterns than with attitude patterns.

Other research issues will focus on the arguments advanced by Morris Janowitz and Charles Moskos and criticized by Alvin Schexnider and John Butler.[7] How many minorities can the military accept and remain socially representative of the larger society? What effect will women have on the military as a fighting force? Another significant issue hinges on the role of women in combat. Their continued exclusion from direct combat units could mean that many military support areas will eventually become all-female corps. There are some indications that army combat arms with their enlistment bonuses attract disproportionate numbers of blacks. Are subtle choices by individuals leading to separate organizations with few social characteristics in common with other military organizations? How will these groups relate to, and support, each other? On the other hand, if women are eventually accepted in the combat areas, how will they affect combat efficiency? Thus, questions about the role of minorities and women in the military have changed, but serious issues are still unresolved. Problems of accommodating minorities and women will be compounded even further by the fact that many of the individuals will be married.

Research hypothesis: The U.S. military must adjust to the fact that it now has a high proportion of married members. A major social issue is the quiet changing of the military from a bachelor institution to a family institution. There has been little recognition of the potential for change posed by this factor, which reinforces, and is reinforced by, the occupational model. The military, both officer and enlisted, is now more than 50 percent married compared with earlier figures of 20 percent.[8] These families have been shaped by the same social forces that generated the demands for rights of minorities and women.

Janowitz forecast a more socially representative officer corps; this meant recruitment from lower social classes than was true in the 1930s. A more socially representative officer corps is now a fact, but there is no analysis of what this has meant to fundamental military traditions and attitudes. As Admiral Miller recognizes in Chapter 22, the military has become more egalitarian as lower social classes have entered the officer corps. Officers and their wives no longer bring to the service those upper-class traditions based on breeding in elitist families. On the other hand, many wives now possess college degrees and feel that they are relatively competent to deal with their own environment. For many of these reasons, the military is no longer viewed as an all-embracing institution. It can no longer approximate a small elite club of people from similar backgrounds. And it can no longer take for granted a group of spouses who are willing to sit at home, take care of the family, and wait for Daddy to return from his twenty-four-hour-a-day job or from an overseas tour. Civilian spouses now are sometimes male, and officers of both sexes have married enlisted members. The entire social composition of the military force has changed, and this change has hardly received public recognition.

The military has discarded almost all of its social ritual of the 1930s. American social values, norms, and dress have penetrated the once separate life-style of the army post. This penetration by different social classes has been reinforced or perhaps even led by the mass nature of American communications, merchandising, and publishing. Societal values, styles, and ideas overwhelm any values generated by the uniqueness of the military profession. Wives work with members of the civilian community, and children go to school with other children from all walks of life. And because of improved pay scales, both single and married members are much more able to live in the civilian community.

Families passively resist moving, changing, and acceding to the demands of the military environment, which requires movement to achieve upward mobility.[9] A single member once made sacrifices with a sense of excitement, but sacrifices become more difficult when married men must account for wives and children. This whole area of research—treated briefly by Hamilton McCubbin and Martha Marsden—may be the most unexplored field in the study of the future military.

Yet another major social issue will face the military in the 1980s. Moskos, Segal, Miller, and Taylor suggest slightly different rationales, but they uniformly imply the need for further research into the pressures toward group representation.

Research hypothesis: The U.S. military will face continuing internal and external pressures for group representation. This is a very uncertain area, and DOD proscriptions against unionism may have quietly put this issue to rest; only time and further exploration will determine the validity of this hypothesis. Interesting developments within the services may also diminish the pressures for military unions, but these developments will have important effects on the nature of military organization.

The military community is conducting management participation experiments among the lowest and the highest ranks. All services work with the concept of organization development through special cadres of management and organization development consultants who bring the latest management and behavioral theory to field units. There is increasing use of surveys to determine the attitudes and beliefs of military populations about issues. Air Force inspectors general, for example, conduct surveys to help commanders measure local satisfaction with particular base facilities and policies. The air force has surveyed all of its commanders and thousands of its members about the quality of their military life.

There are significant attempts to determine the most rewarding aspects of a person's occupation, and deliberate job enrichment programs and flexitime scheduling are becoming more popular. These activities signal a responsiveness to the issue of worker representation, a responsiveness that may dampen the appeal of military unions. But they also signal another factor, highlighted elsewhere in this volume—the local commander's declining control of the policies and destiny of his own organization.

Organizational Dynamics and Change

Research hypothesis: There will be continuing efforts to centralize authority at higher levels in the military and civilian chains of command. If servicewide policies are partially based on surveys of large populations rather than on the consensus of major commanders, other significant issues are worthy of research. Technology permits the highest level of command to determine attitudes and issues, manipulate these data rapidly through the use of computer technology, and then implement servicewide policies. This significantly affects the power, control, and authority of the traditional chain of command, especially local unit commanders. Major research questions related to changes in social organization will come to the forefront if these trends continue.

Admiral Miller makes a pointed and forceful plea for the military to regain its authority or lose its credibility as a valued profession. On the other hand, Toomay, Hartke, Elman, and Hunsicker counterbalance Admiral Miller's arguments with their explanation of centralization and its causes. Clearly, the age of nuclear weapons, computers, instant communications, and everything implied by these technologies are aspects of future military life. The complexities and costs of modern weapon systems and the potential nuclear consequences of battlefield error have affected earlier concepts of the chain of command.

Traditional chains of command have remained intact, and large staffs have continued their functions, but instant communications and computer networks may have made these management elements somewhat anachronistic. Modes of operation tend to centralize functions and choices at higher levels of command and staff. The observations of our contributors point to several research areas. One area might include a clear description of the actual flow of orders and commands through the chain; this description could have implications for the manner in which the military organizes and structures to carry out its commands. This research might suggest the elimination of many intermediate headquarters and chains of command. On the other hand, it might find that decisions made at higher levels may not account for problems and information at lower levels and that centralization may reach a point of diminishing returns. In either instance, this should be an informative undertaking.

We must deepen the examination of the trends toward centralization described in Chapters 15 and 16. There must be more fundamental understanding of the problems faced by small unit and local commanders. They are burdened by responsibility for their organizations, but they control very little of the resources and the individuals provided to them. Military organizations are organized functionally, and functionally specialized individuals are often efficiently assigned from central locations and distributed to the various operating commands and units. Local commanders have little choice in deciding who works for them, how often they will turn over, or what priority is given to their unit needs. Research might enhance understanding of what happens when a functional specialist owes his loyalty both to a functional chain and to his local unit commander, who in turn is responsible to his operational chain for the success or failure of the unit mission.

George Odiorne's provocative chapter describes the problems of individuals when they deal with a faceless, large bureaucracy, such as the military. Research might examine the effects of this bureaucracy on the efficiency of the organization; it might aid in understanding the role of this bureaucratic structure in relation to the occupational malaise found by Segal and to the views of youth as described by Blair.

Developments at the Academies

These same complications seem to appear even at the service academies. The academies have not been spared the bureaucratic problems associated with large, complex organizations manned by specialists and necessarily governed by standardized rules and procedures. In fact, John Lovell suggests in his chapter that perhaps the primary cause of attrition in the academy student bodies is growth in size with concomitant bureaucratization.

Research hypothesis: Significant dissatisfaction and attrition among cadets and midshipmen may be traced to the growth and the impersonal nature of the bureaucratic system. This hypothesis requires further consideration because other factors may not have been fully considered. Public attitudes toward the role of the military in the world and within society may be important factors in determining whether academy attendees believe that their attendance is worthwhile and legitimate. The expansion of the corps has not only. increased bureaucratization but also made positions available to less committed individuals who may seek excellent, free education before they make a firm decision for a military commission. Research might examine whether some entrants use the academies as high-quality, free junior colleges whose reputations permit them to transfer into upper classes at civilian institutions where they might not otherwise be accepted.

Chapters 19, 20, and 21 provide the first published comparative data gathered at all three service academies. These chapters have broken new ground in their attempts to measure the effects of socioeconomic, demographic, and attitudinal variables on career intentions, attrition, and success at the academies. Priest's pioneering study at West Point compares male and female cadets in the first year that women entered the three academies.

Further research might compare these student bodies in greater depth with one another, with typical students at civilian colleges, and with officers recruited from other commissioning sources. The preliminary findings of our authors suggest several important areas of investigation.

Research hypothesis: Graduates of the service academies will (1) generally come from higher social strata and family backgrounds than graduates from all but the most exclusive civilian colleges; (2) generally come from higher social strata and family backgrounds than officers commissioned by the other large commissioning sources, such as ROTC, OTS, and OCS; (3) be more likely to make the service a career and to progress more rapidly than officers commissioned from the other commissioning sources; (4) be more likely to have a career military father than graduates of civilian colleges or officers commissioned from other commissioning sources.

Research hypothesis: Background and attitude variables can help to predict which academy enrollees will remain at the academies and which will perform well at the academies and in the armed services. As our contributors suggest, follow-up research on the relative success of academy graduates will prove interesting. If this additional research is accomplished, we suspect that it will reinforce the conclusions Morris Janowitz expressed in the Foreword. The expansion of the military, the broad injection of technology, and the all-voluۦteer force have altered the organizational essence of the profession of arms since World War II. As the authors imply, this is truly a time to question some of the most fundamental scholarly assumptions about the military institution, civil-military relations, and military professionalism.

New Dimensions of Military Professionalism

The contemporary officer corps is significantly different from the post-World War II corps so well described by Morris Janowitz and Samuel P. Huntington.[10] Expansion of the recruitment base has changed the social composition of the corps, although the military academies still seem to recruit many candidates from the same upper middle class that produced many of the flag officers described by Janowitz. This may partially explain the higher potential of academy graduates for career advancement. Their early upbringing and expectations approximate the social life-style of the general officer.

As a whole, however, the officer corps is much less drawn from a particular segment of society, and its members certainly no longer come disproportionately from the rural South. Further study and analysis must validate theories about the origins of professional officers. Equally informative would be analyses of data on the modern enlisted man. Also of high interest will be the long-term effects brought by the admission of women to the academies and to expanded job responsibilities.

Research hypothesis: As the complexities of military requirements, career patterns, and training increase, professional socialization becomes increasingly more important than personal background variables. Serious study must examine whether regional or rural origins mean much in late twentieth-century America. One might hypothesize further that mass American culture and communications have combined with the demands for technically skilled officers to play down the differences among commissioned recruits. How homogeneous has American culture become? Value systems based on male-female or ethnic-cultural differences may be more important in the future military than traditional concerns.

Even more important differences may continue between the military services and their separate socialization processes, academies, commissioning sources, and professional expectations. Only as we refine our research methods and probe more deeply into these differences can we better understand the military leadership that will be responsible for the nation's defense in the future. Earlier views of the military as a single corporate body must be discarded, and further research must explore these divergences.

Research hypothesis: There is no single U.S. military orientation; instead, important subsets of the modern military have distinctive operating styles, organizations, and procedures. If this volume does anything, it should put to rest the notion that one can generalize about "the U.S. military." Scholars have continually fallen into the trap of studying the U.S. army and generalizing about the U.S. military as a whole. The differences between an army infantry division, a nuclear aircraft carrier, and a strategic missile wing should be self-evident. Sometimes, however, even the people who work in these combat organizations do not completely understand these variances. Perhaps even the most fundamental definition of the military must be challenged.

Research hypothesis: Only a small proportion of the modern U.S. military can be defined as "experts on violence"; individual officers have widely varying personal interests, styles, and values. Defining the U.S. military primarily as the legitimate manager of violence for the state obscures fundamental continuing changes. Indeed, management of violence is the raison d'être of the military, but one must not forget that in the high-technology services, this role is often removed from the daily existence of the vast support forces. Even missile combat crew members and strategic forces, in general, deliver their "violence" by setting switches and following instruments that place weapons of mass destruction on distant targets. In modern warfare, ground forces and tactical air force support of the foot soldier will strike enemy soldiers and tanks at greater distances and with less personal involvement. This is neither good nor bad, but it is a fact of life in the future military.

Will a central concern of the military be the management of support tasks that permit the tip of the spear to perform its institutional role in the management of violence? Must we also research the ability of any individual to serve as a heroic leader and, at the same time, perform efficiently in the role of manager? Who is capable of integrating the talents and functional abilities of large numbers of narrowly specialized individuals? Has combat, especially in the navy and the air force, become so impersonal that the role of heroic leader is less relevant? Does technology demand competent managerial expertise as well as emotional leadership? Does technology combine with higher pay, increased education, and shifting social values to create a work force with needs different from those we historically expected in a manpower-intensive force? Does the modern military leader thus have a more difficult time meeting the higher-order needs of his people? Have many segments of the military become more cognitive than affective? Will the future have groups of decision makers operating within commanders' offices rather than single leaders who make all decisions? These issues suggest fundamental questions about the very nature of military professionalism.

Research hypothesis: Individual officers in the military share few common bodies of knowledge and values; military expertise has become diffuse. The contributors to this volume cause one to wonder whether some of the earliest formulations of military professionalism are still relevant. Has the U.S. military become so advanced that it has civilianized many areas? Do more and more of its tasks and functions approximate the tasks in high-technology civilian occupations? Several research issues flow from any positive answers to these questions. Do military procurement specialists and scientists have more knowledge and values in common with their counterparts in other government agencies or private industry than with army company commanders or navy submariners? Will this be true in many of the support areas that comprise the bulk of the military force? Has the term *military professionalism* become so diluted that it has lost its meaning except in describing discrete organizations and individuals within those units most directly associated with combat functions? On the other hand, any research in this area must also consider whether some of the other suggested dimensions of professionalism—a sense of corporateness and a sense of responsibility—make up for the continuing reduction of shared bodies of military knowledge.

Questioning these earlier assumptions suggests one of the most important issues concerning military professionalism. If gradual civilianization is reshaping professionalism in much of the corps, how does this affect an essential issue in our democracy? How is civilian control of the military maintained under these circumstances?

Research hypothesis: The more the military moves toward civilianization, the more civilian control of the military will depend on a modern version of the citizen-soldier concept. Historically, continuous injection of civilians into a small cadre of military professionals was one way to assure civilian control of the military. This tradition changed after World War II as the cadre of professionals increased in size. The armed forces, however, were still primarily manned in the lowest ranks by nonprofessional officers and selective service draftees. These individuals usually remained in the military for relatively short periods, and they were liberalizing and leavening ingredients. The concept of the ready militia of citizen-soldiers was paramount. Huntington suggested that the military was best subordinated to its civilian political masters through an intense professionalism in which the military focused primarily on its function of managing violence and providing nonpolitical military advice. Janowitz, on the other hand, suggested that the military was best controlled by socially representative recruitment and by military concern with national security matters in the broadest sense. The heroic leader was forced to become the technocrat-manager.

Have world events, technology, centralization, specialization, and the all-volunteer force more or less overtaken both of these formulations? Paradoxically, will civilians control the U.S. military through the emergence of the "soldier-citizen"? Several social scientists expressed early concerns that the all-volunteer force would create a military encamped in ghettos divorced from society. But have the effects of technology and higher wages brought just the opposite? Have military life-styles and functions been increasingly civilianized because most military jobs, except those directly related to combat, increasingly resemble civilian jobs? Have increased military pay and the growth in the numbers of families resulted in broader integration of the military with the civilian community? Have increasing educational levels diminished the potential for a separate "military mind"? Can the military retain a unique, all-encompassing life-style in an era of mass culture, pervasive mass communications, and highly educated officers, enlisted personnel, and spouses? Will civilians control the military in the sense that it increasingly becomes a mirror image of civilian society? Has the boundary separating what is military and what is civilian become so permeable that it is less relevant? In short, is it time to investigate the concept of the "soldier-citizen"—one who wears a uniform but shares virtually all the characteristics of his fellow citizens? Will civilian control of the military become a meaningless concern based on continuing civilianization?

These speculations about the very essence of the military lead to other questions about combat efficiency and effectiveness that might result from such trends. If scholars document more carefully the emerging civilianization of the military, how will this force perform under the emotional tests of combat? To what extent can technology, perhaps a driving factor in these trends, compensate for the diminished institutional character of the military, which formerly held units together under severe combat tests? Will the military segregate itself into clear cut combat and noncombat organizations and functions? Will it more clearly articulate and make explicit numerous discrete recruitment criteria, career and promotion patterns, and life-styles?

To survive the changes suggested in this volume, the military professional must understand them. Thomas W. Carr offers several novel roles for education as a potent force for increasing recruiting opportunities, and education may be an important factor in other areas as well.

Research hypothesis: The military will continue to turn to several forms of education to increase its recruiting potential and its capacity to manage the important changes anticipated for the 1980s. A fundamental dimension of the military's capacity to cope with a complex and changing future will be the requirement for continuing education of its leaders. The military can consciously manage the future only if it is alert and aware of sweeping international, domestic, social, and internal changes. Education may be a primary mechanism for coping with this uncertain future.

Some of the issues raised in this volume are fundamental and profound and cannot be staffed in ninety days. They require careful, objective, in-depth research and education to provide experts and specialists capable of dealing with the future. But, as Carr advocates, an important segment of this research and education must also be dedicated to the humanities and social sciences. From these broader disciplines comes the generalist's capacity to integrate a complex military world and the human resources that populate it. Combat readiness is a critical variable, vital to the survival of the United States and the democratic world in the nuclear age. But perhaps just as crucial is the capacity to understand the degree of combat readiness required and the context in which it will operate.

This helps to explain the reason for this sort of research and the need to ask research questions. Obviously, this volume helps to expand our knowledge and understanding of the U.S. military institution and civil-military relations. There are, in fact, more practical reasons for research, although the expansion of knowledge alone is a worthy achievement.

In the late twentieth century, there appear to be serious threats to the continuing existence of freedom and democracy as forms of thinking and government. As the number of states has increased and as the world has become more complex, more and more states have turned to more authoritarian methods of governing, either to control or to satisfy the desires of their people. At the same time, Western democratic societies control relatively less power than in the past. Democracy is thus threatened in both subtle and explicit ways. As the ultimate defender of U.S. national sovereignty, the U.S. military is an important instrument of national power, but it faces serious problems. Vast international and domestic forces sweeping the world portend a number of changes.

The military will be unable to adjust adequately without at least a minimal understanding of the dimensions and effects of the changes. Research thus fosters more than general human understanding; it can lead to specific understanding of particular military trends and problem areas. Not only must the military as an institution deal with the changes that impinge upon it, but individual members must also cope with an increasingly complex and frustrating world. Even in areas that do not directly affect the military or in areas outside the purview of military control, individual military members can adapt more satisfactorily if they at least understand the dimensions of the world confronting them.

Finally, research of the sort contained in this volume and suggested in this chapter is important to the policy process. In a democratic society, policies are usually made best if they are informed by public debate and information. The most rational policies follow when problems are carefully studied and programs are then designed. Research thus provides information that enhances the rational functioning of the American democratic process.

Unfortunately, the overall content of this volume cannot be considered optimistic; in fact, one can forcefully argue that this is a unique period in U.S. military history. The U.S. military has had prior experiences with the all-volunteer concept; it has actually spent most of its history as an all-volunteer force. And it has always faced shrinking resources and declining numbers after wars have terminated. It has shouldered global responsibilities since the end of World War II, and for the first time in its history, it seeks to recruit manpower as an economic competitor in the American marketplace. The military and the nation are recovering from an unsuccessful and unpopular war, and the American people have witnessed a decline in the nation's relative international power. The United States has faced several of these problems before, but it has never faced all of them at the same time.

This volume represents an attempt to improve understanding of the dimensions of the new era that we will enter in the 1980s. The forecast of the future might appear gloomy, but one may be certain that the 1980s will be dynamic years. During that period, the military will be hard pressed to retain critical institutional values and still not permit these values to interfere with its adaptation to a changing world. Only by understanding trends and defining problems can we focus the enormous resources still available to the U.S. military.

In many respects, the problems are as complex and as potentially unmanageable as any problems facing the military profession in recent years. On the other hand, the modern military may also be more capable of understanding and coping with problems of change. The issues framed in this book are challenging, and they signal that we are entering a phase of major reformulation and rethinking. Indeed, one can only hope, in this third phase of study described by Morris Janowitz in the Foreword, that the best minds inside and outside the military will proceed with this reassessment. The changing world of the American military permits no less.

Notes

1. Major General Robert N. Ginsburgh, USAF (Ret.), made several pertinent comments that should be considered in any discussion of military self-concept or identity crisis. He suggested that social scientists would be more concerned and excited about a military identity crisis than almost every military member. He noted that social scientists (General Ginsburgh is a social scientist) must be cautious about their responsibilities and their potential influence. He questioned, for instance, the complex interrelationships between Morris Janowitz's astute early predictions of trends within the U.S. military and the persuasive power of his words, personality, and military contacts. Did Janowitz predict the trends or did his predictions and subtle influence cause the trends? General Ginsburgh viewed this volume as a much needed work, but he cautioned that we should not forget military capabilities elsewhere in the world. These capabilities are ultimately the most serious threat to the U.S. military and national security.

2. Professor Lucian Pye, MIT, first suggested this explanation—which was borne out in interviews with air force officers and reported in Franklin D. Margiotta, "A Military Elite in Transition," *Armed Forces and Society* 2, no. 2 (Winter 1976):168.

3. The complexities generated by decreased party unity and control in Congress may further complicate research aimed at a deeper understanding of this shifting constitutional balance. Although Congress as a whole seems to be increasing its staff capacities and its power to counter the executive branch, congressional leadership can no longer rely on the solid majorities once gathered by such parliamentary leaders as Cannon, Rayburn, and Johnson. Individual legislators

seem much more independent, and to a certain extent, this may diminish the capacity of Congress to take positive actions.

4. Again, qualifications are appropriate. The executive branch has not tested the constitutionality of the War Powers Resolution in the courts. An astute president might be able to use the resolution politically to unify the country behind a foreign commitment of military forces. For a discussion of this resolution and these issues, see *Department of State Bulletin*, April 9, 1973, pp. 434-439, and November 26, 1973, pp. 662-664; Raoul Berger, "The Constitution Is Clear Enough," *The Nation*, March 26, 1973, pp. 393-397; "A Bad War Powers Bill," *The New Republic*, October 27, 1973, pp. 5-6; Representative Donald M. Fraser, "The Veto Is Wrong," *The New Republic*, November 3, 1973, pp. 9-10; "Congress Sends Nixon a Message," *Newsweek*, November 19, 1973, p. 39; "Limiting the Power to Wage War," *Time*, November 19, 1973.

5. Colonel William Taylor, USA, has suggested that the public recently seems more willing to support the military financially so long as it does not actively participate. To some extent, this qualifies Samuel P. Huntington's conclusions in Chapter 1 that the United States is apathetic about its military in the late 1970s.

6. See, for example, U.S., Congress, Senate, Committee on Armed Services, *All Volunteer Armed Forces: Progress, Problems, and Prospects*, a report prepared by Martir Binkin and John D. Johnston, 93rd Cong., 1st sess. (Washington, D.C., June 1, 1973); Richard V. L. Cooper, *Military Manpower and the All-Volunteer Force*, Rand Report no. R-1450-ARPA (Santa Monica, Calif.: September, 1977); U.S., Congress, Senate, Committee on Armed Services, *Achieving America's Goal: The All-Volunteer Armed Force or National Service?*, a report prepared by William R. King, 95th Cong., 1st sess. (Washington, D.C.: U.S. Government Printing Office, March 2, 1977); U.S. Department of Defense, *The All-Volunteer Force: Current Status and Prospects* (Washington, D.C., December 17, 1976); Thomas A Fabyanic, "Manpower, Military Intervention, and the All-Volunteer Force," in *The Limits of Military Intervention*, ed. Ellen Stern (Beverly Hills, Calif.: Sage, 1977), pp. 281-300.

In addition, there has been a series of congressional hearings on military manpower policies and problems, particularly in the Senate Armed Services Committee. For specific references, see Cooper, *Military Manpower*, p. 406. Finally, another signal of increasing public recognition and attention was the fact that the June 1977 West Point Senior Conference addressed aspects of this issue.

7. Morris Janowitz and Charles C. Moskos, Jr., "Racial Composition in the All-Volunteer Force: Policy Alternatives," *Armed Forces and Society* 1, no. 1 (Fall 1974):109; Alvin J. Schexnider and John Sibley Butler, "Race and the All Volunteer System: A Reply to Janowitz and Moskos," and "Comment," by Janowitz and Moskos, *Armed Forces and Society* 2, no. 3 (Spring 1976): 421-434.

8. These striking changes in military family patterns are carefully described by Nancy L. Goldman, "Trends in Family Patterns of U.S. Military Personnel during the 20th Century," in *The Social Psychology of Miltary Service*, ed. by Nancy L. Goldman and David R. Segal (Beverly Hills, Calif.: Sage, 1976), pp. 119-134. Aside from work done under navy auspices on the effect of separation on navy and prisoner-of-war families, this book contains the first few attempts to gauge the monumental change that has occurred within the military in terms of family patterns. This area promises to be one of the more fruitful areas for research.

9. Major General Robert N. Ginsburgh has suggested that researchers looking into family attitudes should be cautious and recognize the growing acceptance of mobility as a part of American civilian society.

10. Morris Janowitz, *The Professional Soldier: A Social and Political Portrait* (New York: Free Press, 1960); Samuel P. Huntington, *The Soldier and the State: The Theory and Politics of Civil-Military Relations* (Cambridge, Mass.: Harvard University Press, 1957).

Selected Bibliography

Selected Bibliography

Books

Abrahamsson, Bengt. *Military Professionalism and Political Power*. Beverly Hills, Calif.: Sage Publications, 1972.

Ambrose, S. E., and Barber, J. A., Jr., eds. *The Military and American Society*. New York: Free Press, 1972.

Andreski, Stanislav. *Military Organization and Society*. Los Angeles: University of California Press, 1954.

Astin, A. *The College Environment*. Washington, D.C.: The American Council on Education, 1968.

Bachman, Jerald G., and Blair, John D. *Soldiers, Sailors and Civilians: The "Military Mind" and the All-Volunteer Force*. Ann Arbor, Mich.: Institute for Social Research, 1975.

Bachman, Jerald G.; Blair, John D.; and Segal, David R. *The All-Volunteer Force: A Study of Ideology in the Military*. Ann Arbor, Mich.: University of Michigan Press, 1977.

Bachman, Jerald G., and Johnston, Jerome. *Youth in Transition*. Vol. 4: *Young Men and Military Service*. Ann Arbor, Mich.: Institute for Social Research, 1972.

————. *Young Men Look at Military Service: A Preliminary Report*. Ann Arbor, Mich.: Institute for Social Research, 1971.

Barnes, Peter. *Pawns: The Plight of the Citizen-Soldier*. New York: Alfred A. Knopf, 1972.

Bennett, W., et al. *Army Families*. Carlisle Barracks, Pa.: U.S. Army War College, 1974.

Black, Robert B., and Esterline, John H. *Inside Foreign Policy*. Palo Alto, Calif.: Mayfield Publishing Co., 1975.

Bletz, D. *The Role of the Military Professional in U.S. Foreign Policy*. New York: Praeger, 1972.

Bliven, Bruce, Jr. *Volunteers, One and All*. New York: Reader's Digest Press, 1976.

Bradford, Zeb B., and Brown, Frederic J. *The United States Army in Transition*. Beverly Hills, Calif.: Sage Publications, 1974.

Brodie, Bernard. *War and Politics*. New York: The Macmillan Company, 1973.

Burkhead, Jesse. *Government Budgeting*. New York: John Wiley and Sons, 1956.

Burlingham, D., and Freud, A. *War and Children*. New York: International University Press, 1943.

Campbell, Angus; Gurin, Gerald; and Miller, Warren E. *The Voter Decides.* Evanston, Ill.: Row, Peterson, 1954.

Canby, Steven L. *Military Manpower Procurement: A Policy Analysis.* Lexington, Mass.: D. C. Heath and Co., 1972.

Chwat, John Steven, and Collins, John M. *The United States/Soviet Military Balance: A Frame of Reference for Congress.* Washington, D.C.: Government Printing Office, 1976.

Clotfelter, James. *The Military in American Politics.* New York: Harper and Row, 1973.

Coates, Charles H., and Pellegrin, Roland J. *Military Sociology: A Study of American Military Institutions and Military Life.* University Park, Md.: The Social Science Press, 1965.

Cochran, Charles L., ed. *Civil-Military Relations.* New York: Free Press, 1974.

Cooper, Richard V. L. *Military Manpower and the All-Volunteer Force.* Santa Monica, Calif.: The Rand Corporation, September 1977.

Crozier, Michael; Huntington, Samuel P.; and Watanuki, Joji. *The Crisis of Democracy.* New York: New York University Press, 1975.

Dahl, B.; McCubbin, Hamilton; and Hunter, E. *Families in the Military System.* Beverly Hills, Calif.: Sage, 1976.

Dahl, B.; McCubbin, H.; Hunter, E.; Metres, P. J., Jr.; and Plag, J. A. *Family Separation and Reunion.* Washington, D.C.: Government Printing Office, 1975.

Donovan, James A. *Militarism, U.S.A.* New York: Charles Scribner's Sons, 1970.

Ellis, J., and Moore, R. *School for Soldiers: West Point and the Profession of Arms.* New York: Oxford University Press, 1974.

Federman, P. J.; Lautman, M. R.; and Siegel, A. I. *Factors Involved in the Adjustment of Low Aptitude Personnel to the Navy and Their Use for Predicting Reenlistment.* Wayne, Pa.: Applied Psychological Sciences, 1973.

Feldman, K. A., and Newcomb, T. M. *The Impact of College on Students.* San Francisco: Jossey Bass, 1969.

Galloway, K., and Johnson, R. *West Point: America's Power Fraternity.* New York: Simon and Schuster, 1973.

Goldman, Nancy L., and Segal, David R., eds. *The Social Psychology of Military Service.* Beverly Hills, Calif: Sage, 1976.

Gonzales, V. *Psychiatry and the Army Brat.* Chicago: C. C. Thomas, 1970.

Greenstein, Fred I. *Children and Politics.* New Haven, Conn.: Yale University Press, 1965.

Hanson, Elizabeth C., and Russett, Bruce M. *Interest and Ideology: The Foreign Policy Beliefs of American Businessmen.* San Francisco: W. H. Freeman and Co., 1975.

Hauser, William L. *America's Army in Crisis: A Study in Civil-Military Relations.* Baltimore: Johns Hopkins University Press, 1973.

Helmer, J. *Bringing the War Home: The American Soldier in Vietnam and After.* New York: Free Press, 1974.

Hersh, Seymour M. *My Lai 4: A Report on the Massacre and Its Aftermath.* New York: Random House, 1970.

Hill, R. *Families Under Stress: Adjustment to the Crises of War, Separation and Reunion.* New York: Harper and Brothers, 1949.

Huntington, Samuel P. *Changing Patterns of Military Politics.* New York: Free Press, 1962.

_____. *The Soldier and the State: The Theory and Politics of Civil-Military Relations.* Cambridge, Mass.: Harvard University Press, 1957.

Hyman, Herbert. *Political Socialization.* Glencoe, Ill.: Free Press, 1959.

Jacklin, C. N., and Maccoby, E. E. *The Psychology of Sex Difference.* Stanford, Calif.: Stanford University Press, 1974.

Janowitz, Morris. *Military Conflict: Essays in the Institutional Analysis of War and Peace.* Beverly Hills, Calif.: Sage, 1975.

_____. *The New Military.* New York: Russell Sage Foundation, 1964.

_____. *The Professional Soldier: A Social and Political Portrait.* New York: Free Press, 1960.

Janowitz, Morris, and Little, R. *Sociology and the Military Establishment.* Rev. ed. New York: Russell Sage Foundation, 1965.

Karsten, P. *The Naval Aristocracy.* New York: Free Press, 1972.

Katz, D.; Gutek, B. A.; and Barton, E. *Bureaucratic Encounters: A Pilot Study in the Evaluation of Government Service.* Ann Arbor, Mich.: Institute for Social Research, University of Michigan, 1974.

Kemp, Geoffrey; Pfaltzgraff, Robert L., Jr.; and Ra'anan, Uri, eds. *The Other Arms Race: New Technologies and Non-nuclear Conflict.* Lexington, Mass.: D. C. Heath, 1975.

King, William R. *Achieving America's Goals: National Service or the All-Volunteer Force?* Washington, D.C.: Government Printing Office, 1977.

Kinzer, B., and Leach, M. *What Every Army Wife Should Know.* Harrisburg, Pa.: Stackpole, 1968.

Krendle, Ezra S., and Samoff, Bernard. *Unionizing the Armed Forces.* Philadelphia: University of Pennsylvania Press, 1977.

Kronenberg, Philip S., and Lovell, John P., eds. *New Civil-Military Relations: The Agonies of Adjustment to Post-Vietnam Realities.* New Brunswick, N.J.: Transaction Books, 1974.

Ladd, Everett, and Lipset, S. M. *The Divided Academy.* New York: McGraw-Hill, 1975.

Lang, Kurt. *Military Institutions and the Sociology of War.* New York: Sage, 1972.

_____. "Military Organizations." In *Handbook of Organizations,* edited by J. March. Chicago: Rand McNally, 1965.

Lee, Gus C., and Parker, Geoffrey. *Ending the Draft: The Story of the All-Volunteer Force.* Alexandria, Va.: Human Resources Research Organization, April 1977.

Likert, Rensis. *The Human Organization.* Chicago: Rand McNally, 1967.

Little, R., ed. *Handbook of Military Institutions.* Beverly Hills, Calif.: Sage, 1971.

McGregor, Douglas. *The Human Side of Enterprise.* New York: McGraw-Hill, 1960.

Masland, John W., and Radway, Laurence I. *Soldiers and Scholars: Military Education and National Policy.* Princeton, N.J.: Princeton University Press, 1957.

Mills, C. Wright. *The Power Elite.* New York: Oxford University Press, 1956.

Mitchell, Terrence R., and Scott, William G. *Organizational Theory.* Homewood, Ill.: Richard D. Irwin, 1976.

Moskos, Charles C. *The American Enlisted Man.* New York: Russell Sage Foundation, 1970.

Moskos, Charles C., ed. *Public Opinion and the Military Establishment.* Beverly Hills, Calif.: Sage, 1971.

Mueller, John. *War, Presidents, and Public Opinion.* New York: John Wiley and Sons, 1973.

Odiorne, George S. *Management and the Activity Trap.* New York: Harper and Row, 1974.

Oppenheimer, Martin, ed. *The American Military.* New Brunswick, N.J.: Transaction Books, 1971.

Perlmutter, Amos. *The Military and Politics in Modern Times.* New Haven, Conn.: Yale University Press, 1977.

Russett, Bruce M., and Stepan, Alfred, eds. *Military Force and American Society.* New York: Harper and Row, 1973.

Sabrosky, Alan Ned, ed. *Blue-Collar Soldiers?: Unionization and the U.S. Military.* Boulder, Colo.: Westview Press, 1978.

Safilios-Rothschild, C. *Women and Social Policy.* Englewood Cliffs, N.J.: Prentice-Hall, 1974.

Sarkesian, Sam C., ed. *The Military-Industrial Complex: A Reassessment.* Beverly Hills, Calif.: Sage, 1972.

Sarkesian, Sam C. *The Professional Army Officer in a Changing Society.* Chicago: Nelson-Hall Co., 1975.

Schick, Allen. *Congressional Control of Expenditures.* Washington, D.C.: Congressional Research Service, 1976.

Stern, Ellen, ed. *The Limits of Military Intervention.* Beverly Hills, Calif.: Sage, 1977.

Stolz, L. *Father Relations of War-Born Children: The Effect of Postwar Adjustment of Fathers on the Behavior and Personality of First Children Born While Fathers Were at War.* Palo Alto, Calif.: Stanford University Press, 1954.

Stouffer, S. A., et al. *The American Soldier: Adjustment During Army Life.* Princeton, N.J.: Princeton University Press, 1949.

_____. *The American Soldier: Combat and Its Aftermath.* Princeton, N.J.: Princeton University Press, 1949.

Taylor, William J., Jr.; Lockwood, Robert S.; and Arango, Roger J. *Military Unions for the United States: Issues and Alternatives.* Beverly Hills, Calif.: Sage, 1977.

Tax, Sol, ed. *The Draft: A Handbook of Facts and Alternatives.* Chicago: University of Chicago Press, 1967.

Toffler, Alvin. *Future Shock.* New York: Bantam Books, 1970.

Trager, Frank N., and Kronenberg, Philip S., eds. *National Security and American Society: Theory, Process, and Policy.* Lawrence: The University Press of Kansas, 1973.

Van Doorn, Jacques. *The Soldier and Social Change: Comparative Studies in the History and Sociology of the Military.* Beverly Hills, Calif.: Sage, 1975.

Vroom, Victor H., and Yetton, Phillip W. *Leadership and Decision Making.* Pittsburgh: University of Pittsburgh Press, 1973.

_____. *Organizational Dynamics.* New York: American Management Association, 1976.

Weiner, Norbert. *The Human Use of Human Beings: Cybernetics and Society.* 2d ed. Garden City, N.Y.: Doubleday, 1954.

White, Ralph K. *Nobody Wanted War: Misperceptions in Vietnam and Other Wars.* Garden City, N.Y.: Doubleday, 1968.

Yarmolinsky, A. *The Military Establishment: Its Impacts on American Society.* New York: Harper and Row, 1972.

Published Reports

Bachman, Jerald G. *Values, Preferences and Perceptions Concerning Military Service* (NTIS no. AD 763 483). Ann Arbor, Mich.: Institute for Social Research, 1973.

————.*Values, Preferences and Perceptions Concerning Military Service: Part II* (NTIS no. AD 775 205). Ann Arbor, Mich.: Institute for Social Research, 1974.

Bowers, David G., and Bachman, Jerald G. *Military Manpower and Modern Values* (NTIS no. AD 787 826). Ann Arbor, Mich.: Institute for Social Research, 1974.

————. *Navy Manpower: Values, Practices, and Human Resources Requirements* (NTIS no. AD A014 493). Ann Arbor, Mich.: Institute for Social Research, 1975.

Fisher, A. H., Jr. *Army New Standards' Personnel: Effect of Remedial Literacy Training on Performance in Military Service* (HUMRRO Technical Report 71-7). Alexandria, Va.: Human Resources Research Office, 1971.

Franklin, Jerome L., and Drexler, John A. *Influences of Organizational Conditions and Practices on Reenlistment, Operational Readiness, and Satisfaction in the Navy.* Ann Arbor, Mich.: Institute for Social Research, 1976.

Glickman, A. S.; Goodstadt, B. E.; Korman, A. K.; and Romanczuk, A. P. *Research and Development for Navy Career Motivation Program in an All-Volunteer Condition: I. A Cognitive Map of Career Motivation.* Washington, D.C.: American Institutes for Research, 1973.

Goodstadt, B. E.; Frey, R. L., Jr.; and Glickman, A. A. *Socialization Process and the Adjustment of Military Personnel to Army Life.* Washington, D.C.: American Institutes for Research, 1975.

Goral, John. *Major Findings from the May 1974 Gilbert Youth Survey of Attitudes Toward Military Service* (Report no. MR-75-2). U.S., Department of Defense, Manpower Research and Data Analysis Center, 1975.

Goral, John, and Lipowitz, Andrea. *Attitudes of Youth Toward Military Service in the All-Volunteer Force* (Report no. MR-75-1). U.S., Department of Defense, Manpower Research and Data Analysis Center, 1975.

Gunderson, E. K. E. *Biographical Indicators of Adaptation to Naval Service* (Report 63-19). San Diego, Calif.: Navy Medical Neuropsychiatric Research Unit, 1963.

Gunderson, E. K. E., and Sells, S. B. *Organizational and Environmental Factors in Health and Personnel Effectiveness* (Report 75-8). San Diego, Calif.: Naval Health Research Center, 1975.

Holz, R. F., and Gitter, A. G. *Assessing the Quality of Life in the U.S. Army* (Technical Paper 256). Arlington, Va.: U.S. Army Research Institute for the Behavioral and Social Sciences, 1974.

LaRocco, J. M., and Gunderson, E. K. E. *Prediction of Reenlistment: A Discriminant Analysis Approach* (Report 75-21). San Diego, Calif.: Naval Health Research Center, 1975.

Lindquist, R. *Marriage and Family Life of Officers and Airmen in a Strategic Air Command Wing* (Technical Report 5, Air Force Base Project). Chapel Hill, N.C.: Institute for Research in Social Science, University of North Carolina, 1952.

McGoff, R. M., and Harding, F. D. *A Report on Literacy Training Programs in the Armed Forces.* Alexandria, Va.: Air Force Human Resources Laboratory, Manpower Development Division, 1974.

Michaelson, L. K. *Attitudes and Motivations Toward Enlistment in the U.S. Army.*

Princeton, N.J.: Opinion Research Corporation, 1974.

Plag, J., and Goffman, J. M. *The Utilization of Predicted Effectiveness Scores for Selecting Naval Enlistees* (Report 69-6). San Diego, Calif.: U.S. Naval Medical Neuropsychiatric Research Unit, 1969.

Segal, David R., and Diana, Bernard L. *The Social Representativeness of the Volunteer Army* (Memorandum 75-12). Arlington, Va.: U.S. Army Research Institute for the Behavioral and Social Sciences Research, 1975.

Tuttle, T. C., and Hazel, J. T. *Review and Implications of Job Satisfaction and Work Motivation Theories for Air Force Research* (U.S. AFHRL-TR-73-56). San Antonio, Tex.: Lackland Air Force Base, 1974.

Vineberg, R., and Taylor, E. N. *Summary and Review of Studies of the VOLAR Experiment* (HUMRRO Technical Report 72-18). Alexandria, Va.: Human Resources Research Organization, 1972.

Unpublished Reports

Belt, J., and Swenev, A. "The Air Force Wife: Her Knowledge of, and Attitudes Toward, the Air Force." Paper presented at the Military Testing Association Conference on Human Resources, October 1973, San Antonio, Texas.

Blochberger, C. W., Jr. "Military Families: Differential Life-Styles." Ph.D. dissertation, University of California at Berkeley, 1970.

Cabanillas, C. E. "The Army Officer's Wife: Role Conflict and Role Strain." Master's thesis, University of Texas at El Paso, 1975.

Finlayson, E. "A Study of the Wife of an Army Officer: Her Academic and Career Preparation, Her Current Employment and Volunteer Services." Ph.D. dissertation, George Washington University, 1969.

Gard, R. "Applications of Behavioral Science in the Military Environment." Paper presented at the meeting of the American Psychological Association, September 1974, New Orleans.

Jennings, M. K., and Markus, G. B. "The Effects of Military Service on Political Attitudes: A Panel Study." Paper presented at the meeting of the American Political Science Association, 1974, Chicago.

Lyon, W. B. "Some Reactions of Children from Military Families to Family Mobility and Father Absence." Paper presented at the meeting of the American Psychological Association, September 1967, Washington, D.C.

Moskos, C. C., Jr. "Studies on the American Soldier: Continuities and Discontinuities in Social Research." Paper presented at the meeting of the American Sociological Association, 1973, New York.

Picou, J. S., and Nyberg, K. L. "Socialization into the Military: A Study of University Cadets." Paper presented at the meeting of the American Sociological Association, August 1975, San Francisco.

Articles

American Enterprise Institute. "Unions in the Military?" *AEI Defense Review* 1 (1977):1-30.

Bachman, Jerald G., and Blair, John D. "'Citizen Force' or 'Career Force?'

Implications for Ideology in the All-Volunteer Army." *Armed Forces and Society* 2 (1975):81-96.

Bachman, Jerald G., and Jennings, M. K. "The Impact of Vietnam on Trust in Government." *Journal of Social Issues* 31 (1975):141-156.

Bachman, Jerald G., and Johnston, J. "The All-Volunteer Force: Not Whether but What Kind?" *Psychology Today* 5 (1972):113-116.

Bey, D. R., Jr., and Smith, W. E. "Organizational Consultation in a Combat Unit." *American Journal of Psychiatry* 128 (1971):401-406.

Biderman, A. "The Prospective Impact of Large Scale Military Retirement." *Social Problems* 17 (1959):84-90.

Biderman, A., and Sharp, L. M. "The Convergence of Military and Civilian Occupational Structures," *American Journal of Sociology* 73 (1968):381-399.

Booth, R. F., and Hoeberg, A. "Change in Marine Recruits' Attitudes Related to Recruit Characteristics and Drill Instructors' Attitudes." *Psychological Reports* 33 (1973):63-71.

_____. "Structure and Measurement of Marine Recruit Attitudes," *Journal of Applied Psychology* 59 (1974):236-238.

Borus, J. F.; Finman, B. G.; Stanton, M. D.; and Dowd, A. F. "The Racial Perceptions Inventory." *Archives and General Psychiatry* 29 (1973):270-275.

_____. "Racial Perceptions in the Army: An Approach." *American Journal of Psychiatry* 128 (1972):1369-1374.

Boulding, E. "Family Adjustments to War Separations and Reunion." *Annals of the American Academy* 272 (1950):59-67.

Bradford, Zeb B., Jr., and Murphy, James R. "A New Look at the Military Profession." *Army* 19 (1969):58-64.

Brewer, Thomas L. "The Impact of Advanced Education on American Military Officers." *Armed Forces and Society* 2 (1975):63-80.

Brown, Charles W., and Moskos, Charles C., Jr. "The American Volunteer Soldier: Will He Fight?" *Military Review* 56 (1976):8-17.

Butler, John S., and Schexnider, Alvin J. "Race and the All-Volunteer System: A Reply to Janowitz and Moskos." *Armed Forces and Society* 2 (1976):421-432.

Campbell, D. T., and McCormack, T. H. "Military Experience and Attitudes Toward Authority." *American Journal of Sociology* 62 (1957):482-490.

Carroll, R. "Ethics of the Military Profession" *Air University Review* 26 (1974):42.

Clotfelter, James, and Peters, B. Guy, "Profession and Society: Young Military Officers Look Outward." *Journal of Political and Military Sociology* 4 (1976):39-51.

Cortwright, David. "Economic Conscription." *Society* 12 (1975):43-47.

Cutright, P. "The Civilian Earnings of White and Black Draftees and Non-Veterans." *American Sociological Review* 39 (1974):317-327.

Dickerson, W. J., and Arthur, R. J. "Navy Families in Distress." *Military Medicine* 130 (1965):894-898.

Dickson, Thomas I., Jr. "Public Opinion and National Security." *Military Review* 56 (1976):77-81.

Doll, R. E.; Rubin, R. T.; and Gunderson, E. K. E. "Life Stress and Illness Patterns in the U.S. Navy: II. Demographic Variables and Illness Onset in an Attack Carrier's Crew." *Archives of Environmental Health* 19 (1962):748-752.

Dornbusch, S. "The Military Academy as an Assimilating Institution." *Social Forces* 33 (1955):316-321.

Duvall, E. "Loneliness and the Serviceman's Wife." *Marriage and Family Living* 7 (1945):77-81.

Elowitz, Larry, and Spanier, John W. "Korea and Viet Nam: Limited War and the American Political System." *ORBIS* 18 (1974):510-534.

Fabyanic, Thomas A. "Manpower Trends in the British All-volunteer Force." *Armed Forces and Society* 2 (1976):553-572.

Fagen, S.; Janda, E.; Baker, S.; Fischer, E.; and Cove, L. "Impact of Father Absence in Military Families: II. Factors Relating to Success of Coping with Crisis." *Proceedings of the Annual Meeting of the American Psychological Association* 2 (1967).

Feld, M. D. "Military Professionalism and the Mass Army." *Armed Forces and Society* 1 (1975):191-214.

Fiman, G. B.; Borus, J. F.; and Stanton, M. D. "Black-White and American-Vietnamese Relations Among Soldiers in Vietnam." *Journal of Social Issues* 31 (1975):39-48.

Fleishman, E. A. "Leadership Climate, Human Relations Training, and Supervisory Behavior." *Personnel Psychology* 6 (1953):205-222.

Francis, A., and Gale, L. "Family Structure and Treatment in the Military." *Family Process* 12 (1973):171-178.

French, E. G., and Ernest, R. R. "The Relationship Between Authoritarianism and Acceptance of Military Ideology." *Journal of Personality* 24 (1955):181-191.

Gabower, G. "Behavior Problems of Children in Navy Officers' Families." *Social Casework* 41 (1960):177-184.

Gard, Robert F. "The Military and American Society." *Foreign Affairs* 49 (1971): 698-710.

――――. "The Military Profession." *Naval War College Review* 26 (1973):8-15.

Garnier, Maurice A. "Some Implications of the British Experience with an All-Volunteer Army." *Pacific Sociological Review* 16 (1973):177-191.

Goldman, Nancy. "The Utilization of Women in the Armed Forces of Industrialized Nations." *Sociological Symposium* 18 (1977):1-23.

Goldman, N. L. "The Changing Role of Women in the Armed Forces." *American Journal of Sociology* 78 (1973):892-911.

Gunderson, E. K. E. "Body Size, Self-evaluation, and Military Effectiveness." *Journal of Personality and Social Psychology* 2 (1965):902-906.

Gunderson, E. K. E.; Rahe, R. H.; and Arthur, R. J. "The Epidemiology of Illness in Naval Environments: II. Demographic, Social Background, and Occupational Factors." *Military Medicine* 135 (1970):453-458.

Hartnagel, T. F. "Absent Without Leave: A Study of the Military Offender." *Journal of Political and Military Sociology* 2 (1974):205-220.

Hartog, J. "Group Therapy with the Psychotic and Borderline Military Wives." *American Journal of Psychiatry* 122 (1966):1125-1131.

Hoiberg, A.; Hysham, C. E.; and Berry, N. H. "Effectiveness of Recruits Assigned to Academic Remedial Training." *Psychology Reports* 35 (1974):1007-1114.

Huntington, Samuel P. "After Containment: The Functions of the Military Establishment." *Annals* 406 (1973):1-16.

――――. "Power, Expertise and the Military Profession." *Daedalus* 92 (1963): 785-807.

Hyman, Sidney. "The Governance of the Military." *Annals* 406 (1973):38-47.

Janowitz, Morris. "The All-Volunteer Military as a 'Sociopolitical' Problem." *Social Problems* 22 (1975):432-449.

_____. "The Decline of the Mass Army." *Military Review* 52 (1976):10-16.

_____. "Military Institutions and Citizenship in Western Societies." *Armed Forces and Society* 2 (1976):185-204.

_____. "The Social Demography of the All-Volunteer Armed Force." *Annals* 406 (1973):86-93.

_____. "Stabilizing Military Systems: An Emerging Strategic Concept." *Military Review* 55 (1975):3-10.

_____. "The U.S. Forces and the Zero Draft." *Adelphi Papers* 94 (1973).

_____. "Volunteer Armed Forces and Military Purpose." *Foreign Affairs*, April 1972, pp. 428-443.

Janowitz, Morris, and Moskos, Charles C., Jr. "Comment." *Armed Forces and Society* 2 (1976):433-434.

_____. "Racial Composition in the All-Volunteer Force." *Armed Forces and Society* 1 (1974):109-122.

Jordan, Amos A., and Taylor, William J., Jr. "The Military Man in Academia." *Annals* 406 (1973):129-145.

Kourvetaris, George A., and Dobratz, Betty A. "Social Recruitment and Political Orientations of the Officer Corps in a Comparative Perspective." *Pacific Sociological Review* 16 (1973):228-254.

_____. "The Present State and Development of Sociology of the Military." *Journal of Political and Military Sociology* 4 (1976):67-105.

Kraus, John D., Jr. "The Civilian Military College." *Military Review* 56 (1976):77-87.

Lang, Kurt. "Trends in Military Occupational Structure and Their Political Implications." *Journal of Political and Military Sociology* 1 (1973):1-18.

Larson, Arthur D. "Military Professionalism and Civil Control: A Comparative Analysis of Two Interpretations." *Journal of Political and Military Sociology* 2 (1974):57-70.

Lasswell, Harold D. "The Garrison State." *American Journal of Sociology* 46 (1941): 455-468.

Laurance, Edward J. "The Changing Role of Congress in Defense Policy Making." *Journal of Conflict Resolution* 20 (1976):213-253.

Lovell, John P. "Professionalism and the Service Academies." *American Behavioral Scientist* 19 (1976):605-626.

Lyon, W. B., and Oldaker, L. "The Child, the School, and the Military Family." *American Journal of Orthopsychiatry* 37 (1967):269-270.

MacIntosh, H. "Separation Problems of Military Wives." *American Journal of Psychiatry* 125 (1968):260-265.

McKain, J. L. "Relocation in the Military: Alienation and Family Problems." *Journal of Marriage and Family* 35 (1973):205-209.

McNall, Scott G. "A Comment on Research in the Field of Military Sociology." *Pacific Sociological Review* 16 (1973):139-142.

Mahan, J. L., Jr., and Clum, G. A. "Longitudinal Prediction of Marine Combat Effectiveness." *Journal of Social Psychology* 83 (1971):45-54.

Margiotta, Franklin D. "A Military Elite in Transition: Air Force Leaders in the 1980s." *Armed Forces and Society* 2 (1976):155-184.

Miller, A. H. "Political Issues and Trust in Government: 1964-1970." *American Political Science Review* 68 (1974):951-972.

Modigliani, Andre. "Hawks and Doves, Isolationism and Political Distrust: An Analysis of Public Opinion on Military Policy." *American Political Science Review* 66 (1972):960-978.

Moellering, John H. "Future Civil-Military Relations: The Army Turns Inward?" *Military Review* 53 (1973):68-83.

Moos, Felix. "History and Culture: Some Thoughts on the United States All-Volunteer Force." *Naval War College Review* 26 (1973):16-27.

Moskos, Charles C., Jr. "The American Dilemma in Uniform: Race in the Armed Forces." *Annals* (1973):94-106.

——. "The Emergent Military: Civil, Traditional, or Plural?" *Pacific Sociological Review* 16 (1973): 255-280.

——. "The Military." *Annual Review of Sociology* 2 (1976):55-77.

Nathan, James A., and Oliver, James K. "Public Opinion and U.S. Security Policy." *Armed Forces and Society* 2 (1975):46-62.

Owens, A. G. "Job Satisfaction and Reengagement Among Australian Regular Army Soldiers." *Australian Journal of Psychology* 21 (1969):137-144.

Palmer, Bruce, and Tarr, Curtis W. "A Careful Look at Manpower." *Military Review* 56 (1976):3-13.

Powe, Marc B. "The U.S. Army after the Fall of Viet Nam." *Military Review* 56 (1976):3-17.

Reed, Larry W., and Loman, L. Anthony. "The Future of R.O.T.C. on the Small College Campus." *Journal of Political and Military Sociology* 3 (1975):229-236.

Rosser, Richard F. "American Civil-Military Relations in the 1980s." *Naval War College Review* 24 (1972):14-15.

——. "A 20th Century Military Force." *Foreign Policy* 12 (1973):156-175.

Rue, V. M. "A U.S. Department of Marriage and the Family." *Journal of Marriage and the Family* 35 (1973):689-699.

Russett, Bruce M. "Political Perspectives of U.S. Military and Business Elites." *Armed Forces and Society* 1 (1974):79-108.

——. "The Americans' Retreat from World Power." *Political Science Quarterly* 90 (1975):1-21.

Ryan, F., and Bevilacqua, J. "The Military Family: An Asset or a Liability." *Military Medicine* 129 (1964):956-959.

Ryder, N. B. "The Family in Developed Countries." *Scientific American* 231 (1974):122-132.

Sarkesian, Sam C., and Taylor, William J., Jr. "The Case for Civilian Graduate Education for Professional Officers." *Armed Forces and Society* 12 (1975):251-262.

Schexnider, Alvin J., and Butler, John S. "Race and the All-Volunteer System: A Reply to Janowitz and Moskos." *Armed Forces and Society* 2 (1976):421-432.

Segal, David R. "Civil-Military Relations in the Mass Public." *Armed Forces and Society* 1 (1975):215-229.

Segal, David R., and Blair, John D. "Public Confidence in the U.S. Military." *Armed Forces and Society* 3 (1976):3-12.

Segal, David R.; Blair, John; Newport, Frank; and Stephens, Susan. "Convergence, Isomorphism, and Interdependence at the Civil-Military Interface." *Journal of*

Political and Military Sociology 2 (1974):157-172.

Slinkman, John. "Military Unions? A Look at the Consequences." *The Officer* 51 (1976):6.

Taylor, William J., and Bletz, Donald F. "A Case for Officer Graduate Education." *Journal of Political and Military Sociology* 2 (1974):251-267.

Teachers College, Columbia University. *Teachers College Record* 73 (1972).

Van Doorn, Jacques. "The Decline of the Mass Army in the West: General Reflections." *Armed Forces and Society* 1 (1975):147-157.

Public Documents

U.S. Army War College. *Study on Military Professionalism.* Carlisle Barracks, U.S. Army War College, Pa.: 1970.

U.S. Congress. House. Armed Services Committee. *Hearings on the Selective Service System on H.A.S.C. No. 94-36.*

U.S. Congress. Senate. Armed Services Committee. *All-Volunteer Armed Forces: Progress, Problems, and Prospects,* by Martin Binkin and John D. Johnston. 93rd Cong., 1st sess., Washington, D.C.: Government Printing Office, 1973.

U.S. Congress. Senate. Armed Services Committee. *FY 76 and July-September 1976 Transition Period Authorization for Military Procurement, R&D, and Active Duty, Selected Reserve, and Civilian Personnel Strengths. Hearing on S. 920, Part 3: Manpower.* 94th Cong., 1st sess., 1975.

U.S. Defense Manpower Commission. *Defense Manpower: The Keystone of National Security.* Report to the President and Congress. Washington, D.C.: Government Printing Office, 1976.

U.S. Department of the Army. *Leadership for the 1970s.* Carlisle Barracks, Pa.: U.S. Army War College, 1971.

U.S. President's Commission on an All-Volunteer Armed Force. *The Report of the President's Commission on an All-Volunteer Armed Force.* Washington, D.C.: Government Printing Office, 1970.

The Contributors

The Contributors

John D. Blair is a member of the sociology faculty at the University of Maryland. His research interests include military and political sociology, complex organizations, and the sociology of youth. Professor Blair formerly served as assistant study director, Survey Research Center, Institute for Social Research, University of Michigan. His most recent book is *The All-Volunteer Force: A Study of Ideology in the Military*, coauthored with Jerald G. Bachman and David R. Segal.

Thomas W. Carr was director of defense education, Office of the Secretary of Defense. He has served in a variety of governmental posts concerned with education and has written a study on educational leadership and the education of disadvantaged children, *An Education Revolution: The First Year of Title I*. He has been executive director of two presidential advisory councils and was the first director of the White House Fellows Program.

James Clotfelter is professor of political science at the University of North Carolina at Greensboro. Previously, he was director of the Center for Public Service at Texas Tech University, and taught at Emory and Duke universities. Professor Clotfelter is the author of *The Military in American Politics*, coauthor of *Strategies for Change in the South*, and author of several journal articles on defense policy and other topics.

Charles L. Cochran is associate professor of political science at the U.S. Naval Academy. Professor Cochran has been a contributor to several journals and was the editor and contributing author of *Civil-Military Relations: Changing Concepts in the Seventies*. He is also an associate editor of the *Journal of Political and Military Sociology*.

Howard L. Elman is a Reserve officer in the U.S. Air Force and an aeroelastician and rotor dynamicist with Hughes Helicopters. As a historian and museum consultant, he has specialized in the history of aviation and aeronautical engineering. A former executive vice-president of the Bradley Air Museum, he has published many articles on the history of military aviation research and technical articles on helicopter aeroelasticity.

John A. Fitzgerald is associate professor of political science at the U.S. Naval Academy. Professor Fitzgerald has been a contributor to several journals and is the author of *Systems Analysis: Applications to the Non-Western Political Process.*

Major James R. Golden, USA, is associate professor of economics in the Department of Social Sciences at the Military Academy. A field artillery officer with combat experience in Vietnam, he is a graduate of the Army Command and General Staff College, and he holds a Ph.D. degree in economics from Harvard University. He has served as senior staff economist on the President's Council of Economic Advisers and recently chaired a Presidential Task Force on the Administration of Export Controls.

Russell D. Hale has been educated in economics and is the deputy chief for national security affairs, Committee on the Budget, U.S. House of Representatives.

Lieutenant Colonel Richard H. Hartke is on the staff of the President's Committee on Science and Technology. He has served in several air force research and development assignments including a Headquarters Air Force tour in the Science and Technology Division.

Lieutenant Colonel James J. Hogan, USAF, is a former faculty member at the Air Command and Staff College and is now assigned to the Directorate of Concepts, Headquarters, United States Air Force.

Frank R. Hunsicker is an associate professor of business administration and chairman of the Department of Management and Marketing, West Georgia College. A frequent contributor to journals of management, he is also active as a consultant in management and leadership development. His present research emphasis concerns measurement of leadership training effectiveness.

Samuel P. Huntington is Frank G. Thomson Professor of Government at Harvard University. His numerous publications include *The Soldier and the State* and *The Common Defense.* During 1977-1978, Professor Huntington served as coordinator of security planning in the National Security Council.

Leland G. Jordan is a career civil servant in the Department of the Air Force and serves as a budget analyst in the Directorate of Budget,

Headquarters Air Force. Educated as a systems analyst, he has published several financial management articles in professional journals.

John P. Lovell is professor of political science, Indiana University, and is the author of *Foreign Policy in Perspective* and *Neither Athens nor Sparta?* (forthcoming) and many journal articles on the military and U.S. foreign policy.

L. Anthony Loman is associate professor of sociology at Southwest Missouri State University. He has collaborated with Larry Reed on several papers and articles in the field of military sociology; their current research concerns issues of socialization in military life.

Colonel Franklin D. Margiotta is a career air force pilot with an extensive B-52 operational background. Educated in political science at Georgetown University and Massachusetts Institute of Technology, he is research professor of political science at Air University and is director (dean) of curriculum, Air Command and Staff College. His publications include chapters in *Civilian Control of the Military*, *American Defense Policy* (4th ed.), and several journal articles.

Martha A. Marsden is a professional social worker at Mercy Hospital and Medical Center, San Diego, California. She has served as research social scientist in the Family Studies Branch of the Naval Health Research Center. Her articles have appeared in *Army, Navy,* and *Air Force Times* and underscore the importance and needs of the military family.

Hamilton I. McCubbin is a research associate, Family Study Center, University of Minnesota, and associate professor, School of Social Work. He has served as head of family studies, Naval Health Research Center, San Diego, California. His professional writings include *Family Separation and Reunion*, coedited with colleagues at the Naval Health Research Center, and *Families in the Military System*, coedited with Barbara Dahl and Edna J. Hunter.

Vice Admiral Gerald E. Miller, U.S. Navy (Ret.), is a graduate of the U.S. Naval Academy. His military career includes service on cruisers during World War II, combat command of a fighter squadron and a carrier division, and command of the U.S. Second Fleet and the U.S. Sixth Fleet. He served ten years at the Pentagon and two tours at Headquarters Strategic Air Command. Retired in 1974 after thirty-eight years of service, Admiral Miller now works as a private consultant to government and business.

Charles C. Moskos, Jr., is professor of sociology at Northwestern

University. He is the author of *The American Enlisted Man* and *Peace Soldiers: The Sociology of a United Nations Military Force* and editor of *Public Opinion and the Military Establishment.*

Major Gus E. Myers is a T-38 instructor pilot in air force undergraduate pilot training at Reese Air Force Base, Texas. He is a graduate of the Air Command and Staff College; his previous assignments include three years as a physics instructor at the Air Force Academy.

Miroslav Nincic is a lecturer in political science at the University of Michigan.

George S. Odiorne is dean of the School of Business and professor of management at the University of Massachusetts. He has had positions with General Mills, American Management Association, and the American Can Company. He is the author of *Management and the Activity Trap, Personnel Administration, Management by Objectives,* and many articles.

B. Guy Peters is associate professor of political science at the University of Delaware, having formerly taught at Emory University. He is the author of a recently published book on comparative bureaucracy, as well as of a number of articles on public administration, public policy, and European politics.

Robert L. Pfaltzgraff, Jr., is director, Institute for Foreign Policy Analysis, Cambridge, Massachusetts, and associate professor of international politics, The Fletcher School of Law and Diplomacy, Tufts University. He is the president of the Strategic Institute and the editor of *Strategic Review.* His writings include many books and articles on U.S. foreign and defense policy and on the theory and practice of international relations.

Robert F. Priest is a research psychologist in the Office of the Director of Institutional Research at the U.S. Military Academy. He has taught and done research on college student attitudes at the University of Southern California and the University of Missouri. Since 1973, he has studied the values, career motivations, and attitudes of cadets, candidates, and graduates of West Point.

Larry Reed is associate professor of sociology at Southwest Missouri State University. He has collaborated with Anthony Loman on several papers and articles in the field of military sociology; their current research concerns issues of socialization in military life.

Bruce Russett is professor of political science at Yale University, editor of the *Journal of Conflict Resolution*, and president of the Peace Science Society (International). The most recent of his twelve books on international politics and foreign policy is *Interest and Ideology: The Foreign Policy Beliefs of American Businessmen*, coauthored with Elizabeth Hanson.

Sam C. Sarkesian is professor and chairman, Department of Political Science, Loyola University of Chicago; he has served as executive secretary and associate chairman of the Inter-University Seminar on Armed Forces and Society. His publications include *The Military-Industrial Complex: A Reassessment; The Professional Army Officer in a Changing Society; Revolutionary Guerrilla Warfare; Politics and Power: An Introduction to American Government;* and many articles on the military profession and national security.

Major Ronald F. Schloemer is an air force fighter pilot, F-4 instructor, and squadron operations officer at Luke Air Force Base, Arizona. He is a graduate of the Air Command and Staff College; his previous assignments include three years as an air officer commanding at the Air Force Academy.

David R. Segal is professor of sociology and of government and politics at the University of Maryland. From 1973 to 1976, he directed the Army's sociological research program. In addition to writing numerous articles on military sociology and political sociology, he is the author of *Society and Politics*, coauthor of *The All-Volunteer Force: A Study of Ideology*, and coeditor of *The Social Psychology of Military Service*.

Colonel William J. Taylor, Jr., is professor for national security studies and director of the Debate Council and Forum in the Department of Social Sciences, United States Military Academy, and is a member of the Council on Foreign Relations. A frequent contributor to journals and various books, his most recent articles appear in a special edition of *Public Administration Review*, "Professionals in Government" (Fall 1977), and in *American Defense Policy*, 4th ed. (August 1977). He is currently coauthoring a text entitled *The Elements of National Security*.

Major General John C. Toomay, USAF, is the deputy chief of staff for development plans, Air Force Systems Command. He has served in research and development positions from the laboratory system up through high levels in Headquarters Air Force and in the Office of the Director of Defense Research and Engineering.

Robert H. Trice is assistant professor in the Department of Political Science and faculty associate of the Force and Policy Program of the Mershon Center at the Ohio State University. His recent publications focus on the impact of domestic politics on U.S. foreign and defense policy. They include *Interest Groups and the Foreign Policy Process* (1977); chapters in *Oil, the Arab-Israel Dispute, and the Industrial World* (1976), edited by J. C. Hurewitz; and in *Modules in National Security Studies* (1974), edited by David Tarr and Alden Williams; and a number of articles in journals.

Index

Index